Intermediate Creek

The items depicted in this painting by Jonny Hawk are of great significance to the Muskogee (Creek) and Seminole people. Elders, represented by the face in the center, are greatly respected for their knowledge and experience. They provide a connection to the past and can help guide younger people into the future. The keco, kecvpe, and corn signify traditional ways of preparing food. Corn was a mainstay for Creek and Seminole people, and the keco and kecvpe were used to pound it into a form useful for making bread, sofke, and apvske. The ballsticks and turtle shells refer to traditional religious practices. To this day, these items are used during the ceremonial year to promote peace, harmony, and social well-being. Finally, the paper and ink represent the importance of writing for the Creek and Seminole people.

Intermediate Creek

Mvskoke Emponvkv Hokkolat

Pamela Innes, Linda Alexander,
and Bertha Tilkens

University of Oklahoma Press : Norman

Also by Pamela Innes, Linda Alexander, and Bertha Tilkens

Beginning Creek: Mvskoke Emponvkv (Norman, 2004)

Library of Congress Cataloging-in-Publication Data

Innes, Pamela Joan.
    Intermediate creek - Mvskoke emponvkv hokkolat / Pamela Innes, Linda Alexander, and Bertha Tilkens.
        p.   cm.
    Other title: Mvskoke emponvkv hokkolat
    Includes bibliographical references and index.
    ISBN 978-0-8061-3996-8 (pbk. : alk. paper). 1. Creek language—Grammar. 2. Creek language—Conversation and phrase books. 3. Creek language—Study and teaching. I. Alexander, Linda, 1917– II. Tilkens, Bertha, 1936– III. Title. IV. Title: Mvskoke emponvkv hokkolat.
    PM991.I66 2009
    497'.385—dc22

                                                                2008032911

The paper in this book meets the guidelines for permanence and durability of the Committee on Production Guidelines for Book Longevity of the Council on Library Resources, Inc. ∞

1 2 3 4 5 6 7 8 9 10

Contents

Illustrations

Figures

Diagrams

Tables

Preface

This book continues the work started in *Beginning Creek: Mvskoke Emponvkv*, expanding upon some of the linguistic features encountered in the first text and presenting information about creating more complex linguistic constructions. It is expected that students and readers who have worked through the exercises and studied each of the chapters in both this and the first textbook will be able to understand most of the Mvskoke they are likely to hear or read. We strongly advise that readers have a copy of *Beginning Creek* accessible to them as they use *Intermediate Creek*, because we will refer readers back to the first text rather than repeating what is covered in that work.

The conversations, story, and lullaby included on the CD accompanying this text are meant to provide those who do not know fluent Mvskoke speakers with at least a chance to hear the spoken language. If you do not have access to speakers or places where Mvskoke is used, we recommend that you listen closely to the CD so as to pick up the cadence and intonational contours of Mvskoke, as it is spoken by two speakers. Attention to the ways in which Linda and Bertha pronounce words and longer units of speech should help you become acquainted with the way spoken Mvskoke sounds.

Of course the best way to become familiar with the sounds and phrasings of Mvskoke is to spend time in the company of fluent speakers. We highly recommend that you seek out speakers if you can and try using the Mvskoke that you know with them. It is a challenging thing to do, and you will need to be willing to laugh at your own mistakes for quite awhile, but it is the best way to get used to speaking Mvskoke. You may also develop a community of speakers who will help you to learn about more than just the Muskogee.

In the end we hope that this text, along with the first textbook, will help keep the Mvskoke language alive and prosperous. For those who use the book as a teaching or learning tool, we hope that it is encouraging, informative, and challenging enough to enable you to learn and/or teach the language. For those who use this text as a reference, we would caution you that it does not contain every piece of information about the language and its structure, but we hope you will find enough to answer questions about commonly used constructions.

Acknowledgments

Each of the authors is indebted to many, many people who helped us write this book. Our communities of friends and teachers are quite large, and it is nearly impossible for us to thank individually each person who has helped us along the way. For this reason we have short lists of individuals whom we specifically want to acknowledge here, but we want to make certain that all who have given us their friendship, nurturing, and guidance understand that we are tremendously grateful, even if we do not refer to each of you in this section. Please know that your kindnesses and thoughtfulness are remembered by each of us.

Linda Alexander wants to thank her father, Waddie Gibbs, and her *eckuce*, Lena Factor Morgan, for their care and guidance. Waddie taught Linda about traditional practices, demonstrated a high moral character and fairness that she emulates today, and gave her several of the stories that she shares with those who listen. Lena took care of Linda after her mother died, taught her about women's roles in Muskogee life, and gave Linda many of her insights into women's activities. The knowledge about traditional Muskogee life and language that Linda demonstrates today comes from these two great figures in her life.

Linda also wishes to thank her daughter, Bertha Tilkens, for the care and kindness she has shown over the years. Bertha's presence allows Linda to speak Mvskoke on a daily basis, take part in traditional Muskogee practices, and know that her health and well-being are watched after incredibly well. Linda is greatly indebted to Waddie, Lena, and Bertha for all that they have done and continue to do. May others have such good providers and teachers.

Bertha Tilkens wishes to thank her maternal grandfather, Waddie Gibbs, and her paternal grandmother, Rosy Alexander, for teaching her about both the traditional Muskogee ceremonies and Christian traditions among the Muskogee. Both Waddie and Rosy spoke Mvskoke with her, helping her to master the language. Waddie and Rosy also demonstrated several times that the traditional and Christian ways both have good features—that one does not have to make an either-or choice. Her father, Thomas Jones, and her mother, Linda Alexander, also helped instill knowledge and insights that she draws on today. Her father's good, balanced advice and Linda's maintenance of tradition have helped Bertha realize the importance of keeping her language and culture alive.

Pam Innes is deeply indebted to Linda Alexander and Bertha Tilkens for sharing their language, knowledge of Muskogee culture, and friendship. Without Linda's and Bertha's dedication and commitment, it is doubtful that this textbook would have been written. Others in the Muskogee community have also helped Pam learn about the language, including Felix Gouge, Ted Isham, Margaret Mauldin, John Proctor, Lena Tiger, Thomas Yahola, and the late Toney Hill and Tema Tiger. To each of you, and to others, I am very grateful for your patience and tutoring.

Pam also wishes to give her thanks to Terry Zinn, Chester Cowen, and Nancy Laub at the Oklahoma Historical Society Library. Their assistance with the photographic archives was invaluable. Two students from the University of Wyoming are also deserving of thanks: Megan Bolin for her assistance with gathering sources, many of which are to be found in the bibliography; and Amanda Davies for finding illustrations for this book. Your work certainly helped us create a more flowing and interesting text. And thanks to my colleagues in the Anthropology Department at the University of Wyoming, my parents, my partner, and my dear friends in Wyoming and Oklahoma, whose encouragement and support have helped me complete this project.

We all want to thank Marvin Alexander, who donated his time to produce the CD included with the text. His capable direction, great patience, good humor, and willingness to rework the tracks are much appreciated by each of the authors. We also wish to thank Jimmy Gibson for allowing us to include a recording of a stompdance song on the CD. And, finally, our utmost appreciation goes to Jonny Hawk, whose beautiful artwork is featured as the frontispiece for this book. Mvto!

Abbreviations

Each abbreviation in the left column is followed by the phrase or concept it stands for, then a reference to the first page on which the abbreviation is discussed. When an abbreviation was first used in *Beginning Creek*, the page number is preceded by "BC": to show that readers should refer to this work for a discussion of the abbreviation.

(1)	verb stem form for singular subject	26
(2+)	verb stem form for two or more subjects	11
(3+)	verb stem form for three or more subjects	8
1P	first person plural suffix	24
1PII	Type II first person plural prefix	24
1PD	first person plural dative prefix	63
1S	first person singular suffix	BC: 74
1SII	Type II first person singular prefix	BC: 78
1SD	first person singular dative prefix	BC: 101
2persII	Type II second person prefix	59
2persD	second person dative prefix	63
2P	second person plural suffix	24
2S	second person singular suffix	BC: 75
3pers	third person suffix	24
3persII	Type II third person prefix	25
3persD	third person dative prefix	63
app	applicative prefix	66

aux_vb	auxiliary verb	BC: 80
caus	causative suffix	110
cond	conditional suffix	186
ctre	counterexpectational suffix	107
dec	declarative suffix	BC: 34
def_obj	definite object suffix	BC: 49
def_subj	definite subject suffix	BC: 49
dim	diminutive suffix	BC: 52
dir	directional prefix	158
disj	disjointive suffix	138
distr	distributive suffix	6
dp	distant past tense suffix	BC: 135
ds	different subject suffix	174
e_grd	extra-high tone grade	197
emph	emphatic particle	106
fut	future tense suffix	80
hgr	h-grade infix	38
imper	imperative suffix	102
ind_obj	indefinite object suffix	BC: 50
ind_subj	indefinite subject suffix	BC: 50
inf	infinitival suffix	181
instr	instrumental prefix	161
int	interrogative suffix	BC: 179
intent	intentive mood suffix	85
l_grd	lengthened grade	BC: 36
loc	locative prefix	150
mp	middle past suffix	BC: 135
neg	negating suffix	BC: 159
o	object singularity/plurality determines verb form	61
obl	oblique suffix	132
part	participial suffix	176
pl	pluralizing suffix	5
recent	recent past tense suffix	177
rp	remote past tense suffix	BC: 135
s	subject singularity/plurality determines verb form	61
ss	same subject suffix	BC: 80
stat	stative suffix	32
sub	subordinating suffix	174

Intermediate Creek

CHAPTER ONE

Pluralizing Nouns

As we introduced sentences and phrases containing singular nouns in the first textbook, we refer to sections of *Beginning Creek* when a review of materials covered there may help you to understand the new items being discussed in this book. For this reason, we strongly suggest that you have a copy of *Beginning Creek* available for reference.

In this second textbook, we demonstrate the use of plural subject and object noun phrases in sentences. We begin with a discussion in this chapter of how plural noun phrases are formed, with chapters 2 and 3 showing how such phrases are used in the formation of sentences. There are different ways in which the plurality of nouns is indicated in Mvskoke, which we introduce in this chapter. Also, as you will see, in order to know whether the subject and/or object nouns in some sentences are plural, you will have to rely solely on contextual information.

Some nouns in Mvskoke have forms that clearly indicate plurality. These nouns and the features that act as the plural markers are covered first. We then go on to discuss how some adjective forms indicate that multiple items are affected by the adjective. In the second portion of the chapter, we cover how these forms are dealt with in noun phrases.

Nouns with Distinctive Plural Forms

Unlike English nouns, many nouns in Mvskoke do not have forms that indicate the noun is plural. English shows that nouns are plural by modifying the structure of the noun in some way. For example, to show that one is referring to more than one book, English adds a pluralizing suffix (-s) to the noun, which results in the form "books." Unlike English, Mvskoke does not always mark its nouns to show that they are plural. For instance, the Mvskoke noun *efv* 'dog' has this form when one is speaking about a single dog (the **singular number**) and when one is referring to multiple dogs (the **plural number**). In both cases 'dog' and 'dogs' are signified by the same noun form (*efv*) in Mvskoke.

Some nouns, however, do indicate plurality through the application of pluralizing suffixes and infixes (meaningful units placed on the end of or within a word, respectively). These nouns are listed in appendix 1. Many of these nouns concern types of people or positions that people might hold. Acquaint yourself with these nouns, as their use is fairly common in conversational speech. Any conversation about family matters, for example, will probably require the use of plural forms of relative or kinship terms, which have distinctive forms for the singular and plural numbers.

The nouns in appendix 1 are marked for plurality in one of four ways. The first is to use the suffix *–vlk–* on the noun. This suffix is used for nouns referring to an identity that people might have, such as clan name (e.g., *Hvlpvtvlke* 'Alligator clan'), nationality (e.g., *Espanvlke* 'the Spanish'), religious identification (e.g., *Este-Aksomkvlke* 'Baptists'), and/or tribal identity (e.g., *Cvlakkvlke* 'the Cherokee'). The second means of forming plurals on nouns is to add the suffixes *–vke–* or *–vk–*. This suffix is used on nouns that primarily refer to people at various stages of life or to men holding specific positions. 'Boys' *cēpvnvke* is an example of a noun based on a stage of life, while *mēkkvke* 'chiefs' is an example of a noun referring to a social position. Both are pluralized by adding *–vke–* to the singular form of the noun, *cēpvne* and *mēkko* respectively. The third manner of indicating plurality is to add the suffix *–take–* to the noun. This form is used almost exclusively with terms for relatives (e.g., *hopuetake* 'children'), the only exception being the noun *honvntake* 'men,' which also uses this form. The fourth way in which plurality is indicated on nouns is through the use of infixes or processes associated with indicating plural subjects and/or objects on verbs. For example, the plural of 'name' *hocefketv* is formed by the addition of the infix *–ho–* between the /f/ and /k/ of the singular form, leading to *hocefhoketv* 'names.'

Nouns Taking *–vlk-*

As we mentioned above, some Mvskoke nouns indicate that they are plural by adding the suffix *–vlk-* to the noun. This suffix is an "always key" syllable, as we describe in chapter two of *Beginning Creek*. The pitch of the first vowel of the suffix /v/ falls as the suffix is pronounced (you should hear that the pitch goes from a higher to a lower level as you say this vowel), providing the basis for the level of the tone(s) of the noun that come after the *–vlk-* suffix.

The nouns using this suffix to form the plural are listed in the first table of appendix 1. From looking at these nouns, you might think that the final *–e* should be included as part of the pluralizing suffix *–vlk-* (in other words, that the form of the suffix should be *–vlke-*). [Reminder: Examples of incorrect usage or incorrect forms are preceded by an asterisk (*).] However, because there are some words that form a plural through the use of the suffix *–vlk-* but that take the adjectival endings *–at/-an* when they indicate a definite noun, we consider the final *–e* to be separate from the pluralizing suffix.

In chapter 2, for instance, you will be introduced to the pronouns *omvlkackat* and *omvlkat* for 'you (plural)' and 'they' respectively. Notice that both of these words utilize the pluralizing suffix *–vlk-* with the adjectival endings *–at*. This occurs because the noun *omvlke* 'all' is acting as an adjective with the specified noun forms 'you' and 'he/she/it.' *Omvlkack-* and *omvlk-* are thus complete noun phrases that can be translated as 'all of you (plural)' and 'all of them,' with the "all of" portion (*omvlk-*) providing descriptive information about the inclusiveness of the plural "you" and "them." When the adjectival endings discussed in *Beginning Creek*, chapter 4, are added to these words and a few others, the plural suffix (*-vlk-*) occurs without the final *–e*; for this reason, we consider this *–e* to be separate from the suffix itself.

When the suffix *–vlk-* either is the last in the word or is followed only by a suffix marking the noun as indefinite (*–t* or *–n*), an *–e* follows the pluralizing suffix (whose position is denoted by 'pl' in the third line of the examples in which it occurs). Nothing is added to the final *–e* when the noun is a definite subject or object. In example 1 the plural noun plays the role of a definite subject in the sentence, so no other suffix follows the final *–e* on the noun.

1.   Espanvlke lopicvkvtetomvtēs.
      Espan-**vlke**-Ø   lopic-Ø-vk-et-o-mvt-ē-s
      Spanish-pl-def_subj   kind-3pers-distr-ss-aux_vb-rp-stat-dec
      'The Spaniards were kind.'

The verb in example 1 contains a suffix (-*vk*-), identified as 'distr' (for "distributive") in the third line of the example, which shows that the action is distributed over a number of subjects. The distributive suffix (-*vk*-) occurs in all of the sentences containing third person subjects, but we do not explain it in great detail in this chapter. Instead, this suffix and other verbal constructions used with plural subjects and objects are covered in chapters 2 and 3.

Because the noun in example 2 is playing the role of a definite indirect object, it uses the form listed in appendix 1. The object marking prefix indicated in the second line of this example is the initial *em-* on the verb as it appears in the glossary (which also was discussed in *Beginning Creek*, chapter 7).

2.   Mēkkot Fvlvncvlke emmapohicvnks.
      Mēkko-t   Fvlvnc-**vlke**-Ø   em-mapohic-Ø-vnk-s
      chief-ind_sub   French-pl-def_obj   3persD-listen_to-3pers-mp-dec
      'A chief listened to the French people.'

When a plural noun is acting as the indefinite subject or object, the appropriate marker is added to the noun (i.e., -*t* for subjects, -*n* for objects). These suffixes follow the –*e* after the pluralizing suffix. Examples 3 and 4 show the forms for indefinite plural subjects and objects respectively.

3.   Mistvlket tosēnvn hompvketos.
      Mist-**vlke**-t   tosēnv-n   homp-Ø-vk-et-o-s
      man-pl-ind_subj   salt_meat-ind_obj   eat-3pers-distr-ss-aux_vb-dec
      'Men are eating some salt meat.'

4.   Cemme enahvnkvlken encokopericvkes.
      Cemme   e-nahvnk-**vlke**-n   en-cokoperic-vk-Ø-es
      Jimmy   3pers-relative-pl-ind_obj   3persD-visit-distr-3pers-dec
      'Jimmy is visiting his relatives.'

In example 4, the distributive suffix (*-vk-*) has been included on the verb to show that the action of visiting has affected a number of people (Jimmy's relatives). We cover the use of the suffix to demonstrate that an action affects more than one person in chapter 2.

Nouns Taking *–vke-* or *–vk-*

Another group of nouns indicates plurality through the addition of a second pluralizing suffix, *–vke-*. This suffix has a different form, *-vk-*, which is used when the suffix occurs before the diminutive suffix, as in *hoktvkuce* 'girls.' These suffixes are used less commonly than *–vlk-*, as a comparison of the number of nouns in the first and second tables in appendix 1 proves. The *–vke-* and *–vk-* suffixes are used on a fairly limited set of nouns referring to the young and the old (e.g., boys, girls, elders) and men's roles (e.g., chief, peacemaker).

When nouns containing this suffix have the role of definite subjects or objects in sentences, nothing is added to the end of the noun; they retain the construction found in the glossary. A noun pluralized through the addition of the *–vke-* suffix plays the role of the definite subject in example 5.

5.   Cēpvnvke efvn emahkopanvkes.
     Cēpvn-**vke**-Ø   efv-n   em-ahkopan-Ø-vke-s
     boy-pl-def_subj   dog-ind_obj   3persD-play_with-3pers-distr-dec
     'The boys are playing with a dog.'

When a noun containing *–vke-* plays the role of indefinite subject or object in a sentence, it takes either the *–t* indefinite subject suffix or the *–n* indefinite object suffix. Example 6 contains a plural indefinite subject formed with the pluralizing suffix *–vke-*.

6.   Cēpvnvket posuce vpelicvkes.
     Cēpvn-**vke**-t   pos-uce-Ø   Ø-vpelic-Ø-vke-s
     boy-pl-ind_subj   cat-dim-def_obj   3persD-laugh_at-3pers-distr-dec
     'Boys are laughing at the kitten.'

The object noun in example 7 is *hoktvkuce* 'girls.' This noun uses the *–vk-* form of the pluralizing suffix, because it is followed by the diminutive suffix (*-uce*). The final suffix on the noun is the indefinite object suffix, *-n*.

7.   Mvhayv hoktvkucen mvhayemvts.
     Mvhayv-Ø   hokt-**vk**-uce-n   Ø-mvhaye-Ø-mvt-s
     teacher-def_subj   woman-pl-dim-ind_obj   3persII-teach-3pers-dp-dec
     'The teacher taught some girls.'

Nouns Taking *–take-*

The last suffix that shows a noun is plural is *–take-*. This suffix is attached, for the most part, to nouns referring to relatives (e.g., grandchildren, wives, men's sisters, etc.), though it also is used to pluralize the word for 'men' in general. Each of the nouns to which this suffix is added for the plural form is listed in the third table in appendix 1. This is the least used pluralizing suffix of the three we will discuss in this chapter.

Nouns indicating plurality through the application of the *–take-* suffix are treated just like the nouns taking the *–vke-* suffix we described above. In example 8, the noun pluralized with *–take-* plays the role of the definite object.

8.   Honvnwv hopuetake vmelletos.
     Honvnwv-Ø   hopue-**take**-Ø   Ø-vmell-Ø-et-o-s
     man-def_subj   child-pl-def_obj   3persD-point_at-3pers-ss-aux_vb-dec
     'The man is pointing at the children.'

In example 9, the same noun is in the role of the definite subject.

9.   Hopuetake cvmpucen nesvkvnks.
     Hopue-**take**-Ø   cvmpuce-n   Ø-nes-Ø-vk-vnk-s
     child-pl-def_subj   candy-indef_obj   3persII-buy-3pers-distr-mp-dec
     'The children bought some candy.'

Note that because the nouns in both examples were definite, no other suffix follows the pluralizing suffix *–take-*.

When the plural noun fills the role of an indefinite subject or object, however, the suffix *–t* or *–n* is added. In example 10, the plural noun *eccustake* 'a woman's children' is the indefinite subject. In this sentence, it is the form of the verb that indicates that there are three or more children, shown by adding '_(3+)' after the translation of the stem.

10. Cvccustaket rakko hvtkē ohvpoketos.

Cv-ccus-**take**-t	rakko	hvtkē-Ø	ohvpok-Ø-et-o-s
1SII-child-pl-ind_subj	horse	white-def_obj	ride_(3+)-3pers-ss-aux_vb-dec

'My children (three or more) are riding the white horse.' (woman speaking)

Sentence 11 has the noun *ēwvnwv* 'a man's sister' as a plural indefinite object. *Miste* has been included in this sentence to clarify that the dog is barking at a human male's sisters rather than at his own sisters (assuming the dog is male in this case).

11. Efv miste ēwvntaken vwohkvkekotos.

Efv-Ø	miste	ēwvn-**take**-n
dog-def_subj	man/his	male's_sister-pl-ind_obj

Ø-vwohk-vk-ko-t-o-s
3persII-bark_at-dist-neg-ss-aux_vb-dec
'The dog is not barking at his (a man's) sisters.'

Nouns Forming Plurals Based on Verbal Forms

As a look at the fourth table in appendix 1 illustrates, the least common means of indicating plurality on a noun is to modify the form of the noun in a manner similar to that used to denote plural subjects or objects on verbs, which is discussed in chapters 2 and 3. As the discussions in those chapters will demonstrate, several verbs in Mvskoke have distinctive forms when their subjects and/or objects are plural. In many cases, the forms of the verb for singular and plural subjects or objects are very different. When the form of the verb stem is changed significantly without the addition of affixes in order to indicate that the subject or object is singular or plural, it is called a **suppletive verb**. It is precisely because several of the nouns in table 4 of appendix 1 are derived from suppletive verbal structures that they have very different forms in the singular and plural. For instance, *este-capko* 'giant' is derived from the type II verb *cvpkē*, meaning 'long, tall,' which has a very different form (*cvpcvkē*) when plural subjects are long or tall. Rather than concerning yourself with trying to remember which nouns are based on suppletive verbs and which are not, simply memorize the different forms of the nouns for 'giants,' 'members (of a church),' 'names,' 'things,' 'messengers,' and 'widths.' Knowing the plural forms of these nouns is all that you need to concern yourself with at this point.

As you have seen in these examples, any noun that contains the *–vlk-*, *-vke-*, *-vk-*, or *–take-* suffix or that changes its form because it is derived from a verbal construction should be translated as being plural in number. In some sentences, the presence of the plural suffixes or verbally based plural forms will be the only indication that a subject or object is plural. The number of nouns utilizing these suffixes is relatively small, and you should study appendix 1 carefully so as to become familiar with these nouns.

PLURALIZED NOUN PHRASES

There is another way of indicating that nouns are plural in Mvskoke. This involves the use of **suppletive adjectives**, adjectives that have distinct forms showing their subject is plural in number. In many of the examples we present in this section, the noun itself does not have a form clearly indicating plurality and does not take one of the pluralizing suffixes we discussed earlier. Instead, the plurality of the noun is indicated by the inclusion of an adjectival form specifying that the noun being modified by the adjective is plural in number. Adjectives of this type are included in appendix 2.

As we mentioned in textbook 1, chapters 4 and 6, many adjectives are stative in nature and act like type II verbs. As you will see, the adjectives discussed in this section, many of which are type II adjectives, have stem forms that change depending on whether the subject or object is plural. In this section, we will concern ourselves with the formation of noun phrases including suppletive adjectival forms.

An example of a suppletive adjective is presented in example 12 below. Here, the adjective *hvtkē* 'white' has an alternate form when more than one item is described as white. In example 12, multiple horses are described as white, so the form of 'white' is changed to *hvtkvlkē*. (In Linda and Bertha's dialect of Mvskoke, the other plural form of 'white' listed in appendix 2, *hvthvkē*, is used for items made from cloth or material, though this form indicates a plural white noun in other dialects of Mvskoke.) Thus, in this example, it is because *hvtkvlkē* is the form of the adjective in the noun phrase 'white horses' that a listener knows more than one horse is being described as white.

12a. Honvnwv rakko **hvtkvlken** ocetos.
      Honvnwv-Ø   rakko   hvtk-vlke-n   Ø-oc-Ø-et-o-s

| man-def_subj | horse | white-pl-def_obj | 3persII-have-3pers-ss- |
| | | | aux_vb-dec |

'The man has white horses.' (in Linda and Bertha's dialect)

12b. Honvnwv rakko **hvthvken** ocetos.

Honvnwv-Ø	rakko	hvthvke-n	Ø-oc-Ø-et-o-s
man-def_subj	horse	white_(2+)-def_obj	3persII-have-3pers-
			ss-aux_vb-dec

'The man has white horses.' (in other Mvskoke dialects)

In 12b, we show the plural nature of the adjective in the third line by including '_(2+)' after the definition. This marks the adjective as referring to two or more even though it does not include one of the pluralizing suffixes. We will use this type of abbreviation to show that a plural suppletive form of a word is used in a sentence throughout the rest of the book.

When more than one suppletive adjective is contained in a noun phrase with a plural noun, each one will take the form designating that its subject is plural. In example 13, two suppletive adjectives are contained in the noun phrase 'the big, black bears.' Notice that both 'big' and 'black' are taking the forms used with plural nouns (*rakrvkē* and *lvslvtē* respectively).

13.   Nokose **rakrvkē lvslvtat** hompvketos.

Nokose	rakrvkē	lvslvt-at	homp-Ø-vk-et-o-s
bear	big_(2+)-stat	black_(2+)-ind_subj	eat-3pers-distr-ss-
			aux_vb-dec

'Big, black bears are eating.'

To an English speaker, it would seem redundant to include plurality on both adjectives, because the use of one plural form should indicate to a listener that the noun is plural in number. However, in Mvskoke, when an adjective has a suppletive form indicating plurality of its subject, that plural form must be used when its subject noun is plural no matter how many other suppletive adjectives appear in the same noun phrase.

We indicate the definite or indefinite nature of the noun being modified by suppletive adjectives in exactly the same manner we showed you in *Beginning Creek*, chapter 4. Definite nouns are indicated as such through the shortening of the final long /e/ (ē) and the addition of the appropriate role-marking suffix (*-t* or *-n*) on the final adjective modifying that noun. In

example 14, the definite nature of the object "books" is demonstrated
through the structure of the suppletive adjective "heavy," which ends in a
short /e/ and has the object suffix (-*n*).

14.   Miste cokv honhoyen ohlikes.
       Miste-Ø   cokv   honhoye-**n**   Ø-ohlik-Ø-es
       man-def_subj   book   heavy_(2+)-def_obj   3persII-sit_on-3pers-dec
       'The man is sitting on the heavy books.'

When an indefinite noun is modified by adjectives, the final adjective
in the phrase takes either the –*at* or –*an* suffix depending upon whether it
is the subject or object in the sentence. Examples 15a and 15b contain
an indefinite subject, indicated by the addition of the –*at* suffix on the
final adjective. Notice that the two other adjectives in the phrase are
unmodified by the addition of a suffix. Also, since the first adjective 'happy'
is not suppletive, its form is not changed for a plural subject.

15a. Pose afvckē hotosvkē hvtkvlkat cessen vwenayvketos.
       Pose afvckē   hotosvkē   hvtkvlk-**at**   cesse-n
       cat   happy   skinny_(2+)   white_(2+)-ind_subj   mouse-ind_obj
       Ø-vwenay-Ø-vke-t-o-s
       3persII-smell_l_grd-3pers-distr-ss-aux_vb-dec
       'Happy, skinny, white cats smell a mouse.' (in Linda and Bertha's dialect)

15b. Pose afvckē hotosvkē hvthvkat cessen vwenayvketos.
       Pose afvckē hotosvkē   hvthvk-**at**   cesse-n
       cat   happy skinny_(2+)   white_(2+)-ind_subj   mouse-ind_obj
       Ø-vwenay-Ø-vke-t-o-s
       3persII-smell_l_grd-3pers-distr-ss-aux_vb-dec
       'Happy, skinny, white cats smell a mouse.' (in other Mvskoke dialects)

Plural nouns also may be specified by the inclusion of a numerical
term in the adjectival phrase. This is exactly like a construction in English
in which a number precedes the noun (e.g., "we ate *two* eggs" or "the
three boys went fishing"). In such an English construction, the noun still
carries the pluralizing suffix (-s in both examples), so the plurality of the
noun is indicated twice; once through the inclusion of a number greater

than one, and once through the use of the pluralizing suffix on the noun. In Mvskoke, the plural nature of the noun may be indicated in many instances solely through the inclusion of a number greater than one, particularly if the noun does not have a distinctive plural form.

Example 16 presents an object noun phrase containing a numerical adjective. The plural noun in this phrase (*eto*) does not have a distinctive plural form. The numerical adjective makes it clear, however, that the raccoon climbed more than one tree.

16.   Nerē-isē wotko rakkat eto **osten** vcumkvnks.

Nerē-isē	wotko	rakk-at	eto	oste-n	vcumk-Ø-vnk-s
last_night	raccoon	big-ind_subj	tree	four-def_obj	climb-3pers-mp-dec

'Last night, a big raccoon climbed the four trees.'

When used as adjectives, numerical references can indicate the definite or indefinite nature of the nouns they are modifying. In example 16, the definite nature of the noun 'tree' is indicated through the use of the number as it is presented in the dictionary or glossary. When the noun modified by a number is indefinite in nature, the final *–en* of the number is dropped and the appropriate indefinite suffix (*-at* or *–an*) is added. This results in a construction like that shown in example 17, where the number *cahkēpen* 'five' is changed to show that it is modifying an indefinite noun.

17.   Miste vculet ohliketv cahkēpan ohlikemvts.

Miste	vcule-t	ohliketv	cahkēp-**an**	ohlik-Ø-emvt-s
man	old-def_subj	chair	five-ind_obj	sit_on-3pers-dp-dec

'The old man sat on five chairs.'

When a number is used in combination with other adjectives in a noun phrase, the number tends to be the last adjective in the series. This allows the numeral to take the appropriate suffix to mark the role of the noun phrase and indicate whether it is definite or indefinite (i.e., definite or indefinite subject (*-et* or *–at*) or definite or indefinite object (*-en* or *-an*)). In example 18, where *cahkēpen* and the adjective *lowvclokē* 'soft (of two or more things)' are part of the object noun phrase, it is the number, which is the final adjective, that takes the indefinite object suffix:

18.   Miste vculet ohliketv lowvclokē cahkēpan ohlikemvts.

Miste vcule-t   ohliketv lowvclokē cahkēp-**an**   ohlik-Ø-emvt-s
man   old-def_subj   chair   soft_(2+)   five-ind_obj   sit_on-3pers-dp-dec
'The old man sat on five soft chairs.'

This shows that numerical adjectives obey the same rules as all other adjectives, including that of taking the indefinite marker when they are the final adjective in the phrase.

The constructions introduced in this chapter showing that a noun is plural are the only indicators of plurality that occur in the noun phrase itself. Given that there are relatively few nouns with distinct plural forms and a relatively limited number of suppletive adjectives, however, many noun phrases will not contain any indications about the plural or singular nature of the noun. Instead, as you will learn in chapters 2 and 3, plurality of the subject and object nouns is often indicated on the verb in a sentence. Even with these verbal indicators, it can often be unclear whether the subject and/or object is plural.

Contextual information often helps a listener determine whether a subject and/or object noun is plural. Certain kinds of activities require multiple participants or affect multiple objects. For instance, playing ball almost always involves more than one person, so sentences about ball playing frequently involve plural subjects. In some cases, such as playing ball, cultural concepts about the kinds of subjects or objects involved help a listener understand that plurality is inherent in the subject or object noun phrase.

For instance, men use two ball sticks to perform almost every action done to the ball during a stickball game, and it is very unusual for a man to use a single ball stick to complete an action in the course of a game. Thus, when a speaker is describing his own or another man's actions during a ball game, it is understood that two ball sticks will be used to make each action happen unless otherwise specified. While describing how he fought to recover the ball from some grass, a man might say, *"Tokonhen pokkot sonken eshopoyayvnks"* 'With my ball sticks, I looked for the lost ball.' In this sentence, *tokonhe* 'ball stick' is translated in the plural, because it is assumed that a ball player will use both of his sticks to perform an action of this sort during a game. In cases like this, where cultural practices presume the use of plural items, a situation in which the singular number is meant is specified through the inclusion of the numeral "one" in the noun phrase or through the use of the singular verb stem if a suppletive verb is used in the sentence. Thus, if a man speaks about breaking one of his ball sticks, he may state specifically that *one* of his ball sticks broke, as well as using the verb stem specifying that only one long object was broken.

Vocabulary

Natural Objects

English		Mvskoke
moon		hvrēssē
star		kocecvmpv
mountain		kvnhvlwe-rakkē
snow, ice		hetotē
riverbank		hvccenvpv
	or	hvcconvpv
	or	hvcce onvpv
island		ēkvnv otē nvrkvpv
	or	ēkvnv owv ohliketv
sand		oktahv
flower		pakpvkoce
field		cvpofv
ditch, stream		hvccuce
forest		eto-vlke
	or	pelofv
to be piled up (as of laundry, brush, etc.) {II}		tohlicē
	or	tohvpokē
to be dark (as the out-of-doors) {II}		yomockē
	or	yvpockē
to be light (as the out-of-doors, the sun, etc.) {II}		hvyayvkē
to sit up (as from lying down, of one) {I}		aliketv
to sit up (as from lying down, of two) {I}		akaketv
to sit up (as from lying down, of three or more) {I}		a-vpoketv
to be wide (of one) {II}		tvphē
to be wide (of two or more) {II}		tvptvhē
to be deep, not of water (of one) {I}		sofkē
to be very deep, not of water {II}		sofsokē

English	Mvskoke
to be fertile or to be ripe (as of fruit) {II}	lokcē
to sit, be seated (of one) {I}	liketv
to sit, be seated (of two) {I}	kaketv
to sit, be seated (of three or more) {I}	vpoketv
to melt {I}	setēfketv
to freeze something {I;3}	hetoticetv
to open something for someone {I;3;D}	enhvwēcetv
to close something for someone {I;3;D}	em akhottetv

Exercises

EXERCISE 1

Translate each of the noun phrases below. Some noun phrases are ambiguous as to whether the noun is singular or plural. When you are translating phrases of this type, provide both the singular and plural forms in your translations. In noun phrases that clearly identify that plural nouns are involved, specify which word or words in the sentence are clearly indicating that the noun is plural. Two examples are provided for you below:

hopuetake afvcket   the happy children (word indicating plurality is *hopuetake*)

tolose yekcē lanan   a strong, yellow chicken; strong yellow chickens (no word clearly indicates the noun is plural)

1. ēkvnhvlwe lanē hvlhvwat
2. honvntake cvpakhoken
3. eto oklanē tutcēnan
4. hvcce ēpaken lvolvket
5. pelofv yomockat
6. hoktvke hvlvlatken
7. svtv catē lokcan
8. rakko elvwetē pvfpvnet
9. pipuce vholwahokan
10. cokv-hēcv cvfencvkē enhorrē ērolopet

Exercise 2

Translate each of the following sentences. With your translation, you should also provide a list of the morphemes contained in each Mvskoke word in the sentence. In the end, you will have produced lines similar to the second and third lines in each example in this chapter.

1. Cvlakkvlket lvpken opanvks.
2. Cēpvne vhoccickv lvslvtē tutcēnan vslēcekvnks.
3. Cvpvwv kolēppan sulkan vmeliyes.
4. Atomo lvstē cutkat eto mahmvyē hokkolen svcakhemvts.
5. Paksvnkē tēkvnv hotosat cokv-tvlvme osten ohonayvnketos.
6. Opanv locv hvlvlatkē rakrvkan wiyetos.
7. Wakv yekcet nokose cvpakhokē hvthvken vwenayvtēs.
8. Cvrke rvro rakrvkē sulken norihces.
9. Mēkko hvpohayvke afvckē lesleken encokopericvnks.
10. Eco oklanē nehē lopockat owv kvsvppen eskvkekvnks.

Exercise 3

Translate the following sentences into Mvskoke. When you are confronted with a plural subject noun phrase, be certain to modify the verb in the sentence by adding the pluralizing suffix –vk- directly after the verb stem. Break each of the words in your translation into its morphemes after you have formed your Mvskoke sentence. You should end up with lines similar in form to the first two lines in each example in the chapter.

1. The three bears are eating honey.
2. The cold, tired men are dancing.
3. My grandmother baked thick cakes a long time ago.
4. That man just wrote two books.
5. The skinny boys are singing loudly.
6. I did not see the many fat white turkeys.
7. The girl has three orange kittens.
8. Today the black cat chased four slow gray mice.
9. His mother smelled the yellow flowers.
10. The smart students bought ten long pencils.

EXERCISE 4

Each of the noun phrases below contains a singular noun and modifying adjectives. Change the noun phrase from singular to plural. In those noun phrases containing suppletive adjectives, you will need to use the plural form of the adjective to demonstrate that the noun is plural (see appendix 2 for suppletive forms). In those phrases that do not contain a suppletive adjective, add a numerical adjective to indicate that the noun is plural. When you have formed the plural noun phrase, translate it.

1. eslafkv tefnē sopakhvtkat
2. cvmpuce rakkē lanen
3. ervhv holwvyēcet
4. cvnute tvkockē ennokkan
5. hvlpvtv vculē hvlvlatkē lanen
6. efv ewvnhket
7. sokhv vholwvkē nucat
8. ohliketv hvmken fvleknen
9. hvcce tvphē lvoket
10. Espane heromē lopicat

EXERCISE 5

Each of the noun phrases below contains a plural noun and modifying adjectives. Change the noun phrase from plural to singular. In those noun phrases containing suppletive adjectives, you will need to use the correct singular form of the adjective, which may be quite different from the form as it appears in the original form of the noun phrase. You will find each of these adjectives in the Mvskoke-English glossary, as well as in appendix 2. When you have formed the singular phrase, translate it.

1. kocecvmpv hvyayvkē rakrvkan
2. hvcce onvpv hvlhvwen
3. eto-vlke yvmockē leslekat
4. hvpo hvsvthvkē cenvpaket
5. tvstvnvkvlke fekhvmken
6. cvstvlē lanē honhoyē tutcēnen
7. cvpofv tvptvhē tvpeksan

8. nanvke catē kolvpaken
9. sokhv sopakhvthvkē lekvclewē cvfencvkē hokkolat
10. cēpvnvke penkvlen

EXERCISE 6

Translate each sentence considering the subject noun phrase in each to be singular. In some sentences, the object noun phrase is clearly plural, while in others it is ambiguous. In those cases where the object noun phrase is ambiguous, translate it as both singular and plural. Then, for those sentences containing noun phrases that are not clearly plural, come up with some contextual (background) information that would help a listener realize the noun phrase is plural. An example is provided for you.

Efv hotososet sasvkwv oklanē nehen vwohkes. 'The skinny dog is barking at the fat, brown goose.' *or* 'The skinny dog is barking at the fat, brown geese.' One would interpret that the speaker meant 'geese' if they saw the dog barking at a flock of geese. A listener also might hear that a number of geese were disturbed by the dog's barking and know to interpret that the speaker was referring to several geese as the objects of the dog's barking.

1. Hoktē hoktvkucen emponvyemvts.
2. Cvcerwv pakpvkoce pvrkomen vwenvhyekotos.
3. Mistet eppucetake tutcēnen oces.
4. Mvnte enhvyvtke cennahvmkvlken encokopericeckvnks.
5. Tvstvnvke mahat Cekvsvlke mēkkvke emvsehes.
6. Honvnwv cvto tenaspen atvkkeses.
7. Cokv-hēcv cvyayvket eshoccickv lanen vpohetos.
8. Mvt pokkēccvlke Cvlakkvlken kērreckv?
9. Vmmvhayvt cokvn ohhonayvnks.
10. Este vculē erkenvkv cvhkēpen mapohices.

Listening Exercises

Listen to the first conversation on the CD, "Shopping for Groceries" (track 2).

1. As you listen, pay attention to the cadence of the two speakers' voices. Do they speak at the same pace? Does one take more time between her words than the other? Does either of the speakers have a rhythm to her lines?

2. Can you identify the stress and tone patterns within the speakers' turns? Do you hear more or less stress at particular points? Do you hear higher and lower tones in their speech?

3. Are you able to identify any words? It is not expected that you will be able to hear all of the words at this point, and you are not being asked to translate any of the conversation—it is enough for you to try and pick out words that you know. Write down the words that you hear clearly in Mvskoke and be ready to present your list in class. Compare the words that you were able to identify with other students' lists.

Perform the same kind of exercise, answering the same questions, with the second conversation, "Watching TV" (track 3).

Importance of the Environment in Muskogee and Seminole Life

The environment has always been very important to the Muskogee and Seminole people. We are taught from a young age to respect Mother Earth and everything that is in nature. We have been told that if we take care of the earth around us, it will take care of us, too. The earth and everything that it produces is what makes it possible for us to live.

At the Green Corn ceremony, we give thanks to the Creator for everything that has been given to us, including the earth. All of the plants and animals are here for us to use, but only if we respect them and use them as we have been instructed. Whenever we go hunting or fishing or collect plants, we should give thanks to them for letting us take them.

Many of our stories also tell about the characteristics of animals and plants, which we learn about by watching them closely. Some of our stories tell about animals that do not seem to be very smart, yet these stories still provide good information. You can learn something from all things in nature. Sometimes you will not expect what the plants and animals will show you, but you should trust that they know what they are doing. They are guided by the Creator.

It is said that when the owner of a piece of property dies, the land will not be as productive as it was when the original owner was alive. Mother Earth will still let crops grow, but some of the goodness of the ground is lost with a death. This just goes to show the strong connection between Muskogee or Seminole people and the land that they have lived on for their life. This is a strong bond that many people do not value today, but we should be aware of it because it is important for all of us. When someone who cares about the environment, Mother Earth, dies, others need to pick up where that person left off and keep the devotion going. If this is done, the earth can be renewed and may become just as productive as it once was, but it takes effort.

The old teachings tell us that we need to take care of the land, plants, and animals that we rely on for food, shelter, clothing, and medicine. If we do not, all of these things will disappear until we cannot find them anymore. This is happening with some of our medicine plants especially. If we do not pay attention to this and take steps to stop the loss of the environment that supports these plants, we will lose something very important for our culture.

Suggested Readings

More information about formation of plural nouns and noun phrases can be found in Nathan (1977: 58–60). While Nathan's analysis has been done on Florida Seminoles, many of the items she describes are pertinent to Oklahoma Muskogee Creeks and Seminoles, too. Martin (1989) has also written a paper about irregular plurals in Muskogean languages, including Mvskoke that may be of interest to some students of the language. One will need to contact Dr. Martin directly for a copy of the paper, as it has not been published in a book or journal available to the general public.

Nathan's (1977: 58–60) and Martin's (1989: 1–3) information about the formation of plurals in Mvskoke is rather short and should be understandable after reading this chapter. In Martin's (1989) work, there is some use of linguistic notation, but the many examples that he provides are sufficient to allow all readers to comprehend the patterns of plural formation that he is investigating in his paper. Nathan's (1977) work also uses linguistic notation, but the many examples she gives and the narrative that precedes and follows the noun-pluralization section present enough information to make her notations comprehensible.

There are a number of sources containing information about the ways the Muskogees (Creeks) and Seminoles have utilized and cared for the environment in which they have lived both before and after Removal. Early journals kept by travelers through country inhabited by Mvskoke-speaking groups before Removal provide us with interesting insights into their food-procurement strategies, modes and avenues of travel, and other cultural practices. Some of the earliest accounts available are those by men accompanying Hernando de Soto as he attempted to conquer the indigenous inhabitants of the Southeast (Bourne 1922).

Later documents come from naturalists, Indian agents, and traders among the Southeastern groups. The travel diary kept by William Bartram (1928 [1791]), a naturalist, during his travels throughout the Southeast is an interesting, fairly easy to read account of his experiences. Bartram writes about what he observed while visiting with Muskogee towns and individuals, as well as about the local flora, fauna, and geographical formations. Benjamin Hawkins, who was the agent responsible for making treaties and agreements with the Muskogees and Seminoles in the late 1700s, kept detailed journals of his observations and activities, many of which contain descriptions of Muskogee and Seminole towns, agricultural, hunting and trading activities, and other practices that may be of interest to those wanting to know more about Mvskoke speakers' relationship with their local environment (Hawkins 1848, 1980; Henri 1986).

More recent works on the relationship between the Muskogees and Seminoles and their environment include four chapters in the *Handbook of North American Indians* (Innes 2004a; Paredes 2004; Sattler 2004; Sturtevant and Cattelino 2004). In these chapters, the current living conditions—including geographic location, environmental conditions, and interactions with the environment—are described for the western and eastern Creeks and the Florida and Oklahoma Seminoles. Each chapter contains several helpful references for those interested in pursuing further research on this topic.

There are also books in which plant identification and use by Mvskoke-speaking people is described. Lewis and Jordan (2002) give a wonderful account of Creek medicine practices, with a section devoted to listing some of the plants used to cure a variety of illnesses. While the book is primarily about the ways in which Lewis was initiated as a Creek medicine man and how he continues to uphold this role, there are several references to changes he has witnessed in the environment and the ways in which these are affecting Creek medicine. The same can be said for Howard and Lena (1984), in which a Seminole medicine man discusses similar issues from his perspective. Finally, Snow and Stans (2001) are principally concerned with identifying and describing how plants are used medicinally by the Florida Seminoles. Each of these works is very readable and interesting.

CHAPTER TWO

Plural Subjects and Suppletive Verbs

Throughout *Beginning Creek*, you were introduced to sentences containing singular subjects and objects. Now it is time to explore plural subjects and objects. A sentence containing **plural subjects** has more than one person or thing performing the action. In English, the first person plural subject is identified through the use of the pronoun "we," as in the sentence, "*We* went to the store yesterday." When the first person plural subject is indicated by a type I suffix, the position of the suffix will be represented by 1P in the third line of the example. When the first person plural subject is demonstrated through use of a type II prefix, the abbreviation used will be 1PII.

The English pronoun "you" is ambiguous, since it can be used to identify a second person plural subject as well as a second person singular subject, though in some dialects of English a second person plural subject is noted through the use of "you all" or "y'all." When the second person plural subject is shown through use of a type I suffix, its position will be marked by 2P in the third line of the example. As you will see, the second person type II prefix is ambiguous for number, so its presence will always be indicated by 2persII, which does not specify singularity or plurality.

And, finally, English utilizes the pronoun "they" to distinguish the third person plural subject. There is no difference in form between the third person plural and singular type I markers, so the presence of the third person suffix will simply be shown by 3pers in the third line of each example. The same also holds for the type II prefixes, so the presence of such a prefix for a third person singular or plural subject will be represented by 3persII whenever it occurs in an example.

Mvskoke indicates that more than one person or thing is performing the action described in a sentence by making changes to the verb. This differs from English, which marks the plural subjects by modifying the noun phrase. Plural subjects are always indicated on the verb in Mvskoke, and at times plural subjects may also be indicated by marking plurality on the noun phrase.

Some Mvskoke verbs have distinctive forms for two subjects, as opposed to either one subject or three or more subjects. Verbs that have specific forms indicating that two subjects are causing the action to occur are said to have a **dual subject** form. Some Mvskoke verbs have a **dual object** form, which specifies that two objects are being affected by the action, to which you will be introduced in chapter 3. Those verbs that have dual subject or object forms will be explicitly identified in the text and vocabulary sections of each chapter in which they occur, and the dual subject or object form will be listed in the glossary entry for that verb.

Verbs that have a change in stem form depending upon the singular, dual, or plural nature of their subject or object are called **suppletive verbs**. Many of the suppletive verbs in Mvskoke have to do with location or movement and are commonly used in conversation and storytelling. You may have noticed that "(of one)" follows the verb definition presented in the vocabulary and glossary portions of textbook 1 for some of the verbs. Verbs marked like this are suppletive verbs and have different stem forms for plural subjects and/or objects. After you have worked through this book, you will have learned several new forms for verbs you came to know in textbook 1, as the forms indicated in many of the examples and exercises in this book use the suppletive form corresponding with plural subjects and objects. This chapter opens with a discussion of suppletive verbs, because they appear commonly in Mvskoke conversations.

SUPPLETIVE VERBS

Suppletive verbs are verbs that have a number of different stem forms. In Mvskoke, the stem variation depends upon the number of subjects or objects, while in other languages it may depend upon the kind of subject (e.g., first person singular, second person singular, first person plural, etc.). Many languages have suppletive verbs, which are sometimes called

TABLE 2.1. Forms of English 'to be'

Singular subjects		Plural subjects	
1S	I **am**	1Pl	we **are**
2S	you **are**	2Pl	you **are**
3S	he/she/it **is**	3Pl	they **are**

"irregular" verbs. In English, for example, the verb 'to be' is a suppletive verb, having stems with three different present tense forms for singular and plural subjects. These stem forms are presented in table 2.1.

Notice that the verb form used with the second, person singular and first, second and third person plural (2S, 1Pl, 2Pl, and 3Pl) subjects are the same and that the first person singular form is related to this ('am' and 'are' are not so very different). The form used with a third person singular (3S) subject 'is' is quite different from both 'am' and 'are.' It is this variation between verb forms depending upon the subject that leads linguists to identify verbs like this as suppletive verbs.

In Mvskoke, suppletive verbs indicate the number of the subject or object. Mvskoke suppletive verbs do not change their stem form based upon the identity of the subject within the singular or plural category (as English 'to be' changes, based upon the identity of the singular subject— 1S versus 2S versus 3S). Instead, Mvskoke suppletive verbs change their form to indicate that one or more than one person or thing is the subject or object of the verb. Mvskoke verbs can be rather specific about the number of subjects and objects, as some verbs have special stem forms for singular subjects or objects: (the singular stem) two subjects or objects (the dual category), as well as a category for more than two subjects or objects.

Mvskoke suppletive verbs are presented in appendix 2. Verbs that have two stem forms, one for singular and another for plural (2 or more) subjects or objects are listed first. Following that list are those verbs with three different forms used to indicate singular, dual (2), and plural (3 or more) subjects or objects. The grammatical feature determining the use of the suppletive form (whether it is the number of subjects or objects) is also shown for each verb after the English translation. If the translation is followed by "(s)," then it is the number of the subject noun that determines use of the different stems, but if the translation is followed by "(o)," it is the number of the object noun.

You will notice that many of the verbs having a form denoting dual subjects or objects create this by inserting the infix *–ho-* near the end of the verb stem used for singular subjects or objects. This infix becomes part of the verb stem, and its vowel undergoes the changes associated with the lengthening, falling-tone, or h-grades. For this reason, you will need to remain aware of the length and tonal quality of the vowel in this infix when you are pronouncing a dual verb form affected by any of the verb grades listed above. This infix is also modified when the extra-high tone grade discussed in chapter 9, is applied to the verb.

No matter which of the two categories (singular-plural forms or singular-dual-plural forms) under which the verb is found, the stems of these verbs are derived in exactly the same manner as presented in chapters 1 and 6 of *Beginning Creek*. For those verbs ending with the *-etv* suffix, this suffix is removed to find the stem. For verbs ending in a long /e/ (*-ē*), the verb stem is what remains when the *-ē* is removed.

Many of the Mvskoke suppletive verbs have to do with location or movement. These verbs tend to change their stem form based upon the number of subjects causing the action to occur. Others of the verbs have to do with the manipulation of goods and materials commonly used in everyday life. These verbs tend to change their form based upon the number of objects affected by the action. Both categories of verbs are frequently used in conversation, so knowledge of their dual and/or plural forms is necessary if you wish to converse with Mvskoke speakers.

The suppletive forms of some of these verbs are presented three times in this book—in the vocabulary section of each chapter, in appendix 2, and in the glossary. Not all of the verbs presented in appendix 2 are used in the book, but the rules that you learn apply to all of them equally. Thus, knowledge of the verb stems presented in appendix 2 will enable you to use a wider number of verbs than you will be asked to work with in the text itself.

FIRST PERSON PLURAL SUBJECT

The first person plural subject in Mvskoke is equivalent in meaning to English "we." Mvskoke indicates that a first person plural subject is causing the action through the use of a suffix on type I verbs and a prefix on type II verbs (for review of the type I and II verbs, see *Beginning Creek*, chapters 3 and 6). When these markers are added to the verb stem, they

TABLE 2.2. Forms of 1P Subject Marker

Verb Type	1P Subject Marker
Type I	-ē-
Type II	po-
Type I/II or II/I	Either –ē- or po-, depending upon inflection

indicate that more than one person or thing is performing the action, but the exact number of subjects is not specified by the affix. When a verb has distinct forms for dual and plural (three or more) subjects, it is the verb stem itself that specifies whether two or more people or things are included in the first person plural subject.

There are different forms used to specify a first person plural subject, depending upon the type of verb (I, II, I/II, or II/I). The different forms used to mark a first person plural subject on Mvskoke verbs are presented in table 2.2 above.

A discussion of the manner in which these affixes are applied to the verb to indicate a 1P subject follows.

First Person Plural Subject Marking on Type I Verbs

As mentioned above, the marker denoting a 1P subject on type I verbs takes the form of a suffix—a marker placed after the verb stem. The form of the 1P suffix is –ē–. On the verb, the 1P suffix occupies the same position as the singular subject suffixes, demonstrated in diagram 2.1. Notice that the 1P suffix comes between the verb stem and any other suffixes that also are being affixed to the verb. (Remember that anything occurring in brackets in a diagram such as this is not obligatory in the construction. This diagram simply shows the order of affixes when they are placed on the verb, but not all of the spaces need be filled in every instance. Because this is the structure of a verb containing the 1P suffix, it has not been bracketed here.)

[Type D Prefix]	[Type II Prefix]	Verb Stem	Type I (1P) Suffix	[Neg. Suffix]	[Past Tense Suffix]	[Same Subj. Suffix]	[Aux. Verb]	[Dec. or Interr. Suffix]

Diagram 2.1. Order of Affixes on a Type I Verb Inflected for First Person Plural Subject

Example 1, using the verb *fotketv* 'to whistle,' which is a type I verb, includes the 1P suffix:

1.   Pomet fotkēs.
      pom-et   fotk-ē-s
      we-indef_subj   whistle-1P-dec
      'We are whistling.'

Notice that the 1P suffix is located directly between the verb stem (*fotk-*) and the declarative suffix (*-s*).

The plurality of the subject may also be indicated by the inclusion of a pronominal noun phrase before the verb. In example 2, *omvlkēyat* 'all of us' makes it very clear to a listener that the subject is plural in number. Even though a plural subject is specified by *omvlkēyat*, the 1P suffix is still attached to the verb *tasecetv* 'to hop (of 3 or more).' Thus, the plurality of the subject is marked several ways: by the presence of *omvlkēyat*, the use of the plural form of the verb, and the addition of the 1P suffix.

2.   **Omvlkēyat** tasēcēs.
      omvlk-ē-yat   tasēc-ē-s
      all-1P-ind_subj   hop_(3+)_l_grd-1P-dec
      'All of us (3 or more) are hopping.' *or* 'We (3 or more) are hopping.'

The /e/ of the verb stem (*tasec-*) has been lengthened (the stem assumes the form *tasēc-*) due to the lengthened-grade, which indicates progressive aspect (the lengthened-grade (or l-grade), present tense, and progressive aspect are covered in chapter 3 of *Beginning Creek*). The second long /e/ in the verb construction, along with the 1P suffix on the pronominal noun phrase (*omvlkēyat*), both indicate that the subject is first person plural ("we").

Occasionally, you may hear speakers place the 1P suffix on the auxiliary verb, which is also a type I verb. In that case, the sentence in example 2 would take the form shown in 3:

3.   Omvlkēyat tasecetowēs.
      omvlk-ē-yat   tasec-et-ow-ē-s
      all-1P-ind_subj   hop_(3+)-ss-aux_vb_l_grd-1P-dec
      'All of us (3 or more) are hopping.' *or* 'We (3+) are hopping.'

Notice that in examples 2 and 3, the characters '(3+)' are attached to the translation of the verb stem in the third line of both. This notation indicates that the verb has a suppletive form by connecting the plural quality of the verb directly to the translation of the verb stem through the use of the underline (as in 'hop_(3+)'). You should use this format whenever you are called upon to make interlinear translations of sentences in this book.

The placement of the 1P suffix shown in examples 1–3 also occurs in example 4. In this example, the 1P suffix comes between the verb stem and the interrogative suffix. The interrogative suffix has the form *–yv* when it follows the 1P suffix, with the /y/ acting as a glide between the vowels of the 1P and interrogative suffixes.

4.   Omvlkēyat tofkēyv?
        omvlk-ē-yat   tofk-ē-yv
        all-1P-ind_subj   spit-1P-int
        'Are we spitting?' *or* 'Are all of us spitting?'

The auxiliary verb may take the interrogative suffix in a construction utilizing the 1P suffix as well. When this occurs, the 1P suffix also gets moved to the auxiliary verb, as shown in example 5.

5.   Tofketomēyv?
        tofk-et-om-ē-yv
        spit-ss-aux_vb-1P-int
        'Are we spitting?'

When the 1P suffix is added to a verb that is also taking the negating and/or one of the past tense suffixes, the 1P suffix is placed between the verb stem and these suffixes. Thus, when the 1P suffix is part of a construction including the negating suffix, the verb will resemble the form presented in example 6.

6.   Misten entokorkēkotos.
        miste-n   entokork-ē-ko-t-o-s
        man-indef_obj   run_away_from_someone_(2)-1P-neg-ss-aux_vb-dec
        'We (two) are not running away from him.'

The 1P suffix is placed in the same position (between the verb stem and the next suffix) when one of the past tense suffixes is used. In example

7, the verb is inflected with the middle past suffix (see chapters 8 and 9 in *Beginning Creek* for review of the past tense forms). The /y/ between the 1P and past tense suffixes is acting as a glide.

7.   Vpelhoyēyvnks.
      vpelhoy-ē-yvnk-s
      laugh_(2+)-1P-mp-dec
      'We laughed.'

Example 8 shows the placement of the 1P suffix when the negating suffix and a past tense suffix appear on the verb. Recall that when both the negating and a past tense suffix are used in a construction, the negating suffix comes before the past tense suffix. The 1P suffix precedes both of these suffixes in the example. The final –en of *hofonofen* is placed in parentheses, because some speakers do not pronounce them.

8.   Hofonof(en) fullēkvnks.
      hofonof(en)   full-ē-k-vnk-s
      long_ago   wander_(3+)-1P-neg-mp-dec
      'We (3 or more) did not wander a long time ago.'

The 1P suffix is very similar to the singular subject suffixes you learned about in *Beginning Creek* in terms of its location and use on type I verbs. When the verb is suppletive and changes its stem form to denote plural subjects, as in examples 2, 3, 6, 7, and 8, the 1P suffix is placed on the verb in the same location it occupies on verbs that are not suppletive. As the next section shows, the 1P prefixes for use on type II verbs also conform to the pattern you were introduced to for the placement of the singular subject prefixes on type II verbs in the first textbook.

First Person Plural Subject Marking on Type II Verbs

A 1P subject is shown by the prefix *po–* on type II verbs. This prefix occupies the same position as all other type II prefixes introduced in *Beginning Creek* (chapter 6). The order of the affixes on a type II verb with a 1P subject is shown in diagram 2.2. Notice that the 1PII prefix (*po–*) comes after the type D prefix, if one is used, and before the verb stem. This is exactly the same placement that you learned to use for type

II singular subject prefixes in the first text. Whenever they are used, the negating, past tense, stative, same subject, auxiliary verb, and declarative or interrogative suffixes follow the verb stem in the order presented in the diagram. Remember that items appearing in brackets in the diagram are not obligatory for the construction of a complete verbal form, so some of these may not be used in a given sentence.

Type D Prefix	Type II (1PII) Subject	Verb Stem	Neg. Suffix	Past Tense Suffix	Stative Suffix	Same Subj. Suffix	Aux. Verb Suff.	Dec. or Interr. Suffix

Diagram 2.2. Order of Affixes on a Type II Verb Inflected for First Person Plural Subject

Example 9 shows how a type II verb is inflected with the 1PII prefix and the declarative suffix. The verb in this example is *cvpakhokē* 'to be angry (of two or more people),' which begins with a consonant. The 1PII prefix (*po-*) is affixed directly to the initial consonant (*c*) of the verb stem. The declarative suffix is then added to the stem to create a complete sentence. The final long /e/ (*ē*) of this construction is the stative suffix showing that the action is stative in nature—it is a state of being—and is not the type I 1P suffix.

9.   Pocvpakhokēs.
      po-cvpakhok-ē-s
      1PII-angry_(2+)-stat-dec
      'We are angry.'

In example 10, the verb is *enokhokē* 'to be sick (of two or more people),' which begins with a vowel. In cases like this, the initial vowel of the verb stem is deleted and the 1PII prefix is added directly to the consonant that follows that vowel. In this example, the initial /e/ is removed and the 1PII prefix is added to the remaining stem (*-nokhokē*), which contains the stative suffix. The declarative suffix is then added to this construction, leading to the following form.

10.   Ponokhokēs.
      po-nokhok-ē-s
      1PII-sick_(2+)-stat-dec
      'We are sick.'

When suffixes are added to the verb, they take the order indicated in diagram 2.2. Example 11 presents a construction utilizing the negating, distant past, same subject, auxiliary verb, and interrogative suffixes. Notice that the order in which the negating and same subject suffixes appear is exactly like that presented in diagram 2.2. The distant past suffix has been placed on the auxiliary verb between the verb stem and the interrogative suffix.

11.   Posomhokekotomvnkv?
      po-somhok-**eko-t-om-vnk-v**
      1PII-be_lost_(2)-neg-ss-aux_vb-dp-int
      'Weren't we (two) lost some time ago?'

Finally, example 12 presents a type {II;D} verb with the inclusion of a type D object prefix. Because the 1PII prefix begins with a consonant (/p/) the form of the D prefix is taken from the group used when the verb does not begin with *em*– (table 7.2 of *Beginning Creek*).

12.   Cenpomvlostētos.
      cen-po-mvlost-ē-t-o-s
      2persD-1PII-care_for-stat-ss-aux_vb-dec
      'We care for (are fond of) you.'

Notice that the order of the prefixes is second person type D followed by the first person plural type II prefix. The stative, same subject, auxiliary verb, and declarative suffixes follow one another. This is precisely what one would expect from diagram 2.2.

First Person Plural Subject Marking on Type I/II or II/I Verbs

When a first person plural subject is to be marked on a type I/II or II/I verb, the same rules governing the placement and form of the prefix or suffix that we discussed earlier are followed. Generally, if a verb is of this type (I/II or II/I) and is in a construction containing both a subject and an object, the first person plural subject will be shown through the use of the 1P suffix. This allows the object to be the only prefix on the verb, so there is less grammatical information placed at the beginning of the verb structure.

Example 13 provides an example of the structure of a verb containing a 1P suffix and an object prefix. While this verb, *enhomecē* 'to be angry with,' is noted as a type {II;D} form in Martin and Mauldin's (2000) dictionary, it takes a type I suffix to mark the subject in this example. It would appear that some of the verbs marked as {II;D} in the dictionary could be considered as {II/I;D} verbs. Whether such verbs are constructed like {II;D} or {II/I;D} verbs may depend on the dialect of Mvskoke being spoken.

13.   Pomet cenhomecēyēs.
      pome-t   cen-homec-ē-yē-s
      we-ind_subj   2persD-furious_with-stat-1P-dec
      'We are angry at you.'

In this construction, 'we' is marked as the subject through the use of both a pronoun with the subject suffix (*pome-t*) and the inclusion of the type I suffix (-*ē*-) on the verb. The second long /e/, which follows a y-glide in this example, is the stative suffix, showing that the action being discussed is a state of being.

When an object prefix is not used on a type I/II verb, the most common means of showing the first person plural subject marker would be to use *ē*-, the type I suffix. In a sentence containing a type II/I verb without an object, the type II prefix *po*- is used most often to designate a first person plural subject. Remember that these verbs have two ways of showing the subject (I/II *or* II/I) and that the second type of marking will be used in some instances.

For instance, type II/I and I/II verbs may have two slightly different interpretations, depending upon which type of subject marker is used. In examples 14 and 15, the two meanings of the verb *nocicetv* 'to sleep [be asleep], go to sleep (of three or more people/things)' are made evident by the use of two sets of subject affixes. Example 14, which includes the type II prefix, causes a listener to interpret the sentence as 'we were asleep.' While no past tense suffix actually occurs in the sentence, it makes sense that one cannot talk about being asleep while still asleep, so the speaker must have awoken from the state of sleep and the state being discussed is in the past.

14.   Ponocices.
      po-nocic-es
      1PII-to_sleep_(3+)-dec
      'We (3+ people) were asleep.'

In example 15, the use of the type I subject suffix leads a listener to interpret the verb as 'going to sleep,' which is the second definition listed for the verb.

15. Omvlkēyat nocicēs.
     omvlk-ē-yat   nocic-ē-s
     all-1P-ind_subj   go_to_sleep_(3+)-1P-dec
     'We (3+ people) are going to sleep.'

You will find that the use of one of the two types of subject affixes occurring with {II/I} and {I/II} verbs with two slightly different definitions will lead a listener to interpret the verb as having one of the meanings versus the other. Generally, the order of the affixes listed in brackets will correspond with the order of the definitions offered for the verb. In this case, *nocicetv* has the definitions 'to sleep' and 'go to sleep' listed in that order and the order of subject affixes listed is {II/I}. Notice that use of the type II prefix led to the production of a sentence with the first definition of the verb and the use of the type I suffix led to the production of a sentence with the second definition of the verb.

SECOND PERSON PLURAL SUBJECT

The second person plural subject, equivalent to 'you (two or more people)' in English, is marked on the verb in one of three ways in Mvskoke. On type I verbs with or without suppletive forms, this subject is marked by a suffix (–*ack*–). On type II verbs with suppletive plural subject forms, the second person plural subject is marked by the addition of a prefix to the verb. On type II verbs that do not have suppletive forms for plural subjects, the second person plural subject is marked by the affixation of both a prefix and a suffix. The forms of the affixes used to inflect verbs for a second person plural subject are shown in table 2.3.

Second Person Plural Subject Marking on Type I Verbs

The second person plural subject is designated on type I verbs through the application of a suffix (-*ack*-), noted as 2P hereafter. While this suffix sounds as though it should be written as *-atsk-, because only the initial portion of the *c* sound is produced before the *k*, it is always written as

TABLE 2.3. Marking Verbs for a Second Person Plural Subject

Verb Type	Second Person Plural Subject Marker
Type I	-ack-
Type II without suppletive form	second person prefix and –vk-
Type II with suppletive form	second person prefix
Type I/II *or* II/I	Either –ack-, second person prefix alone, *or* second person prefix and –vk-, depending upon verb form

–ack– in the text. The 2P suffix is also noteworthy because it is an always key syllable. Remember that always key syllables are those that take a high tone and influence the tones of those syllables that follow them. Thus, whenever a 2P suffix is part of a verbal construction, it has a high tone and causes a decrease in tone of those syllables that come after it.

Use of the 2P suffix is demonstrated in example 16. The 2P suffix is placed in exactly the same location presented earlier for the 1P suffix in diagram 2.1. Thus, in this example, the 2P suffix comes between the verb stem and the interrogative suffix. The tonal contours of the verb (discussed in *Beginning Creek*, chapter 2) are presented in the third line of the example in order to demonstrate the effects of the inclusion of the 'always key' 2P suffix. The tonal notation shows that the highest tone occurs on the 2P syllable and the interrogative syllable following it has a much lower tone.

16.   Enpefatkackv?
      enpefatk-**ack**-v
      i-2-2-**4**-d
      run_away_(3+)-2P-int
      'Are you (three or more) running away?'

A similar placement of highest tone on the 2P suffix is shown in example 17, where another always key syllable (the negating syllable) is included in the construction of the verb. The tone order of syllables in this structure is indicated in the third line of the example.

17.   Tashokackekotos.
      tashok-**ack-eko**-t-o-s

i-2-4-3-2-d
hop_(2)-2P-neg-ss-aux_vb-dec
'You (two) are not jumping/hopping.'

Because the 2P suffix is the first of the two always key syllables, its tone is highest, while the tone of the negating suffix is the next highest in the word. Any time there is more than one always key syllable in a word, the first is given the highest tone and the others' tones are lower. Also note that the order of the suffixes is following that shown in diagram 2.1. As we presented in that diagram, the 2P suffix immediately follows the verb stem, and is then followed by the negating and same subject suffixes, auxiliary verb, and declarative suffix.

Second Person Plural Subject Marking on Non-Suppletive Type II Verbs

Marking a second person plural subject on type II verbs that do not have suppletive forms is done using both a prefix and a suffix. The prefix set used to mark a second person plural subject is presented in table 2.4. You may notice that these forms are identical to the forms used to mark a second person singular subject on a type II verb, which was introduced in chapter 6 of *Beginning Creek*. Because these sets are the same, you will need to pay attention to whether the distributive suffix, discussed below, has also been affixed to the verb. If a second person subject prefix appears on a non-suppletive type II verb without this suffix, you should consider the subject to be singular.

TABLE 2.4. Second Person Prefix Forms for Use on Non-Suppletive Type II Verbs

Verbs Beginning with consonant or *e*	Verbs Beginning with *ē*	Verbs with Any Vowel Other Than *e* or *ē*
ce-	ecē-	ec-

It is the inclusion of the **distributive suffix** –*vk*- on the stem that makes it clear that the second person subject in the sentence is plural rather than singular. The distributive suffix acts as a means of demonstrating that the action affects or is conducted by a range of objects or subjects. When the type II verb has a suppletive form for plural subjects or objects, it is unnecessary to use the distributive suffix, because the verb stem already alerts a listener to the plurality of the subject or object. However, on verbs that do not have suppletive forms for plural subjects and objects, the distributive suffix alerts the listener that the second person subject or object is plural in nature. The distributive suffix also occurs in constructions indicating a third person plural subject, so learning about its placement and use will also be reinforced in the section discussing constructions for that subject.

The positions of the 2persII prefix and distributive suffix on a type II non-suppletive verb are presented in diagram 2.3. In this diagram and those that follow, the location of the distributive suffix is marked by 'Distr. Suffix' in the diagram. The positions of the second person prefix and distributive suffix marking a second person plural subject are not noted in brackets in this diagram, because the diagram shows specifically where these items occur on the verb.

| $\begin{bmatrix} \text{Type D} \\ \text{Prefix} \end{bmatrix}$ | Type II (2 persII) Prefix | Verb Stem | Distr. Suffix | $\begin{bmatrix} \text{Neg.} \\ \text{Suffix} \end{bmatrix}$ | $\begin{bmatrix} \text{Past} \\ \text{Tense} \\ \text{Suffix} \end{bmatrix}$ | $\begin{bmatrix} \text{Same} \\ \text{Subj.} \\ \text{Suffix} \end{bmatrix}$ | $\begin{bmatrix} \text{Aux.} \\ \text{Verb} \end{bmatrix}$ | $\begin{bmatrix} \text{Dec. or} \\ \text{Interr.} \\ \text{Suffix} \end{bmatrix}$ |

Diagram 2.3. Order of Affixes on a Type II Non-Suppletive Verb Inflected for Second Person Plural Subject

The distributive suffix, shown as 'distr' in the third line of each example in which it appears, is quite different from the other suffixes you have been introduced to thus far, because it is affected by the lengthened- and h-grades. When the distributive suffix is added to a verb, it is so closely associated with the verb stem that its vowel becomes the final vowel in the stem. Thus, when the lengthened grade is applied to that verb, it is the vowel of the distributive suffix that is lengthened. For this reason, you will notice that the form of the distributive suffix is –*ak*- in the examples when the verb has undergone vowel lengthening. The fact that the distributive suffix has undergone lengthening will be shown in the second line of each example through the use of the symbols 'distr_l_grd.'

The distributive suffix is also affected by the h-grade when this is applied to the verb. When the verb is to be modified for the very recent past tense (h-grade), the modifications will be made to the distributive suffix, leading to the form –*vhk*- in the examples. The presence of the h-grade in such examples will be shown by placing '<hgr>' after the abbreviation of the affected morpheme. The characters surrounding 'hgr' in this abbreviation show that it is an infix. In chapter 9, you will be introduced to yet another verb grade affecting the final vowel in the verb stem, which will also cause the vowel in the distributive suffix to be modified.

The ordering of the 2persII prefix and distributive suffix is demonstrated in example 18. The verb in this example (*etkolē* 'to feel cold (of an animate being)') does not have a suppletive form showing that the subject is plural. Thus, both the second person type II prefix (*ce-*) and the distributive suffix (*-vk-*) are used to demonstrate that the 'you' who is feeling cold in this example refers to more than one person.

18.   Cetkolvkēte?
      ce-tkol-**vk**-ēte
      2persII-to_feel_cold-distr-int
      'Are you (plural) feeling cold?'

Due to the presence of both the second person prefix and the distributive suffix, the subject is identified as second person plural. Be certain to note that both the second person and distributive markers occur on the verb when you are asked to identify the meaningful units in a Mvskoke sentence containing a second person plural subject in the chapter exercises in this book.

When a sentence utilizing a type II verb that does not have a suppletive form contains the negating and/or a past tense suffix, these follow the distributive suffix. To ask whether several people were cold in the middle past, the verb would have the following form.

19.   Cetkolvkvnkēte?
      ce-tkol-**vk**-**vnk**-ēte
      2persII-to_feel_cold-distr-mp-int
      'Did you (plural) feel cold?'

Occasionally, a second person plural subject will be shown on non-suppletive {II;D} verbs by the use of the type I suffix (*-ack-*) when a type D prefix is used to indicate an indirect object. In example 20, for instance, the non-suppletive type {II;D} verb *enhomecē* 'furious/mad (at someone)' is inflected with the appropriate D prefix (*vn-*) for the indirect object 'at me,' but the second person plural subject is indicated through the use of the type I suffix instead of the type II prefix.

20.   Vnhomecackēte?
      vn-homec-**ack**-ēte
      1SD-mad_at-2P-int
      'Are you (plural) mad at me?'

The use of the type I suffixes on type II verbs that do not undergo stem changes to indicate plural subjects may be a result of a speaker's wish to make it clear to a listener that the subject is plural. There may be other reasons guiding the use of type I marking on type II verbs as well. No matter what the logic is behind the use of the type I subject-marking system on type II verbs, be aware that it occurs and does not imply these verbs are really type II/I or that the speaker has misspoken.

Second Person Plural Subject Marking on Suppletive Type II Verbs

When a type II verb has a suppletive form for plural subjects, the second person plural subject is marked through the application of the second person prefixes, shown in table 2.4. The distributive suffix is not used in these constructions, because the changes on the verb stem already indicate a plural subject. The order of prefixes and suffixes is exactly that listed in diagram 2.3, except that the distributive suffix is not used.

The prefixes and suffixes shown in example 21 follow the order shown in diagram 2.3. On this type {II} verb, *enokhokē* 'sick (of two or more),' the 2persII prefix is the first item on the verb and the interrogative suffix follows the verb stem.

21.   Cenokhokēte?
      ce-nokhok-ēte
      2persII-sick_(2+)-int
      'Are you (two or more) sick?'

The form of the second person prefix is *ce-* in this example, because the verb stem begins with an *e-*. The verb stem indicates that the subject is plural, so a listener knows to interpret the subject prefix as referring to two or more people or things.

In example 22, the verb (*vholwahokē* 'to be dirty (of two or more)') has a suppletive form beginning with the vowel *v*. This requires that the second person plural prefix take the form *ec-*, as shown in table 2.4. The distant past and declarative suffixes are placed in just the order one would expect from diagram 2.3.

22.   Eceholwahokemvts.
      ec-vholwahok-emvt-s
      2persII-be_dirty_(2+)-dp-dec
      'You (2 or more) were dirty.'

Second Person Plural Subject Marking on Type I/II and II/I Verbs

The second person plural subject is identified on type I/II and II/I verbs in different ways, depending upon the structure of the verb stem and whether an object or indirect object also is contained on the verb. The most commonly used method of indicating a second person plural sub- ject on a type I/II verb is to affix the 2P suffix *–ack–*. This method, which involves the use of the same suffix used on type I verbs, is the preferred form for most speakers. (This is why type I inflection is indicated first in the verb type designation.) However, for those speakers who prefer to treat the verb as type II, the 2persII prefix is used on verbs having a sup- pletive form, while the 2persII prefix and distributive suffix are used together on verbs without a suppletive form.

When no direct or indirect objects are contained on the verb, type II/I verbs will generally take the same kind of marking you learned to use on type II verbs—that is, the 2persII prefix on suppletive verbs, and the 2persII prefix and distributive suffix on verbs that do not have a suppletive form. When an indirect or direct object is identified by a prefix on the verb without a suppletive form, however, the type I suffix (*-ack-*) is fre- quently used to show a second person plural subject. As we discussed pre- viously regarding type {II;D} verbs, using the type I suffix to designate the second person plural subject makes it quite clear to a listener that the subject is, indeed, plural.

THIRD PERSON PLURAL SUBJECT

The third person plural subject is equivalent to 'they' in English. A third person plural subject is indicated on a Mvskoke verb in one of three ways, depending upon the kind of verb being inflected. The different means of

TABLE 2.5. Third Person Plural Subject Marking Constructions

Verb Type	Third Person Plural Subject Marker
Type I or II without suppletive form	null prefix (type II) or suffix (type I) and the distributive suffix -vk-
Type I with suppletive form	null suffix
Type II with suppletive form	null prefix
Type I/II or II/I	Either –vk– or the null prefix or suffix, depending upon inflection

showing that a third person plural subject is performing an action are shown in table 2.5. The third person plural subject is marked by affixing the distributive suffix (*–vk–*) on type I and II verbs that do not have suppletive forms. When type I and II verbs are suppletive for plural subjects, the null third person (3pers) suffix and prefix are used on the verb respectively. When a verb is type I/II or II/I, it will follow whichever rule is appropriate for the verb, depending on whether it is or is not a suppletive verb. We begin with a discussion of type I verbs and the distributive suffix indicating a third person plural subject on these verbs.

Third Person Plural Subject Marking on Type I Verbs

The way in which a third person plural subject is marked on type I verbs depends upon whether the verb has a suppletive form. If the verb stem does not change to show plural subjects, then the third person plural subject is demonstrated by attaching the distributive suffix (-*vk*-) after the null third person suffix. The position of this suffix, as well as all other affixes that may appear on a type I verb inflected for a third person plural subject, is shown in diagram 2.4. Again, the vowel of the distributive suffix

Type D Prefix	Type II Prefix	Verb Stem	Type I (3 pers) Suffix	Distr. Suffix	Neg. Suffix	Past Tense Suffix	Same Subj. Suffix	Aux. Verb	Dec. or Interr. Suffix

Diagram 2.4. Order of Affixes on a Non-Suppletive Type I Verb Inflected for Third Person Plural Subject

will be the one affected by the lengthened grade or h-grade when either is applied to the verb.

Because the third person plural (3pers) type I suffix is a null suffix, meaning that it does not have a form that is pronounced, it is really the inclusion of the distributive suffix that indicates the subject is third person plural. The necessity of including the distributive suffix in order to show the subject is third person plural has caused us to mark the position of the distributive suffix without brackets.

In example 23, the position of the 3pers, distributive, remote past tense, and declarative suffixes follow the order presented in diagram 2.4.

23.   Hofonof hompakemvts.
      hofonof   homp-Ø-ak-emvt-s
      long_time_ago   eat-3pers-distr_l_grd-dp-dec
      'They were eating (a very long time ago).'

Inclusion of the negating suffix leads to the construction demonstrated in example 24, in which the 3pers and distributive suffixes occupy the same positions as in example 23. The distributive suffix in example 24 has the form –vk-, because it has not been modified due to the lengthened grade as in example 23. The past tense and declarative suffixes all come after the negating suffix.

24.   Hofonof hompvkekomvts.
      hofonof   homp-Ø-vk-eko-mvt-s
      long_time_ago   eat-3pers-distr-neg-dp-dec
      'They did not eat (a very long time ago).'

When the type I verb has a suppletive form, the third person subject suffix has a null form (it does not have a form that is audible). Thus, as when inflecting a type I verb for a third person singular subject, it appears as though there is no suffix attached to the suppletive form of the verb. The fact that a listener does not hear a suffix tells her or him that the subject is the third person plural.

An example of the formation of a verb with the null third person plural suffix is shown in 25 below. Both the definite subject and third person plural suffixes, which have null forms, are represented by a zero (Ø) in their positions.

25.   Hoktvkuce efvn eshvkahēces.
       Hokt-vk-uce-Ø   efv-n   Ø-eshvkahēc-Ø-es
       woman-pl-dim-def_subj   dog-ind_obj   3persII-cry_about_(3+)
                                                          _l_grd-3pers-dec
       'The little girls are crying about a dog.'

Because neither the audible first- nor the audible second-person plural subject suffixes are attached to the suppletive verb stem, a listener knows that a
third person plural subject is crying about the dog. In example 25, a plural
subject noun (*hoktvkuce*) precedes the verb, which assists the listener in
identifying the subject as a third person plural. However, a listener would
be able to identify the third person plural subject even without the inclusion of a plural subject noun, so the sentence in example 25 could be said
in the form shown in 26.

26.   Efvn eshvkahēces.
       efv-n   Ø-eshvkahēc-Ø-es
       dog-ind_obj   3persII-cry_about_(3+)_l_grd-3pers-dec
       'They are crying about a dog.'

Third Person Plural Subject Marking on Type II Verbs

Type II verbs that do not have a suppletive form are inflected for a third
person plural subject by adding a null third person subject prefix and the
distributive suffix to the verb stem. Examples 27 and 28 show how a non-
suppletive type II verb is inflected for a third person plural subject.

27.   Yvlahv kvmoksvkēs.
       Yvlahv-Ø   Ø-kvmoks-vk-ē-s
       orange-def_subj   3persII-sour-distr-stat-dec
       'The oranges are sour.'

Neither the noun phrase nor the verb stem shows that the subject is
plural, so it is only the inclusion of the distributive suffix on the verb that
specifies a plural subject. Given that Mvskoke nouns are not always
marked for plurality and not all verbs are suppletive, you will need to be
aware of and pay attention to the use of the distributive suffix.

The verb stem in example 28 is different from its infinitive form (*nekattetv*) because of the use of the h-grade, not because the verb is suppletive.

28. Tēkvnvlke tutcēnat vnnekatiyes.

tēkvn-vlke	tutcēn-at	vn-Ø-nekatiy-es
deacon-pl	three-def_subj	1SD-3persII-nod_once<hgr>-dec

'The three deacons nodded once at me (just now).'

In this example, it is only audible features on the noun phrase that let a listener know that the subject is plural. First, the noun itself is marked for the plural by the *–vlke-* suffix. The noun phrase includes the numeric adjective 'three' specifying the number of deacons who are nodding. Due to the presence of these plural indicators on the subject noun phrase, it is not necessary to mark plurality on the verb, so the distributive suffix does not appear in this example.

When a type II verb is suppletive, a null prefix is added to indicate a third person plural subject. In essence, the lack of any other prefix on the suppletive verb form indicates that a third person plural subject is performing the action. All other plural subjects have prefixes that one can hear on the suppletive verb stem.

Examples 29 and 30 demonstrate how suppletive verbs are inflected for third person plural subjects. Example 29 uses several suffixes but only the third person (null) prefix in its construction.

29. Hofonof konot fvmfvpekotomvtēs.

hofonof	kono-t	Ø-fvmfvp-eko-t-om-vtē-s
long_time_ago	skunk-ind_subj	3persII-smelly_(2+)-neg-ss-aux_vb-rp-dec

'A long, long time ago, skunks were not smelly.' (as in a story)

In example 30, the first person type D and the 3persII prefixes are used. The position of the null third person prefix is indicated in the third line of the example, even though it does not have an audible form on the verb.

30. Vncvpvkhokēte?

vn-Ø-cvpvkhok-ēte

1SD-3persII-mad_at_(2+)_l_grd-int

'Are they mad at me?'

Third Person Plural Subject Marking on Type I/II and II/I Verbs

On type I/II and II/I verbs, the third person plural subject is most frequently marked according to the manner indicated by the number appearing before the slash. Thus, on type I/II verbs the third person plural subject will be shown most commonly through the affixation of the 3pers and distributive suffixes (-Ø- and -vk- respectively) on those verbs whose stems do not change for plural subjects. On {I/II} verbs that are suppletive when plural subjects are performing the action, the third person plural subject is indicated by the 3pers (null) suffix. On type II/I verbs, a third person plural subject is indicated by the use of the 3persII (null) prefix and distributive suffix on verbs that do not have suppletive forms and by the 3persII (null) prefix on verbs that are suppletive.

In the end, it is necessary to have some knowledge of the suppletive verb forms in order to correctly understand a speaker of Mvskoke. The majority of suppletive verb forms in Mvskoke are listed in appendix 2, in order of English translation. Suppletive forms of verbs used in this text, listed according to their Mvskoke spelling, are provided in the Mvskoke to English glossary, with an entry for each form of the verb stem provided there. The number of verbs having suppletive forms is fairly large, but their frequency of use in the language should assist you in memorizing many of those listed in the Mvskoke to English glossary and in appendix 2.

Vocabulary

ANIMALS

English		Mvskoke
duck		foco
	or	fuco
toad *or* frog		sopaktv
snake		cetto
rattlesnake		cetto hvce svkvsicv
opossum		sokhv-hatkv
owl, screech owl		efolo
turkey		penwv
hawk		ayo

eagle		lvmhe
squirrel		ero
worm		cuntv
turtle		locv
gopher		ekvn(v) rolahvlēcv
	or	hvcetekv
	or	vcetekv
mole or vole		tvko
skunk		kono

VERBS

English		Mvskoke
to jump, hop (of one) {I}		tasketv
to jump, hop (of two) {I}		tashoketv
to jump, hop (of three or more) {I}		tasecetv
to wriggle {I}		fekefeketv
	or	wenowēyetv
to climb up, of one {I;3}		vcumketv (Seminole)
		vcemketv (Muskogee)
to climb up, of two {I;3}		vcumhoketv (Seminole)
		vcemhoketv (Muskogee)
to climb up, of three or more {I;3}		vcumecetv (Seminole)
		vcemecetv (Muskogee)
to come down, of one {I}		ahvtvpketv
	or	akhvtvpketv
to come down, of two {I}		ahvtvphoketv
	or	akhvtvphoketv
to come down, of three or more {I}		ahvtvpecetv
	or	akhvtvpecetv
to whistle {I}		fotketv
to run away from someone, something (of one) {I;D}		enletketv
to run away from someone, something (of two) {I;D}		entokorketv
to run away from someone, something (of three or more) {I;D}		enpefatketv
to spit {I;II}		tofketv
to carry, catch one object {I;II}		esetv
to carry, catch two or more objects {I;II}		cvwetv

Exercises

EXERCISE 1

Create ten sentences using plural subjects on type I verbs that do not have suppletive forms. Two of the three plural subjects you have learned to use in this chapter should be present in three of your sentences, and one should be present in four sentences. Some of your sentences should also utilize the negating and/or past tense suffixes. Use the recent past (h-grade) in one sentence as well. After you have formed your sentences, break each word into its morphemes, as has been done in each of the examples in the chapter. Then provide a translation of each sentence.

EXERCISE 2

Create ten sentences using plural subjects on type I verbs that have a suppletive form showing plural subjects. (A list of suppletive verbs is presented in appendix 2.) Two of the three plural subjects you have learned to use in this chapter should be present in three of your sentences, and one should be present in four sentences. Some of your sentences should also utilize the negating and/or past tense suffixes. Use the recent past (h-grade) in one sentence as well. After you have formed your sentences, break each word into its morphemes, as has been done in each of the examples in the chapter. Then provide a translation of each sentence.

EXERCISE 3

Create ten sentences using plural subjects on type II verbs that do not have suppletive forms. Two of the three plural subjects you have learned to use in this chapter should be present in three of your sentences, and one should be present in four sentences. Some of your sentences should also utilize the negating and/or past tense suffixes. Use the recent past (h-grade) in one sentence as well. After you have formed your sentences, break each word into its morphemes, as has been done in each of the examples in the chapter. Then provide a translation of each sentence.

EXERCISE 4

Create ten sentences using plural subjects on type II verbs that have suppletive forms. (A list of suppletive verbs is presented in appendix 2.) Two of the three plural subjects you have learned to use in this chapter should be present in three of your sentences, and one should be present in four sentences. Some of your sentences should also utilize the negating and/or past tense suffixes. Use the recent past (h-grade) in one sentence, as well. After you have formed your sentences, break each word into its morphemes, as has been done in each of the examples in the chapter. Then provide a translation of each sentence.

Exercise 5

Each of the sentences below has been inflected for a first person singular subject. Using the verb that occurs in the original sentence, inflect the verb for a first person plural subject. When a verb has a suppletive form for a dual subject, inflect the verb for that subject as well. Translate each sentence once you have completed the various inflections. An example is provided.

Tulsa ayis.	Tulsa vhoyēs.	Tulsa vpēyēs.
I am going to Tulsa.	We (2) are going to Tulsa.	We (3 or more) are going to Tulsa.

1. Cetto hvce svkvsicvn pohis.
2. Cvlvwēs.
3. Tasikis.
4. Cvholwvkekotos.
5. Foco hecimvts.
6. Eton vcemkis.
7. Eton pvfnēn vcemkiyvnks.
8. Vcohohkes.
9. Honvnwv vculē emvpelis.
10. Cēwvnwv encvcvpakkekotos.

Exercise 6

Each of the sentences below has been inflected for either a second person singular or a second person plural subject. If the subject in the sentence is second person singular, inflect the verb that occurs in the original sentence for a second person plural subject. If the subject in the sentence is second person plural, inflect the verb for a second person singular subject.

When a verb has a suppletive form for a dual subject, inflect the verb for that subject as well. Translate each sentence once you have completed the various inflections. An example is provided.

Tvkon hēceckv?   Tvkon hēcackv?
Do you (singular) see the mole?   Do you (plural) see the mole?

  1. Cefvckvkēte?
  2. Fullackekvnks.
  3. Mvhakv-cuko yefolikeckv?
  4. Fekefēkackvtēs.
  5. Yvhiketvn cvyayakusēn yvhikecketomvts.
  6. Eton ahvtvphokackvnkv?
  7. Cewvnhkēte?
  8. Cehathvwvks.
  9. Rakko lvstē rakkan emenhoteckēte?
10. Paksvnkē wakkeckvnks.

EXERCISE 7

Each of the sentences below has been inflected for a third person singular subject. Inflect the verb that occurs in the original sentence for a third person plural subject. If the verb has a suppletive form for a dual subject, inflect the verb for that subject as well. None of the subject nouns presented in these sentences have forms indicating plurality, so you need not alter the form of any of the nouns in these sentences. Translate each sentence once you have completed the various inflections. An example is provided.

Poset lētketos.   Poset tokorketos.   Poset pefatketos.
The cat is running. The (2) cats are running. The (3+) cats are
                                            running.

  1. Sopaktvt taskeks.
  2. Nokoset lvmhen homipv?
  3. Svtv lowvckekomvts.
  4. Eto mahat lvtikes.
  5. Mēkko vmmērrvtēs.

6. Cvcket wakvpesēn asvnwiyes.
7. Svtv cvlaknētos.
8. Cokv-hēcv vhoccickv lvstan vslēces.
9. Foco lekothofv fvccvn tvmketos.
10. Wotkot eton ahvtvpkekvnks.

EXERCISE 8

Read the following short story. Use information from the story to answer the questions that follow it. Answer the questions in complete sentences, as your teacher may ask you to read your answers aloud in class.

Tom tvlofvn yvkapet ayetos. Tom Cemme hēces. Cemme rakko hvtkan ohlikes. Tom "Hensci!" kihcetos. Cemme "Hensci!" kihcetos. "Stvmen ayeckv?" Tom kihces. "Tvlofvn ayis. Stvmen ayeckv?" Cemme kihcetos. "Tvlofvn ayis. Cvhotosēs. Paksvnkē yekcēn vtotkiyvnks. Paksvnkē cvrke emvniciyvnks. Mucv-nettv vcen vyocēyvnks," Tom kihcetos. "Rakko yekcētos. Cēmeu rakkon ohḻikeckes. Rakko ohkakēs." Cemme kihcetos. Cēpvnvke hokkolat tvlofvn vhoyvnks.

1. Estvmen Cemme vyvnkv?
2. Estimvt rakkon ohlikv?
3. Tom estonko?
4. Nakstomen Tom hotosēte?
5. Cemme lopicēte?
6. Estomē cēpvnvke tvlofvn vhoyv?

Listening Exercises

Listen again to the first conversation on the CD, "Shopping for Groceries" (track 2). Have ready the list of words you recognize that you wrote out for the listening exercise in chapter 1.

Now, listen to the first ten sentences in this conversation one by one (tracks 9–19). Listen for individual words within the sentences. Listen to the sentences as many times as you need to in order to get a sense of what the speakers are saying. Are there any words that you do not recognize even after listening to the sentences several times? If so, make note of the sentence in which these words occur and approximately when in the sentence they do so. Ask your teacher or a fluent speaker of Mvskoke to listen to the sentences and help you with the pronunciation and translation of these words. With this help, are you able to get a sense of what the speakers are talking about?

Working with a classmate, take turns reciting sentences 1–6 from "Shopping for Groceries" (tracks 9–15). Begin by having one of you repeat the sentences spoken by the first speaker, while the other participant takes the sentences spoken by the second speaker. When you are fairly comfortable repeating those sentences, take the other speaker's role. If you cannot pronounce all of the words exactly, try at least to mimic the intonational contours of the words. Be ready to recite these sentences in class as best you can. Your teacher may allow you to recite along with the CD, or you may be asked to recite as much as possible from memory.

Use of Herbs to Catch Fish in the Old Days

People used to catch fish a lot in the old days. Whenever the crops were sturdy enough that they could be left for a day or two, families would meet on the bank of one of the rivers or streams. Usually this would be two or three families. There was lots of work to be done.

The day before the fishing was scheduled to take place, one of the men would gather some herbs or weeds. These weeds are known by the name *hvloneske* or *hvnoleske* (called "Devil's Shoestring" in English). They look like string. These would be collected and then beaten against a log or fence rail. When the plant was beaten, it would fray and split open a little so that the inside was exposed.

The beaten plants would then be put in a tub of water. The amount of water depended on how big the stream was that you were going to fish at. The tub was left in the sun all day. By evening, the top was frothy, kind of like the foam that collects on a lakeshore after a big windstorm. The men would load the tub into a wagon and take it to the streambed.

When everyone was gathered at the stream, the men, women, and children would gather willow branches. These were made into a fence across the stream by sticking the bigger poles into the bottom and weaving the others from one big pole to the next. When this was done, the willows

Three young fishermen, ready to shoot, August 27, 1924. *Jennie Elrod Collection, Courtesy of the Oklahoma Historical Society. Negative #20382.950.*

acted like a fence across the stream. A fence was put in upstream and downstream from where the men would be fishing.

Two or three men who could swim would then take the tub and pour it out in the stream, moving from one side to the other. As soon as the herb water hit the stream water, the fish would start to rise to the surface. The fish acted like they could not really swim anymore. Men on the banks would shoot their arrows at the fish and kill them that way. When the shooting was done, everyone would go to the stream or river and collect the fish that had been shot. Each family would claim its fish, which they could identify because of the markings on the arrows.

Usually, the families would have a big fish fry right there. Kettles would be brought out, and the fish would be fried at the riverbank. Most families brought pancakes or pan-made corn bread to eat with the freshly fried fish. Whatever was not eaten right there could be taken home, though usually there was not much left after a fish fry. The families might stay together for the night or go home that same day. Either way, it was a nice way to visit with other families and have some fun.

Waiting to go into the water. Ground Devil's Shoestring in the tubs. August 27, 1924. *Jennie Elrod Collection, Courtesy of the Oklahoma Historical Society. Negative #20382.946.*

Suggested Readings

Information about forming sentences with plural subjects may be found in Nathan (1977: 93–103), Bosch (1984: 35), and Harwell and Harwell (1981: 23–25). Nathan's (1977) work explores the ways in which sentences containing plural subjects are formed in Florida Seminole. Several of the items discussed in that work are treated here, and they appear to work similarly for speakers of Mvskoke from Oklahoma and Florida. There are a few slight differences, however, so readers should be aware that the two regional dialects of Mvskoke are not completely alike.

Both Bosch (1984) and Harwell and Harwell (1981) are texts produced in order to facilitate language classes at Bacone College. The material contained in these works provides a basis to which a language instructor would add more information and explanation. Both works offer further examples of sentences inflected for plural subjects, but the reader may find that the narrative in the sections in which plural subject sentences are discussed does not cover the verb inflection and sentence formation rules in enough detail to be satisfactory. However, these books may be useful as additional resources against which to check the information presented in this text, particularly as they contain further examples of plural subject sentences.

The importance of farming and hunting to the Muskogee and Seminole way of life, from the archaeological past to the present, has been well documented. While there is some uncertainty about exactly which archaeological sites are associated with the Muskogee Creek, Seminole, and other Southeastern tribes, it is clear that agriculture was practiced by the ancestors of the Mvskoke-speaking people. Welch (1991) and Blitz (1993), among others, provide clear evidence of farming in Mississippian archaeological sites dating from about A.D. 900 to the early 1500s.

Growing crops, gathering wild foods, and hunting game were carried out during the years preceding and following Removal to Oklahoma, as evidenced by travelers' descriptions of food-procurement strategies carried out by Mvskoke-speaking people. Thomas Nairne's journals (1988), kept while he journeyed from South Carolina to the Mississippi River in 1708, give us an early glimpse at some of the agricultural and hunting practices of several Southeastern peoples, including the Muskogees. At the time, Europeans did not recognize the Muskogees as a unified people, and they may not have been, so his descriptions are of individual groups (the Ochessees, Talapoosies) who later became part of the Muskogee people. He describes the hunting and farming practices that he witnessed in some detail. A little later in time, William Bartram (1928[1791]) speaks about the same issues among the pre-Removal Muskogees and Seminoles.

It appears that the Muskogee and Seminole people attempted to resume their agricultural ways after Removal, as evidenced by the descriptions in the journals of E. A. Hitchcock (1996) and the writings of Alex Posey as presented and analyzed by Littlefield (1992). Both authors found that the Muskogees and Seminoles continued to rely on agriculture and on hunting and fishing to meet their subsistence needs. The tenacity and resourcefulness of the Mvskoke-speaking people was clearly evident as they learned how to survive in an environment very different from that in Georgia, Alabama, and Florida. The fact that they were capable farmers, fishermen, and gatherers made it possible for them to flourish in a new land. Lest you get the idea that traditional ways of doing things were only helpful in the past, we would point out that the relevance of traditional tools and ways of doing things is still recognized by the Muskogee Creek and Seminole people, as indicated by items like those in the *Muscogee Nation News* (2007).

CHAPTER THREE

Plural Direct and Indirect Objects

When someone or something is directly affected by the verb, that noun is considered to be the **direct object** of the action. In the English sentence "Joe is eating the apple," 'the apple' is the direct object because it is the thing being eaten by Joe. In *Beginning Creek*, chapter 7, you were introduced to the way in which singular direct objects are shown on Mvskoke verbs. In this chapter, you will learn how plural direct objects are indicated.

This chapter also covers another class of objects, **indirect objects**, which are nouns that are affected by the action in an oblique (indirect) way. Frequently, indirect objects are people or things that are the recipients of an action or provide a directional focus for the action. The sentence "Her brother handed the baby to me" contains an indirect object ('me'), who is the recipient of the action of 'handing,' while 'the baby' is the direct object. In the sentence "The boy chased the horse away from us," 'us' is the indirect object and provides a sense of the direction in which the horse was being chased. We will begin with a discussion of the ways in which plural direct objects are indicated in a Mvskoke sentence, then we will move on to plural indirect objects.

PLURAL DIRECT OBJECTS

As we mentioned previously, direct objects are those that are immediately affected by the action specified in the sentence. They are the items upon which the action is performed. Plural direct objects are indicated in

57

Mvskoke sentences by affixing either a type II or a type D prefix to the verb, depending upon whether the primary verb is type {I;II}, {I;D}, or {II;D}. The distributive suffix is also added when the direct object is second or third person plural.

There are also suppletive verbs in Mvskoke that change their stem form when plural objects are affected by the action. Verbs with suppletive plural object forms take the type II and type D prefixes, but the distributive suffix is not added to these verbs. There is no question about the plural nature of the object on these verbs, so the presence of the distributive suffix, which helps to indicate plurality of subjects and objects, is not necessary.

Marking Verbs For Type II Plural Direct Objects

Type {I;II} verbs that do not have a suppletive form for plural objects denote a plural direct object through the use of type II prefixes and, in the case of second and third person plural objects, the distributive suffix. The form of the plural type II prefix varies somewhat depending upon the first sound of the verb stem. The abbreviations that will be used in the third line of each example to refer to the category of person (first, second, third) of the object, different forms of the type II plural direct object prefixes, and the association of the second and third person prefixes with the distributive suffix are shown in table 3.1.

As you can see, it is the first sound of the verb stem that determines the form of the plural direct object prefix. For verbs beginning with a consonant or *e*, the second and third person prefixes are exactly like those showing a singular direct object. The inclusion of the distributive suffix is the only difference between a verb form marked for plural second and third person objects rather than a singular object. First person plural direct objects, however, are marked by prefixes quite different from those showing first person singular direct objects.

The type II plural prefixes are attached to type {I;II} verbs in the same position and manner as is demonstrated in chapters 6 and 7 of *Beginning Creek*. The order of the affixes is presented in diagram 3.1. The positions of the type II direct object prefix, distributive suffix, and type I subject suffix are not placed in brackets, because diagram 3.1 is specifically indicating where these affixes occur on the verb. Example 1 shows the second person plural direct object prefix attached to *hecetv* 'to see.' Note that the 2persII prefix is attached directly to the verb stem. The distributive and type I subject suffixes follow the verb stem and are, in turn, followed by the declarative suffix.

TABLE 3.1. Ways of Marking Plural Direct Objects on Type II Verbs That Do Not Have Suppletive Forms for Plural Objects

Verb Stem First Sound	Person Abbreviation	Plural Direct Object Translation	Mvskoke Direct Object Prefix Form
Consonant or *e*	1PII	us	(e)po-
	2persII	you (plural)	ce- and distr. suffix –vk-
	3persII	them	Ø and distr. suffix –vk-
Any vowel except *e*	1PII	us	ep-
	2persII	you (plural)	ec- and distr. suffix –vk-
	3persII	them	Ø and distr. suffix –vk-

Type II direct object prefix	verb stem	distributive suffix	TypeI subject suffix	neg. suffix	past tense suffix	declarative or interrogative suffix

Diagram 3.1. Order of Constituents on a Type {I;II} Verb with a Direct Object

The 2persII prefix has the form *ce-* because it is attached to a verb that begins with a consonant. The distributive suffix has the form *–ak-*, because it has been affected by the lengthened grade.

1. Omvlkackan cehecakis.
    omvlk-**ack**-an   ce-hec-**ak**-i-s
    all-2P-def_obj   2persII-see-distr_l_grd-1S-dec
    'I see all of you (plural).'

In this example, the plurality of the object 'you' is demonstrated through the application of the distributive suffix on the verb and the use of a plural pronoun *omvlkackan* 'all of you,' which contains the second person plural type I suffix. Mvskoke speakers often clarify that a second and third person direct object is plural through the use of a separate pronoun, and they may use a separate pronoun to indicate that a first person direct object is plural, too.

The sentence in example 2 demonstrates the inclusion of a third person plural pronoun (*mistvlken*) that helps to specify that the object of the sentence is plural. As we discussed above, this appears to occur in order to make it clear to listeners that the object is plural.

2.   Mvn mistvlken kerrakeckv?
      mvn   mist-**vlk**-en   Ø-kerr-**ak**-eck-v
      those   man-pl-ind_obj   3persII-know-distr_l_grd-2S-dec
      'Do you know those men?'

Because the type II prefix indicating a third person direct object is a null prefix, it has no form that is pronounced. A listener knows that the third person object is plural, because of the combination of the plural noun *mistvlken* and the inclusion of the distributive suffix on the verb, which again has the form –*ak*- due to the lengthened grade. You will find that many speakers in the Muskogee and Seminole communities, when referring to a plural third person direct object, will often mark the object's plurality through the use of a plural noun form and the appropriate verbal form for plural objects.

The first person plural prefix is attached directly to the verb stem in example 3, in keeping with the order of affixes presented in diagram 3.1. At first glance, it would appear that the form of the first person direct object plural (1PII) prefix to be used on this verb should be *ep-*, because the verb looks as though it begins with the vowel *i*. However, the initial *i* is a prefix that is moved from the verb stem when another prefix is applied. Thus, the form of the 1PII direct object prefix ((*e*)*po*-) applied to this verb is that used on verbs beginning with a consonant or *e*-. The initial *e* of the 1PII prefix is then replaced by the initial *i* from the verb.

3.   Omvlkackat ipomapohicackes.
      omvlk-ack-at   **ipo**-mapohic-ack-es
      all-2P-def_subj   1PII-eavesdrop_on-2P-dec
      'You (plural) are eavesdropping on us.'

This same prefix form (*e*)*po*- also appears in examples 4a and 4b. The initial *e* of the prefix is in parentheses because some speakers do not pronounce it. The verb in examples 4a and 4b (*celayetv* 'to touch, feel') takes this form of the 1PII prefix, because it begins with a consonant. Speakers will pronounce the sentence in the two ways, presented in 4a and b, depending upon whether they pronounce the initial vowel of the prefix. Note that the plurality of the subject is not shown on the verb by the presence of the distributive suffix (–vk-). Instead, the plural nature of the subject is demonstrated by the addition of a plural adjective following the subject noun. First person plural objects do not use the distributive suffix to show they are plural.

4a.   Wotko sulkat epocelayetos.
      wotko   sulk-at   **epo**-celay-Ø-et-o-s
      raccoon   many-ind_subj   1PII-touch-3pers-ss-aux_vb-dec
      'Raccoons are touching us.'

4b.   Wotko sulkat pocelayetos.
      wotko   sulk-at   **po**-celay-Ø-et-o-s
      raccoon   many-ind_subj   1PII-touch l_grd-3pers-ss-aux_vb-dec
      'Raccoons are touching us.'

Both sentences are exactly the same in meaning, despite the differences in pronunciation of the 1PII prefix.

When a verb begins with any vowel besides *e*, the form of the 1PII prefix attached to the verb is *ep-*. Example 5 demonstrates the application of this prefix on *akketv* 'to bite':

5.   Efv epakkvnks.
      efv-Ø   **ep**-akk-Ø-vnk-s
      dog-def_subj   1PII-bite-3pers-mp-dec
      'The dog bit us.'

Type II Object Prefixes on Suppletive Verbs

Some verbs in Mvskoke change their form when the object is plural. These suppletive verbs are presented in appendix 2, with an (o) following the English translation. We have already introduced you to the verbs that change their form when the subject is plural, shown by the (s) following their translation. For those verbs marked with an (o) following their translations, the change in the verb stem clearly indicates to a listener that the object is plural.

The type II prefixes attached to those verbs with suppletive forms for plural objects are the same as those attached to verbs that do not change their form. Thus, the prefixes shown in table 3.1 are used on the suppletive verbs. The distributive suffix is not used to indicate plural second and third person objects, as the verb stem makes this evident. In example 6, the suppletive verb form demonstrates that the object is plural, so there is no need to use a pronoun or the distributive suffix to indicate this fact. In effect, the object prefix simply helps to indicate whether the plural object is first, second, or third person.

6.   Hoktē coko sulke hvsvthicekvnks.

hoktē-Ø	coko	sulke-Ø	**Ø-hvsvthic-Ø-ek-vnk-s**
woman-def_subj	house	many-def_obj	3persII-clean_(2+)-3pers-neg-mp-dec

      'The woman did not clean the houses.'

While *coko* 'house' does not have a form showing plurality, the inclusion of the modifying adjective *sulke* 'many' and the change in the verb stem tell a listener that the woman did not clean several houses.

      In example 7, the fact that the 'you' indicated through the use of the prefix *ce-* is referring to more than one person is indicated by the form of the verb stem. *Svholwahuecetv* is used when more than one object is being dirtied, so it is unnecessary to use *omvlkacken* to indicate the plurality of the second person direct object. The initial *sv-* on the verb stem is actually a pair of prefixes, which we discuss in detail in chapter 7. These prefixes, whose positions are shown by 'instr' and 'app' in the third line are moved to precede the object prefix.

7.   Pipuce svceholwahuecvnkv?

pipuce-Ø	s-v-**ce-holwahuec**-Ø-vnk-v
baby-def_subj	instr-app-2persII-make_dirty_(2+)-3pers-mp-int

      'Did the baby make you (plural) dirty?'

As you might imagine, use of these suppletive verbs makes it obvious to listeners when a plural object is affected by the action specified in the sentence. These verbs are listed in appendix 2, and you are encouraged to become familiar with them.

INDIRECT OBJECTS

Indirect objects are those that are obliquely or indirectly affected by the action in the sentence. In English, indirect objects frequently follow prepositions, as in the sentence "Jimmy kicked the ball **at me**." In this sentence, "Jimmy" is the subject, "the ball" is the direct object, and "me" is the indirect object. "Me" is providing a directional focus for the action (notice that it follows the preposition "at"), but this person is neither performing the action nor being directly affected by the kicking. When a noun plays only a peripheral role in the performance of the action in the sentence, we consider it to be an indirect object.

In Mvskoke, indirect objects are signified primarily through the use of the Dative prefix set. Verbs that take indirect objects of this type have the notation {I;3;D} or {II;D} in their glossary entry. When the indirect object is second or third person plural, the distributive suffix is used in conjunction with the appropriate D prefix. The prefix set shown in table 3.2 is used with both {I;3;D} and {II;D} verbs and also indicates that the distributive suffix is used with the second and third person prefixes to mark the plurality of the object. The choice of prefix form depends upon whether the prefix is attached to a verb stem beginning with *em-* or to some other combination of sounds. This becomes an important point when working with type {I;3;D} verbs beginning with *em-*, as these take the third person (null) type II prefix to mark the direct object. Because the third person type II prefix is null, the indirect object prefix will always be of the form that attaches to *em-*. For type {I;3;D} verbs beginning with *em-* and taking the first or second person type II prefix, the D prefix will always be taken from the column showing forms affixed to anything but *em-*, as these type II prefixes have audible forms.

Examples 8 through 10 demonstrate the use of type D prefixes on type {II;D} verbs that do not have suppletive forms for plural objects. The first verb *em penkvlē* 'to be afraid of' and the verb in example 10 *em enhotetv* 'to be uneasy about' both begin with *em-*. Because there is no type II prefix coming between the type D prefix and the verb stem, the type D prefixes used in these examples are from the middle column of table 3.2. In example 9, the verb *enhomecē* 'to be angry at' begins with *en-* and takes the type D prefix from the last column in table 3.2. The verb in example 9 does not have a suppletive form, nor does it take the distributive suffix. In this

TABLE 3.2. Type D Prefix Forms for Plural Indirect Objects

Prefix Abbreviation and Translation	Form Affixed to *em-*	Form Affixed to Anything but *em-*
1PD "to us, at us, etc."	(e)pom-	(e)pon-
2persD "to you (plural), at you (plural), etc."	cem- and distr. suffix (-vk-)	cen- and distr. suffix (-vk-)
3persD "to him/her/it, at him/her/it, etc."	em- and distr. suffix (-vk-)	en- and distr. suffix (-vk-)

case, the context in which the sentence is used is the only way a listener can be certain about the plurality of the subject and/or object.

8.   Mv hoktet pompenkvlētos.
        mv   hokte-Ø   **pom-Ø-penkvl-ē-t-o-s**
        that   woman-ind_subj   1PD-3persII-afraid_of-stat-ss-aux_vb-dec
        'That woman is afraid of us.'

9.   Erkenvkv cenhomēcvkētos.
        erkenvkv-Ø   **cen-Ø-homēc-vk-ē-t-o-s**
        preacher-def_subj   2persD-3persII-angry_at-distr-stat-ss-aux_vb-dec
        'The preacher is angry at you (plural).'

10.   Penwv konon emenhotvkēs.
        penwv-Ø   kono-n   **em-Ø-enhot-vk-ē-s**
        turkey-def_subj   skunk-ind_obj   3persD-3persII-uneasy_about-distr-
                                            stat-dec
        'The turkey is uneasy about the skunks.'

    Notice that no plural pronouns are used in any of these sentences. The use of such pronouns is unnecessary, because the first person plural indirect object marker is quite different from the singular form and the second and third person plural indirect object forms include the distributive affix, which helps distinguish these from singular forms. It would be possible for a speaker to include a plural pronoun or modify the object noun with a suppletive adjective in order to be absolutely clear about the plurality of the indirect object in the sentence, as we discussed in the section on direct objects. For instance, sentence 9 could be rephrased with a pronoun as in example 11, to make it absolutely clear that the indirect object is plural.

11.   Erkenvkv omvlkackan cenhomēcvkētos.
      erkenvkv-Ø   omvlk-**ack**-an   **cen**-Ø-homēc-vk-ē-t-o-s
      preacher-def_subj   all-2P-ind_obj   2persD-3persII-angry_at-distr-stat-
                                                        ss-aux_vb-dec
      'The preacher is angry at all of you.'

Marking Verbs for Both Plural Subjects and Objects

There are occasions when it will be necessary to include a plural subject and object in a sentence. When the subject is plural first person, there is no uncertainty about this, as the plural first person forms for these roles are quite different from other plural subject and object prefix forms. Examples 12 and 13 show how the first person plural subjects on both type I and type II verbs are quite distinct from the plural object markers that may occur with them.

12.   Hoktvke omvlkan emmapohicētos.
      hokt-vke   omvlk-an   em-mapohic-ē-t-o-s
      woman-pl   all-ind_obj   3persD-listen_to-1P-ss-aux_vb-dec
      'We are listening to the women.'

13.   Mistvlken encvpvkhokēyētos.
      mist-vlk-en   en-cvpvkhok-ēy-ē-t-o-s
      man-pl-ind_obj   3persD-mad_at_(2+)-1P-stat-ss-aux_vb-dec
      'We are mad at them.'

Notice that the distributive suffix does not occur on the verb in example 12, even though the object is third person plural. In this case, the plural marking on the noun itself (*hoktvke*) makes it apparent that the object is plural and allows a speaker to leave the distributive suffix off of the verb.

When the plural object is first person, the forms of the type II and D prefixes make it clear to a listener that the first person plural is being used. Thus, in examples 14 and 15, the plural first person prefixes make it obvious that the object being discussed is first person plural in nature. The initial *as-* of *aswiyetv* is another of the prefixes that is moved to a position before any object marking prefixes, which we will discuss further in chapter 7. In this example, its position is marked by the abbreviation 'app.'

14.   Honvntake aspomwiyiyes.
      honvn-take-Ø   as-**pom**-wiyiy-Ø-es
      man-pl-def_subj   app-1PD-pass_to<hgr>-3pers-dec
      'The men passed it to us.'

15.   Pohehcackv?
      po-hehc-ack-v
      1PII-see<hgr>-2P-int
      'Did you (plural) see us (just now)?'

When a second person plural subject is indicated on a type I verb, the plurality of the subject is easy to hear, thanks to the distinctive form of the 2P suffix. When a third person plural object is added to a verb containing the second person plural suffix, the distributive suffix stands out as the marker of the plurality of the object, because it does not co-occur with the 2P suffix. In example 16, the verb is conjugated for a second person plural subject and a third person plural object. You will note, however, that the distributive suffix does not appear on the verb. The plural form of the object noun makes it possible for a speaker to leave off the distributive suffix in this case, though it is not always the practice with other statements.

16.   Mēkkvken pohackv?
      mēkk-vk-en   Ø-poh-**ack**-v
      chief-pl-ind_obj   3Pldo-hear-2Pl-int
      'Do you (plural) hear the chiefs?'

It can be difficult to tell when a third person plural object has been added to a type II verb conjugated for a second person plural subject. This uncertainty occurs because the second person plural subject is denoted by the combination of the second person prefix (*ce-*) and the distributive suffix (*-vk-*). When a third person plural object is added to this existing form, there appears to be no change, as the only difference is a null prefix placed at the beginning of the verb. The distributive suffix has already been added to the verb as one part marking the second person plural subject. Because of the ambiguity in a verb conjugated for a second person plural subject and a third person plural object, the plural subject and object noun phrases are frequently specified in the sentence, as in example 17.

17. Omvlkackat hvtekpikv sulken ceyvcakēte?
     omvlk-**ack**-at   hvtekpikv   **sulk**-en   Ø-ce-yvc-ak-ēte
     all-2P-def_subj   pants   many-ind_obj   3persD-2persII-want-
                                                            distr_l_grd-int
     'Do you (plural) want the pants?'

In this case, as in many others, the plurality of the subject noun phrase is marked by a pronominal form of *omvlke* and the plurality of the object noun phrase is indicated by the use of the word *sulken* 'many.'

When a type {II;D} verb is conjugated for a second person plural subject and a plural third person plural object, the subject may be indicated by the use of the type I suffix. Using the second person plural type I suffix form makes the plurality of the subject very clear to a listener. It also makes the use of the distributive suffix a feature that can only be marking the plurality of a third person plural object.

The easiest way to make it obvious that a verb has been conjugated for plural third person subjects and objects is to specify the plurality of the subject and object in noun phrases before the verb. An example of this is shown in example 18, where *sulke* 'many' has been included in the object noun phrase and the subject noun has a distinctive plural form.

18. Cēpvnvke svtv sulken hompvhkes.
     cēpvn-**vke**-Ø   svtv   **sulk**-en   Ø-homp-Ø-vhk-es
     boy-pl-def_subj   apple   many-ind_obj   3persII-eat-3pers-distr<hgr>-dec
     'The boys ate the apples (just now).'

Both the subject and object, being third person plural, take the distributive suffix to demonstrate their plural nature on the verb. When a listener may have difficulty knowing whether the distributive suffix is referring to the subject, the object, or both, a speaker can make it clear by including a noun phrase that is already marked as plural, as was done in this case. The distributive suffix has a distinctive form in this example, because the h-grade has been applied to it.

Vocabulary

CLOTHING

English		Mvskoke
shoe/shoes		estelepikv
sock/socks		(estele) svhocackv
	or	svhocickv
pants		hvtekpikv
skirt		honnv-lecv
	or	honnv kocoknosat
dress		honnv
shirt		yokkofketv
hat		kvtopokv
	or	kvpotokv
glasses, eyeglasses		torsakhēckv
watch		hvse-eskērkuce
ring		estenkesakpikv
tie, scarf, anything worn around the neck		ohenockv
underwear		ofiketv
glove		(e)stenke-hute
coat		kapv
vest		sakpv-seko
boots		estelepik morvfkv
	or	sohtēhkv
quilt		telomhv

VERBS

English	Mvskoke
to sew (one item) {I;3}	vhoretv
to sew (two or more items) {I;3}	vhorhuecetv
to fold {I;3}	pvkohlicetv
to put on clothing that slips over the head or is wrapped around the body (one subject) {I;3}	vccetv
to put on clothing that slips over the head or is wrapped around the body (two or more subjects) {I;3}	vchoyetv

to put on one shoe or one item pulled up on a body part, to put one item in another {I;3}	vpiketv
to put on pants or two things pulled up on a body part, to put two or more items in another {I;3}	vtehketv
to take off one's own clothes {I}	ēkayetv
to take off one piece of clothing {I;3}	roketv
to take off more than one piece of clothing {I;3}	rokruecetv
to wash (one object or subject) {I;II}	okkosetv
to wash (two or more objects or subjects) {I;II}	okkoskuecetv
to iron {I;3}	tenēpicetv
to dry one item {I;3}	kvrpēcetv
to dry two or more items {I;3}	kvrkvpēcetv
to be dirty, unclean {II}	svholwvkē

Exercises

EXERCISE 1

Translate these sentences. Identify each of the morphemes in the Mvskoke words, then provide a morpheme-by-morpheme analysis before you list the English translation. In the end, you should have lines similar to the second, third, and fourth lines of each example in this chapter.

1. Cēmet wakvpesē nehan aspomwiyeckes.
2. Hokte mahet honnv osten lvpkēn vhorhuehceks.
3. Pakpvkoce lanan ceyvcakēte?
4. Omvlkackat kapvn okkoskuecackv?
5. Sakpv-sekon vcceckes.
6. Yokkofketv sulken rokruecekotomis.
7. Hoktvkucet kapv pvkohlicvketomv?
8. Efv cvpakhokat vpowohecemvts.
9. Nokose sopakhvthvkat hvtekpikv holatten homipvkes.
10. Honnv hvmken vhoris.

EXERCISE 2

Each of the sentences below has been formed with a plural direct object. Change each of the sentences so that it has the correct form for a singular direct object. Use the same number of person marking on the direct object as you change the sentence. For instance, if the original direct object is first person plural, you should change the object to first person singular; second person plural changes to second person singular; and third person plural changes to third person singular. In some cases, you may need to change the form of the direct object noun when one is included in the sentence.

 1. Estelepik morvfkvn somhuecackvnkv?
 2. Sakpv-seko ēpaken nesimvts.
 3. Eslafkv fvsfvkē ocecketos.
 4. Hoktucet enhonnv-lecv hokkolen neseks.
 5. Omvlkackan kerriyatēs.
 6. Estelepikv vtēhkis.
 7. Honvnwv vculat nokose tutcēnen hehces.
 8. Nokose tutcēnet hopuetaken vwenayaks.
 9. Hopuetaket honvntake vcule sulken emmapohicakekotos.
10. Hoktē mahat ohenockv ofiketv svhocackv tepakat okkoskueces.

EXERCISE 3

Translate the following sentences from English to Mvskoke. In order to be certain that you have not omitted any pertinent features from the verb, we suggest that you separate each of the morphemes in the verb, as has been done in the second line of each example in this chapter. Your teacher may require that you do this when the exercise is assigned.

 1. I gave them five oranges yesterday.
 2. Mother folded four of my shirts just now.
 3. Did you (plural) iron our pants?
 4. We are not afraid of the skinny dogs.
 5. Those two children are dirty.
 6. The girls did not eat all five pies just now.
 7. Some ducks are flying north.
 8. Those six rivers are deep.
 9. You (plural) did not listen to the preacher on Sunday.
10. The two boys are hanging up their hats.

EXERCISE 4

Each of the following sentences contains a singular indirect or direct object. Change these sentences so that they have plural objects. Use the same number of person marking on the indirect object as you change the sentence. For instance, if the original indirect object is first person singular, you should change it to first person plural; second person singular changes to second person plural; and third person singular changes to third person plural. In some cases, you may need to change the form of the indirect object noun when one is included in the sentence.

1. Oponayv cvyayvkēn vmponvhyes.
2. Vcvtofihkeckv?
3. Hoktvlan vsse asemwiyis.
4. Cofe rakrvkē hokkolat ecohvthoyvtēs.
5. Cēpanat torsakhēckv mvhayvn ehmes.
6. Pipucet tolose lanan empenkvlētos.
7. Pome cemmērrēkotomēs.
8. Mv honvnwvt vmvkeriyices.
9. Hoktē ehesset efv ennokkan emmērrosēte?
10. Cvpvwvn esvmfekcakhēte?

EXERCISE 5

A list of subjects, direct objects, indirect objects, and verbs is provided. Where prefix or suffix forms are suggested (as for a first person singular subject or object), the abbreviation for that subject or object (e.g., 1S, 2S, 2P, etc.) is used in the appropriate column. From this list, construct ten sentences made up of some combination of the elements. You will need to decide what tense you will use in each of the sentences, and some of your sentences may include negation. You may also construct questions.

You should have used every item in the list after you have constructed all of the sentences. The number of different sentence constructions you could make from the items provided is quite large, though you should try to construct sentences that make some sense. After you have constructed your ten sentences, you should be prepared to say them out loud in class. Your teacher may have you translate other students' sentences, too, so be

ready to listen closely to your classmates' sentences and recall the meanings
of the vocabulary and morphemes we have listed below.

Subject Nouns	Direct Object Nouns	Indirect Object Nouns	Verbs
penwv	estenke-hute	ēwvnwv	emetv
cokv-hēcv	cvtvhakv	2P	vpefatecicetv
foco	owvlvste eshoccickv	2S	ohtvmhoketv
epose	ofiketv	1S	em vcvnēyetv
1P	hvtekpikv	mvhayv	tenēpicetv
mistvlke	cesse	3pers (singular)	ēkayetv
2S	vce	3pers (plural)	hompetv
kaccv			pvkohlicetv
mēkko			em mapohicetv
hoktvke			aswiyetv

EXERCISE 6

Each of the sentences below has been formed with a singular direct
object. Change each of the sentences so that it has the correct form for a
plural direct object. Use the same number of person marking on the
direct object as you change the sentence. For instance, if the original
direct object is first person singular, you should change the object to first
person plural; second person singular changes to second person plural;
and third person singular changes to third person plural. In some cases,
you may need to change the form of the direct object noun when one is
included in the sentence.

   1. Hvtekpikvn okkosis.
   2. Omvlkackat cvnvfkackvnks.
   3. Hoktuce hotosat yokkofketv sopakhvtken tenēpicekomvts.
   4. Cecket pipucen asvmwiyetos.
   5. Cēpvnvke hokkolat kvnhvlwen vtokorkvtēs.
   6. Efv oklanat cvhēhkes.
   7. Rakko hvtket eto lanen ahvlvtes.
   8. Omvlkat cehecakes.
   9. Ervhvlke rakrvket vcvhopvkvkvnks.
   10. Penwv holwvyēcē vculat cetakikv?

EXERCISE 7

Create your own story about family gatherings. This story should contain at least twelve sentences, half of which must have either plural objects or plural indirect objects. You may write the story in either the present or the past tense or employ a combination of both. Be prepared to tell the story to your classmates should your teacher ask you to do so.

EXERCISE 8

Each of the following sentences contains a plural indirect object. Change these sentences so that they have singular indirect objects. Use the same person marking on the indirect object as you change the sentence. For instance, if the original indirect object is first person plural, you should change it to first person singular; second person plural changes to second person singular; and third person plural changes to third person singular. In some cases, you may need to change the form of the indirect object noun when one is included in the sentence.

1. Cvrket pommēkusapemvts.
2. Hvse-eskērkuce osten omvlkackan ecohfolhuecvkis.
3. Pipuce ennokket omvlkan ohhaktēsikvks.
4. Kapvn omvlkackan cencvwakis.
5. Hoktuce cahkēpet pakpvkocen omvlkacken cehmvkes.
6. Efvn cvpakkat pofvccvn alētkes.
7. Erkenvkvt tohwelēpkvn sulke mistvlken emvkvnks.
8. Cerket wakv-pesē nehan aspomwihyes.
9. Mēkko honvntake omvlken cvyayvkēn emponayaketos.
10. Mv hoktet hopuetakuce elvwvkan tvklik-cvmpen hompicvkvnks.

Listening Exercises

Listen again to the second conversation on the CD, "Watching TV" (track 3). Have ready the list of words you recognize that you wrote out for the listening exercise in chapter 1.

Now, listen to the first ten sentences in this conversation one by one (tracks 33–43). Listen for individual words within the sentences. Listen to the sentences as many times as you need to in order to get a sense of what the speakers are saying. Are there any words that you do not recognize even after listening to the sentences several times? If so, make note of the sentence in which these words occur and approximately when they occur the sentence. Ask your teacher or a fluent speaker of Mvskoke to listen to the sentences and help you with the pronunciation and translation of these words. With this help, are you able to get a sense of what the speakers are talking about? If there are constructions in the sentences that you do not understand, make note of them and ask your teacher about them in class. Some of these constructions may require review of *Beginning Creek*, while others will be covered later in this book, so your teacher may ask you to keep your notes and questions as you continue to work on the language. In some cases, though, your teacher may want to discuss the structures at the time.

Working with a classmate, take turns reciting sentences 1–6 from "Watching TV" (tracks 33–39). Begin by having one of you repeat the sentences spoken by the first speaker, while the other participant takes the sentences spoken by the second speaker. When you are fairly comfortable repeating those sentences, take the other speaker's role. If you cannot pronounce all of the words exactly, try at least to mimic the intonational contours of the words. Be ready to recite these sentences in class as best you can. Your teacher may allow you to recite along with the CD, or you may be asked to recite as much as possible from memory.

Listen to the fifth conversation on the CD, "Health" (track 6).

   1. As you listen, pay attention to the cadence of the two speakers' voices. Do they speak at the same pace? Does one take more time between her words than the other? Do either of the speakers have a rhythm to their lines? Do any of these turns sound different from the others? Why might that be?
   2. Can you identify the stress and tone patterns within the speakers' turns? Do you hear more or less stress at particular points? Do you hear higher and lower tones in their speech?
   3. Are you able to identify any words? It is not expected that you will be able to hear all of the words at this point, and you are not being asked to translate any of the conversation—it is enough for you to try

and pick out words that you know. Write down the words that you hear clearly in Mvskoke and be ready to present your list in class. Compare the words that you were able to identify with other students' lists.

Patchwork

The Muskogees and Seminoles are known for their patchwork clothing. Clothing made with patchwork is very colorful. The colors and patterns in patchwork are meaningful to the Muskogee Creek and Seminole people.

Patchwork is made by sewing narrow strips of fabric together lengthwise to form strips of fabric three, four, or more colors wide. Think of the strips below as five long, narrow strips of fabric. When the strips are sewn together, they will make the form in the next picture.

Blue	Red	White	Red	Blue

Blue
Red
White
Red
Blue

Long pieces of fabric like this are cut top to bottom to make narrow strips again, this time with all of the colors in a strip. The strips from one or more of the multicolored strips are then pieced back together, with some rotated or moved up or down a strip to make the pattern. The next picture shows how these little strips would be pieced together to make a pattern. The pieces shown here are from three different multicolored strips. One is just like the long piece shown above; another has the colors in the order blue, white, red, white, blue; and the third has the colors arranged as blue, black, black, black, blue. If narrow strips are cut from these multicolored strips and rearranged, they can end up in the pattern below:

From strip 3	From strip 2	From strip 1	From strip 2	From strip 3	From strip 3	From strip 2	From strip 1	From strip 2	From strip 3
Blue	Blue	Blue	Blue	Blue	Blue	Blue	Blue	Blue	Blue
Black	White	Red	White	Black	Black	White	Red	White	Black
Black	Red	White	Red	Black	Black	Red	White	Red	Black
Black	White	Red	White	Black	Black	White	Red	White	Black
Blue	Blue	Blue	Blue	Blue	Blue	Blue	Blue	Blue	Blue

These strips are then sewn onto vests, jackets, and skirts. When people wear clothing with these colorful pieces, they look happy, healthy, and active. Some of the patterns also tell something about a person. There are patterns that symbolize a clan or the fire, both of which are important to traditional Muskogee Creek and Seminole people. You can tell a lot about a person wearing patchwork if you know what the patterns mean.

Suggested Readings

The readings that we suggested in chapter two, Nathan (1977), Bosch (1984) and Harwell and Harwell (1981), also cover constructions with plural objects. As we stated in chapter two, Nathan's (1977) work is the most thorough of the three, with some discussion of the intricacies of inflecting verbs for both plural subjects and objects. Nathan presumes that the reader has some knowledge of linguistic terminology and notation, which can make reading this text a little difficult, but the narrative that precedes and follows the section in which she discusses inflecting verbs for plural subjects and objects can make much of her terminology and notation clear to a reader.

Bosch (1984) and Harwell and Harwell (1981) are materials meant to supplement a language class led by a teacher with knowledge of the language, and they may not be as explanatory as a reader might wish. The examples offered in these works do allow readers of this textbook to see that the affix positions and their uses are consistently followed on verbs other than those in our examples. Thus, these books, while perhaps raising more

Martha Holata's dress, made by June Lee. Mekusukey Mission, Oklahoma, July 13, 1999. *Photograph by Chester R. Cowen. C. R. Cowen Collection, Courtesy of the Oklahoma Historical Society. Negative #19687.IN.FC5.12.11.*

questions than they are able to answer, can be helpful when used in conjunction with this textbook.

Those interested in patchwork designs and their manufacture have a number of outside resources to investigate. The history of patchwork, which was begun by the Florida Seminoles in the 1800s, and a study of several designs is presented in Rush and Wittman (1994). The authors give instructions for the creation of patchwork strips and their application to clothing of several types. The directions are easy to follow, and the rationale behind the construction of strips is explained nicely.

Two Web sites that readers may find helpful are Preston and Hannigan (1998) and Blackard and West (2004). The first is a copy of a paper in which the mathematics of Seminole patchwork are explained, accompanied by analysis of a number of designs and the stories that go with those designs. Blackard and West (2004) present a historic overview of the development of patchwork and its application to a variety of clothing styles. This page is part of the Seminole Tribe of Florida Web site and has links to several other interesting fields for those who would like to learn more about the tribe.

CHAPTER FOUR

Future Tense and Intentive Mood

Now that you are acquainted with several features of verbal conjugation in Mvskoke, we will introduce two more verbal suffixes, one indicating future tense and another that indicates intentive mood. Both of these suffixes can be used to refer to actions that will take place in the future, but only the future tense suffix makes it absolutely clear that the action being discussed will be occurring in the future. The intentive mood suffix indicates that the subject is intent upon and has the resources available to perform the action. Use of this suffix in a sentence often causes people to translate the sentence as though it is indicating that the action has yet to happen and, therefore, implies that the sentence is referring to the future tense. While this is often a correct reading of the sentence, the intentive suffix really has no clear future tense reference.

FUTURE TENSE

Unlike the past tense forms (discussed in *Beginning Creek*, chapters 8 and 9) which are used based on the length of time elapsed between the occurrence of the action being discussed and the discussion itself, the future tense suffix does not indicate how far in the future the speaker expects the action will take place. Adverbial time marking words may be included in a sentence when a speaker desires to communicate that a specific time frame in the future is part of the statement. In the English sentence "I will go to the store tomorrow," the word "tomorrow" acts as an adverbial time marking phrase that makes it quite clear to a listener that the action will be occurring at a specific time in the future.

If no time marking phrase is included, as in the sentence "I will go to the store," the length of time into the future at which the speaker will go to the store is not made clear to a listener. Addition of the future tense suffix to a verb in Mvskoke would lead a listener to interpret the sentence in the manner of this second sentence. A listener can only determine a particular time in the future when an action will occur if a speaker includes a time marking phrase along with the future tense suffix in a Mvskoke sentence.

On a type I verb, the future tense suffix is placed on a verb before the same subject, auxiliary verb, 2nd declarative or interrogative suffix. It follows each of the other suffixes that you have learned about to this point: distributive, type I subject, and negating. The location of the future tense suffix on a type I verb is shown in diagram 4.1.

Type D Prefix	Type II Prefix	Verb Stem	Distr. Suffix	Type I Subject Suffix	Neg. Suffix	Future Tense Suffix	Declarative or Interrogative Suffix

Diagram 4.1. Order of Affixes on a Type I Verb Conjugated for Future Tense

The future tense suffix is not included in brackets in diagram 4.1, because its position is being shown in the table. As it is an optional suffix, it will be presented in brackets in later diagrams.

The form of the future tense suffix is *–vrē-*, and its presence in an example will be shown by 'fut' in the third line. When the future tense suffix comes after the 1S suffix, the first vowel of the future tense is lengthened. In effect, it absorbs the vowel sound of the 1S suffix (*-i-*) and becomes *–arē-* as a result. With all other subject suffixes, however, it continues to have a short vowel. Example 1 demonstrates the use of the future tense suffix with a verb conjugated for a first person singular subject. Note that while the positions of the 1S and future suffixes are indicated in the third line of the example, these two are actually combined within the long *a* of the future suffix.

1.   Cehecarēs.
      ce-hec-**arē**-s

2persII-see-1S-fut-dec
'I will see you.'

Example 2 is exactly like example 1, except that it includes the adverbial phrase *pvkse* 'tomorrow,' stating when the action will be accomplished. **Adverbial phrases** in Mvskoke, as in English, provide information about how an action is accomplished. In this case, the adverbial phrase, which can be one word or more in length, specifies the time at which the action will take place. An adverbial phrase specifying time is often marked with a suffix (*-n*), designating that it plays an oblique role in the sentence—it is informative but quite secondary. When this suffix appears in an example, its position will be marked by 'obl' in the third line.

2. Pvksen cehecarēs.

    pvkse-n   ce-hec-arē-s
    tomorrow-obl   2persII-see-1S-fut-dec
    'I will see you tomorrow.' *or* 'Tomorrow, I will see you.'

When the future tense suffix is added to a verb conjugated for a subject other than first person singular, the suffix has a short initial vowel. Examples 3 and 4, which have second person singular and third person plural subjects respectively, include the form of the future tense suffix that does not contain a lengthened initial vowel.

3. Rakko catan ohlikeckvrēs.
    rakko   cat-an   Ø-ohlik-eck-**vrē**-s
    horse   red-def_obj   3persII-ride-2S-fut-dec
    'You will ride the red horse.'

4. Honvntake cvtvhakvn hompvkvrēs.
    honvntake-Ø   cvtvhakv-n   Ø-homp-vk-Ø-**vrē**-s
    men-def_subj   blue_bread-ind_obj   3persII-eat-distr-3pers-fut-dec
    'The men will eat blue bread.'

Generally, an auxiliary verb is not used when the future tense suffix is affixed to the primary verb, but there are times when the future tense suffix can be affixed to the auxiliary verb. When this is the case, all other suffixes will remain on the primary verb, as shown in diagram 4.2. The other suffixes are affixed to the primary verb in the order in which they regularly occur. In this diagram, you will notice that several elements that have been shown as optional (they appear in parentheses in other diagrams) are not optional in this case. The first two, the type I subject and same subject suffixes, are always included on the primary verb when an auxiliary verb takes the future tense, so there is no choice but to use them in this kind of construction. The auxiliary verb stem, the future tense, and the declarative or interrogative suffixes also have to appear in a structure of the kind that we are discussing here in some specificity, so they are shown without parentheses around them.

[Type D Prefix]	[Type II Prefix]	Verb Stem	[Distr. Suffix]	Type I Suffix	[Neg. Suffix]	Same Subj. Suffix	Aux. Verb	Future Tense Suffix	Declarative or Interrogative Suffix

Diagram 4.2. Location of Future Tense and Other Affixes on a Type I–Auxiliary Verb Construction

Example 5 shows the structure of a verbal construction in which the future tense suffix has been affixed to the auxiliary verb and the subject and negating suffixes are attached to the primary verb. When the future tense suffix is added to the auxiliary verb, it implies that the action will be carried out some time between now and the future. Thus, when the negating suffix is added to the main verb and the future tense suffix is on the auxiliary verb, as in example 5, it is interpreted as meaning that the subject will never perform the action (he or she will not perform the action from now into the future).

5.   Mvhakv-cuko vyvkotomvrēs.
      mvhakv-cuko-Ø   vy-v-ko-t-om-**vrē**-s
      school-def_obj   go-1S-neg-ss-aux_vb-fut-dec
      'I will never go to school.'

Notice that the first vowel of the future tense suffix (-*vrē*-) has not been changed to a long *a* in example 5. This is because the subject marker for first person singular remains on the primary verb, while the future tense suffix has been placed on the auxiliary verb. When there is distance between the first person singular suffix's position and that of the future tense suffix, no change is made to the form of the future tense. It is only when the two occur side by side, as when the subject and future tense suffixes are both affixed to the primary verb, that the vowel of the future tense suffix is lengthened.

Example 6 demonstrates the location of several suffixes on the primary verb, as you have seen them in past chapters. The future tense suffix is located on the auxiliary verb as you were shown in example 5.

6.   Cvnahvnkvlken vnokecvkecketomvrēte?
        cv-na-hvnk-vlk-en   Ø-vnokec-vk-eck-et-om-**vrē**-te
        1S-body-one-pl-ind_obj   3persII-love-distr-2S-ss-aux_vb-fut-dec
        'Will you always love my relatives?'

When the interrogative suffix follows the future tense, it takes the form used when the final sound in the word is either /t/ or /i:/ (ends in *t* or *ē* in written form). If you need some further discussion of this form of the interrogative suffix, please see pages 181–82 in *Beginning Creek*.

When the future tense suffix is affixed to a type II verb, its location is as specified in diagram 4.3. While the position of the future tense suffix is not included in brackets in this diagram, it will be placed in brackets in future diagrams, because it is an optional suffix on the verb. Generally, an auxiliary verb is not used in future tense constructions with type II verbs. For this reason, the positions of the same subject suffix and auxiliary verb stem are not shown in this diagram. If you do speak with or listen to someone who creates future tense sentences with type II and auxiliary verbs, the position of the two verbs (primary and auxiliary) and the locations of the same subject and future tense suffixes will be as shown in diagram 4.2 for type I verbs, with the only difference being that no type I subject suffix will appear in the construction.

Type D Prefix	Type II Prefix	Verb Stem	Distr. Suffix	Neg. Suffix	Future Tense Suffix	Declarative or Interrogative Suffix

Diagram 4.3. Position of Future Tense and Other Affixes on a Type II Verb

The form of the future tense suffix on type II verbs is always –*vrē*-. The suffix never undergoes the vowel lengthening that it does on a type I verb, as it never immediately follows after the first person singular subject marker. In example 7, for instance, the future tense suffix has its usual form, because the first person singular subject prefix is at the beginning of the verb and is not next to the future tense suffix.

7. Fvccvlik-hoyanen cvhotosvrēs.
    fvccvlik-hoyanen   cv-hotos-**vrē**-s
    afternoon   1S-tired-fut-dec
    'I will be tired this afternoon.'

The same form of the future tense occurs in example 8, in which the verb is conjugated for a third person plural subject.

8. Omvlkat vnheromosvkvrēte?
    omvlk-at   vn-Ø-heromos-vk-**vrē**-te
    all_of_them-def_subj   1SD-3persII-kind_to-distr-fut-int
    'Will all of them be kind/generous to me?'

With the future tense suffix, you are now able to construct sentences that refer to actions that have yet to be performed. This suffix, along with the four past tenses and the lengthened grade, are the means by which Mvskoke speakers indicate the time to which the sentence refers—past, present, or future. The next suffix to be discussed is also used to indicate the time frame during which the action will take place, though it does not act specifically to indicate the time. However, as it is often used to indicate that a future action is being discussed, we introduce it in this chapter.

INTENTIVE MOOD

The future tense suffix that you have just been introduced to lets a listener know that an action is yet to happen. The **intentive mood**, indicated by a suffix on the verb, means that the speaker has the intention and the resources available to pursue the action being discussed, which tends to imply that the speaker will be performing it in the future. It is precisely because the speaker is indicating that he or she has a particular view in regard to the activity being discussed—that is, that he or she intends to undertake the action—that this suffix is noted as an indicator of the **mood**. Because it is the speaker's intention that is the primary piece of information indicated by this suffix, linguists consider it to be a mood suffix, not a tense suffix. However, this suffix is most frequently used by speakers to talk about actions that they have not yet performed, so it takes on the sense of future tense in that respect. That is why we are presenting it in this chapter.

Discussion of this suffix also raises the issue of **agentivity**. This is the quality of being purposeful or in control of the action. Generally, when Mvskoke speakers use the intentive mood suffix, they are indicating that they have some level of control regarding whether or how the action will take place. Agentivity is of some importance in Mvskoke, as one of the primary distinctions between type I and type II verbs has to do with agentivity. You may have noticed that many of the type II verbs concern actions about which the speaker or subject does not or cannot have total control, such as being large or small (the type II verbs *rakkē* and *cutkē*). Thus, it appears that within the language, the sense of whether the subject is able to cause an action to happen is a meaningful characteristic that governs the categorization of verbs and indicates whether the future tense or intentive mood suffix should be used to denote actions that will take place at some later time.

Agentivity should not be assumed to imply that the subject has absolute control over the performance of the action. In the English sentence "John will drive to the store tomorrow," we infer that John has the means of driving to the store and desires to do so. However, as we all know, circumstances may arise that will keep John from driving to the store tomorrow. Constructions asserting subject agentivity, in both Mvskoke and English, should not be considered to guarantee that the subject will successfully complete the activity, just that she or he has the resources and desire to do so at the time when the utterance is made.

The intentive mood suffix is *–vhan-*. In the second line following each example in this text in which the intentive mood suffix appears, "intent" is the abbreviation that will be used to designate where this suffix occurs on the verb. We will be using the abbreviation "intent" for intentive rather than "int" since "int," is already used to show the position of the interrogative suffix.

It should be noted that we are including the intentive mood suffix in our discussion of future tense constructions, because that is the way in which the suffix is used most commonly in Mvskoke sentences. As we mentioned earlier, affixing the intentive mood suffix on a verb indicates, in most cases, that the action has not been undertaken at the time the statement is made. However, other authors, such as Nathan (1977:120–21), have discussed this suffix as simply indicating the agentivity of the subject, not the future tense. Indeed, it is possible to form a sentence including the intentive mood suffix and the past tense, as in example 9, but the future tense is more commonly implied by the use of the intentive mood suffix. Thus, while we are discussing the intentive mood suffix as a means of indicating future tense in Mvskoke sentences, you should be aware that it is really indicating the subject's intention and ability to complete the action and can be used with other tenses.

9.   Cufet vyvhaneks.
        cufe-t   vy-vhan-Ø-ek-vnk-s
        Rabbit-ind_subj   go-intent-3pers-neg-mp-dec
        'Rabbit did not intend/want to go.'

Unlike the future tense suffix, the intentive mood suffix is often used in sentences containing an auxiliary verb. Thus, in diagram 4.4, you are shown that the intentive mood suffix (designated as the Intent. Suffix) follows the type I verb stem and precedes the Type I subject suffixes, negating suffix, same-subject suffix, the auxiliary verb, and the declarative and interrogative sentence markers.

On Type I Verbs

Type D Prefix	Type II Pref.	Verb Stem	Distr. Suffix	Intent. Suff.	Type I Subj. Suffix	Neg. Suffix	Past Tense Suffix	Same Subj. Suffix	Aux. Verb	Dec. *or* Interr. Suffix

On Type II Verbs

Type D Prefix	Type II Pref.	Verb Stem	Distr. Suffix	Intent. Suffix	Neg. Suffix	Past Tense Suffix	Same Subj. Suffix	Aux. Verb	Dec. *or* Interr. Suffix

Diagram 4.4. Order of Affixes on Type I and Type II Verbs with Intentive Mood Suffix

Example 10 presents a sentence containing the intentive mood suffix. The inclusion of the intentive mood suffix shows that the police officer has the desire and/or the ability to arrest the thief. In order to signal this intent and ability, the English translation of the sentence includes the verb "will," which also implies that the action has yet to happen. When the intentive mood suffix appears in Mvskoke sentences that do not contain any tense suffixes, translate the sentence as though it implies the future tense and the agentivity of the subject by using the verb "will" or the verb phrase "is/are going to," as shown in the alternative translation of example 10.

10. Estewvnayv horkopv svlvfkēcvhanes.
     estewvnayv-Ø   horkopv-Ø   Ø-svlvfkēc-Ø-vhan-es.
     police_officer-def_subj   thief-def_obj   3persII-arrest-intent-3pers-dec
     'The police officer will arrest the thief.' *or*
     "The police officer is going to arrest the thief."

Generally, when declarative sentences containing the intentive mood suffix are translated in this book, the translations will use the verb "will" to denote the subject's agentivity and the future nature of the action.

To demonstrate the placement of the pluralizing suffix and intentive mood suffix, the sentence from example 10 has been conjugated with a plural subject in example 11. In this case, the distributive suffix (-vk-) occurs before the intentive mood suffix on the verb. The sentence also has been turned into a question by replacing the declarative suffix with the interrogative suffix.

11. Estewvnayvlke horkopv svlvfkēcvkvhanv?
     estewvnay-vlke-Ø   horkopv   Ø-svlvfkēc-vk-vhan-Ø-v
     police_officer-pl-def_subj   thief-def_obj   3persII-arrest-distr-intent-3pers-int
     'Will the police officers arrest the thief?' *or*
     'Are the police officers going to arrest the thief?'

In this case, the distributive suffix used with either plural subjects or objects comes before the intentive suffix.

When the subject marking suffix following the intentive mood suffix is third person (a null suffix), the form of the interrogative suffix is –v. When the interrogative suffix follows any other subject suffix attached to the intentive mood suffix, the interrogative form is –isv. When the –isv form of the interrogative suffix follows a subject suffix that ends in a vowel, as do 1S and 1P (-i- and ē- respectively), then a y-glide is inserted between the vowel of the subject suffix and the i of the interrogative. Examples 12–17 show constructions using each of these subjects in Mvskoke. Table

Table 4.1: Forms of the Interrogative Suffix on Intentive Mood Constructions with Singular and Plural Subjects

1S	verb_stem-vhan-i-yisv	1P	verb_stem-vhan-ē-yisv
	verb_stem-intent-1S-int		verb_stem-intent-1P-int
2S	verb_stem-vhan-(e)ck-isv	2P	verb_stem-vhan-ack-isv
	verb_stem-intent-2S-int		verb_stem-intent-2P-int
3S	verb_stem-vhan-Ø-v	3P	verb_stem-vk-vhan-Ø-v
	verb_stem-intent-3pers-int		verb_stem-distr-intent-3pers-int

4.1 shows the order of suffixes and the variation in interrogative suffix forms on constructions for all possible subjects.

The following examples show these suffix orders and the forms of the interrogative. Because their structure has been discussed in the previous paragraph and in table 4.1, there is no discussion between any of these examples.

12.   Tvklik-cvmpvn epoyvhaniyisv?
       tvklik-cvmpv-n   epoy-vhan-i-**yisv**
       cake-ind_obj   win-intent-1S-int
       'Am I going to win a cake?'

13.   Vcen lokcicvhan(e)ckisv?
       vce-n   lokcic-vhan-(e)ck-**isv**
       corn-ind_obj   farm/grow-intent-2S-int
       'Are you going to farm/grow corn?'

14.   Mvt fayv eco fayvhanv?
       mv-t   fayv-Ø   eco-Ø   fay-vhan-Ø-**v**
       that-indef_subj   hunter-def_subj   deer-def_obj   hunt-intent-3pers-int
       'Is that hunter going to hunt deer?'

15.   Somecicvhanēyisv?
       somecic-vhan-ē-**yisv**
       lose-intent-1P-int
       'Are we going to lose (this game)?'

16.   Rvro emakwiyvhanackisv?
      rvro-Ø   em-akwiy-vhan-ack-**isv**
      fish-def_obj   3persII-fish_for-intent-2P-int
      'Are you (plural) going to go fishing?' *or* 'Will you (plural) go fishing?'

17.   Vlēkcv omvlkat cvcvfeknicvkvhanv?
      vlēkcv   omvlk-at   cv-cvfeknic-vk-vhan-Ø-**v**
      doctor   all-def_subj   1SII-heal/cure-dist-intent-3pers-int
      'Will all the doctors cure me?'

At times, the intentive mood suffix can be attached to the auxiliary verb. When a type I verb is the primary verb in a construction of this sort, the intentive mood, subject, and declarative or interrogative suffix is placed on the auxiliary verb, while all other suffixes remain on the primary verb. If the verb is type II, the subject prefix and distributive suffix (if used) remain on the primary verb and the intentive mood and declarative or interrogative suffixes move to the auxiliary verb.

Example 18 presents a type I verb conjugated for a single subject in the intentive mood. The intentive mood, subject, and declarative suffixes are located on the auxiliary verb. All other suffixes are found in the order one would expect on the primary verb.

18.   Pvkse vsimv Okmvlke vyetomvhanis.
      pvkse-vsimv   Okmvlke-Ø   vy-et-om-**vhan**-i-s
      day_after_tomorrow   Okmulgee-def_obj   go_(1)-ss-aux_vb-intent-1S-dec
      'I will go to Okmulgee the day after tomorrow.'

Example 19 presents a sentence very similar to that in example 18, except for the inclusion of the negating suffix. Notice that the negating suffix remains on the primary verb.

19.   Pvkse vsimv Okmvlke vyekotomvhanis.
      pvkse-vsimv   Okmvlke   vy-eko-t-om-**vhan**-i-s
      day_after_tomorrow   Okmulgee-def_obj   go_(1)-neg-ss-aux_vb-intent-
                                                1S-dec
      'I will not go to Okmulgee the day after tomorrow.'

Example 20 shows a construction involving the movement of the intentive mood and interrogative suffixes to the auxiliary verb when the primary verb is type II. The type D and type II prefixes remain on the primary verb, as do the negating and past tense suffixes.

20.   Hofonof cēpvnvke cecvpakkvkekvnketomvhanisv?
       hofonof   cēpvn-vke-Ø
       long_time_ago   boy-pl-def_obj
       Ø-ce-cvpakk-vk-ek-vnk-et-om-**vhan**-isv
       3persD-2persII-mad_at_(1)-dist-neg-mp-ss-aux_vb-intent-int
       'You weren't going to get mad at the boys a long time ago?'

Generally, the intentive mood is not used with many type II verbs. The majority of type II verbs are stative in nature; that is, they are states of being and are caused by factors outside of the control of the person whose body or mood is affected by these factors. Because subjects often do not have agentive control over type II verbal states, it is uncharacteristic for a Mvskoke speaker to use the intentive suffix, as this suggests that the subject has control. For those type II verbs that do allow some control by the subject, such as the verb used in example 20, *cvpakkē* 'to be mad,' the order of affixes follows the order shown in diagram 4.4.

More about Agentivity

The guidelines for use of the intentive mood and future tense suffixes rely on a subject's ability to complete the action being discussed. In many cases, the sense that the subject of a sentence is both desiring and able to cause the action to occur is similar for Mvskoke and English speakers. There are some cases, however, in which sentences about items that English speakers generally do not view as having intentionality include the intentive mood suffix.

For instance, example 21 describes the growth of a pecan tree.

21.   Ocē-cvpkuce mvpe rakkē hakvhanētos.
       ocē-cvpkuce-mvpe   rakkē-Ø   Ø-hak-**vhan**-ē-t-o-s
       pecan_tree   big_(1)-def_subj 3persII-grow-intent-stat-ss-aux_vb-
                                             dec
       'The pecan is going to become a big tree.'

Most English speakers would not consider pecan trees to have intentionality, as this is most often reserved for those things we consider to be sentient (thinking) beings. For the Muskogees, as for many other Native American peoples, the elements and forces of nature are thought to be directed by a higher power (*Hesaketvmesē*). Thus, you may hear many speakers use the intentive mood suffix to discuss activities relating to natural forces or involving elements of nature.

When faced with the choice of whether to use the future tense or intentive mood suffixes in sentences about upcoming actions, there are certain features that may help you decide to use one suffix versus the other. If the subject is human, the focus is on whether the person has both the intention and the resources necessary to perform the action. If she or he does, use the intentive mood suffix. If the subject lacks either or both of these qualities, use the future tense suffix.

If the subject of the sentence is a nonhuman animate being (plant or animal), you should determine whether the activity is regularly carried out by the subject. If the being usually performs the activity (e.g., dogs almost always chase rabbits when they see or smell them), the intentive suffix is appropriate to talk about that action. If the being only occasionally performs the activity (e.g., bears stand upright at times but generally stay on all fours), the future tense suffix would be best to use when you speak about the being performing this behavior at some later time.

And finally, if it might seem as though there is some kind of driving force behind the action, whether involving an animate or inanimate subject, then the intentive mood suffix may be used. For instance, if the sky has become very cloudy and the atmosphere is very damp, you could use the intentive mood suffix in a sentence stating that it is going to rain. While we all know that rain does not always come, even under the most promising circumstances, the fact that the Mvskoke worldview considers natural elements like rain to be governed to some extent by natural forces or powers, and that there are sets of signs (like clouds and a damp atmosphere) that presage rain, makes the use of the intentive mood suffix appropriate in these situations.

Vocabulary

OCCUPATIONS

English		Mvskoke
farmer		naklokcicv
worker		vtotkv
cook		hompetv hayv
nurse		nokke-vfastv
	or	enokkvlke-vfastv
doctor		vlēkcv
policeman		estewvnayv
fireman		totkv-vslēcv
secretary		cokv-hayv
hunter		fayv
fisherman		rvro akhopoyv
	or	rvro em akwiyv
salesperson/shopkeeper		nakwiyv
lawyer		vhakv-hayv

VERBS

English		Mvskoke
to argue {I;D}		isemayecetv
to argue with each other {I}		etem vyoposketv
to farm/grow things {I;3}		lokcicetv
to heal, cure (one person) {I;II}		cvfeknicetv
to heal, cure (two or more) {I;II}		cvfencicetv
to arrest {I;II}		svlvfkēcetv
to let go, untie someone {I;D}		enrecvpetv
	or	ayēccicetv
to hunt {I}		fayetv
to fish {I}		rvro em akwiyetv
(one person) to show someone something {I;II}		nak en hecicetv
(two or more persons) to show someone something {I;II}		nak en hecicēyetv
to win {I}		epoyetv
	or {I}	vkosletv

to lose (as a game or a single item) {I;3}	somecicetv
to lose (two or more things) {I;3}	somhuecetv
to help someone {I;D}	em vnicetv

Exercises

EXERCISE 1

Translate the following sentences from Mvskoke into English. As you work through each sentence, begin by dividing the Mvskoke words into their morphemes, as is done in the second line of each example. Then show the abbreviation for each morpheme as it appears in the third line of each example in the text. Finally, formulate a complete English sentence that provides a close translation of the Mvskoke sentence. An example is provided.

Mvskoke sentence:	Pvksen rvro emakwiyeckvrēte?
Divide into morphemes:	pvksen rvro-Ø em-akwiy-eck-vrē-te
Identify morphemes:	tomorrow-obl fish-def_obj 3persII-catch_fish-2S-fut-int
English translation:	'Are you going fishing tomorrow?'

1. Cokv-hayvt mvt cokvn ohhonayvhanetos.
2. Cufet Econ encokopericvhanes.
3. Cvhecackvrēs.
4. Nakwiyvt vmvnicekvhanekotos.
5. Vhakv-hayvke hokkolat ispomayecvkvhanetos.
6. Wotko rakrvkē fo-encvmpē hompvkvhanv?
7. Eto pvsvtkē tutcēnat pvlvtkvrēs.
8. Nokke-vfastv lopicat honvntaken cvfencicvkvrēs.
9. Vtotkvlket mēkusvpkv-cukon hayvkvhanes.
10. Wakv cvhecicvrēs.

EXERCISE 2

Write a story about something you wanted to do when you were younger. Your story should be at least eight sentences long. In the sentences, you must use the future tense and intentive suffixes each at least one time. If you want to use vocabulary for terms or activities that you cannot find in the glossaries of this book or in *Beginning Creek*, refer to Jack Martin and Margaret Mauldin's *A Dictionary of Creek/Muskogee* for these words. You may also look them up in R. M. Loughridge and David M. Hodge's *Dictionary of Muskogee and English*. When you have written your story, practice telling it out loud, as you may be asked to recite your story to your classmates.

EXERCISE 3

Translate the following sentences from English to Mvskoke. Each sentence will require the use of either the future tense or intentive mood suffix. For each sentence, state why you chose to use the suffix that you did. An example is provided for you.

English sentence: The farmer will grow potatoes next year.
Mvskoke translation: Ohrolopēyof naklokcicv vhv lokcicvrēs.
Reason: The future tense suffix was used in this case, because
                                the farmer is making a decision about what crop to
                                grow a year ahead. He may change his mind, or
                                something might happen that will cause him to
                                decide on a different crop.

1. The preacher is going to write a sermon.
2. Some gophers are going to whistle.
3. Ice will melt today.
4. My daughter will wash two quilts.
5. That cat is going to spit at you.
6. Those five firemen are going to drive to town tomorrow.
7. I will iron the shirts.
8. The little boy will lose his gloves.

EXERCISE 4

Change the following present tense Mvskoke sentences into sentences indicating that the action will take place in the future. In doing this, you may opt to use the future tense or intentive mood suffixes to indicate that the action has not yet occurred. As you modify the sentences, think about whether your decision to use the future tense or intentive mood suffix has some bearing on how a person would interpret the sentence. For instance, using the intentive mood suffix on sentence 1 indicates both that the man has yet to build the house and that the speaker believes he has the desire and resources available to do so. Be prepared to talk about these kinds of underlying assumptions for each sentence.

1. Honvnwvt cuko hayetos.
2. Naklokcicvlke wotkvlken hopoyvketos.
3. Cufet tashokeks.
4. Nokke-vfastv cemvnicvketos.
5. Henehvlket elvwēcētos.
6. Ecerwvn vsēkvkotos.
7. Vcvkerriceckv?
8. Sokhvt a-vpokes.
9. Cēpanat morvfkvn vtehkes.
10. Hoktvket telomhv tutcēnen vhorhuecekotos.

Exercise 5

The following story is three paragraphs long. The first two paragraphs have been translated for you. Translate the third paragraph. Be certain that you can read the story aloud, as your teacher may ask you to do so in class. The character Poca Rakko is Wolf, often referred to by this phrase in Rabbit stories and others of this sort.

Cufet Poca Rakko Sahkkopanes

Cufet arvtēs. Cufet rakko rakket hecvtēs. 'Tehoyvnvtēs. Ayvtēs. Mont Cufet enhesse Poca Rakko vnrvpvtēs. "Vnhesse, nake ceyaceton hehcis!" Cufet maketos. "Rakko elan hehcis." Momen, "Vhoyvkēs!" Poca Rakko maketos.

Yefolhokvtēs. Rakko elen hecvkvtēs. Rakko elen wakketos. "Esokso hompeckes. Vnet ehvckon homparēs." Cufet makvtēs. "Hēnretos." Poca Rakko kicvtēs. Mowen, rakko hvcet nekēyvtēs. "Hotvlē rakko hvcen nekēyicetos." Cufet makvtēs. "Cetorofvn cemvrokafvhanes. Hvcen cemvwvnvyvhanis. Mowof, hvcen nekēyekvrēs."

Poca Rakko ahuervtēs. Cufet vwvnayvtēs. Poca Rakkot rakko esokson enkecētkvtēs. Rakko ataskvtēs. Mowen rakkot Poca Rakkon esletkvtēs. Poca Rakkot rakkon wvnvkvkvtēs. Cufet vpelicvtēs.

Rabbit Plays a Trick on Wolf

Rabbit was wandering around. Rabbit saw a big horse. He passed it by. He went on. Then, Rabbit met his friend Wolf. "My friend, you'll like what I just saw!" said Rabbit. "I just saw a dead horse." Then, "Let's go!" said Wolf.

They went back. They saw a dead horse. The dead horse was lying down. "You eat his hip. I'll eat his ears," Rabbit said. "That's good," said Wolf. Then, the horse's tail moved. "The wind moved the horse's tail," Rabbit said. "It will slap you in your face. I'll tie the tail to you. Then, when it happens, the tail won't move."

Listening Exercises

Listen again to the fifth conversation on the CD, "Health" (track 6). Have ready the list of words you recognize that you wrote out for the listening exercise in chapter 3.

Now, listen to all of the sentences in this conversation one by one (tracks 80–87). Listen for individual words within the sentences. Listen to the sentences as many times as you need to in order to get a sense of what the speakers are saying. Are there any words that you do not recognize, even after listening to the sentences several times? If so, make note of the sentence in which these words occur and approximately when the sentence occurs. Ask your teacher or a fluent speaker of Mvskoke to listen to the sentences and help you with the pronunciation and translation of these words. With this help, are you able to get a sense of what the speakers are talking about? If there are constructions in these sentences that you do not understand, make note of them and ask your teacher about them in class. Some of these constructions may require review of *Beginning Creek*, while others will be covered later in this book, so your teacher may ask you to keep your notes and questions as you continue to work on the language. In some cases, your teacher may want to discuss the structures at that time.

Working with a classmate, take turns reciting the sentences from "Health" (tracks 80–87). Begin by having one of you repeat the sentences spoken by the first speaker while the other participant takes the sentences spoken by the second speaker. When you are fairly comfortable repeating those sentences, take the other speaker's role. If you cannot pronounce all of the words exactly, try at least to mimic the intonational contours of the words. Be ready to recite these sentences in class as best you can. Your teacher may allow you to recite along with the CD, or you may be asked to recite as much as possible from memory.

Listen to the story "Turtle's Shell" (track 89). As you listen, pay attention to the cadence of Linda's voice. Does she always speak at the same pace? Is there a rhythm to her speech? Does her speech as she tells this story sound different from the way she spoke in the conversations? Why might that be?

Are you able to identify any words? It is not expected that you will be able to hear all of the words at this point, and you are not being asked to translate any of the conversation — it is enough for you to try to pick out words that you know. Write down the words that you hear clearly in Mvskoke and be ready to present your list in class. Compare the words that you were able to identify with other students' lists. If you like, listen to the rough translation that Linda gives on track #90. This may give you some idea of words to listen for in the Mvskoke version.

Careers and Jobs

Webster's Third New International Dictionary defines education as "developing the mind, knowledge, or skill." Our ancestors and elders are teachers, although most do not have college educations or degrees. In the old days, they drew from their experiences to teach the young men how to hunt, fish, and identify certain plants to be used as medicine. Women taught their daughters how to cook and preserve wild game how to and use the hides for clothing. They also showed girls how to identify edible plants and preserve them for future use. This is how our ancestors educated their young people in the ways of tribal life. Education has always been part of every culture in existence, including the Muskogee Creek and Seminole cultures.

Then the removal of tribes from their homelands brought new experiences. They were introduced to religion and schools. The children were sent to schools to learn English and forget their language and culture. This created a hardship for the children, as the elders and leaders of the tribes did not want the children to forget their culture.

We know now that education is the way of the future. Slowly, the elders came to see that their children would have to learn the new ways in order to survive. They hoped that the children could learn the new things and still keep their culture. To ensure this would happen, they took the time to tell children stories and take them out with them to experience Muskogee Creek and Seminole ways of being in the world when they came home from school.

Today, the gates are open to young people to make their way in the world through education. With their education, they can develop careers and find jobs in fields that are interesting and useful. Grants are available to them, along with assistance from some tribes, to help pay for college and graduate education.

Tribal members in general can benefit from the education of our young people. A lot of our young people come back to work with their tribes. Sometimes, though, there can be a clash between the older and newer ways of doing things. This can be overcome if we stop to think about ways our older values can be interwoven with education.

Life offers a way to develop our skills, knowledge, and minds to create our way in this world. Getting an education will lead to jobs and careers and can really help students, their families, and their tribes.

Suggested Readings

Interestingly, despite the fact that there are two ways of indicating that an action will take place in the future in Mvskoke usage, there has been little written about this phenomenon. Michele Nathan's dissertation (1977) explores the future tense and intentive mood suffixes in separate sections. Hers is the only easily accessible analysis that covers both of these suffixes in detail. Nathan (1977: 111) discusses the future tense suffix, noting that the future tense form can vary between –vrē- and –vhē- in Florida Seminole Mvskoke. Among Oklahoma speakers of Mvskoke, the –vhē- form of the future tense suffix is almost never heard.

Nathan (1977: 120–21) also describes two forms of the intentive mood suffix. Both of these forms, used by speakers of the Florida Seminole dialect

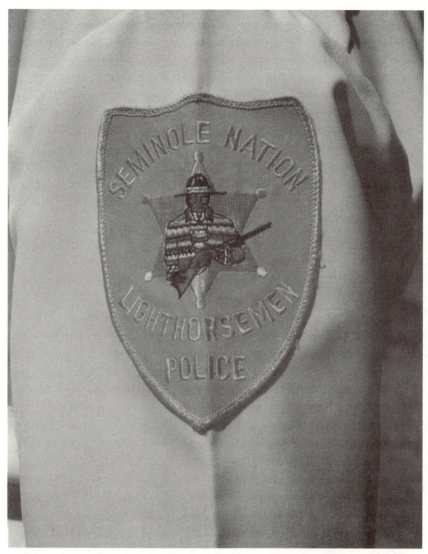

Seminole Lighthorsemen's Patch. Mekusukey Mission, Oklahoma, July 13, 1999.
*Photograph by Chester R. Cowen. C. R. Cowen Collection, Courtesy of the Oklahoma
Historical Society. Negative #19687.IN.FC5.12.1.*

of Mvskoke, are different from the form of the intentive mood suffix used by Mvskoke speakers in Oklahoma. While the actual suffixes used to mark intentive mood differ in Florida and Oklahoma speakers, much of Nathan's discussion about the uses of these suffixes applies equally to speakers in both communities. Speakers and listeners in both Mvskoke-speaking communities interpret the use of the intentive mood suffix(es) to indicate that the subject of the sentence has the means and intention to cause the action to happen and/or that the subject will pursue the action in the future. Nathan notes that Florida speakers interpret the use of the intentive mood suffixes as indicating that the action will take place in the very near future. This differs somewhat from Oklahoma speakers' use, in which the intentive mood suffix can be used for actions that will take place more than a day or two in the future.

There are several excellent sources available for those interested in learning about employment opportunities and economic activities of the Mvskoke-speaking peoples. Readers interested in understanding how the Muskogee Creeks and Seminoles made their living both before and after Removal are directed to Fogelson (2004). In this book, the lifeways and practices of several Southeastern groups are explored in detail. We suggest the following chapters, as these concern Mvskoke-speaking groups in particular: Finger and Perdue (2004: 152–62); Fixico (2004: 162–73); Walker (2004: 373–92); Innes (2004a: 393–403); Paredes (2004: 404–406); Sturtevant and Cattelino (2004: 429–49); and Sattler (2004: 450–64).

These chapters explore a number of aspects of cultural, social, and economic life among the Oklahoma and Alabama Muskogee Creeks, and the Oklahoma and Florida Seminoles from the very distant past to the present. The chapters by Finger and Perdue and by Fixico provide a general overview of the historical events that have affected Muskogee Creek and Seminole life since the time of Removal, providing a basis against which the observations specific to the Muskogee Creeks and Seminoles can be compared. The chapters by Walker, Innes, and Paredes focus on the Oklahoma and Alabama Muskogee Creek communities. The historic and current circumstances of the Oklahoma and Florida Seminole communities are discussed in the chapters by Sturtevant and Cattelino and by Sattler. In all, it becomes very clear that those within the Muskogee Creek and Seminole communities have weathered several changes in economic opportunities by being flexible and resilient.

The newspapers of the Muscogee (Creek) and Seminole Nations of Oklahoma (the *Muscogee Nation News* and *Cokv Tvleme* respectively), and the Seminole Tribe of Florida (the *Seminole Tribune*) provide a wealth of information about employment and educational opportunities available to tribal members. Each one frequently includes articles discussing important economic, employment, and educational achievements of tribal members. These newspapers will keep you informed about all aspects of tribal life that are important for members today, including careers, housing, education, social-welfare programs, and more.

CHAPTER FIVE

Commands and Causatives

We will begin this chapter by introducing you to the way in which Mvskoke speakers give commands to others. In linguistic usage, commands are often called "imperatives." **Imperatives** are sentences in which the speaker is ordering another person to undertake an action. An example of an imperative in English is "Sit down!" The most forceful examples of English imperatives are those that contain only a verb. However, it is possible to construct forceful imperatives with a verb and object, such as in "Pick it up!" With these very short forms an English speaker makes it clear that he or she is ordering the listener to perform the action, even though the subject of the sentence is not indicated.

A Mvskoke speaker can indicate that he or she is commanding the listener to do the action by adding the suffix –vs to the end of the verb. When a Mvskoke speaker commands a listener NOT to do something, the negating suffix is followed by –t to end the command. (In the third line of the examples, the position of the imperative suffix (-vs in the case of positive commands, -t in the case of negative commands) is indicated by the abbreviation "imper" for "imperative." As commands in Mvskoke are often given with a different tone of voice and greater emotional force than are declarative sentences, exclamation points act as a further indicator that this form is being used in written texts.) Mvskoke imperatives, like those in English, frequently leave out the subject suffix. Thus, a mother might say the sentence in example 1 to her child.

1. Nocvs!
    noc-**vs**
    sleep_(1)-imper
    "Go to sleep!"

Even though the mother is speaking directly to her child, she does not conjugate the verb for second person singular ("you"). Instead, she is simply presenting the action that she expects her child to perform by using the verb stem with the imperative suffix.

This is the general pattern of imperative formation in Mvskoke. The imperative suffix is added directly to the verb stem, without the addition of a tense or subject affix. The only other affix that occurs with any frequency with the imperative suffix in Mvskoke is the negating suffix, which is added between the verb stem and the imperative suffix. Example 2 shows how a command including the negating suffix is formed.

2. Eccekot!
    ecc-eko-**t**
    shoot-neg-imper
    "Don't shoot!"

When an object is included in the imperative form, the appropriate object prefix will be included on the verb stem. For instance, in example 3 the object "us" is indicated by the addition of the first person plural type II prefix to the verb. Thus, the only difference between example 3 and example 2 is the inclusion of the object prefix.

3. Epoccekot!
    epo-cc-eko-t
    1PII-shoot-neg-imper
    "Don't shoot us!"

When a command in Mvskoke involves the use of a suppletive verb, the verb stem used to create the command depends on the number of either the subject or the object. Examples 4, 5, and 6 present the forms a Mvskoke speaker would use to command that one, two, or more than two people are supposed to stand up.

4. Ahuervs!
    ahuer-vs
    stand_up_(1)-imper
    "Stand up!"

5. Asehokvk(v)s!
    asehok-vk-(v)s
    stand_up_(2)-distr-imper
    "Stand up (to two)!"

6. Asvpaklvk(v)s!
    svpakl-vk-(v)s
    stand_up_(3+)-distr-imper
    "Stand up (to three or more)!"

Because the verb stem varies according to the number of subjects and it is the listener(s) at whom the command is directed who will take on the role of subjects, the verb stem to which the imperative suffix is added depends on the number of people to whom the speaker is giving the command. Because the speaker giving the commands in examples 5 and 6 expects that all those who are being spoken to will follow the directive, the distributive suffix is included. This makes it clear that all of those being told to perform the action should pay attention—the command applies equally to all in the group.

When a command is given that includes a verb for which there are different stem forms depending on the number of objects, the appropriate form is chosen for the number of things on which the speaker wants the listener to perform the action. Examples 7, 8, and 9 all contain different forms of the verb "to set (something) down," because the number of objects is different in each sentence.

7. Cokv-tohahwvn ataklicvs!
    cokv-tohahwv-n   **ataklic**-vs
    paper-box-ind_obj   set_down_(1)-imper
    "Set/put down the paper bag!"

8. Cokv-tohahwvn atakkayvs!
    cokv-tohahwv-n   **atakkay**-vs

paper-box-ind_obj   set_down_(2)-imper
"Set/put down the (two) paper bags!

9.   Cokv-tohahwvn atakvpoyvs!
    cokv-tohahwv-n   **atakvpoy**-vs
    paper-box-ind_obj   set_down_(3+)-imper
    "Set/put down the (three or more) paper bags!"

Thus, as examples 7 through 9 demonstrate, the choice of which of a suppletive verb's stems to use is based on the number of objects affected by the action that the listener is being commanded to perform in the imperative sentence.

An imperative containing a verb that does not have suppletive forms for plural subjects or objects will use the distributive suffix to show that the subject or object noun is plural. The imperative suffix (-vs) then follows the distributive suffix. Note that when the imperative suffix comes after the distributive suffix, the initial v of the imperative suffix is not pronounced.

10.   Hompvks!
    homp-vk-**s**
    eat-distr-imper
    "(you plural) Eat!"

In cases like that in example 10, the use of a more forceful tone of voice helps to make it clear that this is an imperative rather than a declarative statement.

When a verb that does not have suppletive forms is being used in a negative command, the distributive suffix is again added to the verb stem. The negating suffix follows the distributive suffix and, finally, the imperative –t is added. This leads to the form in example 11.

11.   Emonayvkekot!
    em-onay-vk-eko-ŧ
    3PD-tell_them-distr-neg-imper
    'Don't tell them!'

Commands created by adding the imperative suffix alone—or negating and imperative suffixes in combination—to the verb stem are forceful. Often, just as with English commands, imperative forms in Mvskoke are given in a louder and "sharper" tone of voice than are less emotionally laden sentences. Mvskoke speakers can add further information about the speaker's emotional commitment to the imperative through the addition of the emphatic particle *ci*. (The particle can also be pronounced as *cē*, which is the form in which the particle is entered in the Martin and Mauldin dictionary [2000]. However, because the most often heard form is *ci*, we will use that notation to mark the inclusion of this particle in the sentences in this book.)

The element *ci* is called a **particle** because it does not have a meaning of its own, as a word does, yet it stands alone in the sentence and, thus, is not considered to be an affix. Its inclusion in a sentence makes a difference in the emotional tone but does not significantly alter the overall meaning of the sentence. When a Mvskoke imperative verb is followed by *ci*, it indicates that the speaker is very emphatic about what he or she is saying (hence, the abbreviation 'emph' for this particle in the third line of each example). If the imperative is being offered as an extension of friendship or camaraderie, as in example 12, where one is being told to eat and take advantage of the host's generosity, the inclusion of *ci* tends to signify that the speaker is truly stating the imperative out of concern for the listener's welfare.

12.   Hompvks ci!
       homp-vk-s **ci**
       eat-distr-imper emph
       "(you plural) Eat!"

When the emphatic particle follows an imperative form that is issued out of a sense of anger, hostility, or derisiveness, the particle serves to underline that the speaker is issuing the command in no uncertain terms. In effect, the listener had better comply with the command or else! An example of this type of command, to which *ci* has been added, occurs in example 13.

13.   Vyvs ci!
       vy-vs ci
       go_(1)-imper emph
       "Go!"

The command given in example 13 would be used when telling an unwanted guest to leave. It is a very direct order and shows that there is no love lost between the speaker and the listener.

The use of the imperative suffix and the emphatic particle allows Mvskoke speakers to create very forceful commands indeed. However, there are situations in which speakers may want to lessen the emotional tone of the imperative somewhat, as we do in English by preceding the command form with "Please," as in "Please, sit down." The addition of "Please" suggests that the listener has far more leeway to do something else and that the speaker is not really demanding that the listener do as he or she has been told. Mvskoke also has a way of making a command less forceful by including a suffix *(-ep(o)-)* indicating that the speaker recognizes that the listener has the option to not follow the command. The position of this suffix will be marked by the abbreviation 'ctre' for "counterexpectational," following the usage in Hardy (2005: 224–25).

The counterexpectational suffix has a range of meanings, most of which revolve around the idea that the action specified by the verb to which the suffix has been attached is not going as would usually be expected. When the suffix is attached to imperative constructions of the sort that we are considering here, it gives the sense that the speaker is aware that the listener has the option of performing the action or not. Thus, by including the counterexpectational suffix in imperatives, the speaker leaves the listener with the option of choosing whether or not to do what is being commanded.

The sentence in example 14 is commonly heard when one visits a Mvskoke speaker.

14. Likepvs ci!
     lik-**ep**-vs ci
     sit_(1)-ctre-imper emph
     "Sit down!"

This sentence is uttered when the host wants the guest to make her- or himself comfortable by taking a seat. Despite the fact that the sentence has all of the markings of a strong imperative (it contains the imperative suffix and the emphatic particle), the presence of the counterexpectational suffix makes it clear that the guest is under no obligation to take a seat, so the host is not really issuing a strong command to the guest. The difference between the sentence in example 14 and the same construction without the counterexpectational suffix ("Likvs ci!") is similar to the difference between "Please, sit down!" and "Sit down!" in English. Including the counterexpectational suffix makes the tone of the command much more polite and less commanding.

In many lullabies, like that on track 7 of the CD accompanying this book, the counterexpectational suffix is used to soften a command. As you might expect, in a song like a lullaby the singer will often tell the child,

15.   Nocepvs!
       noc-**ep**-vs
       sleep-ctre-imper
       "Go to sleep!"

This actually serves to change the meaning of the word slightly, from 'sleep' to 'go to sleep.' By including the counterexpectational suffix in the command, the singer is, to some extent, inviting or encouraging the listener to go to sleep, rather than demanding that the listener do so. Using the softer form of the command also allows that the listener may or may not fall asleep, which makes sense, as one cannot always predict that babies and young children (to whom one would generally sing a lullaby) will go to sleep when you want them to.

Generally, when you want to express a command that will get the listener's attention and quick response, you should use the form with only the verb stem, the distributive suffix (if you are speaking to plural listeners), and the imperative suffix. Adding the emphatic particle to the imperative verb can either make the command even more intense (as in imperatives offered in an unfriendly manner) or show that you sincerely care about the listener's following your direction (as when using the imperative with a friend). In the latter case, the emphatic particle demonstrates that you are using the imperative form based on your desire for the listener to benefit from the action. Inclusion of the counterexpectational suffix serves to soften the tone of the imperative. This suffix makes it clear that you leave the decision up to the listener as to whether she or he will perform the action. Knowledge of these various ways of constructing imperatives in Mvskoke is important, as it will help you to identify whether speakers are being very direct and forceful in their comments or are making suggestions from the perspective of a friendly host.

Causatives

Causatives are constructions in which the subject of the sentence is not the beneficiary of the action. Generally, in causative sentences the subject is either making another entity perform the action or is actively performing the action on another being. Think of the meanings of the following English sentences:

16. "The man eats bananas."
17. "The man is making you eat bananas."
18. "The man is feeding you bananas."

In sentence 16, which is not a causative, the man is performing the act of "eating" on bananas and, as a result, is the sole beneficiary of the action of eating. In sentences 17 and 18, however, "you" are the beneficiary or recipient of the action, not the man. In sentence 17, the man is making or causing you—hence the term 'causative'—to perform the action of eating the bananas. This means that it is you, and not the man, who reaps the benefits of this activity. In sentence 18, you again are the recipient of the action, as it is you who are the recipient of the man's act of feeding you.

When the person or thing that is being caused to do something (the causee) is being made to take an active role in the completion of the action specified in the causative construction, this is called a **direct causative**. Sentence 17 above is an example of a direct causative, because in order for the action to take place, "you" have to do the eating of the bananas. This does not mean that the causee cannot resist the action, nor should it be taken to imply that the causee necessarily wants to comply with the activity. But in all cases of direct causatives in Mvskoke, there is the sense that the causee plays an active role in the performance of the activity.

Indirect causatives are those in which the causee does not play a very active role in performing the action. Sentence 18 is an example of an indirect causative, in that the action is really being performed on the recipient. In sentence 18, the man (the causer) is the one doing the feeding of "you" (the causee), so the causee only plays an indirect role in the performance of the action. In indirect causatives, the causer or some other entity is the one who is really in control of the action.

The causative suffix in Mvskoke has two forms, -ec- and –yc-. The position of the causative suffix will be shown by the inclusion of 'caus' in its position in the third line of each example. The choice of which of these forms to use on a verb depends, to a great extent, on the sounds preceding the location of the causative suffix. Below, we discuss tendencies governing which of the two forms is used, covering the vast majority of the cases. However, as there are some verbs that do not follow this general pattern, you will have to pay attention as you interact with Mvskoke speakers in situations in which sentences containing causative verbal constructions are used.

Stem vowels

Before we begin discussing how speakers determine which of the two forms of the causative suffix to use with a given verb, we must introduce the idea of a final vowel on Mvskoke verb stems. To this point, you have been told that the verb stem is what remains after the infinitival suffix has been dropped from the form of the verb that appears in the glossary. On most type I verbs, the infinitival suffix is –etv, and on type II verbs it is –ē. Deleting or dropping the infinitival suffix from the verb form presented in the vocabulary lists and glossary has been all that you have had to do to prepare the verb for the addition of the prefixes and suffixes that you have seen to this point.

When the causative suffix is added to the verb, however, the most reasonable and elegant explanation for three of the four phonologically different forms that it has relies upon the existence of a final stem vowel that does not appear in the general form of the infinitive. In essence, there is an argument (presented by Haas [1948], Booker [1980], and Martin [1991]), that the stems of Mvskoke verbs used to end in vowels that reappear when the causative suffix is to be added to a verb. In forming causative sentences, then, you will have to take into consideration a final vowel that is no longer found in the infinitive form of the verb, and it is this vowel that we will consider to be the final **stem vowel** in this section of the text.

Luckily, most Mvskoke verbs follow a set of patterns in regard to determining what the final stem vowel is. We will discuss each of these patterns in the next few paragraphs. While it is true that these patterns apply to the majority of Mvskoke verbs, you should keep in mind that there are some that do not seem to conform to these patterns, so it is possible that you will encounter some causative forms that you would not expect from the discussion that follows.

TABLE 5.1. Means of Determining the Final Stem Vowel

When the Final Vowel in the Infinitive Is	And the Final Consonant in the Infinitive Is	Then the Vowel to Be Added to the Stem Is
v, a, o, e, *or* ē	Neither p *nor* k	e
Either v *or* a	Either p *or* k	o
o	Either p *or* k	v
Either ē *or* e	Either p *or* k	Either e *or* o

Table 5.1 shows the general pattern for determining the final vowel of the verb stem. Notice that the final vowel depends on the vowel that appears to be last in the infinitival form (e.g., the vowel *o* of *hocetv* 'to pound or beat something in a container') and on the final consonant in the infinitival form (e.g., the consonant *c* of *hocetv*). Because of this vowel-consonant ending in the infinitive form, the final vowel to be added to the verb stem (infinitive form minus infinitival ending) is *e*, leading to the form *hoce-*, to which the causative suffix will be added.

Table 5.2 provides examples of each of the verb structures listed in table 5.1 in the order in which they were presented. Thus, the first two lines in table 5.2 show the results of putting two verbs ending in v and a, and whose stems do not end in the consonants p or k, through the process of determining the final stem vowel. The modified stem form, showing the addition of the final vowel, is given in the third column of the table for each of the verb stem examples. This format is repeated for every other combination of vowel and consonant listed in table 5.1 above.

The final vowel of the verb stem is important, as this vowel determines which of the two forms of the causative suffix (*-ec-* or *–yc-*) will be used on the verb. The *–ec-* form is used when the final vowel of the verb stem is *v* or *e*. A final vowel of *o* takes the *–yc-* form of the suffix. The application of the suffix causes some changes in pronunciation of the stem vowel, which we have described below for each form of the suffix.

The –ec- form of the causative suffix

As stated above, the *–ec-* form of the causative suffix is used when the stem vowel is *v* or *e*. When the *–ec-* form comes after a *v* stem vowel, its own vowel (*e*) combines with the final stem vowel (*v*) to create the sound of the

TABLE 5.2. Examples of Final Vowel Addition to Verb Stems

Stem Form (Final Vowel and Consonant in Infinitive Form)	Exemplary Verb Stem	Resulting Stem with Final Vowel
Stem vowel *v*, final consonant is not *p* or *k*	pvcc- 'to pound, shatter'	pvcce-
Stem vowel *a*, final consonant is not *p* or *k*	fay- 'to hunt'	faye-
Stem vowel *o*, final consonant is not *p* or *k*	okkos- 'to wash (one object)'	okkose-
Stem vowel *e*, final consonant is not *p* or *k*	es- 'to take'	ese-
Stem vowel *ē*, final consonant is not *p* or *k*	mvnhēr- 'to enjoy'	mvnhēre-
Stem vowel *a*, final consonant is either *p* or *k*	task- 'to hop (of one)'	tasko-
Stem vowel *v*, final consonant is either *p* or *k*	ewvnhk- 'to be thirsty'	ewvnhko-
Stem vowel *o*, final consonant is either *p* or *k*	homp- 'to eat'	hompv-
Stem vowel *e*, final consonant is either *p* or *k*	vyep- 'to leave, go away from (of one)'	vyepe- *or* vyepo-
Stem vowel *ē*, final consonant is either *p* or *k*	hvtēsk- 'to sneeze'	hvtēske- *or* hvtēsko-

vowel *i*. Thus, in example 19, the vowel in the causative suffix is written and pronounced as *i*, because it results from the combination of the *v* final stem vowel of *hompv-* and the initial vowel (*e*) of the causative suffix (*-ec-*).

19.   Cecke tvklike cehompices.
      ce-cke-Ø   tvklike-Ø   Ø-ce-homp-ic-Ø-es
      2SII-mother-def_subj   bread-def_obj   3persD-2persII-eat-caus-3pers-dec
      'Your mother fed you the bread.'

You should note that the "causer" in this and the following examples is indicated by the type I subject suffix on the verb. The "causee" is denoted through the use of the type II prefix on the verb. When necessary, the item upon which the "causee" is performing the action is shown by the use of the type D prefix.

Example 20 presents another case in which the action of placing the –*ec*- form of the causative suffix after a stem ending in –*v*- leads to the vowel sound *i* between the stem and the causative.

20.   Uewvn okofkiciyvnks.

uewv-n   Ø-okofk-**ic**-v-k-vnk-s
water-indef_obj   3persII-muddy-caus-1S-neg-mp-dec
'I did not make the water muddy.'

In this example, you can also see that the causative suffix occurs before the 1S subject suffix on the verb. Following the subject suffix are the negating, middle past, and declarative suffixes, which are in the order you were shown in *Beginning Creek*, chapter 10. Note also that *v* was identified as the final stem vowel, because the last vowel of the infinitive verb form is *o* and the last consonant in the infinitive stem is *k*. Even though another consonant, in this case *f*, comes between the last vowel in the infinitive form of the verb and the *k*, this does nothing to alter the choice of *v* as the final stem vowel when you are getting ready to add the causative suffix.

The verb in example 20 also shows that type II verbs are taken through the same steps as type I verbs when you are determining the final vowel and adding the causative suffix. The verb stem is found by deleting the final long *ē* from the end of the infinitive form. The determination of the final stem vowel is then made on the basis of the remaining sounds. Thus, in example 20, the stem of the verb *okofk*- was derived from *okofkē*, and the final vowel was then shown to be *v*, because the last vowel in the infinitive stem is *o* and the final consonant is *k*. When a type II stem is presented in an infinitive form that ends in –*etv*, follow the steps already given for determining final vowels on type I verbs.

When the –*ec*- form of the causative suffix is added to a verb stem that ends in the vowel *e*, the two vowels combine to create a long *ē* sound before the *c* of the causative suffix. In example 21, this is what has happened to cause the form of the causative to be heard as *ēc*-.

21.   Hvset cvhiyēcetos.
      hvse-t   cv-hay-**ēc**-Ø-et-o-s.
      sun-indef_subj   1SII-warm-caus-3pers-ss-aux_vb-dec
      'The sun is making me warm.'

Given the number of verb stems whose final vowel is *e*, it will come as no surprise that this is the most common form of the causative that you are likely to encounter when listening to or talking with Mvskoke speakers.

The –*yc*- form of the causative suffix

The other form of the causative suffix is –*yc*-. This form is used when the final vowel of a verb stem is *o*. When this form of the causative is placed after the *o* of the verb stem, it can modify the sound of this vowel so that it sounds like the /oy/ of the English word "boy." In the speech of many speakers, though, this combination of final stem vowel *o* and the *y* of the causative are pronounced like the English word "way."

It is because of the first pronunciation described above that linguists consider the form of the causative added to verbs with final stem vowel *o* to be –*yc*-. For this reason, when the position of this suffix is shown in the second line of each example in which it occurs, the stem vowel *o* will be shown on the verb stem and the causative will be indicated as –*yc*-. Remember that this is the case, even though the stem vowel *o*-causative suffix combination will always be represented as –*uec*- in the Mvskoke writing system, as in the verb *ohfolhuecetv* 'to make (two or more) return something,' which has this form in its glossary entry. Example 22 presents a verb, ending in a final *o*, to which the –*yc*- form of the causative suffix has been attached. Notice that the manner of representing the stem vowel and causative suffix in the second line of the example follows the format we have just described.

22.   Cesse cvtaskuecetos.
      cesse-Ø   cv-tasko-**yc**-Ø-et-o-s
      mouse-def_subj   1SII-jump-caus-3pers-ss-aux_vb-dec
      'The mouse made me jump.'

In cases where the final vowel of the verb stem may be either *o* or *e* (when the verb infinitive form has a final vowel of *e* or *ē* and the final consonant is either *p* or *k*), causative constructions with these verbs may take either the *–ec-* or *–yc-* forms. The first is used when the final vowel is *e*, the second when the final vowel is *o*. Thus, it is possible for speakers to create either of the sentences in examples 23 and 24 when they want to explain what it was that made the woman sneeze.

23. Homucet hokten hvtēskuecvnks.

homuce-t	hokte-n	Ø-hvtēsko-**yc**-Ø-es
black_pepper-indef_subj	woman-indef_obj	3persII-sneeze-caus-3pers-mp-dec

'Black pepper made the woman sneeze.'

24. Homucet hokten hvtēskēcvnks.

homuce-t	hokte-n	Ø-hvtēsk-**ēc**-Ø-es
black_pepper-indef_subj	woman-indef_obj	3persII-sneeze-caus-3pers-mp-dec

'Black pepper made the woman sneeze.'

Because of this alternation, Mvskoke speakers will understand both kinds of causative formations, but people generally prefer to use one over the other. In Oklahoma Mvskoke-speaking communities, there appears to be a shift toward the use of the *–ec-* form of the causative in these cases. Whether you use the *–ec-* or *–yc-* form of the causative suffix with verbs that allow for the use of either one, you will be understood, though you may find that most of the speakers with whom you interact prefer one version over the other.

Further Considerations

There are some other features of verbs that play a role in determining which version of the causative suffix to use with a given verb. Both of the items we will deal with here have to do with suppletive verbs. The way in which a verb changes to denote the plurality of its subject can make a difference in which form of the causative suffix is used with the plural verb stems.

First, as you may have noticed in looking over the verbs listed in appendix 2, several verbs change from a singular to a plural form by adding the suffix *–ho-* to the verb stem. For instance, the verb *vpeletv* 'to smile, laugh' has a plural form *vpelhoyetv*. In creating causatives with the plural form of verbs that have *ho* followed by *y* at the end of their infinitive form (such as *vpelhoy-* from the infinitive *vpelhoyetv*), no further vowel is added to the stem formed when *–etv* has been dropped from the infinitive form. With verbs of this sort, the *–yc-* form of the causative suffix is added directly to the verb stem that results from dropping the infinitival suffix. This leads to the following differences between causative structures made from the singular and plural forms of 'to laugh' in examples 25 and 26.

25. Posucet vmvpelēcvnks.
     pos-uce-t   vm-vpel-**ēc**-Ø-vnk-s
     cat-dim-ind_subj   1SII-laugh/smile_(1)-caus-3pers-mp-dec
     'A kitten made me smile/laugh.'

26. Posucet vmvpelhuecvnks.
     pos-uce-t   vm-vpelho-**yc**-Ø-vnk-s
     cat-dim-ind_subj   1SII-laugh_(2+)-caus-3pers-mp-dec
     'Kittens made me smile/laugh.'

Generally, when the plural form of a verb is differentiated from its singular form by the inclusion of *ho* in the stem, the *–yc-* form of the causative is used even when a consonant besides *y* follows the suffix *ho* in the infinitive. Thus, in constructing a causative statement with the verb *enokhokē* 'sick (of two or more),' the final *k* of the stem derived from the infinitive form is dropped before the *–yc-* version of the causative suffix is added. This leads to the structure shown in example 27.

27. Wakvpesē toksat ponokhuecvnks.
     wakvpesē   toks-at   po-nokho-**yc**-Ø-vnk-s
     milk   sour-def_subj   1PII-sick_(2+)-caus-3pers-mp-dec
     'The sour milk made us sick.'

A further element must be kept in mind about suppletive verbs that have different forms for singular, dual, and plural subjects or objects. In many cases, verbs with three distinct forms will have a plural form that includes something that could be construed as the causative suffix. For instance, the verb 'to sleep (of three or more)' has the structure *nocicetv*. When the stem of 'to sleep (of three or more)' is separated from the infinitival suffix, the resulting form is *nocic-*, which sounds as though it ends with the causative suffix (cf. examples 19 and 20).

TABLE 5.3. Causative Forms for Verbs with Plural Stems That Could Be Mistaken for Causative Forms

Verbal Infinitive Forms (Singular, Dual, Plural)	Verb Stems Derived from the Infinitives	Causative Stem Forms
ropottetv 'to go through, pass through (of one)'	ropott-	ropottecic- 'to make (one) go through, pass through'
ropothoyetv 'to go through, pass through (of two)'	ropothoy-	ropothoyc- 'to make (2+) go through, pass through'
ropotecetv 'to go through, pass through (of 3+)'	ropotec- (could be taken as a causative)	
nocetv 'to sleep (of one)'	noc-	nocecic- 'to make sleep (of one)'
nochoyetv 'to sleep (of two)'	nochoy-	nochoyc- 'to make sleep (of 2+)'
nocicetv 'to sleep (of 3+)'	nocic- (could be taken as a causative)	

Verbs whose plural stems end in a final syllable that could be mistaken for the causative suffix tend to have special causative forms. Table 5.3 shows the way in which Mvskoke marks the causative form on two different verbs whose plural stems end in sounds that could be confused with the causative. The rationale for using a special, long form of the causative on the singular forms of verbs such as those in table 5.3 is to make it clear to a listener that one is using the causative on the singular stem, rather than the noncausative plural. For instance, if *ropottetv* did not have a long causative form, one would think that the causative of this stem would be *ropottēc-*, which is very close to the plural form of the noncausative verb stem *ropotec-*. The only difference between the two is the length of the final vowel (the long *ē* of the causative form versus the short *e* of the plural, noncausative form), which does not provide much for a listener to use in determining whether a speaker is using the causative singular form or the noncausative, plural form.

The use of special structures in the case of causatives leads to the very clear differences among the verbal forms shown in examples 28–32, which provide sentences containing both causative and noncausative forms of the singular, dual, and plural forms of *ropottetv*. Examples 28–30 give you non-causative sentences, while examples 31–32 give you causative sentences.

28.   Eto-vlke tvphan ropottimvts.
       eto-vlke   tvph-an   ropott-i-mvt-s
       tree-pl   wide-def_obj   pass_through_(1)-1S-dp-dec
       'I passed through the wide forest.'

29.   Cēpvnvke eto-vlke tvphan ropothoyemvts.
       cēpvn-vke-Ø   eto-vlke   tvph-an   ropothoy-Ø-emvt-s
       boy-pl-def_subj   tree-pl   wide-def_obj   pass_through_(2)-3pers-dp-dec
       'The (2) boys passed through the wide forest.'

30.   Cēpvnvke eto-vlke tvphan ropotecemvts.
       cēpvn-vke-Ø   eto-vlke   tvph-an   ropotec-Ø-emvt-s
       boy-pl-def_subj   tree-pl   wide-def_obj   pass_through_(3+)-3pers-dp-dec
       'The (3+) boys passed through the wide forest.'

31.   Hoktvlēt eto-vlke tvphan cvropottecicemvts.
       hoktvlē-t   eto-vlke   tvph-an   cv-ropott-**ecic**-Ø-emvt-s
       old_woman-ind_subj   tree-pl   wide-def_obj   1SII-pass_through_(1)-
                                                             caus-3pers-dp-dec
       'An old woman made me pass through the wide forest.'

32.   Hoktvlēt cēpvnvke eto-vlke tvphan ropothuecemvts.
       hŏhoktvlē-t   cēpvn-vke   eto-vlke   tvph-an
       old_woman-ind_subj   boy-pl-def_obj   tree-pl   wide-def_obj
       Ø-ropotho-**yc**-Ø-emvt-s
       3persII-pass_through_(2+)-caus-3pers-dp-dec
       'An old woman made the (2 or more) boys pass through the wide forest.'

Notice that the causative in example 32 covers plurals of 2 or more. When a verb has a long causative form in the singular, there is only one plural causative form, even though the noncausative form of the verb may have different stems for singular, dual, and plural.

The rules governing the production and use of the command and causative forms that you have learned in this chapter cover most of the verb forms in Mvskoke. However, there are some irregular causatives and command forms with which you will undoubtedly be confronted as you interact with Mvskoke speakers. As long as you are aware of the general forms of the command and causative suffixes, you should be able to discern when one of these kinds of sentences has been constructed, even though it does not conform exactly to the patterns you have been shown to this point.

Indirect Causatives

Direct and indirect causatives differ in that the causer tends to have an active role in making the action happen in direct causatives, while in indirect causatives, the causer has an oblique role in the performance of the action. In a direct causative, there is little doubt that the causer is directly responsible for making the causee do the activity. In an indirect causative, the causer may provide the suggestion that the causee pursue the activity or may play a role in helping the causee perform the action. When the causer plays a helping or supporting role in carrying out the action, the causative is indirect in form.

The Mvskoke causative examples that you have seen to this point are almost all direct causatives. The sole exception is example 19, in which 'your mother' (the causer in this sentence) is feeding 'you' (the causee) some bread. In this case, the causer is providing the food for your consumption, even to the point of moving the food to your mouth, but it is up to 'you' to do the chewing and swallowing that completes the action. In this case, while we may think that 'your mother' is being very active in carrying out the activity of the sentence, it is really up to the one being fed to do the consuming of the food, so this is considered an indirect causative.

In most other cases, the fact that one is faced with an indirect causative is indicated by the inclusion of the counterexpectational suffix in the causative construction. As we mentioned earlier, the counterexpectational suffix indicates that the action may not go exactly as one would expect or that the person performing the action has the possibility of not complying with expectations. Including this suffix in a causative sentence demonstrates that the causee has a real role in determining whether the action happens or not, which—as one might expect—places the causer in the position of being less directly responsible for seeing that the activity takes place.

When the counterexpectational suffix, like the distributive and causative suffixes, is the last one on the stem before the negating or tense-marking
suffixes, it is affected by the changes caused by the application of verb
grades to the stem. Given that the counterexpectational suffix generally
comes before the causative suffix in a causative construction, it is rarely in
the position affected by the verb-grade changes. Occasionally, though, the
counterexpectational suffix may come after the causative. When this occurs,
you will need to pay attention to any changes to the form of the suffix
resulting from the lengthened-grade, falling-tone grade, or h-grade.

The inclusion of the counterexpectational suffix before the causative
also leads to the use of a form of the causative that you may not expect.
With the counterexpectational suffix added to the verb stem (thereby
becoming part of it), it would appear that the form of the stem vowel
should be *–e-*, which, when melded with the vowel of the causative suffix,
would make the causative be pronounced as *–ēc-*. However, in this case
the final stem vowel is actually *–v-*, which leads to the pronunciation *–ic-*
when the causative suffix has been applied. Thus, whenever you create a
causative in which the counterexpectational suffix precedes the causative
suffix, the latter will be written and pronounced as *–ic-*.

Examples 33 and 34 present the different forms of direct and indirect
causatives respectively. Note the difference in interpretation of the two sentences. While both lead to the same English sentences in the fourth line of
the examples, the ways in which the man is going to cause the boy to dance
are quite different. In example 33, for instance, the man is making the boy
dance through direct physical contact. In example 34, however, the man is
doing something that leads the boy to begin to dance, but the man is not
entirely responsible for the boy's actions.

33.   Mvt mistet cēpanan opvnēcvhanes.

    mvt   miste-t   cēpan-an   Ø-opvn-**ēc**-vhan-Ø-es
    that   man-ind_subj   boy-def_obj   3persII-dance-caus-intent-3pers-dec
    'That man is going to make the boy dance.'
    (By bouncing the boy up and down on his knee, for instance.)

34.   Mvt mistet cēpanan opvnepicvhanes.

    mvt   miste-t   cēpan-an   Ø-opvn-**ep**-**ic**-vhan-Ø-es
    that   man-ind_subj   boy-def_obj   3persII-dance-ctre-caus-intent-
                                                            3pers-dec

'That man is going to make the boy dance.'
(By playing music that would make the boy dance, for instance.)

It will be necessary to consider how the causer is managing to persuade the causee to do the action whenever you are trying to interpret an indirect causative. Generally, the context in which the action is occurring will give you enough information to be able to infer how the causer is indirectly making things occur.

The directive and command forms that you have just learned are used rather more frequently in Mvskoke interactions than you might expect. Directive constructions are used when interacting with guests, both familiar and unfamiliar, so if you go to visit Mvskoke speakers, you will undoubtedly be hearing and responding to politely offered directives to sit down and/or eat. Causative constructions are also used with some frequency in conversations, particularly when the speaker is relating what has happened to other people.

Vocabulary

TOOLS

English		Mvskoke
hammer		svtokuce
nails/nail		vcokv
	or	vcopv
saw		esfokv
ladder		vccakv
screwdriver		nak (e)sem vfiyetv
screw/screws		(e)sem vfikv
gun		eccv
bullet, arrow		rē
bow		cvkotvkse
arrow		cvkotvkse enrē
fishhook		rvro rakcvwetv
	or	cufokonhe
net		hoyv
knife		eslafkv

English	Mvskoke
pen/pocket knife	eslafkuce
axe	woceswv
or	pocoswv

VERBS

English	Mvskoke
to pound or shatter (as with a hammer or mallet) {I;3}	pvccetv
to pound or beat (as corn with a *keco* and *kecvpe* or seeds with a mortar and pestle) {I;3}	hocetv
to saw {I;3}	foyetv
to carry (one item) {I;II}	esetv
to carry (two or more items) {I;II}	cvwetv
to drop (one item) {I;3}	awiketv
to drop two items {I;3}	atakkayetv
to drop three or more items {I;3}	atakpvlvtetv
to fire, shoot {I;II}	eccetv
to catch a fish {I;3}	rvro esetv
or {I;3}	rvro aswiketv
to build one thing {I;3}	hayetv
to build two or more things {I;3}	hahicetv
to tear down something {I;3}	letvfetv
to screw in {I;3}	(e)sem vfiyetv
to unscrew something {I;3}	(e)sem vfikv em esetv
to cut something (once) {I;3}	tvcetv
to cut something (several times) {I;3}	waretv
to drill a hole/holes {I;3}	polletv
to carve something {I;3}	kvlvfetv
to chop (wood) {I;3}	cvsketv

Exercises

EXERCISE 1

Change each of the following sentences into a causative, making five
sentences that include the counterexpectational suffix with the causative

suffix and five others using only the causative suffix. Provide a translation for each sentence, including those provided as your starting point. For each indirect causative sentence that you construct, provide an explanation as to how the causer is making the causee perform the action. An example has been provided for you.

Original sentence:	Causative form:
Honvnwvt vccakvn awikvnks.	Cvpvwvt honvnwvn vccakvn awikepicvnks.

Translation:	
A man dropped a ladder.	My maternal uncle made a man drop a ladder.

Explanation for the indirect causative:
My maternal uncle came around a corner and scared the man so much that he dropped the ladder.

1. Ceckuce telomhv hokkolan vmvhorhvkvhanetos.
2. Honvntake coko tutcēnen hahicvkvrēs.
3. Sopaktv tashokes.
4. Cēpvne mahat vcopv cvcaweks.
5. Rvro em akwiyv hoyv tvphan cvhwes.
6. Wotko nehat pvfnēn lētketos.
7. Honvnwv ēwvnwvt yvlahv ponesemvts.
8. Hoktvlat kapv cekfan rokiyes.
9. Cvcket vcen hocekotos.
10. Foco ostvpakat tvmēces.

EXERCISE 2

Construct ten different directive sentences using the verbs, nouns, and adjectives listed below. Five of the sentences can contain only a verb, while the other five directives can contain a noun, too. Of the five sentences with nouns, include at least one adjective in three of the sentences.

	Verbs	Nouns	Adjectives
1.	ahvtvpecetv	yokkofketv	holattē
2.	em akhottetv	eto	hvtkē

	Verbs	Nouns	Adjective
3.	okkosetv	sokhv	hvsvtkē
4.	vcumhoketv	vccakv	hvsvthvkē
5.	foyetv	hvccuce	cvpakkē
6.	kaketv	tvklike	mahē
7.	enrecvpetv	(ē)kvnhvlwuce	kvrpē
8.	vtehketv	enke	kvmoksē
9.	waretv	vhvoke	polokē
10.	pvkohlicetv	svhocackv	cvhkēpen

EXERCISE 3

Come up with ten or more directives you are likely to use in the course of one or two days. Write these down in a list that you can turn in to your teacher. Over the course of one or two days, be certain to use these directives whenever an appropriate situation arises. You may recite them only to yourself or, if you are in the presence of another Mvskoke speaker, you should say them out loud. Keep track of some of the situations in which you have used the directives and describe these on the same sheet on which you have written the list of directives, so that you can hand these in to your teacher, too. Your teacher may ask you to share your list of directives and the descriptions of how and when you used them with other members of your class. Be prepared to say your directives aloud at that time.

EXERCISE 4

Think about all that you did or that you observed others doing over the past two days. Based on what you recall about how your and others' activities were performed, write out ten causative sentences that relate to your experiences. If you need vocabulary items not included in the glossary of this text, we suggest that you consult *Beginning Creek*, the Loughridge and Hodge dictionary (1890 [1964]), or the Martin and Mauldin dictionary (2000). After you have written down your ten causative sentences, provide sufficient contextual information so that another person can imagine how and why the causer made the action occur. Your instructor may ask you to pronounce your sentences in class and provide some background information, so you might want to practice saying the sentences that you have formed.

EXERCISE 5

Separate out and then identify each morpheme in the sentences below. Follow this with an English translation. When you have done so, you will end up with a structure similar to the second, third, and fourth lines of each of the examples in this chapter. An example is provided for you.

Example: Hvse hiyat sokhv-hatkv ewvnhkēcvrēs.

hvse	hiy-at	sokhv-hatkv-Ø	Ø-ewvnhke-ec-Ø-vrē-s
sun	hot-def_subj	possum-def_obj	3persII-thirsty-caus-3pers-fut-dec

'The hot sun is going to make the possum thirsty.'

1. Totkv hiyat vssen morēcetos.
2. Miste vculet cēpvnvke cvyayvhokan eton pvfnēn cvskepicvnks.
3. Wakvpesē-neha asvmwiyvs!
4. Vhakv-hayv cvpakkat cempenkvlēcetisv?
5. Cemvhayv hoktuce hokkolan hoccicepihces.
6. Poposet cvcerwvn pohvpo ponhayepihces.
7. Vpokepvks ci!
8. Efv vculet wakv lvsten yvkvpēcvhanes.
9. Hofonof Cufe Nokose elvwēcvtēte?
10. 'Sem vtehkv hompvks ci!

EXERCISE 6

Translate the following causative sentences into Mvskoke, constructing an indirect and a direct form of the causative for each sentence. When you have done this, describe some context that would explain the indirect form (the context should make it clear how the causer made the action occur indirectly).

1. A naughty boy made the little girl cry.
2. The dog made two squirrels climb that tree.
3. My older brother made me carry my younger brothers. (Man speaking.)
4. I made them tear down the arbor.
5. The fireman made the thin old woman open the door.

Listening Exercise

Listen to track 5 on the CD that accompanies this textbook. This is a conversation regarding food preparation, and in it one of the speakers uses some directives and causatives. Tracks 64–79 present each speaker's turns in order. Listen closely to these tracks and identify at least four sentences that contain either a directive or a causative construction. Be prepared to state the sentences out loud in class, so that your classmates can understand why you think that it is an example of a causative or directive construction.

      Listen for directives in "Turtle's Shell" (track 89). When do they occur? Who is the recipient or target of the directives and who is giving them? Are these directives very forceful, or do they contain the counter-expectational suffix? Does Linda's voice change in any way when she is using these directives in the story? You may find that listening to the English translation is helpful in identifying approximately where the directives occur in the Mvskoke version.

      What role does Turtle's inappropriate response to the directives play in the story? What is the outcome of his inattention to the directives? Do you think the fact that Turtle ignores the directives makes this story a useful teaching tool? What audience might need to be taught about the importance of paying attention to directives? Be prepared to discuss your answers in class.

Tools and Their Maintenance

Tools that are used to sustain life require maintenance. The Indians knew that in order to sustain themselves, they needed to keep their tools and weapons in good working order. This meant that every person had to be careful to use tools appropriately and treat them with care.

      The men used knives, bows, arrows, and tomahawks for hunting and protecting the tribe. Bows and arrows were used mainly for hunting. With these implements, they hunted rabbit, squirrels, deer, and fish. They were very good at hunting and managed to keep the tribe fed year-round. They also knew ways of using plants to assist them in their hunting.

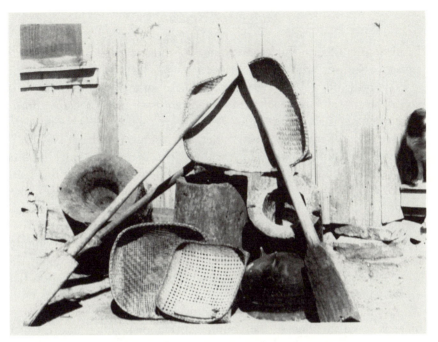

Three basket sieves, three wood mortars and pestles, and an iron pot, Lydia Larney's home, March 2, 1923. *Photograph by Jennie Elrod. J. Elrod Collection, Courtesy of the Oklahoma Historical Society. Negative #20382.80.*

Women used knives, baskets, clay pots, and grinders. The grinders that women used in the old days are nothing like those we use today. Grinders used to be made out of a mortar made from a hollowed-out log, called a *keco*, and were used in conjunction with a pestle, also made from wood, called a *kecvpe*. Women used this to grind corn by putting the corn in the *keco* and pounding on it with the *kecvpe*. Corn could be ground into different sizes, such as coarse meal for hominy or *sofke*, or really fine grinds for corn meal or *ecko*.

Hollowed-out gourds were used as dippers for ladling water or soup. Baskets and clay pots were also part of the items used by women as they fixed food for their families. The Creator gave us each of these things and showed us how to use them to survive. If we did not keep our tools in good condition and use them with respect and care, it could have cost our lives. It is clear that our ancestors maintained their tools well, since we are still here.

Suggested Readings

Readers interested in the various usages of the counterexpectational and causative suffixes are referred to Nathan (1977), Cohn (1987), Martin (1991) and Hardy (1988, 1994, 2005). These sources treat the suffixes in very different ways, but each raises important issues and provides informative discussions about the suffixes as they are used in speech within the Muskogee and Seminole communities. For instance, Nathan (1977: 123) identifies the suffix that we have called "counterexpectational" in this work as the "middle voice" in her book. She demonstrates that this same suffix (*-ep(o)-*) is used to show that the subject is affected by his or her action or that the subject is benefiting from the action taking place. Nathan does not specifically address the issue of including this suffix in the formation of commands, but she does show how it is used in conjunction with the causative suffix (Nathan 1977: 75–76). In the latter, she comes to many of the same conclusions about causative formation that we have presented in this book.

Cohn (1987) focuses almost exclusively on the causative suffix, although there is some mention of the counterexpectational suffix (again, called "middle voice" in this chapter). Cohn is interested in two aspects of causative structures in Mvskoke. The first aspect concerns the patterning of the pronominal suffixes and prefixes in verbs that contain the causative suffix. The second feature involves analyzing the order of suffixes in causative constructions and the interpretations that result from different organizational structures. Cohn (1987: 61–63) provides a nice discussion of the differences in meaning associated with the direct and indirect causatives, which may be of interest to those intrigued by this structure.

Hardy (1988) is concerned with many of the same issues that Cohn covers and goes into even more detail about each of them. Hardy's work is more technical in nature, so it may be a little more difficult to comprehend at first, but those interested in the subject will find Hardy provides excellent insights into the morphological issues associated with the formation of causatives in Mvskoke. Hardy's (1994) article, "Middle Voice in Creek," covers some aspects of causative formation in pages 52–66 but is primarily concerned with investigating the occurrence and meaning of a suffix that indicates middle voice. In this case, Hardy's (and others') definition of middle voice is very different from what Cohn is referring to by the same term or what we have called the counterexpectational.

Martin (1991) is another source concerning the use of the counterexpectational and causative suffixes, though only in regard to the ways in which these suffixes work to create causative sentences. Martin makes the argument that the relationship of the subject to the action changes when the counterexpectational suffix is included in a causative structure. In his discussion of the subject-to-action relationship, Martin (1991: 214–15) shows that the subject does, as Nathan suggests, become the beneficiary of the action. However, Martin demonstrates that the subject plays a more active role in the performance of the action when the sentence contains both the counterexpectational and causative suffixes than when only the causative suffix is used, so he goes beyond what Nathan covers.

In the most recent work on causative forms, Hardy (2005: 224–25) proposes that the primary use of the counterexpectational (-ep(o)-) suffix is to show that something is unexpected or there is the possibility that the action will not occur as expected. He offers little discussion of whether the subject benefits from or is affected by the action denoted by the verb to which the suffix has been attached. In the section on the counterexpectational suffix, however, Hardy speaks about three different meanings that the suffix can indicate. Each of these meanings, except for the strictly counterexpectational, has been covered in this chapter.

The types of tools and the ways in which they are used by Muskogee people, both historically and currently, are discussed in several sources. The information about tools and their use is sporadic in the readings listed below, but there is a good deal of detail provided in each source. The most authoritative work on the types of tools used by the Muskogees before Removal is Swanton (1928a). Tool types and their use are covered as Swanton presents historic and ethnographic details about each of the areas of life in which they were used. Unfortunately, he does not provide a single section devoted solely to material culture of the pre-Removal Muskogees, but the information available throughout his report is insightful.

Information regarding tools, their use, and technological changes occurring after Removal may be found in a variety of sources. Reports of tools bought for the use of tribal members, means of training individuals to use the tools, and the success and productivity resulting from such training are to be found in the Muscogee (Creek) Nation and Seminole Nation files at the Oklahoma Historical Society. These reports were compiled by leaders of the two nations or their representatives and were offered as evidence of the success (or lack thereof) of federally sponsored training and modernization programs.

Baker and Baker (1996) is a second source providing some information about technological items and their uses by the Muskogee people. Some members of the Muscogee (Creek) and Seminole Nations were slave owners who had brought their slaves with them to Indian Territory (Oklahoma) during Removal. Some of the narratives presented in this work, which are reminiscences of individuals who had been slaves among the Creeks and Seminoles, describe their general activities and the tools with which they performed these activities in often considerable detail.

CHAPTER SIX

Postpositions and Compound Noun Phrases

In this chapter, you will be introduced to postpositions and compound noun phrases. **Postpositions** and **postpositional phrases** are means of indicating the location of one noun phrase in relation to another noun phrase. **Compound noun phrases** are noun phrases that have more than one type of noun contained within the phrase.

The term **postposition** refers to words that perform the same function as prepositions do in English. In most cases, postpositions in Mvskoke indicate the relationship of one noun phrase to another as the preposition does in the English phrase "the man *behind* the counter." The combination of postposition and the noun phrase that it is modifying is called a **postpositional phrase**. Words and phrases demonstrating the spatial relationship of nouns within a Mvskoke sentence are called postpositions or postpositional phrases because the directional words always follow the noun phrase that they modify, rather than coming before them as in English. Examples 1 and 2 show the difference in location of the positional words in first an English then a Mvskoke sentence. The positional word in each is in boldface, and the noun phrase modified by the positional word is italicized. The postpositional phrase is made up of both the postposition and the underlined noun phrase in example 2.

1. Grandfather's dog is lying **under** *the chair.*

2. Poca emefvt *ohliketv* (**e**)**lecvn** wakkes.
    Ø-poca   em-efv-t   ohliketv-Ø   Ø-(e)lecv-n

> 3persII-grandfather   3persII-dog-ind_subj   chair-def_obj   3persII-under-obl
> wakk-Ø-es
> lying_down_(1)-3pers-dec
> 'Grandfather's dog is lying under the chair.'

Notice that *lecvn* 'under' follows the noun phrase *ohliketv* 'the chair,' which it modifies.

In the second and third lines of example 2, the postposition is shown as having a null prefix and a suffix. The prefix, when one is used, is taken from the type II prefix set. When the noun phrase modified by the post-position is denoted by a first- or second-person pronoun, it is marked by the inclusion of a type II pronominal prefix in Mvskoke sentences. Thus, example 3 presents a Mvskoke sentence with a second person pronoun as the object of the postposition.

3.   Cēpvnet ceyopvn hueretos.

     cēpvne-t   **ce**-yopv-n   huer-Ø-et-o-s
     boy-ind_subj   2persII-behind-obl   stand_(1)-3pers-ss-aux_vb-dec
     'A boy is standing behind you.'

The suffix shown on the postposition (called the **oblique** and indicated by 'obl' in the third line of each Mvskoke example) helps to show a listener that the items affected by the postposition are playing a secondary role in the sentence in relation to the performance of the action. In essence, using this suffix makes it clear that the position of the items in the noun phrase is included as informative material, but that this information is not directly connected with the activity being discussed in the sentence. This suffix is used at some times and not others by Mvskoke speakers, and its inclusion or exclusion does nothing to change the meaning of the sentence. As examples, the sentences in examples 4 and 5 are exactly alike in meaning and tone, except that the oblique suffix is included in example 4 but not in example 5.

4.   Poset coko homvn likvnks.

     pose-t   coko-Ø   Ø-homv-n   lik-Ø-vnk-s
     grandmother-   house-def_obj   3persII-in_   sit_(1)-3pers-mp-dec
       ind_subj   front_of-obl
     'Grandmother sat in front of the house.'

5.   Poset coko homv likvnks.

   pose-t   coko-Ø   Ø-homv   lik-Ø-vnk-s
   grandmother-   house-def_obj 3persII-in_front_of sit_(1)-3pers-mp-dec
      ind_subj
   'Grandmother sat in front of the house.'

When the object of the postpositional phrase is identified by a pronoun, as in example 3, the pronoun prefix is taken from the list presented
in table 6.1. The pronominal prefixes shown here are identical to the type
II prefix set used on verbs. Notice that there is no clear way to tell whether
a second or third person object noun is plural or singular. The distributive
suffix is not used with postpositions, only the type II prefix, so there is no
distinction between the second or third person singular and plural forms.

TABLE 6.1. Pronominal Prefixes Used with Postpositions

Object Noun	Abbreviation	Postpositions Beginning with a Consonant or *e*	Postpositions Beginning with Any Vowel Other Than *e*
1S 'me'	1SII	cv-	vc-
2pers 'you'	2persII	ce-	ec-
3pers 'him/her/it'	3persII	—	—
1P 'us'	1PII	po-	pom-
2pers 'you (plural)'	2persII	ce-	ec-
3pers 'them'	3persII	—	—

You also may have noticed that the noun phrase modified by the
postposition in examples 2 through 5 has appeared as a definite object in
each case. This is standard for noun phrases modified by postpositions.
When the noun phrase includes adjectives, as in example 6, the final
adjective takes the –*an* suffix, showing that it is a definite object.

6.   Eshoccickvn cokv holattē rakkan onvpvn ascvnwiyvs!

   eshoccickv-n   cokv   holattē   rakk-**an**   Ø-onvpv-n
   pencil-ind_obj book   blue   big-def_obj   3persII-on_top_of-obl
   Ø-as-cvn-wiy-vs
   3persII-to-1SD-pass_something-imper
   'Pass me the pencil on top of the big blue book!'

It is possible to create sentences containing multiple numbers of post-positional phrases, similar to the English sentence "The boy ran behind the rock in front of the house." The Mvskoke translation of this sentence is shown in example 7.

7.   Cēpvne cvto yopvn encoko ehomvn letikes.

cēpvne-Ø	cvto-Ø	**yopv-**n	en-coko-Ø	**ehomv-**n
boy-def_subj	rock-def_obj	behind-obl	3persII-house-def_obj	in_front_of-obl

letik-Ø-es
run_(1)<hgr>-3pers-dec
'The boy ran behind the rock in front of the house.'

Notice that the order of the postpostional phrases is the same in the Mvskoke example as it is in the English translation. The fact that the boy is running *behind the rock* is mentioned first, then that the rock is located *in front of the house*. This ordering presents the most important information first (that the boy is running behind a rock) and then provides less relevant information (specifics about exactly where the rock is located). Thus, if you are confronted with a Mvskoke sentence in which one or more postpositional phrases follow a first phrase, translate them as you would the prepositional phrases in an English sentence. The first postpositional phrase has the most important information for understanding and completing the sentence, with later phrases adding descriptive material.

Occasionally, English sentences containing prepositions will be translated without using a postpositional phrase in Mvskoke. In example 8, *ofv* 'in' does not occur in the Mvskoke sentence but does appear in the English translation. Instead of a direct translation of "in" from the English, Mvskoke speakers will form locational phrases using verbs to denote the position of the object noun.

8.   Cokv sokcv vtehken tohahwv yopvn eslikes.

cokv-Ø	sokcv-Ø	**vtehke-**n	tohahwv-Ø
book-def_subj	bag-def_obj	be_inside_a_container_(2+)-obl	box-def_obj

yopv-n	eslik-Ø-es
behind-obl	be_situated_(3+)-3pers-dec

'The books are in the bag behind the box.'

In this example, the fact that the books are located inside the bag is shown through the use of the stem from *vtehketv* 'to be inside a container (of two or more objects),' to which the oblique suffix *–n* has been added.

Verbs describing the location of one item in regard to another, like *vtehketv*, show up rather frequently in Mvskoke constructions that require the use of prepositions in their English translations. Often, the verbs in such constructions will have the structure described in example 8, where the oblique suffix has been affixed to the verb stem. The form has been mentioned here to make you aware of this means of demonstrating the locational relationships between nouns in Mvskoke sentences. It will be discussed in greater detail in chapters 8 and 9, where we cover the formation of sentences containing multiple verbs.

Compound noun phrases

At times, more than one noun may be included in a noun phrase. When this is the case, a **compound noun phrase** is formed. In Mvskoke, the way in which a compound noun phrase will be indicated depends on whether the noun phrase is conjoined or disjoined. In the case of **conjoined noun phrases**, the nouns are considered to be part of a single group, as in the English sentence *"The man and his dog* were running." In this sentence, the subject noun phrase consists of both 'the man' and 'his dog,' making it compound in nature, and the man and the dog are performing the action together, indicating that the nouns in this phrase are conjoined.

A disjoined object noun phrase occurs in "You use either *a saw or an axe* to chop wood." In a **disjoined noun phrase**, the nouns are not considered to be part of the same group. Disjoined noun phrases lead the hearer to conclude that at least one of the items will not be part of the subject, direct object, or indirect object noun phrase when the action takes place. In the English sentence given above, a listener would know that only one of the items specified in the disjoined noun phrase 'a saw or an axe' will be used to chop the wood.

Conjoined noun phrases

When a Mvskoke speaker creates a conjoined compound noun phrase, the nouns that a listener is to perceive as part of the same grouping are listed one after another. Often, the nouns take the definite subject or object suffix and there is no inclusion of a connective word similar to the English 'and.' The fact that a number of nouns are spoken one after another, along with the proper form of the verb (if suppletive), is enough to demonstrate to a Mvskoke listener that the speaker is creating a conjoined noun phrase. An example of this construction in presented in example 9.

9.   Foco sasvkwv tvmēcetos.
       foco-Ø   **sasvkwv-Ø**   tvmēc-Ø-et-o-s
       ducks-def_subj   geese-def_subj   fly_(3+)_l_grd-3pers-ss-aux_vb-dec
       'Ducks and geese are flying.'

When the nouns are marked as indefinite subjects or objects, all nouns in the noun phrase will be marked in the same way. Thus, in example 10, each of the nouns is marked as an indefinite object (each one ends with the indefinite suffix –*n*). As in example 9, it is simply the fact that a string of nouns, marked in the same way, occurs in the sentence that indicates it is a compound, conjoined noun phrase.

10.   Ecket tvkliken tosēnvn tafvmpen wares.
       ecke-t   tvklike-**n**   tosēnv-**n**   tafvmpe-**n**
       mother-ind_subj   bread-ind_obj   salt_meat-ind_obj   onion-ind_obj
       Ø-war-Ø-es
       3persII-slice_(2+)_l_grd-3pers-dec
       'Mother slices the bread, salt meat, and onions.'

Occasionally, a conjoined noun phrase consisting of only two nouns will be marked as such by the inclusion of the word *tepvkē* 'together' in the sentence. This word is used very much as though it is an adjective in that it follows the two nouns that it modifies. Also, when it is marked as definite, it takes the form *tepvkat/tepvkan*, but when it is marked as indefinite, it takes the form *tepvket/tepvken*, as other type II adjectives do (see *Beginning Creek*, chapter 4, for review of this structure). In example 11, *tepvkē* marks the conjoined nature of the noun phrase in that it shows that the shirt(s) and socks, together, are considered to be the objects of the sentence.

11.   Cēpanat yokkofketv estele-svhocackv tepvkan vpvlvtetos.

cēpan-at   yokkofketv   estele_svhocackv   tepvk-**an**
boy-def_subj   shirt   socks   together-def_obj

Ø-vpvlvt-Ø-et-o-s
3persII-throw_away_(3+)-3pers-ss-aux_vb-dec
'The boy threw away his shirt(s) and socks.'

Notice that the verb takes the form for three or more objects, even though the use of *tepvkan* would make it seem as though only two things are being thrown away. The 3+ form of the verb makes it clear that the number of items being discarded is at least three.

Mvskoke speakers also may indicate that they are forming a conjoined noun phrase by adding the suffix –o- 'and' to the nouns. When this suffix is added to nouns in a string, it is usually preceded by –t- (which will be grouped together with the 'and' suffix in the second line of each example) and followed with the appropriate subject/object ending (-t/-n). When a speaker uses this suffix on nouns in a conjoined phrase, he or she will usually place it on each noun except the final one in the phrase. If a speaker adds another noun to the phrase, rather as if he or she had forgotten one item on the list, the speaker will often place the 'and' suffix on this noun, too. You can hear an example of this sort of structure on track 11 of the CD included with this text, in which Bertha is listing off several items she will buy, obviously adding meat to the list almost as an afterthought. The written version of this line is presented in example 12.

12.   Wakvpesēton, wakvnehaton, custaken, vpeswvton vpohvhanetowis.

wakvpesē-**to**-n   wakvneha-**to**-n   custake-n   vpeswv-**to**-n
milk-and-ind_obj   butter-and-ind_obj   egg-ind_obj   meat-and-ind_obj

vpoh-vhan-et-ow-i-s
buy-intent-ss-aux_vb-1S-dec
'I will buy milk, butter, eggs, and meat.'

Disjoined Noun Phrases

Mvskoke uses three different constructions for disjoined, compound noun phrases. One way of demonstrating that at least one of the nouns in a compound noun phrase is to be considered separately from the others, as in an 'either-or' sentence, is to insert the word *monkat/monkan* 'or' between the nouns in the phrase. Examples 13 and 14 show sentences in which the disjoined noun phrase is marked by the use of this word.

13. Cvrke nockv-coko monkan hompetv-hakcokofv yvkapes.
     cv-rke-Ø   nockv-coko   **monk-an**   hompetv-hak-coko-(o)fv
     1SII-father-def_subj   sleep-room   or-def_obj   food-make-room-in
     Ø-yvkap-Ø-es
     3persII-walk_(1)_l_grd-3pers-dec
     '(My) father is walking in either the bedroom or the kitchen.'

14. Kafen uewvn monkan wakvpesēn ceyacv?
     kafe-n   uewv-n   **monk-an**   wakvpesē-n   Ø-ce-yac-v
     coffee-   water-ind_obj   or-def_obj   milk-ind_obj   3persD-2persII-
       ind_obj   want-int
     'Do you want coffee, water, or milk?'

Notice that *monkan* comes just before the final noun in the phrase in example 14. This is the usual position of *monkat/monkan* when it is used to show a noun phrase is disjoined.

   A second means of showing that the nouns are disjoined may be combined with the use of *monkat/monkan* to make it even clearer that one of the nouns should be thought of as separate from the others in the phrase. This is done by adding the disjointive suffix *–tis* to each of the nouns in the phrase. The appearance of this suffix is marked by the use of 'disj' for 'disjointive suffix' in the third line of the examples in which it appears, beginning with number 15.

15. Sokhvtis monkat wakvtis vce hompvkvnks.
     sokhv-**tis**   **monk-at**   wakv-**tis**   vce-Ø   Ø-homp-vk-Ø-vnk-s
     pig-disj   or-def_subj   cow-disj   corn-def_obj   3persII-eat-distr-
                                                             3pers-mp-dec
     'Either the pigs or the cows ate the corn.'

The use of this suffix plus *monkat/monkan* makes it very clear to a listener that only a subset of the nouns in the phrase should be considered to be playing the role of subject, object, or direct object in the sentence. At least one of the nouns marked by the suffix *–tis* is to be separated from the others.

It is possible to use the disjointive suffix by itself, too. Example 16 presents a sentence in which the disjoined noun phrase is indicated solely by the use of *–tis.*

16.　Focotis sasvkwvtis hvcce onvpvn tvmhohkes.
　　　foco-**tis**　　sasvkwv-**tis**　hvcce　　onvpv-n　　tvmhohk-Ø-es
　　　duck-disj　　goose-disj　river　　over-obl　　fly_(2)<hgr>-3pers-dec
　　　'Two ducks or geese just flew over the river.'

A listener knows that *hvcce* is not part of the disjoined noun phrase, because the disjointive suffix has not been added to it. Therefore, it is part of another noun phrase playing a different role in the sentence.

Vocabulary

BUILDING FEATURES

English		Mvskoke
house		coko
	or	cuko
door		vhvoke
window		vhvokuce
floor		taktopvtake
roof		coko-onvpv
	or	coko-ohrvnkv
ceiling		cokofv-ohrvnkv
	or	vtopv
bathroom		cokuce
bedroom		nockv-coko
	or	wakketv-cokofv
kitchen		hompetv-hakcoko
	or	hompetv-coko
hallway		etehoyvnēcv
chimney, fireplace		totkv-hute

Postpositions

English	Mvskoke
above, over	onvpv
because of, in order, for	vrvhkv
behind, in back of	yopv
below, under, beneath	(e)lecv
between	(e)tennvrkvpv
or	(e)tenrvwv
by, next to	vfopkē
close to, near	tempē
in back of a building	topvrv
in front of	(e)homv
inside of, during	ofv
on the other side of	pvrvnkē
place, location	miyewv
or	mi
to the right	kvperv fvccvn
to the left	kvskvnv fvccvn

Verbs

English	Mvskoke
to open (a door, window, etc.) {I;3}	hvwecetv
to close (a door, window, etc.) {I;3}	vkhottetv
to hang up one item {I;3}	vtvretv
to hang up two or more items {I;3}	vtvrticetv
to take down (one item) {I;3}	aesetv
to take down two or more items {I;3}	acvwetv
to paint (a picture, a house) {I;II}	vhayetv
to cover {I;II}	ohranetv
to uncover one item {I;II}	ohrvnkv esetv
to uncover two or more items {I;II}	ohrvnkv cvwetv
to break, crack (one egg, glass, etc.) {I;3}	tvkocetv
to break, crack (two or more eggs, glasses, etc.) {I;3}	tvkohlicetv
to be level {II}	tvpeksē
to be uneven {II}	etemontvlē

Exercises

EXERCISE 1

Translate each of the following sentences from English into Mvskoke.

1. Your glasses are lying to the right of the paper.
2. My older brother built a house in the woods. (a man speaking)
3. I made her hang the dresses in front of the shirts.
4. A hawk and an eagle flew behind that mountain.
5. The man dropped the nails to the left of the hammer.
6. A hunter hung his bow above the door.
7. Six skunks just ran under the house.
8. The old dog lay down between the tree and the car.
9. The women are sitting under the arbor behind the house.
10. Yesterday, I walked near your house.

EXERCISE 2

Identify each morpheme within the following sentences, provide the linguistic notation for each morpheme, then translate each sentence from Mvskoke to English. As you perform this exercise, you should produce lines similar to the second, third, and fourth lines found in the examples in this chapter. The following is an example of what your answers should look like.

Original sentence:
   Oponvkv hērv honayetv nak-eshoccicetv cokv lecvn wakketos.
Morphemes:
   oponvkv hērv honayetv-Ø nak-eshoccicetv cokv-Ø lecv-n wakk-Ø-et-o-s
Linguistic notation:
   sermon-def_obj notebook-def_obj under-obl lying_down_l_grd-
   3pers-ss-aux_vb-dec
Translation: The sermon is lying (is located) under the notebook.

1. Estelepikv vhvoke yopvn tohlikētos.
2. Cēpanat cuntvn enke ofvn cawetos.
3. Nokke-vfastvt vlēkcv kvskvnv fvccvn hueres.

4. Naklokcicv ēkvnv coko ehomvn tvpeksēpicvhanes.
5. Cēpvnvke hoktvkuce mvhakv-cuko topvrvn ahkopvnaketos.
6. Vhvokuce totkv-hute tempen vhayēyvnks.
7. Mēkko henehvlken kvperv fvccvn liketos.
8. Vhvoke nockv-coko etehoyvnēcv etennvrkvpvn hvwecvs!
9. Vmmvhayv cokv eto lecvn ohonvhyes.
10. Kocecvmpvn kvnhvlwe-rakkē onvpvn hecvkvtēs.

EXERCISE 3

Translate the following sentences into Mvskoke.

1. The moon and stars were bright last night.
2. Eagles eat rabbits, mice, and gophers.
3. Our mother bought apples and oranges yesterday.
4. The chief, warriors, and speaker are sitting under the arbor.
5. Open the door and the window!
6. He has a white car and a blue car.
7. I lost my coat and my gloves.
8. The fire burned the roof and one wall.
9. The boys carried the nails and the screwdriver.
10. A doctor cured my older sister and my mother.

EXERCISE 4

Translate each of the sentences in the exercise and then form a sentence containing a disjoined noun phrase in either the subject or the object position that follows from the first sentence. Translate the sentence that you create and be prepared to describe how it relates to the first one. An example is presented below.

Original sentence: Hoktvkucet hompetv hahihces.
Translation: The girls just made the meal.
Second sentence: Helen monkat Jane vpeswvn wahres.
Translation: Either Helen or Jane sliced the meat.
Discussion: The second sentence provides information about which of two girls had the responsibility for preparing the meat for the meal.

1. Omvlkat cemvnicvkeks.
2. Nake poheckvnkv?
3. Estenkesakpikv somhuecēs.
4. Mv hoktēt cenhonnv-lecv sulkan tenēpicvhanes.
5. Rakko lvstat enletkekotos.
6. Ēwvntake hokkolat akaketos.
7. Stimvt vhvokucen hvwecvnkv?
8. Estvmen vpēyētomv?
9. Cufet tasecekotomvtēs.
10. Cvcerwv mvnetosat eton vcemketos.

Exercise 5

Translate the following sentences into Mvskoke.

1. I want either *sofke* or water.
2. That man carves wood and stone.
3. Mother will buy either a ring or a watch today.
4. A boy and a girl are walking to school.
5. Horses and cows are afraid of bears.
6. We will go to town on Wednesday or Thursday.
7. July and August are hot.
8. Eat the cookies and candy!
9. The old woman will sew a shirt, dress, or pants for you.
10. They made me carry the tall ladder and the sharp saw.

Exercise 6

Below are several nouns, adjectives, postpositions, and verbs. Using these words, create ten sentences. At least five of your sentences should have postpositions, with two of these sentences containing more than one postposition. At least six of your sentences should contain either conjoined or disjoined compound noun phrases in either the subject or object position. You do not have to use only the listed nouns as the subjects or objects in your sentences, as you may conjugate the verbs for subjects using type I suffixes and/or type II prefixes. Be prepared to say your sentences out loud in class and to translate your sentences for the other students.

Nouns	Adjectives	Postpositions	Verbs
hetotē	yvpockē	lecvn	enrecvpetv
sokhv-hatkv	fvmpē	ofv	tvcetv
taktopvtake	pohkē	onvpv	vchoyetv
sote	afvcfvkē	tempē	eteyametv
cvkotvkse	honnē	yopv	hvsvthicetv
Este-Aksomkvlke	oklanē	etennvrkvpv	eyvcetv
torkowv	cutkosē	ehomv	sehoketv
ekv	lopicē	vrvhkv	cvfencicetv
eslafkv	mahmvyē	vfopkē	setēfketv
vhakv-hayv	vcvkē	pvrvnkē	vsēketv
eckuce	hotosvkē		em enhonretv
ohenockv	tvskocē		takketv
Ohkalvlke			
hockvte			
kvtopokv			
vlēkcv			
fayv			
vhvoke			

EXERCISE 7

Write a story about a group that you interact with regularly. Describe where your group meets, the kinds of people who attend the meetings, and the topic that brings you together. If there is a leader in your group, discuss the kinds of things that this person can make others do. Provide information about any projects or activities your group plans to accomplish in the future. Be prepared to tell your story to the class and to help other students comprehend all that you talk about in your story. If you need assistance with vocabulary that you have not encountered in this text or *Beginning Creek,* you should look at Loughridge and Hodge's *Dictionary of Muskokee and English* (1890 [1964]) and/or Martin and Mauldin's *A Dictionary of Creek/Muskogee* (2000).

Listening Exercises

Listen to the individual turns in the conversation about food preparation (tracks 64–79) on the CD included with this book. Does either of the speakers use any postpositions in their sentences? In cases where you are able to figure out the object nouns of the postpositions, write down the track in which it occurs. Also, write down or memorize the entire postpositional phrase, including the object noun and the postposition. Are you able to understand how the postpositional phrase fits into the rest of the sentence in which it occurs? If so, write this down for the appropriate track number. If you have difficulty with this for any of the tracks, remember which tracks cause you the most problems and ask your teacher or another fluent Mvskoke speaker for help in understanding these tracks.

Still listening to tracks 64–79 on the CD, do you hear any compound noun phrases in the speakers' turns? If so, make note of the track number and write down or memorize the compound noun phrase that you hear on that track. (If you write out the compound noun phrase, you may do so in either Mvskoke or English.) Do any of these compound noun phrases occur in connection with the postpositions you identified in the previous exercise? Are you able to understand any of the tracks better after having listened closely to them?

Listen to "Turtle's Shell" (track 89). Does Linda use any postpositions in this story? As best you can tell, do these postpositional phrases play a crucial role in the story? Or does their occurrence simply add secondary information that is not central to the story? It may help to listen to track 90, a loose English translation of the story, in order to identify which postpositions occur in the Mvskoke version. Write down or memorize which postpositions appear in the story.

Buildings

A long time ago, the Muskogee Creeks lived in villages, each village surrounded by a fence. The buildings were made of limber tree limbs that were bent to form a house with a rounded shape, covered with animal hides. Each family had its own space within the fence in which it could build its houses. As a result, every family within a village had several buildings within its area. Some of these buildings were made to store food for the village.

Villagers also erected a building where the men met to discuss the problems faced by the village or the larger tribe. Some of the issues that the men would discuss included where and when to go hunting for food, whether to face other tribes who came into their area with hostility or generosity, and the arrangements necessary to conduct important ceremonies. Women were not generally allowed to take part in these meetings, though they could enter the house to bring in food or drink to the men and, at times, older women could offer their ideas about the topic being discussed.

Women had their cooking houses, in which they performed many of their activities. Many times, there was an area in front of this house where all work like fixing corn, sewing, and making baskets and cooking pots was done. This meant that any trash from these activities stayed outside the houses, and the women could enjoy being outdoors while they worked.

The Seminoles lived in *chickees* in Florida. These were built off the ground to keep wild animals and insects from getting into the house. Poles were used to hold up the roof and floor. They used leaves to cover the roof. Since they lived in swampy areas of Florida, no walls were built. This let any cooling breeze come right through the house, while the roof kept the burning sun and strong rain off them and their belongings.

Especially after Removal to Oklahoma, both tribes began to build homes like we see today. Now, both tribes have beautiful buildings on their properties in Oklahoma and Florida. You can still see a *chickee* occasionally in Florida, but most Muskogee Creeks and Seminoles now live in the kind of houses that you are used to. This, along with other steps the Muskogee Creek and Seminole tribes have taken to adapt to living in the modern world, has helped both tribes to continue growing and taking their place in history.

Suggested Readings

Further information about Mvskoke postpositions can be found in Nathan (1977: 129–30) and Hardy (2005: 239). Hardy introduces *vrvhkv, ofv, elecv, ehomv, eyopv,* and *vfopke* in his work, while Nathan covers each of these and three other postpositions. The only postposition discussed in this chapter and not represented in either of these works is *etennvrkvpv*. Hardy and Nathan have different opinions about what we have identified as the oblique suffix (following Nathan), with Hardy finding that this suffix is similar in nature to the indefinite object suffix (labeled as 'accusative' in Hardy's work). Hardy's argument is persuasive, but we have chosen to use Nathan's terminology, as there do seem to be some differences between the ways in which the suffixes are used on postpositions and nouns. In all other respects, the information provided in both works is similar in scope and detail and is consistent with what has been presented in this chapter.

Several sources contain descriptions of prehistoric, early historic, and modern Muskogee and Seminole buildings. Archaeological analysis of Mississippian sites always includes some discussion of the remains of buildings and their contents. Readers interested in building methods and technologies used by the Mississippian and earlier inhabitants of the American Southeast are directed to Hally and Mainfort (2004). This work, particularly pages 274–80, provides a nice overview of the ways in which Southeastern groups arranged their communal space, and it is replete with citations. As readers find their interest piqued about any particular aspect of spatial arrangement and building technologies, they are advised to check the sources listed within the text for more information.

Many of the early travelers, traders, and agents in Muskogee and Seminole territory left written descriptions of the buildings and communities that they visited. Of these, William Bartram's *Travels* (1928 [1791]) is among the most informative and engaging. Bartram describes how the Muskogee communities fit within the landscape and how buildings were arranged within the villages he visited. He also provides an occasional illustration and notes on activities he witnessed taking place around various structures.

Swanton (1928a) relied heavily on Bartram and others' accounts of pre-Removal village layouts and building technologies, which he included in his ethnography of the post-Removal Muskogee Creeks. Swanton provides several photographs of stompground and church structures throughout this work, discusses their spatial arrangements, and considers how the organization he saw reflected earlier patterns. The form and construction of the ground and church buildings photographed by Swanton in the 1920s can still be seen at most Muskogee Creek and Seminole stompgrounds and churches today. Walker (2004: 377–79) provides additional detail to the information provided by Swanton and deserves attention.

Modern-day buildings and their roles within Muskogee Creek and Seminole life are discussed, although generally only briefly, in Innes (2004a),

Sturtevant and Cattelino (2004), and Sattler (2004). In each of these works, photographs are provided of buildings recently constructed by or for members of the tribes. Each work includes some discussion of the technologies now used in building construction and the importance of buildings in the maintenance of community relationships. For even more on current-day structures, readers are directed to the *Muscogee Nation News, Cokv Tvleme,* and *Seminole Tribune,* which run stories almost every month on housing conditions for each group.

CHAPTER SEVEN

Locatives

Postpositions are not the only way in which Mvskoke speakers can include locational information in sentences. Mvskoke has a set of prefixes, called **locatives**, which indicate where an action is taking place or the location of an object affected by the action. We also will discuss other verbal prefixes that provide information about things such as whether an action is being performed with an object, by both subjects on each other, or toward the subject or object of the sentence. Many of these prefixes will already be familiar to you, as you have seen them on several verbs by now. We will concern ourselves with the locative prefixes first, then the other prefixes.

LOCATIVE PREFIXES

Locative prefixes are attached to verbs in order to indicate the location where an action is taking place or the location of an object affected by the verb to which the prefix has been affixed. These prefixes are commonly placed on verbs concerning location, movement, or placement. Whenever a locative prefix has been attached to a verb, any Dative and type II prefixes come before the locative prefix. In effect, the locative prefix can be considered as closely joined to the verb stem, with other prefixes having to take positions further away from the stem. Thus, the order of the Dative, type II, and locative prefixes on a verb always follows the pattern shown in diagram 7.1.

The locations of the Dative and type II prefixes and of distributive, negating, and tense suffixes are shown in brackets in diagram 7.1, because these prefixes and suffixes are optional when constructing a verb phrase. The location of the locative prefix in relation to the other prefixes and verb stem is not contained within brackets, because the placement of the locative prefix is the focus of this table. However, you should keep in mind that the use of a locative prefix is optional and would be shown as such by being framed in brackets if this diagram were presenting the position of any of the other elements instead. The placement of the interrogative, same-subject, or declarative suffix is not included in brackets, because it is necessary to include one of these suffixes in a complete verb phrase.

| [Dative Prefix] | [Type II Prefix] | Locative Prefix | Verb Suffix | [Distributive, Negating, and/or Tense Suffixes] | Interrogative, Declarative, or Same-Subject Suffix |

Diagram 7.1. Order of Locative and Object Prefixes

There is a limited set of locatives in Mvskoke, listed in table 7.1, with distinct locational references.

TABLE 7.1. Locative Prefixes

Locative Prefix Form	Translation/Locational Reference	Notation Indicating the Use of This Prefix
ak-	in water or mud, in a low place	water
tak-	at ground level, around a house or structure	ground
oh-	on top of something	on
v-	away from	away

The form of each prefix presented in table 7.1 is used consistently with all verbs to which the prefixes have been attached. There are some variants in the meanings associated with these prefixes, but the most important and frequently used meanings have been presented in the table. As we discuss each prefix separately, we will talk about other meanings that occur less frequently. Finally, the notation used to show the position of each of these prefixes will be shown by 'loc' in the third line of each example when a locative prefix occurs on the verb.

The prefix *ak-*

The prefix *ak-* has a variety of meanings, all of which imply that the action takes place in or is somehow associated with water, mud, or a ditch or other low place. For instance, the difference in meaning between examples 1 and 2 is directly tied to the occurrence of *ak-* in the second sentence.

1.   Honvnwv lētketos.
       honvnwv-Ø   lētk-Ø-et-o-s
       man-def_subj   run_(1)_l_grd-3pers-ss-aux_vb-dec
       'The man is running.'

2.   Honvnwv aklētketos.
       honvnwv-Ø   **ak**-lētk-Ø-et-o-s
       man-def_subj   loc-run_(1)_l_grd-3pers-ss-aux_vb-dec
       'The man is running (in water *or* a low place).'

In a case such as this, the action's occurrence in water or a low area has been specified by the addition of the locative prefix.

    The addition of this prefix may also show that the activity will result in something's being in water or a low place. Example 3 presents a sentence in which the rabbits will end up in water as a result of having jumped.

3.   Cufe aktashokvhanes.
       cufe-Ø   **ak**-tashok-Ø-vhan-es
       rabbit-def_subj   loc-jump_(2)-3pers-intent-dec
       'The (2) rabbits are going to jump (into water or a low place).'

At times it is helpful to specify exactly where the subject or object will end up, despite your having added the *ak-* prefix to the verb. The sentence in example 3 may be modified slightly with the addition of *ēkvn-korke* 'hole dug in the ground' to lead to the sentence in example 4. Notice that the verb in example 4 is exactly the same as in example 3, but the insertion of *ēkvn-korke* causes one to reinterpret the meaning of the prefix *ak-*.

4.   Cufe ēkvn-korken aktashokvhanes.
       cufe-Ø   **ēkvn-korke-**n   **ak-**tashok-Ø-vhan-es
       rabbit-def_subj   ground-hole_in-ind_obj   loc-jump_(2)-3pers-intent-dec
       'The (2) rabbits are going to jump into the hole in the ground.'

When *ak-* is affixed to a verb concerning vision or looking, it indicates that the subject is gazing into or toward water or a low place. Example 5 presents a sentence in which the direction of the speaker's gaze is specified by the use of this locative prefix.

5.   Paksvnkē mv hvccucen akhecvkotomvnks.
       paksvnkē   mv   hvcc-uce-n   **ak-**hec-v-ko-t-om-vnk-s
       yesterday   that   river-dim-ind_obj   loc-look-1S-neg-ss-aux_vb-mp-dec
       'I didn't look in that creek (or ditch) yesterday.'

Adding *ak-* to verbs about removing items from a place or vacating a space causes them to mean that the action originates in the water or low area. With this change in meaning, the item is considered to be removed from water or the subject is vacating a space in water or in a low lying area. Examples 6 and 7 contain verbs that concern removing items and vacating a space respectively. In example 6, the verb form without *ak-* is *esetv* 'to hold, catch, or take (one).' The addition of the prefix leads to *akesetv*, which means 'to take (one) from water or a low place'. Notice that in this instance, water is specifically mentioned as being the element from which the apple is being taken.

6.   Svtvn owv akesvhaneckv?
       svtv-n   **owv-**Ø   **ak-**es-vhan-eck-v
       apple-ind_obj   water-def_obj   loc-take_(1)-intent-2S-int
       'Are you going to take the apple out of the water?'

Example 7 involves the movement of a person out of the water. The unmodified form of the verb *ossetv* means that one gets out of jail or some confined space. With the addition of *ak-* to this verb, the resulting form means that one gets out of water or out of a low place.

7.   Rvro akhopoyvt akosseks
       rvro-ak-hopoyv-t   **ak-**oss-Ø-ek-s

fish-loc-seeker-ind_subj   loc-get_out_(1)-3pers-neg-dec
'A fisherman is not getting out (of water *or* a low place).'

You will find several examples of verbs whose meanings change slightly with the addition of *ak-* in appendix 2. Whether a verb is suppletive or not, affixing this prefix to the verb will lead a listener to infer that water or a low place is somehow associated with the activity being discussed.

The prefix *tak-*

Tak- alerts a listener to the fact that the action to which this prefix has been added is taking place on or near the ground or ground level. For instance, in example 8, adding *tak-* to the verb *lomhetv* 'to lie down (of three or more)' makes it clear that the hunters are lying on the ground, not on a bed or some platform above ground level.

8.   Fayvlke taklomhes.
      fay-vlke-Ø   **tak**-lomh-Ø-es
      hunter-pl-def_subj   loc-lie_down_(3+)_l_grd-3pers-dec
      'The hunters are lying down on the ground.'

It is possible to be even more specific by including *ēkvnv* 'ground' before the verb, resulting in a sentence like that shown in example 9. This sentence would be translated as saying the same thing as the sentence in example 8, but the fact that the hunters are lying on the ground is related twice in the sentence in example 9.

9.   Fayvlke ēkvnvn taklomhes.
      fay-vlke-Ø   **ēkvnv**-n   **tak**-lomh-Ø-es
      hunter-pl-def_subj   ground-ind_obj   loc-lie_down_(3+)_l_grd-3pers-dec
      'The hunters are lying down on the ground.'

With some verbs, the inclusion of *tak-* means that performance of the action results in the subject or object's being on or near the ground. The verb *yurketv*, when not modified with *tak-*, means 'to fall (of two).' When the prefix *tak-* is added to the verb, the resulting form is *takyurketv*, whose meaning is 'to fall on the ground or floor (of two).' The addition of *tak-* to this verb helps to locate the position of the falling subjects once they have finished the action, whereas the unmodified version does not provide this information about where the falling items come to rest.

Affixing *tak-* to a verb of seeing or looking causes the subject's gaze to be directed toward the ground or to ground level. This is similar to the change made by affixing *ak-* to a verb of seeing. The similarity between *tak-* and *ak-* does not end here, however. Adding *tak-* to a verb regarding movement of an item from someplace leads a listener to interpret the movement of the item as being from the ground to another place. The same holds true when a subject is vacating a space; adding *tak-* to the verb changes the meaning to that of leaving the ground or a ground-level position.

In some cases, *tak-* adds the meaning of performing the action of the verb in an enclosed space or building. The verb *fulletv* 'to go about, wander, be located (of three or more)' changes its meaning when it becomes *takfulletv*. With the addition of *tak-*, it can mean either 'to be around at ground level or on the floor (of three or more)' as well as 'to be around in an enclosed space/building (of three or more)'. Affixing *tak-* thus allows a speaker to talk about someone's being at home or in another building without having to specify exactly which building the subject is occupying. Examples 10 and 11 give versions of sentences with very similar meanings. The only difference is that in example 10, exactly which building the men are in has not been specified, though often listeners will infer that it is the subject's home.

10.   Hofonofvn honvntaket takfullvtēs.
       hofon-ofv-n   honvn-take-t   **tak**-full-Ø-vtē-s
       long_ago-during-obl   man-pl-ind_subj   loc-be_around_(3+)-3pers-rp-dec
       'Men were at the house/building a long, long time ago.'

11. Hofonofvn honvntaket cokon takfullvtēs.
       hofon-ofv-n   honvn-take-t   **coko**-n   **tak**-full-Ø-vtē-s
       long_ago-   man-pl-ind_subj   house-ind_obj   loc-be_around_(3+)-
         during-obl   3pers-rp-dec
       'Men were at the house/building a long, long time ago.'

The prefix *oh-*

You have seen the locative prefix *oh-* on several verbs by now. This prefix specifies that the location of the action or the position of the object as a result of the action is above normal ground level or is on top of another object. Often, the object on top of which the action is occurring or on which the object comes to be positioned is explicitly stated in the sentence, though this need not always be done.

Oh- is most commonly interpreted as demonstrating that the action is occurring on something. The verb *ohliketv*, which we have translated as 'to ride (of one)' to this point, may also mean 'to sit on (something) (of one).' If you think closely about riding a horse, it is reasonable to assume that 'to sit on (something)' was the original meaning and that this was expanded to cover sitting on a horse while riding it. The sense of 'riding' has since been broadened to include riding in an automobile as well. Given the multiple meanings associated with *ohliketv*, it is wise to include the object upon which one is sitting or riding so that your listeners will understand what you mean, as examples 12 through 14 show.

12. Cēpvne rakko sopakhvtken ohliketos.
    cēpvne-Ø   rakko   sopakhvtke-n   **oh**-lik-Ø-et-o-s
    boy-def_subj   horse   grey-ind_obj   loc-sit_(1)-3pers-ss-aux_vb-dec
    'The boy is riding a grey horse.'

13. Cēpvne atomo sopakhvtken ohliketos.
    cēpvne-Ø   atomo   sopakhvtke-n   **oh**-lik-Ø-et-o-s
    boy-def_subj   car   grey-ind_obj   loc-sit_(1)-3pers-ss-aux_vb-dec
    'The boy is riding in a grey car.'

14. Cēpvne ohliketv sopakhvtken ohliketos.
    cēpvne-Ø   ohliketv   sopakhvtke-n   **oh**-lik-Ø-et-o-s
    boy-def_subj   chair   grey-ind_obj   loc-sit_(1)-3pers-ss-aux_vb-dec
    'The boy is sitting on a grey chair.'

If the object upon which the action is occurring is not specified, one would only know that the boy is sitting on or riding something.

The second most common meaning attributed to *oh-* is that the action results in one item's being on top of another. Using *ohkayetv* 'to set (two items, something made of cloth) on top of (something else)' provides information about where the object(s) being set down are located when the action is completed. Example 15 shows a sentence using this verb.

15.   Cecke hvtekpikvn topvn ohkayvnks.

ce-cke-Ø	hvtekpikv-n	topv-n	Ø-**oh**-kay-Ø-vnk-s
2persII-mother- def_subj	pants-ind_obj	bed-ind_obj	3persII-loc-set_ (cloth)-3pers-mp-dec

'Your mother set some pants on top of a bed.'

In rare circumstances, speakers may leave out the object being moved onto something else. This usually only happens when the listener already knows what the subject is likely to be moving or when the context makes it clear.

Affixing *oh-* to verbs of vision tells the listener that the subject's gaze is directed down onto something or that the subject is looking over the top of something. The use of *oh-* with *hecetv* 'to look, see' in example 16 makes possible both translations given in the fourth line of the example.

16.   Miste vculat ēkvnhvlwe onvpvn ohhēces.

miste-Ø	vcul-at	ēkvnhvlwe	Ø-onvpv-n	**oh**-hēc-Ø-es
man	old-def_ subj	hill	3persII-on_ top_of-obl	loc-look_l_grd- 3pers-dec

'The old man is looking down from the hilltop.' *or*
'The old man is looking over the hilltop.'

With some verbs of movement, the affix *oh-* is used to indicate that the direction of the movement is toward some other entity. For instance, adding *oh-* to *tvmketv* 'to fly (of one)' changes the meaning to 'to fly toward/over (of one).' Sentences showing the difference in meaning and usage between *tvmketv* and *ohtvmketv* respectively are presented in examples 17 and 18.

17.   Ayot tvmketos.

ayo-t   tvmk-Ø-et-o-s
hawk-ind_subj   fly_(1)-3pers-ss-aux_vb-dec
'A hawk is flying.'

18.   Ayot vcohtvmketos.

ayo-t   vc-**oh**-tvmk-Ø-et-o-s
hawk-ind_subj   1SII-loc-fly_(1)-3pers-ss-aux_vb-dec
'A hawk is flying toward me.' *or* 'A hawk is flying over me.'

The prefix v-

As listed in table 7.1, the addition of the prefix v- to a verb alerts the listener that the focus of an action is away from where the action originates. The verb vmelletv 'to point at' will be used as the first example of the way in which application of v- alters the meaning. With the addition of the prefix v- to the verb melletv 'to point,' the focus of the action is no longer placed on the person or thing doing the pointing (and originating the activity), but is placed instead on the person or thing at whom the pointing is directed. Similarly, lvtketv 'to fall (of one)' changes to vlvtketv 'to fall against (of one)' when the prefix is added and the place to which the object is falling becomes of central interest.

This prefix and the three others we discuss above are considered as part of the same set here, because they take a position between the object prefixes and the verb stem. Also, as each one relates some information about the location where the action is taking place or where its object will be found, they fulfill the role of locatives generally. The prefix v- is the least used of these four prefixes, as you will find, but it is worth mentioning in conjunction with the others.

OTHER VERBAL PREFIXES

Other prefixes exist that provide information about how an action is proceeding. Not only do these differ from the locative prefixes in meaning, but their position relative to the verb stem is unlike that of the locative prefixes. Whereas the locative prefixes come between any object prefixes and the verb stem, the other verbal prefixes do not do so. Instead, they appear before the object prefixes. Due to this, when you are faced with choosing the correct form of the object prefix, use the first sound of the verb stem, not the first sound of the verbal prefix as a guide.

The order of prefixes on verbs to which the verbal prefixes have been attached is shown in diagram 7.2. Only the positions of the various prefixes that may be added to verbs are shown. As each of these prefixes is optional in constructing a well-formed verb phrase, their positions are indicated within brackets.

Directional Prefix	Instr. Prefix	Applic. Prefix	Type D Prefix	Type II Prefix	Locative Prefix	Verb Stem

Diagram 7.2. Positions of All Verbal Prefixes

Directional prefixes

As their name implies, **directional prefixes** give some indication of the direction taken in the performance of an action or the amount of distance covered by the action. It may seem as though the directional prefixes, presented in table 7.2, are somewhat similar to locative prefixes, as both sets provide information about the performance of an activity within space. However, there are two aspects of the directional prefixes that set them apart from the locative prefixes.

First, directional prefixes, whose position will be marked by 'dir' in the third line of each example in which they occur, always come before type D and type II prefixes attached to the verb, as shown in diagram 7.2. Directional prefixes, when included in the glossary and dictionary entries of verbs like *awiyetv* 'to hold out (a hand, a paper, etc.),' look as though they are firmly attached to the verb stem. However, when one adds a type II and/or D prefix to verbs with directional prefixes, the type II and/or D prefix comes between the directional prefix and the verb stem. Example 19 shows how the direct object prefix is sandwiched between the directional prefix *a-* and the verb stem *wiyetv* in a sentence.

19.   Cēpvne svtokucen acenwiyekotomvnks.
       cēpvne-Ø   svtokuce-n   a-cen-wiy-Ø-eko-t-om-vnk-s
       boy-def_subj   hammer-ind_obj   dir-2persII-hold_out-3pers-neg-ss-
                                             aux_vb-mp-dec
       'The boy was not holding out a hammer to you.'

The second way in which directional prefixes differ from locative prefixes is that they can occur in combination with locative prefixes. Two locative prefixes cannot appear on the same verb stem, but it is possible for a directional prefix to be used in association with a locative prefix. Thus, it is permissible to have forms such as *a-ohyvkvpetv* 'to walk a short distance toward (of one).' In the infinitival verb form, the long-distance

TABLE 7.2. Directional Prefixes

Directional Prefix Form	Translation/Directional Reference
ra- rah- (some speakers use this form before *o* and *a*)	a longer distance covered between initiation and completion of the activity than is indicated by *a-/ah-*
a- ah- (some speakers use this form before *o* and *a*)	a short distance covered between initiation and completion of the activity *or* action directed toward the speaker or another person
er- (before consonants) r- (before vowels) ·	arrival at a point while moving away from a reference point
ye- (before consonants) y- (before vowels)	arrival at a point while moving toward the destination

directional prefix is clearly present as *a-*, but when the 2persII prefix is inserted between the directional and locative prefixes, this prefix combines with the initial /i/ of the 2persII prefix to create the sound /e:/ (written as *i* in the Mvskoke orthography). Example 20 provides a sentence with the resulting verbal form.

20. Hofonofvn omvlkackan icohyvkvpvkayvnks.
     hofon-ofv-n   omvlk-ack-an   **a-ec-oh-**yvkvp-vk-a-yvnk-s
     long_time_ago   all-2P-def_obj   dir-2persII-loc-walk_(1)-distr-1S-mp-dec
     'I walked a short distance toward you (plural) a while ago.'

Examples 19 and 20 have shown you sentences in which an audible object prefix appears between the directional prefix and either the verb stem or a locative prefix. When a type II third person prefix is used, however, it will seem as though there is nothing coming between the directional prefix and what follows it, because third person object prefixes are null (they do not have an audible form). When it comes to working through the exercises, however, you should be certain to include the position of the type II third person prefix to indicate that you know where such a prefix is located.

Examples 19 and 20 have presented sentences containing the first directional prefix listed in table 7.2. The last two prefixes listed in the table, *er-/r-* and *yi-/y-*, deserve some discussion, due to their reliance on a given reference point for comprehension. *Er-/r-* is used to indicate that the action, usually involving movement of something, has begun at one point (the reference) and ended at another. For instance, the meaning of the verb *oretv* 'to reach, achieve (a goal, a position, etc.)' becomes 'to arrive, get to (a location)' with the addition of the *r-* directional prefix. In common usage, the resulting verb form, *roretv*, is taken to imply that one has arrived at a location as a result of having moved away from another point (the reference). Thus, in narratives, one would be likely to hear sentences like those presented in example 21, in which the first sentence provides the location from which Rabbit is going (the hill), the second notes that Rabbit saw Bear's house a moderate distance away, and the third tells a listener that he arrived at Bear's house after having left the hill. It is also possible for a narrator to specify the reference point in the same sentence, which is a construction that will be covered in chapter 8.

21.   Cufet ēkvnhvlwe onvpvn huervtēs.

cufe-t	**ēkvnhvlwe-Ø**	onvpv-n	huer-Ø-vtē-s.
rabbit-ind_subj	hill-def_obj	on_top-obl	stand_(1)-3pers-rp-dec

Cufet Nokose encoko rahecvtēs.

cufe-t	nokose-Ø	en-coko-Ø	ra-Ø-hec-Ø-vtē-s.
rabbit-ind_subj	bear-def_obj	3persII-house-def_obj	dir-3persII-see-3pers-rp-dec

Cufet Nokose encoko rorvtēs.

cufe-t	nokose-Ø	en-coko-Ø	r-or-Ø-vtē-s.
rabbit-ind_subj	bear-def_obj	3persII-house-def_obj	dir-arrive_(1)-3pers-rp-dec

'Rabbit stood on top of the hill.
Rabbit saw Bear's house some ways away.
Rabbit arrived at Bear's house (after leaving the hill).'

The final directional prefix *ye-/y-* is used to indicate that the subject arrives at a location in the course of moving toward a destination. The destination point used as the reference for this prefix will have been provided either in earlier sentences of a narrative or within the same sentence (a construction covered in chapter 9). Example 22 presents a collection of sentences that resemble what one might hear as a speaker uses the *ye-/y-* prefix on a verb. In this example, the first sentence provides information about where Bear is moving from, the second introduces Rabbit's position as the reference point, and the third includes the verb with the directional prefix.

22.   Nokose encokofvn likvtēs.

nokose-Ø   en-coko-ofv-n   lik-Ø-vtē-s
bear-def_subj   3persII-house-in-obl   sit_(1)-3pers-rp-dec

Nokose Cufen coko ehomvn hecvtēs.

nokose-Ø   **cufe-n**   **coko**   **ehomv-n**   Ø-hec-Ø-vtē-s
bear-def_subj rabbit-ind_obj house   in_front-obl 3persII-see-3pers-
                                                               rp-dec

Nokose yossvtēs.

nokose-Ø   y-Ø-oss-Ø-vtē-s
bear-def_subj   dir-3persII-go_out_(1)-3pers-rp-dec

'Bear was sitting in his house.

Bear saw Rabbit in front of his house.

Bear went out (toward Rabbit).'

Finally, concerning directional prefixes, be aware that many speakers delete the initial vowel of a verb stem beginning with *v-* before adding the prefixes (*a-*) and (*ra-*) to the verb stem—but only when this vowel is not the one affected by the lengthened grade in the progressive aspect. When such speakers add either of these prefixes to the verb *vwenayetv* 'to smell, sniff,' for instance, the first vowel of the verb stem is deleted, giving –*wenayetv*, and the prefix is then added. Thus, the Mvskoke verb 'to smell (something) from a short distance' for many speakers will be pronounced as *awenayetv* rather than *a-vwenayetv*. While this is true of most speakers, some will pronounce the prefix as a separate entity, so it is possible that you may hear some speakers say *a-vwenayetv*, but this is an uncommon occurrence. For those speakers who delete verb-initial *v-* when these prefixes are added, the type II or D prefix closest to the verb stem will be taken from the set occurring before consonants.

Instrumental prefix (*e*)*s-*

Another adverbial prefix we will discuss is the **instrumental prefix**, (*e*)*s-*. This prefix, noted as 'instr' in the third line of each example, indicates that the action is being carried out through the use of an object or instrument (hence the name for this prefix). It may also indicate that the subject has an instrument in his, her, or its possession while performing the activity, as when walking with a bag of groceries. As shown in diagram 7.2, this prefix follows any directional prefixes also attached to the verb but precedes other prefixes. Very often, speakers will omit the initial *e* of this prefix. When the instrumental prefix is presented in an example without the initial *e*, an apostrophe will precede the *s*. You should remember that the apostrophe signals that the *e* has been dropped in this case, as all words containing the instrumental prefix are shown with the *e* intact in the glossary.

Generally, when the instrumental prefix is added to a verb, the instrument being used to conduct the action will be specified in the sentence if it is not absolutely clear from the surrounding context. When the instrument is specified, it often takes the indefinite object suffix, showing that it is part of the verb phrase. Example 23 shows how a sentence containing the instrumental prefix and the instrument noun is constructed.

23.   Ceckuce vloson hakkvn 'seteyametos.
      ce-ck-uce-Ø   vloso-n   **hakkv-n**
      2persII-mother-dim-def_subj   rice-ind_obj   **spoon-ind_obj**
      's-Ø-eteyam-Ø-et-o-s
      instr-3persII-stir-3pers-ss-aux_vb-dec
      'Your aunt stirs rice with a spoon.' *or* 'Your aunt uses a spoon to stir rice.'

When a directional prefix and the instrumental prefix occur on a verb at the same time, the instrumental prefix always follows the directional prefix. The verb in example 24 contains directional, instrumental, Dative, and type II prefixes. The order of these prefixes is made obvious in the third line of the example. Note that this use of the instrumental relates to the fact that the boy would have been carrying out the act of passing the ball stick to you by having the stick in his possession. This is the second meaning associated with the instrumental prefix we described in the opening paragraph of this section.

24.   Mvt cēpvne tokonhen asponwiyekotomvnks.
      mvt   cēpvne-Ø   tokonhe-n
      that   boy-def_subj   ball_stick-ind_obj
      a-s-pon-Ø-wiy-Ø-eko-t-om-vnk-s

dir-instr-1PD-3persII-pass_to-3pers-neg-ss-aux_vb-mp-dec
'That boy did not pass a ball stick to us.'

The instrumental prefix can also appear on a verb containing a locative prefix. When this is the case, the instrumental prefix moves to the left of any Dative or type II prefixes, while the locative prefix remains attached directly to the verb stem. An example of a sentence containing a verb with the instrumental and 'on' locative prefix is presented in example 25. In this example, as in example 24, the instrumental prefix indicates that a bag or some kind of container is holding the potatoes, as there would be no reason to use the prefix in this sentence if the potatoes were loose. Because there is only one bag being set down in this instance, the singular object form of 'to set (something) down' (*eslicetv*) is used in this sentence. If two bags were being discussed, the dual form of this verb (*eskayetv*) would have been used instead.

25. Vhvce-rēhe ohhompetvn 'sohlicvs!

vhvce-rēhe-Ø	ohhompetv-n	(e)s-Ø-oh-lic-vs
Irish_potato-def_obj	table-ind_obj	instr-3persII-loc-set_down_
		(1)-imper

'Set the potatoes down on the table!'

Applicative prefixes

The two applicative prefixes we discuss here add information concerning how the subject(s) are performing the action. The position of both of these applicative prefixes will be indicated by 'app' in the third line of each example in which they occur. The first prefix to be discussed is the reciprocal prefix *ete-*. This prefix is used most commonly to demonstrate that all members included in a plural subject are performing the actions on one another. Bear and Rabbit are known to be looking at one another in example 26, because of the addition of this prefix to the verb *hecetv*.

26. Nokose Cufe etehecakvtēs.

nokose-Ø	cufe-Ø	ete-hec-ak-Ø-vtē-s
bear-def_subj	rabbit-def_subj	app-see-distr_l_grd-3pers-rp-dec

'Bear and Rabbit looked at each other.'

This prefix may also be used when all members of a plural subject are acting together to perform the action. The prefix is used in this manner in example 27, in which Rabbit and Bear are fishing.

27. Cufe Nokose tepvkat rvron etemakwiyakvnks.
     cufe   nokose tepvk-at   rvro-n ete-m-akwiy-ak-vnk-s
     rabbit bear   together-def_subj fish-def_obj app-3persD-catch_fish-
                                       distr_l_grd-mp-dec
     'Rabbit and Bear were catching fish.'

For some speakers, the initial *e* of this prefix may be dropped when speaking, so it would also be possible to hear the sentence in example 27 pronounced as presented in example 28.

28. Cufe Nokose tepvkat rvron temakwiyakvnks.
     cufe   nokose tepvk-at   rvro-n   te-m-akwiy-ak-vnk-s
     rabbit bear   together-def_subj fish-def_obj app-3persD-catch_fish-
                                       distr_l_grd-mp-dec
     'Rabbit and Bear were catching fish.'

The second applicative prefix to be presented in this chapter is the reflexive prefix *ē-*. This prefix tells a listener that the subject of the sentence is performing the action upon itself. In example 29, the fact that Bear is seeing himself in the water is made clear through the use of the reflexive prefix.

29. Nokose owv ofvn ēhēcvtēs.
     nokose-Ø   owv-Ø   ofv-n   ē-hēc-Ø-vtē-s
     bear-def_subj water-def_obj in-obl   app-see_l_grd-3pers-rp-dec
     'Bear was seeing himself in the water.'

The prefixes covered in this chapter are widely used and add important information to the verb phrase. The locative and directional prefixes, along with the postpositions that you learned about in the last chapter, allow you to specify the location of items in space and the direction of movement of those items. The other prefixes make it possible for you to now specify that an action was performed with the assistance of some instrument, that the action involved the participation of all members included in a plural subject, or that a subject performed the action on itself. Such details, which can provide interesting and necessary information to a listener or reader, can be provided through the use of prefixes on the verb phrase.

Vocabulary

FOODS

English	Mvskoke
boiled meat (meat that has been dried, then boiled, ground, and cooked with onions)	vpeshockē
onions/onion	tafvmpe
Irish potatoes	vhvce-rēhe
rice	vloso
gravy	okneha
carrots	yvlonkv-lanet
pickles	takompv (Seminole)
or	kakompv-saktehke (Mvskoke)
grape dumplings	pvrko-svpkonepke
or	pvrko-sakporoke
or	pvrko-afke
pig intestines, cleaned well and fried	fekce
apple	svtv
orange (fruit)	yvlahv
bananas	penanv
cookie	tvklik-cvmpuce
cake	tvklik-cvmpv
pie	(e)sem vtehke
or	(e)sem vtehkv

VERBS

English	Mvskoke
to boil, make bubble {I;3}	morecetv
to cook, bake {I;3}	noricetv

English	Mvskoke
to roast, broil, bake {I;3}	hotopetv
to stir things {I;3}	eteyametv
to grind (coffee, corn, etc.) {I;3}	enfolotetv
to wash over and over (as when preparing *fekce*) {I;II}	okkoset mēcetv
to mash (potatoes), grind meat {I;3}	cetvketv
to be thick (like material, paper, gravy) {II}	cekfē
to be thin (like gravy) {II}	kvsvmrē
or {II}	wētvlkē
to be sour (not of milk) {II}	kvmoksē
to be sour (of milk) {II}	toksē
to be tender (of meat), soft (of one) {II}	lowvckē
to be tough (as of meat or clay) {II}	tvlvswē
to burn {I;II}	nokricetv
or {I;II}	nekricetv
to crumble {I;3;D}	tofvpetv

Exercises

EXERCISE 1

Each of the sentences below has a locative prefix on the verb. Identify each of the morphemes in the sentence, show the linguistic notation for each morpheme as it occurs, and then give a rough translation of the sentence. In some cases, you may find that more than one translation is possible. When this is the case, list all translations that make sense. In the end, you will have produced a set of lines similar to the second, third, and fourth lines of each example in this chapter.

1. Hoktucet rvron akcelahyes.
2. Kapvn ēkvnv takkayekot!
3. Cēpvne elvwvkat topvn ohtasecvrēs.
4. Rakko hotosvkē hiyat owvn aksvpakletos.
5. Sally ecerwvn hvccucen akemēhetos.
6. Eshoccickvt cokv lvsten onvpvn ohwakkvnks.

7. Lvmhet mvn eto onvpvn ohvpoketowv?
8. Henehv ehopvn cvyayvkēn takpahses.
9. Nokoset ēkvnhvlwen vhecvtēs.
10. Honvnwvt taktopvtake takliketos.

EXERCISE 2

Translate the following English sentences into Mvskoke. These sentences will require you to use the locative and/or other prefixes discussed in this chapter.

1. The woman's older sister put the cake on the table.
2. We walked a little distance yesterday.
3. Jimmy made me hit his brother with a stick.
4. My dad used a ladder to paint above the windows.
5. The ducks flew toward the river a long time ago.
6. A young boy dropped his coat into the water.
7. His grandmother picked the coat up from the water.
8. Grandfather rode a long distance today.
9. The rocks dropped a short distance into the stream.
10. The eagle saw the deer from a long way away.

EXERCISE 3

Working with another student in your class, create a conversation about a topic that would involve the use of locative and/or directional prefixes on the verbs. Some possible topics include: camping, playing with children, gardening, cooking, or fishing. Locative or directional prefixes should appear on at least twelve of the verbs in your conversation, six that you use and six used by your colleague. Practice your conversation until it sounds natural, as your instructor may ask you to perform it for the other students in your class.

EXERCISE 4

In Mvskoke, describe some work that you have done around your home recently. Your narrative should be at least twenty-five sentences long. Be certain to include locative prefixes and other prefixes on at least twelve of the verbs that you use in your narrative. Recite your narrative out loud a few times before bringing it to class, as your instructor may ask you to read it to your fellow students.

Exercise 5

Make up ten directions for a Simon Says game. Be prepared to state your directions to your classmates when your teacher calls on you. Be certain that five of your directions involve the use of locative or other prefixes. If any of your directions involve the use of props, be certain that these props are available in your classroom (e.g., if you direct students to pick up paper from the floor, be sure there is paper on the floor).

Exercise 6

Make up a story about Rabbit and some other character. Rabbit almost always tries to pull tricks on others or does things that will allow him to get his way. Sometimes things work out as he wants them to, but at other times he ends up looking silly, greedy, or thoughtless. Rabbit stories may be mostly for fun or they may be stories with a moral to them. Whatever kind of story you come up with, make sure that you include locative and other prefixes on at least ten of your verbs. Then, be prepared to tell your story out loud to your fellow classmates. Hopefully, you will all laugh and learn from Rabbit's adventures!

Listening Exercises

Listen to track 2 of the CD. Do the speakers use locatives or other verbal prefixes in this conversation? Which one(s) seem to be used more often than others? What kind(s) of prefix(es) are used most—locative, directional, instrumental, applicative? Why do you think that is? Now that you are more aware of these kinds of prefixes and what they indicate in Mvskoke, are you able to understand more of any of this conversation?

Perform the exercise above while listening to track 3 of the CD. Draw from what you hear on track 3 to answer all of the questions presented in the above exercise. Are the most frequently used prefix(es) the same in the conversations? Why do you think this is so?

Perform the first exercise presented above while listening to track 5 of the CD. Use what you hear on track 5 to answer the questions in the first listening exercise. Compare the most used prefixes from this track and from the conversation on track 2. Are they the same? Why do you think this is the case?

Listen to track 89, "Turtle's Shell," on the CD. Do you hear any of the prefixes discussed in this chapter in the story? Which of the prefixes appear? What kind of information are they adding to the verb? Remember some of the prefixes that you hear on the track and ask your classmates whether they heard the same ones.

The Importance of Corn in the Muskogee Diet

You will find that corn is the most used ingredient in a lot of Indian foods. The Seminoles and Muskogee Creeks used a lot of corn in their food. Also, in the first textbook, the Green Corn dance was mentioned as the most sacred of all the dances. The green corn, when first harvested, was used to honor or give thanks to the Creator.

Corn was dried and stored for future use. It was used by cooking it with meat or as a drink. The following are some of the ways corn was used in the past and continues to be used today.

Sofke is a drink. It is cooked in a large kettle. Water is put in the kettle, the corn is added, and it is cooked slowly until it begins to soften. Ash drippings, called *kvpe* among the Seminoles and *ēsso* among the Muskogee Creeks, are added to give it flavor.

What are ash drippings? During the period of time when cooking was done over an open fire, ashes from the fire were saved in a covered container. Even now, some people save their ashes. To make the drippings, the ashes are put in a clean cloth and hot water is strained through the cloth until a tan or brown liquid comes out. Ashes from blackjack or hickory wood make the best ash drippings. The drippings are stored in glass jars until they are needed.

To make *sofke* using today's modern way of cooking: Fill a 4-quart Crock-Pot about ¾ full of water. Add 2½ cups of dry hominy or white corn. Cook for 2½ hours, then add the ash drippings until the flavor is right and the mixture looks a little cloudy. Cook until the corn is soft, then serve either hot or cold.

Lydia Larney sifting *sofke* meal for *sofke*, April 17, 1923. *Photograph by Mrs. Jennie Elrod. J. Elrod Collection, Courtesy of the Oklahoma Historical Society. Negative #20382.140.*

Another dish that uses dried corn is hominy with pig feet. Brown the pig feet before placing them in a Crock-Pot. Add 2 cups of corn and fill the Crock-Pot about ¾ full with water to cover the pig feet and corn and cook until the corn is soft. To add flavor, use bacon drippings and salt to taste.

This is a recipe to make dried corn. Using fresh corn, cut the corn off the cob. Dry the corn in the sun, turning or agitating it at times so that it gets dried evenly. Store the corn in a container until you are ready to use it. This is very good with stew meat.

Dried corn is used in making another good dish called blue bread. Take the dried corn and grind it until you have a very fine meal, like corn meal. The meal will be white or maybe slightly tan in color. To make the bread blue, color is added by using dry bean hulls. After the bean hulls are dried, the hulls are burned and the resulting ashes are added to the corn meal. The ashes look grey when they are just burned, but they give the bread a blue color upon cooking.

To cook the blue bread, put water in a pot (the amount of water and size of the pot depend on how much blue bread you plan to make) and bring it to a rolling boil. Use some of the water to mix with the dried corn/bean hull mixture. Add just enough so that the dough sticks together, about the consistency of pie dough. When it comes to the right consistency, pinch off golfball-sized pieces of the dough, roll it in your hands, and pat it to flatten it somewhat, then drop the dough in the boiling water. This makes a very moist bread that is done when the dough has floated in the water for some time.

Two dishes that do not use corn but that are traditional foods, too, are grape dumplings and wild onions. Grape dumplings are made from what we call Possum Grapes. These are grapes that grow in the wild and that ripen in the fall. They grow on vines that creep into the treetops. Pick the grapes from the vine, wash them, place them in a pot of boiling water, and cook until it comes back to a boil and you see thick juice. Let the liquid cool and then strain it to remove the seeds from the grapes. Use the liquid to make grape dumplings. Make the dumplings by mixing some flour and grape juice until you have a dough that you can handle. Bring some grape juice to a boil. Roll out the dumplings, pretty thin, and drop them into the boiling juice until they are cooked through. You can add some sugar to the juice, if it is sour.

Wild onions are found in early spring, around small creeks or in areas where the ground stays pretty moist. Dig them up and clean them like you would garden onions (remove the outermost skin and wash them well). Cut them up, place them in a skillet with cooking oil, and add water. Cover the pan and let it simmer until the heads (white parts) of the onions are transparent. Add beaten eggs and cook until the eggs are done. Serve with salt pork or bacon.

Suggested Readings

Hardy (2005: 227–30) offers a clear and concise discussion of the locative, directional, and applicative prefixes. He provides examples of each, as we have done in this text, and he speaks briefly about the uses and meanings of each. There are some major differences between Hardy's treatment of these prefixes and that we offered in this chapter. For instance, he does not consider *v-* to be a locative prefix, whereas we do. He also does not consider two of the prefixes referring to the distance over which an action has occurred (*er-/r-* and *ra-*). The last difference concerns the instrumental prefix, which we have given its own treatment, but that is considered to be an applicative prefix by Hardy.

Nathan (1977) discusses the prefixes in several different parts of her dissertation. The locative prefixes (including *v-*) are covered on pages 77–82, the directional prefixes designating the distance over which an action occurs are described on pages 83–85, and the instrumental prefix is discussed on page 104. Nathan does not include the applicative prefixes found in this chapter, so readers wanting more information about these are referred to Hardy (2005).

Those with a particular interest in the directional prefixes are directed to Booker (1984). Booker's analysis of these prefixes is concise and clear. Examples and explanations of each of the prefixes are provided in the paper, and the majority of readers should find it to be understandable and informative. She presents a cogent argument that several of the most-used directional prefixes have very little to do with the distance over which the activity occurs, but are instead more concerned with the focus of the action toward or away from a given point.

Those interested in finding out more about Muskogee cooking and recipes are directed to the following sources. Cox and Jacobs (1991) is a cookbook containing some Muskogee Creek and Seminole recipes, as well as recipes from several other tribes. Information about the ingredients and/or traditions surrounding the prepared food is included with each recipe, providing nice background for those preparing the dish.

The Seminole Tribe of Florida has recipes for fried bread and *sofke* on their website. Readers are referred to www.Seminoletribe.com/culture/recipes.shtml for more information. The recipe for *sofke* on the Seminole website is very similar to that provided in this book, but the recipe for fried bread differs from the one offered in *Beginning Creek* in that it calls for self-rising flour and water rather than flour, baking soda, and buttermilk. In either case, we are certain that you will find traditional Muskogee foods to be delicious and worth trying.

CHAPTER EIGHT

Sentences with Multiple Clauses

All of the sentences that you have seen to this point have contained only one verb. In this chapter, we will introduce you to the ways that sentences in which more than one verb occurs are formed, necessitating a discussion of clauses. **Clauses** are sentences containing a subject and a verb. In a sentence containing two or more clauses, the one that includes the main verb of the sentence is called the **primary clause. Embedded clauses** are those incorporated within the main clause. There are several ways in which Mvskoke embeds one clause within another, each of which we will discuss in this chapter.

An element of Mvskoke grammar that comes into play when multiple clauses are included in sentences, and which you will need to understand in order to interpret all of the examples in this and later chapters, is switch-reference. **Switch-reference** refers to the practice of marking whether the subjects of the verbs in a sentence are the same or different. Mvskoke has a system of switch-reference marking that appears on the verbs preceding the main verb of the sentence. You have already been introduced to this in *Beginning Creek*, pages 80–81, when auxiliary verbs were discussed. At that time, the **same-subject suffix** (*-et/-t*), which comes between the main verb of the sentence and the auxiliary verb, was described as a suffix indicating that the main verb and the auxiliary verb share the same subject.

This same suffix is used on verbs in embedded clauses, when the subject of the embedded and primary clauses is the same. When the subjects are different, a **different-subject suffix** (-*en*/-*n*) is used to show that the subjects of the verbs in the embedded clauses are not the same as those in the primary clause. The positioning of these suffixes and the rationale for using the two different versions of each will be discussed in the following sections. When a different-subject suffix appears in the examples, its location will be marked by the use of 'ds' in the third line of each.

THE SUBORDINATING SUFFIX

Perhaps the most frequently used means of forming an embedded clause is to use the subordinating suffix. The **subordinating suffix** (-*at*) shows that the verb to which it is affixed is not the primary verb of the sentence. This suffix also serves to indicate that the clause in which it occurs is a subsidiary or subordinate piece. When this suffix appears in sentences, its position will be marked by 'sub' in the third line of each example. The subordinating suffix occasionally appears as –*an*, but the reasons for using this form instead of –*at* are not understood well enough to be discussed in this chapter. Simply be aware that –*an* is another form of this suffix, even though we will not delve into its use here.

The subordinating suffix is often used when a complete clause modifying a noun is included in a larger sentence. Example 1 presents a Mvskoke sentence containing a subordinate clause modifying a noun. The embedded clause is italicized in both the Mvskoke sentence and the English translation.

1.   *Honvnwv kvtopokvn kvtopoyat* vmvpēles.
     honvnwv-Ø   kvtopokv-n   kvtopoy-**at**   vm-vpēl-Ø-es
     man-def_subj hat-ind_obj   wearing_a_hat-sub 1SD-smile_(1)-3pers-dec
     '*The man wearing a hat* is smiling at me.'

It should be pointed out that the final consonant of the subordinating suffix is not marking that the embedded clause is the subject of the sentence. Instead, it appears that this suffix ends in /t/ most of the time, even when the suffix occurs on a verb in a clause that relates to the object of the primary sentence, as in example 2.

2.   *Cofonwv ohhompetv ohlomhat* kvrkvpēciyvnks.
     cofonwv-Ø   ohhompetv-Ø   oh-lomh-**at**   Ø-kvrkvpēc-i-yvnk-s
     fork   table   loc-lie_down   3persII-dry_(2+)-1S-mp-dec
                                 _(3+)-sub
     'I dried *the forks lying on the table*.'

The forks whose location is described in the embedded clause serve as the object of the verb in this sentence, yet the subordinating suffix still has the form –*at* rather than –*an*. This suggests that the final consonant of this suffix does not really work to show that either the subjects of the embedded clause's verb and the primary verb are the same or that the noun that is the subject of the embedded clause is also the subject in the primary sentence.

PARTICIPIAL PHRASES

The subordinating suffix also works to indicate participial phrases. **Participial phrases** are those containing or made up of a word that has attributes of both an adjective and a verb. Most of the adjectives that you have seen to this point in *Beginning Creek* and this book are participles, type II verbs that can be used to modify nouns. Earlier, we had discussed the use of the suffixes –*at* and –*an* as a means of showing that the final adjective in a string is referring to a definite subject or object respectively. However, -*at* and -*an* can be added to a fully conjugated verb so as to indicate 'the one who (verbs)' or 'the (verb) one.' Affixing this suffix to verbs to form participial phrases that do not include a noun has the effect of changing the verbs into nounlike forms.

Examples 3 and 4 contain sentences in which the two forms of the suffix are used to form participial phrases. Notice that in these examples, changes to the verb stem due to the use of the recent past (h-grade) and incompletive aspect (l-grade) have been made to the participle to which the subordinating suffix has been added. In example 3, the participial phrase is the subject of the sentence and thus takes the –*at* form of the suffix. The participle in this sentence has been modified to show the recent past, as has the main verb.

3.   Yefolhohkat emmvyattēhcvkes.
      yefolhohk-**at**   em-mvyattēc-vhk-Ø-es
      go_back_(2)<hgr>-sub   3persD-wave_at-distr<hgr>-3pers-dec
      'The ones going back (just now) waved at him/them.'

In example 4, the participial phrase is affected by the lengthening grade and includes the distributive suffix to demonstrate that there are multiple objects in this case. Notice that because the participial phrase concerns the objects of the main sentence, the form of the subordinating suffix in this case is *–an*.

4.   'Ponvyakan kērritos.
        'ponvy-ak-**an**   Ø-kērr-i-t-o-s
        talk-distr_l_grd-sub   3persD-know_l_grd-1S-ss-aux_vb-dec
        'I know the ones who are talking.'

The participial phrase is affected by the h-grade and lengthened grade, when it is appropriate to include these features (e.g., when the subject of the phrase is 'the one(s) who just *verbed*' or 'the one(s) who is/are *verbing*').
    Participial phrases may also be constructed by applying a participial suffix (*ē*) to a verb, which changes the verbal meaning to 'the *verb* one(s).' This suffix is used primarily with stative verbs, whereas the subordinating suffix is used with active verbs. Its position in sentences in which it appears will be marked by the use of 'part' in the third line of each such example. Examples of participial phrases using this suffix are supplied in examples 5 and 6.

5.   Pvfnē epoyvkvnks.
        pvfn-ē-Ø   epoy-vk-Ø-vnk-s
        fast-part-def_subj   win-distr-3pers-mp-dec
        'The fast ones won.'

6.   Honvnwvt fvskē eswahres.
        honvnwv-t   fvsk-ē-Ø   es-wahr-Ø-es
        man-ind_subj   sharp-part-def_obj   instr-cut<hgr>-3pers-dec
        'A man was just cutting with the sharp one.'

As you may have noticed in these sentences, the indefinite subject and object suffixes were not used on the participles. Occasionally, the indefinite subject suffix does get used on participles, while the indefinite object suffix is almost never used in these constructions. This may be the case because the use of this suffix could cause the participle to be confused with an adverbial phrase (see *Beginning Creek*, chapter 5, for further details about adverbial phrases).

Tense marking may take place on participles formed by adding the participial suffix. If the participle is marked for tense, the participial suffix can be used with verbs that are not stative. When a participle is formed with a recent past tense marker and the *ē* suffix, it requires the use of a different form of the recent past tense—not the h-grade. Instead, the verb stem is affected by the lengthened grade, and a recent past suffix (*-is*) is applied after the distributive and subject suffixes and before the participial suffix. The position of this suffix in examples in which it appears will be shown by 'recent' in the third line of each. The order of affixes on a verb using this form of the recent past is shown in diagram 8.1. As presented in the diagram, the verb stem may be preceded by the directional, instrumental, object, and locative prefixes. Thus, in forming a participle, you may add a significant amount of information through the use of affixes.

[Directional Prefix]	[Instrumental Prefix]	[Object Prefix]	[Locative Prefix]	Verb Stem (1-grade)	[Distr. Suffix]	[Type I Subject Suffix]	Recent Past Suffix	Participial Suffix

Diagram 8.1. Order of Affixes on a Participle Including Recent Past *–is*

Participles formed in this way tend to be used to modify nouns and thus help to form embedded clauses. An embedded clause including a participle marked for the recent past tense and using the participial suffix is shown in the subject position in example 7. The noun, in this instance, has been marked with the indefinite subject suffix (*-t*) even though this suffix does not appear on the participle. A noun modified by a participle that is marked this way in the primary sentence is not unusual, though speakers appear to have some leeway in choosing whether to mark the noun or not. Generally, though, it is only the noun that is so marked, not the participle. Also, note that the same form of the recent past is used on the main verb of the sentence, as well as on the participle.

7. Hoktēt 'sesketv sulkē kvrkvpēcisē ēponvyis.
    hoktē-t   'sesketv   sulkē-Ø   Ø-kvrkvpēc-Ø-is-ē
    woman-ind_subj   cup/glass   many-def_obj   3persII-dry_(2+)_l_grd-
                                                                  3pers-recent-part

    ē-ponvy-Ø-is
    app-talk_to_someone-3pers-recent
    'A woman drying the glasses was talking to herself.'

Example 8 presents a sentence in which the recent past tense suffix follows an audible subject suffix. Notice that the noun modified by the participle is marked for its role as object in the primary sentence, but that the indefinite object suffix does not appear on the participle.

8.   Ecke oknehan kvsvmrē morececkisē eshecis.
     ecke-Ø   okneha-**n**   kvsvmrē   Ø-morec-**eck-is-ē**
     mother-def_subj   gravy-ind_obj   thin   3persII-boil-2S-recent-part
     Ø-eshec-Ø-is
     3persII-find-3pers-recent
     'Mother just found the thin gravy that you boiled.'

If the participle is to be marked for the middle past tense, then the participial suffix follows the middle past suffix *–vnk*. In example 9, this tense is used on a participle constructed from a stative verb. This example differs from examples 7 and 8 in that the noun in the embedded clause is marked as a definite subject in the primary sentence.

9.   Honvnwv cvpakkvnkē epohyvkvpvnks.
     honvnwv-Ø   Ø-cvpakk-**vnk**-ē   ep-oh-yvkvp-Ø-vnk-s
     man-def_subj   3persII-angry-mp-part   1PII-loc-walk_(1)-3pers-mp-dec
     'The man who was angry walked toward us.'

If the tense marker were not used, it would be possible to restructure this sentence as in example 10. Note that in this case, the subordinating suffix is used instead of the participial suffix.

10. Honvnwv cvpakkat epohyvkvpvnks.
     honvnwv-Ø   Ø-cvpakk-at   ep-oh-yvkvp-Ø-vnk-s
     man-def_subj   3persII-angry-sub   1PII-loc-walk_(1)-3pers-mp-dec
     'The angry man walked toward us.'

FORMING COMPLEMENTS OF VERBS OF SPEAKING, THINKING, AND WANTING

Verbs of speaking, thinking, and wanting have to be accompanied by whatever was said or thought. The quotations and summaries of thoughts that appear in sentences containing verbs of speaking or thinking are called the **complements** of these verbs. This section will demonstrate how complements of verbs of speaking, wanting, and thinking are constructed in Mvskoke.

When a verb of speaking is included in the primary sentence, the complement (the quoted portion) is formed just as it would be if it were a sentence all on its own. Subject, direct and indirect object, and instrumental noun phrases will precede the verb within the quote. The verb will have been fully inflected for number, tense, and aspect and will include the appropriate ending (declarative, interrogative, imperative). Thus, the quoted portion will be a completely formed sentence embedded within the larger sentence, whose main verb concerns speaking. An example of this kind of sentence is shown in example 11.

11.   "**Totkvn vslēcackvnkv?**" porket epvpohvnks.
      totkv-n   Ø-vslēc-ack-vnk-v   po-rke-t   ep-vpoh-Ø-vnk-s
      fire-ind_obj   put_out_fire-2P-   1PII-father-   1PII-ask-3pers-mp-dec
                     mp-int   ind_subj
      '"Did you (plural) put out the fire?" our father asked us.'

The same structure works when one is using *kicetv* or *maketv* 'to tell, say (to someone)' and 'to tell (no one in particular)' respectively.

12.   "**Cvhotosētos**," erkenvkv makis.
      cv-hotos-ē-t-o-s   erkenvkv-Ø   mak-Ø-is
      1S-tired-stat-ss-aux_vb-dec   preacher-def_subj   say-3pers-recent
      '"I'm tired," said the preacher.'

Occasionally, the speaker and the one to whom the speech is directed may be specified before the complement is presented. When this is the case, the noun phrases identifying the speaker and the listener are generally followed by *oketv* 'to say, mean,' conjugated for the number of speaker(s) and listener(s) and suffixed with the subject form of the subordinating suffix (-*at*). An example of this type of construction is presented in example 13.

13.   Cufet Nokose lvsten okat, "Svtv lokcē catat ascenwiyvhanis."
      cufe-t   nokose   lvste-n   **Ø-ok-Ø-at**   svtv   lokcē
      rabbit-   bear   black-   3persII-say-   apple   ripe
        ind_subj   ind_obj   3pers-sub

cat-at   a-s-cen-wiy-vhan-i-s
red-sub   loc-instr-2SII-pass_something-intent-1S-dec
'Rabbit says to Black Bear, "I will pass you the red, ripe apple."'

Some speakers may also separate the speaker's and listener's noun phrases in the larger sentence. When this is the case, the speaker's noun phrase, followed by the appropriate form of *oketv*, will always precede the quotation. The listener's noun phrase and a verb of speaking will signal the end of the primary sentence. In example 14, this is the structure that has been used.

14.   **Cufet okat**, "Svtv lokcē catat ascenwiyvhanis," **Nokose lvsten kicis**.
       cufe-t   Ø-ok-Ø-at   svtv   lokcē   cat-at
       rabbit-ind_subj   3persII-say-3pers-sub   apple   ripe   red-sub
       a-s-cen-wiy-vhan-i-s   nokose   lvste-n
       loc-instr-2SII-pass_something-intent-1S-dec   bear   black-ind_obj
       Ø-kic-Ø-is
       3persII-say-3pers-rec
       'Rabbit said, "I will pass you the red, ripe apple," to Black Bear.' *or*
       'Rabbit said to Black Bear, "I will pass you the red, ripe apple."'

In a sentence structured with *oketv* and another verb of speaking, only one reference to speaking need appear in the English translation, even though there are two instances of verbs about speaking in the Mvskoke version.

Verbs of thinking and wanting show a similar manner of constructing sentences with complements, when the subject of the dependent verb and the subject of the main verb in the primary sentence are NOT the same. In such cases, a fully formed sentence is used to show the complement of the verb of thinking or wanting. In example 15, the subject of *kometv* 'to think, try, hope, want,' the main verb, is different from the subject of the verb within the complement clause. Because the subjects differ, the complement is a well-formed sentence with noun phrases and verbal inflection that one would expect in a complete sentence.

15.   "**Cvccus hoktē** wakvpesē toksan pvlvtvrēs," **ecket** komis
       cv-ccus hoktē-Ø   wakvpesē   toks-an   Ø- pvlvt-Ø-vrē-s
       1SII-daughter-def_subj   milk   sour-def_obj   3persII-pour_out-
                                                               3pers-fut-dec

ecke-t   kom-Ø-is
mother-ind_subj   think-3pers-rec
'"My daughter will pour out the sour milk," thought her mother.' *or*
'Her mother thought, "My daughter will pour out the sour milk."' *or*
'Her mother thought she [the daughter] will pour out the sour milk.'

In the first two translations, the complement clause appears in quotations, because the structure in Mvskoke is giving a direct statement of the thought going through the mother's mind. However, the third translation contains all the relevant pieces of information from the original sentence and is perfectly permissible, depending on the context in which the translation is to be understood. You may present your translations in either form, as you work with similar kinds of sentences in the examples and the rest of the text.

This format of having a completely conjugated verb in the complement clause also works with *eyvcetv* 'to like, want, need,' when the subject of the verb in the complement clause is different from the subject who is wanting or needing the complement. Example 16 contains a sentence in which the policeman wants the young man to open the door.

16. **Honvnwv mvnettat vhvoken enhvweces** estewvnayv eyahces.

     honvnwv   mvnett-at   vhvoke-n   en-hvwec-Ø-es
     man   young-def_subj   door-ind_obj   3persD-open_for-3pers-dec
     estewvnayv-Ø   eyahc-Ø-es
     policeman-def_subj   want<hgr>-3pers-dec
     'The policeman wanted/needed the young man to open the door for him.'

When the subjects of the verb in the complement and the thinking or wanting verb in the primary sentence are the same, then a different construction is used. In this case, the verb in the complement appears in its infinitive form with the addition of the oblique suffix –*n*. The verb in the dependent clause in example 17 shows how this construction appears in a sentence in which the one thinking about doing something and the one who would do it are one and the same. The position of the infinitival suffix is shown in the third line of this and following examples by the inclusion of 'inf.'

17. Letketvn komētos.

     letk-**etv-n**   kom-ē-t-o-s

run-inf-obl   think-1P-ss-aux_vb-dec
'We are thinking about running.'

This same structure is used when the main verb is *eyvcetv* 'to want, like,' as example 18 shows.

18.   Yvhiketvn ceyvcvkvnks.
       yvhik-**etv-n**   ce-yvc-vk-vnk-s
       sing-inf-obl   2persII-like-distr-mp-dec
       'You (plural) used to like singing.' *or* 'You (plural) used to like to sing.'

SWITCH-REFERENCE MARKED VERBS

Yet another means of marking that a clause is included within a larger sentence is to use switch-reference marking on the verbs coming before the primary verb. As we mentioned previously, switch-reference marking is a way of indicating whether the subject of the marked verb is the same or different from the subject of the main verb in the sentence. When the subjects of the switch-reference marked verb and the main verb are the same, the suffix used is *–et* (*-t* after the 1S suffix), and its position on the verb will be noted by 'ss' in the third line of each example in which it occurs. When the subjects of the marked verb and the main verb are different, the suffix is *–en* (*-n* after the 1S suffix), and its location on the verb will be shown by 'ds' in the third line of each example in which it appears.

Switch-reference marking is common in Mvskoke speech. It is used on **independent clauses**, which are able to stand alone as sentences, even though they may be contained within larger sentences. Despite the fact that switch-reference marked clauses are independent in Mvskoke, they may be translated as though they are **dependent clauses** (unable to stand alone as sentences, depending on another element in the sentence for their meaning). In English, dependent clauses are commonly introduced by words such as "after," "as," "because," "before," "if," "since," "than," "that," "until," "when," "where," "which," "while," or "who," among others. Notice that you have already seen several of these words in the examples included in the section about the subordinating suffix.

An example of this difference between what the Mvskoke sentence is actually saying and how the translation may alter that is shown in example 19. In this example, the fact that the house is situated somewhere can stand as its own sentence. However, as its role is to specify what Rabbit was passing by, it sounds better to make it appear as though it is dependent in the translation. The literal translation given in the fourth line of the example presents the clause containing the switch-reference marked verb as clearly independent. The looser translation, which may sound better to speakers of English, changes the independent clause into a dependent one through the use of "that."

19. Hofonofvn Cufet **coko rakkan liken** hoyvnvtēs.

hofon-ofv-n   cufe-t   coko   rakk-an   lik-**en**
long_ago-during-obl rabbit-ind_subj house   big_(1)-sub sit_(1)-ds
hoyvn-Ø-vtē-s
pass_by_(1)-3pers-rp-dec
Literal: 'A long time ago, Rabbit passed by a big house located there.'
Loose: 'A long time ago, Rabbit passed by a house that was (located) there.'

The switch-reference marking suffix used in example 19 shows that the subject of *liketv* is different from that of *hoyvnetv*. The house is the subject of the clause in which *liketv* appears, whereas Rabbit is the subject of the primary clause, which includes *hoyvnetv*. When the two subjects are different, as in this case, the two subjects are often specified in their respective clauses so as to lessen any confusion about who is doing what.

Example 20 presents a sentence in which three verbs appear. The subjects of the first and main verb are the same, but the subject of the second verb is different. The first verb is marked with the same-subject suffix not because its subject is the same as the verb that follows it, but because its subject is the same as the main verb. The switch-reference markers, then, are used in reference to the subject performing the final action in the sentence, not in regard to the next-occurring verb.

20. Efolot eton ohliket wotkot rvro hompen hēcvnks.

efolo-t   eto-n   oh-lik-Ø-**et**   wotko-t
owl-ind_subj   tree-ind_obj loc-sit_(1)_l_grd-3pers-ss   raccoon-ind_subj
rvro-Ø   Ø-homp-**en**   Ø-hēc-Ø-vnk-s
fish-def_obj   3persII-eat_l_grd-ds   3persII-see-3pers-mp-dec
'An owl sat in the tree and watched a raccoon eating a fish.'

When the subjects of two or more verbs in a sentence are the same, as in examples 21 through 23, there really is no reason to restate the subject in each clause. Thus, you will notice that Rabbit is only mentioned once in example 21, even though he is the subject performing both verbs.

21. **Cufet** Poca Rakkon hēcet vsēkvtēs.

cufe-t	poca_rakko-n	hēc-Ø-et	Ø-vsēk-Ø-vtē-s
rabbit-ind_subj	wolf-ind_obj	see_l_grd-3pers-ss	3persII-greet-3pers-rp-dec

'Rabbit saw Wolf and greeted him.'

In examples 22 and 23, the subject is presented through the use of a subject suffix with an audible form. The difference between these two sentences is that in example 22, both verbs are displaying the subject suffix, whereas in example 23, only the final verb carries the subject suffix. Both constructions are possible, though the form in example 23 is the more common of the two.

22. Likit honvnwv vculen emmapohicayvnks.

lik-**i**-t	hovnvwv	vcule-n	em-mapohic-**a**-yvnk-s
sit_(1)_l_grd-1S-ss	man	old-ind_obj	3persD-listen_to-1S-mp-dec

'I sat and listened to the old man.'

23. Liket honvnwv vculen emmapohicayvnks.

lik-et	honvnwv	vcule-n	em-mapohic-**a**-yvnk-s
sit_(1)_l_grd-ss	man	old-ind_obj	3persD-listen_to-1S-mp-dec

'I sat and listened to the old man.'

In examples 20–23, the switch-reference marked verbs are affected by the lengthened grade. This is done when the actions are performed at almost the same time, with only a slight delay between them. The time frame in which the actions took place (recent, middle, distant or remote pasts, present, or future) is indicated by the placement of the appropriate tense marker on the final verb in the sentence. The lengthened grade on the embedded verbs makes it clear to a listener that the actions specified by them took place at nearly the same time as that indicated on the main verb.

A different construction is used in conjunction with the switch-reference suffixes, when one action follows shortly after another. When this is the case, the first action that occurred is usually stated as the embedded verb, while the action that followed this one appears as the main verb. The first verb is modified with the h-grade or the recent past suffix, and the second verb includes the appropriate tense marker for the point in time in which its action took place. Examples 24 and 25 present a sentence in which these features may be seen. The difference between the two examples is that 24 uses the h-grade and 25 uses the recent past suffix to mark the sequential nature of the actions being discussed.

24.   Fekcen okkoset mēhcecken svkmorecvkarēs.
       fekce-n   okkoset_mēhc-eck-en   Ø-svkmorec-vk-a-rē-s
       intestines-ind_obj wash_repeatedly<hgr>-2S-ds 3persII-fry-distr-1S-fut-dec
       'You will wash the intestines and I will fry them.'

25.   Fekcen okkoset mēceckisen svkmorecvkarēs.
       fekce-n   okkoset_mēc-eck-**is**-en   Ø-svkmorec-vk-a-rē-s
       intestines-ind_obj wash_repeatedly-2S-rec-ds   3persII-fry-distr-1S-fut-dec
       'You will wash the intestines and I will fry them.'

In these examples, the speaker openly declares that the washing of the *fekce* precedes frying the *fekce*, by using the h-grade or recent past suffix on the verb for washing. Even though the h-grade/recent past is used on the first verb, the action to which it has been attached is still considered to be taking place in the future, as the time of its occurrence is specified through the use of the future tense suffix on the main verb. In this case, the h-grade/recent past is simply showing that the two actions being spoken about in the sentence occur in sequence, not at the same time.

Switch-reference suffixes are also used when forming sentences with two or more clauses linked by "but" rather than "and." In sentences of this type, the switch-reference suffixes are attached to the auxiliary verb. Because the auxiliary verb is going to take the switch-reference suffixes, among others, the verb stem will have the form *om-/ow-*, depending upon which dialect of Mvskoke is being spoken. The verb directly before the auxiliary verb will have the same-subject suffix on it, as the auxiliary clearly relates to the same subject as the verb to which it is attached. Example 26 shows how a sentence is formed with the auxiliary verb denoting that the conjunction joining the clauses in this sentence is "but."

26.   Tvlofvn vyetv cvyacetowen cvrket vyetv yacekis.

tvlofv-n	vy-etv	cv-yac-et-**ow-en**	cv-rke-t
town-ind_obj	go_(1)-inf	1S-want_l_grd-ss-aux_vb-ds	1SII-father-ind_subj

vy-etv	Ø-yac-ek-is
go_(1)-inf	3persII-want_l_grd-neg-recent

'I wanted to go to town but my father didn't want to go.'

It is permissible to include the recent past or h-grade on the auxiliary verb, if desired. In example 27, the recent past nature of the embedded and final verbs is marked by placing the recent past suffix on both. This makes it very clear to a listener that both actions were occurring at about the same time, though it is possible to leave this to the listener's interpretation, as in example 26, where the recent past only appears on the main verb.

27.   Honvnwv owv hvtvm yacetowisen nvcomusēt owvn owis.

honvnwv-Ø	owv-Ø	hvtvm	Ø-yac-et-ow-**is**-en
man-def_subj	water-def_obj	again	3persII-want_l_grd-ss-aux_vb-recent-ds

nvcomusē-t	owv-n	ow-Ø-**is**
little_bit-ss	water-ind_obj	to_be-3pers-recent

'The man wanted water again, but there was just a little bit.'

CONDITIONAL SUFFIX

The conditional suffix, -*nowat*, is used when the sentence contains conditional relations between the clauses. **Conditional relations** mean that the performance of one activity relies on the performance of another. The most common type of conditional sentence in English is an 'if-then' sentence such as, "If you buy the meat, then I will cook it." In this sentence, 'I will cook the meat' will happen on the condition that you have already bought it.

The conditional nature of the relationship between two or more verbs in a sentence is indicated by affixing the conditional suffix (-*enowat*) to those verbs that have to happen before the final action takes place. The position of the conditional suffix is shown by the placement of 'cond' in the third line of each example in which it occurs. Example 28 shows how this suffix is used in a sentence containing one conditional relationship.

28. Cvrket eto cvskenowat totkvn etecvhanis.

cv-rke-t	eto-Ø	Ø-cvsk-Ø-**enowat**	totkv-n
1SII-father-ind_subj	wood-def_obj	3persII-chop-3pers-cond	fire-ind_obj

Ø-etec-vhan-i-s
3persII-light-intent-1S-dec

'If father chops the wood, then I will light a fire.'

It is possible to have more than one conditional relation in the sentence. In such a situation, all of the verbs preceding the main verb carry the conditional suffix. An example of this kind of sentence is shown in example 29.

29. Cvrket eto cvskenowat, cēmet owvn 'svcvlvkeckenowat, vssen morecvhanis.

cv-rke-t	eto-Ø	Ø-cvsk-Ø-**ēnowat**	cēme-t
1SII-father-ind_subj	wood-def_obj	3persII-chop-3pers-cond	2persII-ind_subj
owv-n	's-vc-vlvk-eck-**enowat**	vsse-n	Ø-morec-vhan-i-s
water-ind_obj	instr-1S-bring_to-2S-cond	tea-ind_obj	3persII-boil-intent-1S-dec

'If father chops the wood and if you bring me the water, then I will boil some tea.'

When the verb stating the condition (the one following "if") is a stative verb, it shows up in its infinitive form and the same subject suffix is added to it. At these times, the conditional suffix appears to stand alone. We will present this construction as shown in example 30, though you should understand that placing *nowat* as a particle is not commonly recognized in the linguistic literature. It may be that a change is occurring in the use of this suffix, but this has not been sufficiently described to make the categorical claim that it is the case. However, as this construction is heard in common speech, we present it here for your consideration.

30. Cehotosēt nowat, cokon refolhokētos.

ce-hotosē-t	**nowat**	coko-n	re-folhok-ē-t-o-s
2persII-tired-ss	cond	house-ind_obj	dir-return_(2)-1P-ss-aux_vb-dec

'If you are tired, then we will go back home.'

The conditional suffix is also used in 'when-then' sentences. In such sentences, one activity is known to take place after the other. The idea that one action takes place before the other is similar to the idea of the 'if-then' sentence, which may explain why the conditional suffix is used to mark the sequential relation between verbs. Example 31 shows how a sentence containing a when-then relationship between the verbs is formed.

31.   Vmefv hotosēt nowat rvmvlaketos.

vm-efv	Ø-hotosē-t	**nowat**	r-vm-vlak-Ø-et-o-s
1SII-dog	3persII-tired-ss	cond	dir-1SD-return_(1)_1_grd-3pers-ss-aux_vb-dec

'When my dog is tired, (then) he comes back/returns to me.'

Using each of the structures presented in this chapter will allow you to create sentences with greater complexity than those you have been able to form previously. Each structure builds upon the grammatical rules that you have seen up to this point but will let you use those rules to present even more information to your listeners and readers in a single sentence. If you review the conversational sentences on the CD-ROM included with this book or the conversational sentences contained in *Beginning Creek*, you will notice that several of the forms discussed here are contained in those dialogues. This is the case because speakers make frequent use of these structures as they talk with others.

Vocabulary

DISHES AND SERVING UTENSILS

English	Mvskoke
plate, dish	pvlaknv
fork	cofonwv
teaspoon	hakkuce
spoon, ladle	hakkv
knife	eslafkv
serving bowl	hompetv-vcvnetv
or	avtēhkv

English	Mvskoke
cereal bowl, small bowl	avtēhkuce
cup, glass	(e)sesketv
platter	pvlaknv-rakko
pan	nak-vtehetv
or	halo-pvlaknv
stove	totkv-hute
or	cvto
oven	tvklik-noricv
or	norickv-hute
frying pan	nak-svkmorēcv
bag	sokcv

VERBS

English	Mvskoke
to store, protect, or save something {I;3}	vcayēcetv
to take out of (a container) {I;II}	acvwēcetv
or {I;3}	iem esetv
to lose one thing {I;3}	somecicetv
to lose two or more things {I;3}	somhuecetv
to find something {I;3}	eshecetv
to stack one thing on top of another {I;3}	etohlicetv
to stack two things on top of another {I;3}	etohkayetv
to stack three or more things on top of another {I;3}	etohvpoyetv
to dry one thing {I;3}	kvrpēcetv
to dry two or more things {I;3}	kvrkvpēcetv
to be dull {II}	tefnē
to be sharp {II}	fvskē
to pour liquid out (as when emptying a bucket or jar) {I;3}	pvlvtetv
to light a fire/stove {I;3}	etecetv
or {I;3}	tak-etecetv
to put out a fire {I;3}	vslēcetv

Exercises

EXERCISE 1

Translate the following sentences from Mvskoke into English. Before you provide the translation, show each of the morphemes in the words and provide the linguistic notation for each one. In the end, you will have created lines similar to the second, third, and fourth line in each example in the text. Practice saying the Mvskoke sentences, too, as your instructor may ask you to read them out loud in class.

1. Cvrvhvt cofonwvton eslafkvton hompetv-vcvnetv kvrkvpēcen pvlaknvn etohvpohyis.
2. Vhvce-rēhe cetvkat ceyacv?
3. Pose rakkē oklanat elvwētowisen foswvn esekotowis.
4. Cvstvlē lokcēt nowat hompvhanēs.
5. Popose okat, "Honnv catat vnnesvhaneckes komis," pomeckucen kihces.
6. Cēpvne efv lvsten ocat cokv-tohahwv vloso cvwat ohhompetvn ataklihces.
7. Pvrko-svpkonepken morecekonowat nak-vtehetvn iemesekot.
8. "Likepvs ci!" tēkvnv hvse-eskērkucen vccat omvlkēn kicvnks.
9. Tvklik-svkmorke, tosēnv, tafvmpuce hahyecken, cenahvmkvlke omvlken cencokopericvkvhanetos.
10. Svtv sulke lokcēt ēkvnv takpvlvtkvrēs.

EXERCISE 2

Translate the following sentences into Mvskoke. Be prepared to discuss why you use the constructions that you do and to say your own sentences aloud to your classmates. You may find that some of your sentences differ from your colleagues' sentences, depending on how you chose to interpret the embedded clauses.

1. The man wearing the blue coat and the man wearing the green vest greeted one another.
2. "When will you (plural) return home?" asked the boys' mother.

3. A hawk carrying a mouse just flew over me.
4. The old woman doesn't like to eat watermelon.
5. If you sew me a vest, then I will wear it.
6. Yesterday, I sawed wood and Jimmy painted the window above the door.
7. A pig dug a hole under the tree that stands in front of our house.
8. When we go to town, I need to buy some nails.
9. My teacher asked me, "Did you write this?"
10. The boy jumped from behind the chair, but his sister was not scared.

EXERCISE 3

The following is another version of the story to which you were introduced in chapter four. In this version, several of the sentences are conjoined, making this story much more similar to what you are likely to hear when listening to speakers tell narratives in a natural context than would a story cut into shorter sentences. The two activities to complete using this story are listed below.

Cufet Poca Rakko Sahkkopanes

Cufet arenowat rakko rakrvkan hecvkvtēs. Rakko oklanat, hvthvkat svpaklen, rakko lvstē hvmkat wakkis. Tehoyvnvket, ayvtēs. Mont Cufet enhesse Poca Rakko vnrvpvtēs. "Vnhesse, nake ceyaceton hehcis! Rakko elan hehcis," Cufet maketos. "Henrētos. Vnet, cvhiwv, cvhopuetake sulkē epolvwētos. Fayetv vyitowis, eco, sasvkwv, sokhv eccakekvnks," Poca Rakko maketos. Momen, "Vhoyvkēs!" maketos.

Yefolhoket, rakko lvstē elen wakkat hecvkvtēs. "Esokso hompecken vnet ehvckon homparēs." Cufet makvtēs. "Henrētos. Esokso cvyacetos," Poca Rakko komvtēs. Mowen, rakko hvcet nekēyvtēs. "Hotvlē rakko hvcen nekēyicetos." Cufet makvtēs. "Cetorofvn cemvrokafvhanes. Hvcen cemvwvnvyvhanin hvcen nekēyekvrēs."

Poca Rakko ahueren Cufet hvcen vwvnayvtēs. Poca Rakkot takliket rakko esokson enkecētvtēs. Esokso enkecētenowat, rakko ataskvtet Poca Rakkon esletkvtēs. Poca Rakko cvpakkat rakko empenkvlat wvnvkvkvtēs. Cufet Poca Rakkon vpelicat vyvtēs.

Part 1. Translate the story and describe how this version differs from that presented in chapter four. Do all sentences in the two versions have the same meanings? Are there new or different pieces of information in this version? Which one is easier for you to say? Why is that?

Part 2. Answer the following questions in Mvskoke. Formulate answers that are complete sentences.

    1. Stimvt rakkon hēcvtēte?
    2. Poca Rakkot rakko ehvckon vwvnayvtēte?
    3. Nake rakko taskuecvtēte?
    4. Stomen Cufe vpelvtēte?
    5. Nake rakko mēcenowat Cufe hecvtēte?
    6. Cufet Poca Rakko enhesse henrētowv?
    7. Nake rakko hvce nekēyicetos Cufe makvtēte?
    8. Stimvt elvwēte?
    9. Nakstomen Cufet Poca Rakkon rakko lvstan wvnvkvkisv?

EXERCISE 4

Write a story about an experience that you have had or an activity in which you were involved. Be certain that your story contains several sentences with multiple clauses, including some that involve speaking, thinking, or wanting. Also try to incorporate some participle phrases in your story. Be prepared to tell your story to your classmates in Mvskoke. They may ask you to help them translate some portions, so be prepared to offer explanations about what you wanted to say. If you need assistance with vocabulary, you might look at the glossaries in this text and *Beginning Creek*, Loughridge and Hodge's *Dictionary Muskokee and English* (1890 [1964]), or Martin and Mauldin's *A Dictionary of Creek/Muskogee* (2000).

Listening Exercises

Listen to track 89 "Turtle's Shell" from the CD included with this book. You have listened for particular linguistic features in this story in several of the preceding exercises, so you should be getting very familiar with the narrative. As you listen to it this time, listen for switch-reference marked verbs. Do they appear in the story? Do they seem to occur more or less frequently than verbs marked with the declarative, interrogative, or directive suffixes? Why do you think that is the case? Do you hear participial phrases or the conditional suffix in the story?

Using what you have been asked to write down or memorize about the story (track 89) as a result of doing the listening exercises in this chapter and chapters 4, 5, 6, and 7, formulate your own loose translation of the Mvskoke version that Linda tells. Does your translation change any when you compare notes with some of your classmates? How does your translation differ from the loose translation that Linda offers on track 90? Be ready to discuss your answers to these questions in class.

Listen to track 4 on the CD, "Attending Dances." How much of this conversation are you able to understand? (You may listen to this track more than once before answering. Also, you may listen to the individual speakers' turns on tracks 47–63.) Do your best to come up with a loose translation of the conversation. You may work with another student as you do this. This is a complex task, so do not get too frustrated if it does not come easily. You are still training your ear, so you should not expect to get every nuance in the conversation. If you are able to get the general gist, you are doing well!

Traditions Surrounding Serving Food

Food is an important and obvious symbol of health and generosity among the Muskogee Creek and Seminole people. Everyone who is a friend will be offered food and drink when they come to a person's home. It is considered rude and unfriendly if you do not take what is offered. If you ever enter an Indian home and are offered food or drink, be courteous and take whatever is given to you. This is true for most tribes, not just the Muskogee Creeks and Seminoles.

At a family meal, the father and other men are always served first. When the men have taken what they want, the women and children serve themselves. At a meal at a stompground or a church, visitors will often be told "Hompvks ci!" and are expected to go to one of the camps that are serving visitors. When visitors come to a camp, the hosts will take care of

Full-blood Creek Indian girls showing the famous Creek pottery. September 1902. *Twin Territories: The Indian Magazine Collection, Courtesy of the Oklahoma Historical Society. Negative #21178.4.260.*

everything for the visitors and will do whatever they need to do to make their guests comfortable. After the guests have eaten, the family members will eat and clean up from the meal.

One of the customs of both the Creeks and the Seminoles was that when a woman was having her menstrual cycle, she did not eat at the table or out of the serving dishes used by the men. Instead, she had her own plates and her own chair upon which she sat at this time of the month. Some families even constructed small houses for women to use at this time, so that they could remain away from the men while sleeping and doing their daily activities that were done in the house.

This was the tradition, because the men used medicine to keep themselves healthy and help them with hunting and other activities. This medicine was given by the Creator and was considered sacred. When a woman was having her menstrual cycle, she was considered unclean, and it was thought she might contaminate the men and spoil their medicine. Very few people follow this tradition today at their homes, though many still practice this division of plates, utensils, and seating at the grounds, since medicine is being used by everyone there.

Suggested Readings

Those interested in knowing more about the various means of creating multiclausal sentences in Mvskoke are directed to Bosch (1984), Hardy (1988, 2005), Harwell and Harwell (1981), and Nathan (1977). Each of these works discusses several of the constructions used to form and join clauses presented in this chapter. The terminology used to discuss the suffixes or structures differs from one text to the next. Bosch's and the Harwells' books refer to the various types of clauses and their means of formation in a way that is best understood by one fluent in Mvskoke and grammatical analysis. Both of these books were apparently written for teachers intent on having their students do grammatical analysis of Mvskoke, rather than for those intent on learning the language.

Nathan's and Hardy's texts speak about the structure of multiclausal sentences in a way more like that used in this textbook. Each presents examples and demonstrates how the various verbal features are arranged. The explanations of exactly what these features mean differ somewhat from what you have been told here, for reasons that have to do with the authors' theoretical outlook. Generally, however, their analyses are compatible with what has been presented in this chapter.

Schuetze-Coburn (1987) differs from the preceding sources in that he focuses solely on switch-reference marking suffixes and does not discuss conditional or participial suffixes in any real detail. He presents excellent examples and provides understandable explanations for his findings. His discussion includes a description of how these markers work in larger units of discourse, which we will be covering in the next chapter, so it delves into uses of switch-reference that we have not raised here. Students who have studied this chapter should be able to grasp Schuetze-Coburn's arguments though, so we offer this as another text that interested readers might investigate.

There are a number of references discussing social relationships among the Muskogee Creeks and Seminoles, particularly in regard to gender relations. Swanton (1928a, 1928b), Speck (1907), Spoehr (1941a, 1942, 1947), Bell (1990), and Innes (2006) all discuss men's and women's roles among the Muskogee Creeks and/or Seminoles. Swanton (1928a) provides insights as to older forms of Muskogee Creek gendered behaviors, as remembered and related by his informants in the 1920s. The second work by Swanton (1928b) gives both detailed descriptions and analyses of Muskogee Creek medicine-making activities and beliefs. Readers interested in the rationale behind separating menstruating women from men are directed to Swanton (1928a: 358–62).

Speck's (1907) work is similar in nature to that of Swanton, though without quite as much detail. He describes the roles and responsibilities of both men and women in Taskigi Town, as well as beliefs and practices that members of this town share with other Muskogee Creeks.

Spoehr's texts from 1941 and 1942 are primarily concerned with describing and analyzing the kinship systems of the Muskogee Creeks, and the Oklahoma and Florida Seminoles. Within these reports, there are descriptions of how the kinship system serves to regulate and structure male-female relationships in the communities under study. In his 1947 publication, Spoehr does a nice job of comparing the kinship systems of the Muskogee Creeks and two other Southeastern groups. He also compares the kinship structures observed at that time with what he had observed earlier. In this comparison, he charts changes in the gender and generational relationships among the Muskogee Creeks and provides readers with a baseline against which they can compare the kinship practices of the Muskogee Creeks today.

Bell's (1990) and Innes's (2006) works highlight the importance of ideology in shaping Muskogee Creek and Seminole gender relations. The two authors focus on an activity closely associated with Muskogee Creek and Seminole women: gossip. Bell and Innes have different outlooks on what gossip is, whether it is a valuable activity, and what it does for the community. Both works are accessible and interesting, and they may cause readers to reevaluate gossip's importance in their own community.

CHAPTER NINE

Discursive Structures

This chapter will present information about a verb grade, demonstrating that the activity is occurring for a markedly long time or is happening in an intense manner. Then we will discuss constructions that are frequently used in creating narratives and other forms of lengthy discourse. With this chapter, you will have been introduced to the majority of features and structures that you are likely to encounter in conversations with Mvskoke speakers.

EXTRA-HIGH TONE GRADE

The one verbal grade that has not been discussed previously is the extra-high tone grade, which is often also referred to as the rising tone grade. Like the other verb grades, this one modifies the meaning of the verb stem to some degree. When the verb stem is affected by the **extra-high tone grade**, it demonstrates that the activity continues/continued for a long time, or that it was performed or felt in a very intense way. The position of the extra-high tone grade will be shown in examples in which it occurs by the placement of 'e_grd' in the third line.

The extra-high tone grade causes the final vowel of the verb stem to be lengthened even more than it is in the lengthened grade. The vowel sound is held about one count longer than when the verb is affected by the lengthened grade, which is, in itself, noticeable. The extra-high tone grade is marked by two other features, as well. First, while the vowel is held extra long, it is nasalized. **Nasalization** adds an "n-ish" quality to the vowel. If you compare your pronunciation of the vowels in "on" and "ah," you will notice that the vowel of "on" is produced with an /n/ quality to it. This is the kind of change that happens to the vowel affected by the extra-high tone grade. The final element that helps to mark this grade is that the tone of this vowel is quite high. Some speakers even begin the vowel with a high tone and go yet higher as they hold the vowel, which is why this grade is commonly identified as the rising tone grade. The combination of these three distinctive features is enough to clearly mark the extra-high tone grade when it is used.

If a speaker wishes to indicate that an action being discussed happened over a very long time, the extra-high tone grade is used to mark it. In some versions of the story describing how the Mvskokes came to occupy the Southeast, for instance, the extra-high tone grade is used to emphasize that the people walked for a very long time. Example 1 is from a version of this story.

1.   Hvsossv fvccvn Mvskokvlke ohyvkvpakvtēs.

hvsossv   fvccv-n   mvskok-vlke-Ø   ohyvkvp-**ak-Ø-**vtē-s
east   toward-obl   Mvskoke-pl-def_subj   walk_toward-**distr_e_grd-**
                                                  3pers-rp-dec

'The Mvskokes walked a long time toward the east (a very long time ago).'

In this case, the vowel of the distributive suffix is the final vowel on the verb stem (remember that the distributive, counterexpectational, and causative suffixes are affected by each of the verb grades), so it has become extremely long, has a high/rising tone, and is nasalized. This combination of features on the vowel of the suffix alerts a listener to the fact that this activity took place over a long, long time. The exact amount of time that an action takes is not specified by the application of the extra-high tone grade, but further details in the narrative often help to give the suggestion of just how long the action took place. In the narrative from which this sentence is taken, a listener knows that the Mvskokes left someplace mountainous in the west and were walking east in a large group, so it must have taken them at least several months, if not some years to get to the Southeast.

This is not to suggest that the extra-high tone grade is only used when the activity takes place over several months or years. Speakers may use the extra-high tone grade to emphasize that an activity took much longer than it usually does. For instance, the sentence in example 2 could be offered when one responds rather sarcastically to the question "Have you been waiting long?" The *y* between the 1S and recent past suffixes is a glide that arises between these two suffixes when they co-occur.

2. Ehi, heyv likiyis.
    ehi   heyv   **lik-iy-is**
    yes   here   **sit_(1)_e_grd**-1S-recent
    'Yes, I've been sitting here for a long time.'

A speaker could also use this type of structure when wanting to point out that it took longer for her or him to perform an activity than is usual. When this is the reason for using the extra-high tone grade, the speaker does not necessarily mean that it took years to perform the activity, but just that it took longer than normal. In some cases, this may be due only to the speaker's perception and may not really be referring to the actual time involved. The speaker can indicate in this way that it appeared to take a great deal longer than normal, even though the real time it took to do the activity may not have been much longer than usual. Example 3 presents a sentence of this type, in which the speaker is noting that it is apparently taking the woman longer to wash clothes than it normally does.

3. Hoktēt honnv yokkofketv hvtekpikv okkoskueces.
    hoktē-t   honnv   yokkofketv   hvtekpikv   **Ø-okkoskuec-Ø-es**
    woman-   dress   shirt   pants   3persII-**wash**_(2+)_e_grd-
     ind_subj   3pers-dec
    'The woman is washing dresses, shirts, and pants (for a long time).'

This verb grade may also be used to indicate the increased intensity of an activity. For this reason, it is commonly used in the introductory word of stories that happened a very long time ago. Example 4 presents the first sentence in a story about Rabbit and Bear. Notice that the extra-high tone grade is used on the first word of the sentence, which introduces the entire story as something that happened a long, long time ago. In this case, the verb grade is marking that the length of time referred to by "long ago" is quite long—it has intensified the sense of this time marker.

4.   Hofonof Cufet arvtēs.
       hofon-of   cufe-t   ar-Ø-vtē-s
       long_ago_e_grd-during   rabbit-ind_subj   wander_(1)_l_grd-3pers-rp-dec
       'A long, long time ago, Rabbit was wandering around.'

Intensification is also marked in constructions describing states of being. When one wants to emphasize that the subject noun is *really* big, small, tired, and so forth, then one applies the extra-high tone grade to the stative verbs applying to it. For instance, in example 5, the fact that Rabbit was extremely tired is signaled by the use of the extra-high tone grade on *hotosē*.

5.   Cufet hotosetowvtēs.
       cufe-t   Ø-**hotos**-et-ow-vtē-s
       rabbit-ind_subj   3persII-**tired_e_grd**-ss-aux_vb-rp-dec
       'Rabbit was really tired.'

When the stative verb to which the extra-high tone grade applies is one in a string referring to the same subject, the grade is only found on those states that are intensely felt. If other states within the string of verbs are not so intensely felt, these do not show the changes associated with the extra-high tone grade. Example 6 presents a sentence in which Rabbit is feeling his tiredness very deeply, while registering his hunger and warmth at a more usual level. In this case, the extra-high tone grade is applied only to *hotosē* 'tired' and is not to be found on *elvwē* 'hungry' or *hayē* 'hot.'

6.   Cufet vkerricat, "Cvlvwēt, cvhiyēt, cvhotosēs," kowvtēs.
       cufe-t   vkerric-at   cv-lvw-ē-t   cv-hiy-ē-t
       rabbit-ind_subj   thinking_about-sub   1SII-hungry-stat-ss   1SII-hot-stat-ss
       cv-**hotos**-ē-s   kow-Ø-vtē-s
       1SII-**tired_e_grd**-stat-dec   think-3S-rp-dec
       'Rabbit thought, "I'm hungry, I'm hot, and I'm really tired."'

In example 6, the most stressed state of being occurs last in the string. This is a pattern that appears frequently in narratives when one wants to stress something—that element either appears at the beginning or end of a line of speech. In this way, it stands out for the listener's attention. As you listen to spoken Mvskoke, it should be easy to tell when a speaker has used the extra-high tone grade. However, as there are no special diacritic marks to show that the tone height is quite high or that the vowel is even longer than a normal long vowel, you will have to use your intuition about the use of the extra-high tone grade when reading Mvskoke narratives. For the most part, Mvskoke speakers will use the extra-high tone grade to specifically emphasize states of being that affect the characters and/or flow of events in a narrative. You will find that the kind of points that Mvskoke speakers emphasize in this way are quite similar to those emphasized by English speakers, so trust in your abilities to determine whether particular verb states or durations are important in the narrative as you read Mvskoke.

On the CD included with the book, there are several examples of verbs affected by the extra-high tone grade, particularly within "Attending Dances" on track 4. In this narrative, you will hear Linda using the extra-high tone grade as she speaks about feeling good when she attends dances or thinks about young people carrying on tradition. Pay attention to tracks 53, 55, and 61, each of which comes from "Attending Dances" and in which the extra-high tone grade affected verbs are clearly discernable. There are further examples of the extra-high tone grade throughout other portions of the CD as well, so do not be surprised if you hear verbal forms that stand out because of the length, high tone, and nasalization of the vowel.

Narrative Conjunctions

Just as in English narratives, Mvskoke speakers have several ways to connect portions of their narratives together. In this section, we will present examples that oftentimes will be more than one sentence long, so as to show how these conjunctions serve to keep the narrative flowing across clausal and sentence boundaries. While we will discuss how these conjunctions work to keep narratives such as stories going, you should keep in mind that these same conjunctions are used in general speech, particularly when speakers are connecting several turns of talk or are constructing extended segments of discourse.

One of the most commonly used means of showing that segments of speech are connected is to rely on the switch-reference marking system to relate the subjects. It is quite common for speakers to produce several clauses in a row, with only the final one having the verb marked with the

declarative, interrogative, or directive suffix. Each of the verbs coming
before the final verb ends with a switch-reference marker, showing how
its subject relates to that of the final, marked verb.

This structure appears in stories or other narratives where a speaker's
ability to keep going is fairly certain, for the speaker must get to the final
verb in order to make all of the relationships among the subjects and
verbs that have come before it completely obvious. Thus, if a speaker is
concerned that his or her turn will be cut short, the speaker will generally
stick with marking each verb for mode (declarative, interrogative, or
directive), so that listeners will know what has happened to whom in each
instance, even if the speaker is interrupted at some point. When the
speaker is comfortable that his or her turn will not be cut short, however,
he or she may create strings of discourse like that shown in example 7.

7.   Hofonof Cufet arvtēt.
       "cvlvwēt, cvhiyēt, cvhotosēs," kowet.
       "stofvn cokon likat hehcit, fekhonnvhanis," Cufe kicvtēs.
       hofon-of   cufe-t   ar-Ø-vtē-t
       long_ago_e_grd-during rabbit-ind_subj go_about_(1)_l_grd-3pers-rp-ss
       cv-lvw-ē-t   cv-hiy-ē-t   cv-hotos-ē-s   kow-Ø-et
       1SII-hungry- 1SII-hot-   1SII-tired_e_grd-stat-ss   think-3pers-ss
        stat-ss   stat-ss
       stofvn   coko-n   Ø-hehc-i-t   fekhonn-vhan-i-s   cufe
       when   house-ind_obj 3persII-see<hgr>-1S-ss stop-intent-1S-dec rabbit
       kic-Ø-vtē-s
       think-3pers-rp-dec
       'A long time ago, Rabbit was going around.
       "I'm hungry, I'm hot, and I'm really tired," he thought.
       "When I see a house I will stop," Rabbit said.'

In this and other multiclause examples that follow, each clause is
given its own line. The ends of some clauses are marked with commas,
indicating that the intonation of such a clause marks it as one that is part
of a larger sentence. Other clause ends are marked with a period, question mark, or exclamation point, not because each is a completely formed
sentence (remember, the verbs are not necessarily marked for subject, tense,
or mode), but because they are pronounced with an intonation like that one
hears given to a complete sentence. The same convention is followed in the

TABLE 9.1. Mvskoke Narrative-Conjunction and Transition Words

Mvskoke Conjunction	English Translation
ehen	um, uh
monkv	so, therefore
momet/mowet	and (with the same subject in the following clause)
momen/mowen	and (with a different subject in the following clause)
momis/mowis	but, however

English translation of each clause. Despite the punctuation, it should be remembered that the speaker has not completed the entire clause chain until the clause containing the final, fully inflected verb is produced.

Mvskoke also has several words that may be used to connect sections of narrative or to mark transitions between sections or sentences within a narrative. These words are used in ways that are nearly identical to the use of their translations in English narratives. Some speakers also appear to use these words as a means of keeping the floor while taking time to formulate their next utterance, much as English speakers use the interjections "um," "uh," or "eh." These hesitations allow a speaker time to construct his or her next statement before making it.

Table 9.1 provides a list of the narrative-conjunction words commonly used in Mvskoke speech. The translations are shown to the right of the Mvskoke words. These words may be used to begin entirely new sentence structures or to transition between clauses within the same sentence. As you listen to the conversations included on the CD, you will hear each of these conjunctions used by both Linda and Bertha as they compose their narratives.

Ehen is an interjection used within and between clauses. This interjection allows a speaker to compose his or her next statement, much as its English equivalents do. The longer segments of narrative spoken by Linda in "Food Preparation" (track 5) on the CD contain several instances where she uses *ehen*. In this portion of the CD, Bertha is asking Linda about how she prepares several types of traditional foods. Linda's answers are quite detailed and, as you might expect, Linda takes care to see that the information she is relating is correct. This causes her to use interjections such as *ehen*, um, and ah (the latter two may or may not be intrusions from English) in order to choose her words carefully and ensure that she is saying what she intends. Tracks 65, 67, and 71 present Linda's responses to Bertha's questions about making dried beef, sour corn bread, and dried corn, and *ehen* occurs frequently in these individual tracks.

Monkv does not appear in the conversations on the CD. However, it is commonly used in narratives and sentences when an action derives from something that had happened previously. For instance, the sentence in 8 would follow those presented in example 7.

8.   Monkv, stofvn Cufet Nokose encoko likat heciset, ohyvkvpvtēs.
       monkv   stofvn   cufe-t   nokose   en-coko   lik-at
       so   when   rabbit-ind_subj   bear   3persII-house   be_located-sub
       Ø-hec-Ø-is-et   Ø-ohyvkvp-Ø-vtē-s
       3persII-see-3pers-recent-ss   3persII-walk_toward_(1)-3pers-rp-dec
       'So, when Rabbit saw Bear's house there, he walked toward it.'

In this case, given what Rabbit had thought to himself in the sentence in example 7, it makes perfect sense that Rabbit would take the action described in example 8. In this case, *monkv* shows the relationship between what had just been discussed in the sentence from example 7 and what is being described in example 8.

Monkv may also appear between clauses within the same sentence. This occurs in example 9, which follows the sentence from example 8.

9.   Nokoset Cufen coko ehomvn heciset, monkv yossvtēs.
       nokose-t   cufe-n   coko   ehomv-n   Ø-hec-Ø-is-et
       bear-ind_subj   rabbit-ind_obj   house   in_front-obl   3persII-see-3pers-
                                                                              recent-ss

       monkv   y-Ø-oss-Ø-vtē-s
       so   dir-3persII-go_out_(1)-3pers-rp-dec
       'Bear saw Rabbit in front of his house, so he went out.'

Again, the clause introduced by *monkv* follows logically from the clause that precedes it. If Bear had not seen Rabbit in front of his house, then he might not have had any other reason to go outside.

The conjunctions *momet/mowet* and *momen/mowen* are marked to show that the subject of the clause they open is the same as or different from that in the clause immediately preceding it. These two conjunctions are used in the narrative segment in example 10, which follows the narrative structure already begun in examples 7, 8, and 9. The more direct translation of the clauses is presented in the twelfth line of the example. The translation presented in the thirteenth line deletes the second "and" (*momen*) in order to make the sentence less like a run-on in English. If you work with many texts or written documents, you may find it to be more stylistically pleasing to overlook *momet* and *momen* occasionally if you are translating these items into English. In Mvskoke, however, the formation of fairly long clause chains linked together with *momet* and/or *momen* is both permissible and stylistically pleasing.

10. Nokose Cufe vsēken,
       momet "likepvs ci!" kicen.
       momen Cufe okat, "mvto, vnhesse," kicvtēs.
       nokose-Ø   cufe-Ø   Ø-vsēk-Ø-en
       bear-def_subj   rabbit-def_obj   3persII-greet-3pers-ds
       mome-t   lik-ep-vs   ci   Ø-kic-Ø-en
       and-ss   sit-ctre-imper   emph   3persII-say-3pers-ds
       mome-n   cufe-Ø   Ø-ok-Ø-at   mvto   vn-hesse
       and-ds   rabbit-def_subj 3persII-say-3pers-sub thank_you   1SII-friend
       Ø-kic-Ø-vtē-s
       3persII-say-3pers-rp-dec
       'Bear greeted Rabbit and said, "Sit down!" and Rabbit said, "Thank you, my friend."'
       'Bear greeted Rabbit and said, "Sit down!" Rabbit said, "Thank you, my friend."'

It may seem a little odd that the different subject suffix appears on the verbs in the first two clauses, yet the conjunction introducing the second clause has the same subject suffix. Remember that the same or different subject marker on the verb indicates whether the subject performing that action is the same as the subject performing the activity of the main verb in the sentence. Bear is greeting Rabbit and inviting him to sit down, but it is Rabbit who is saying "thank you" at the end of the sentence. Thus, the first two verbs are marked with the different subject suffix, but because it is Bear performing both activities in the first and second clauses, the conjunction between these uses the same subject suffix.

You were introduced to one means of forming sentences implying the conjunction "but" in the last chapter. A second manner of creating

sentences with this conjunction is to use the word *momis/mowis* to introduce the object clause. A sentence using this construction is shown in
example 11, which continues the narrative from examples 7 through 10.

11.   Nokose okat, "hompetv cehayvhanit,
       mowis vpeswv vlkēn hompitos."
       nokose-Ø   Ø-ok-Ø-at   hompetv-Ø   ce-hay-vhan-i-t
       bear-def_subj 3persII-say-3pers-sub food-def_obj 2SII-make-intent-1S-ss
       mowis   vpeswv   vlkē-n   homp-i-t-o-s
       but   meat   only-ind_obj   eat-1S-ss-aux_vb-dec
       'Bear said, "I will make you some food, but I eat only meat."'

With these conjunctions, you are now able to construct and follow
long stretches of discourse in which the relationships between topics and
ideas are maintained across clause boundaries. The constructions presented in this chapter are commonly used, so you should hear them nearly
every time that you interact with Mvskoke speakers. Some speakers will use
these constructions more than others, depending upon how capable as
speakers they are, the context within which they are speaking, and the topic
about which they are conversing. You will also find that some speakers
use some of these constructions and conjunctions more than others, just
as speakers of English tend to have different patterns of use for joining or
establishing the connections between clauses. As you speak Mvskoke with
others, you will find which conjunctions and constructions are most comfortable for you.

Vocabulary

GOVERNMENT

English	Mvskoke
town	tvlofv
clan	em vliketv
leader	enhomahtv
chief	mēkko
House of Kings	coko enmēkko

House of Warriors	coko entvstenvke
district	ēkvntvckv
or	'kvntvckv
band	meteliketv
chairman, chairperson	ohliketv-ohlikv
vice-chairman, vice-chairperson	ohliketv-ohlikv-vpoktv
general council	nak-vfastv
council meeting	nak-vfastv-emetohkvlketv
law	vhakv
constitution	vhakv-empvtakv
judge	fvccēcv
council house	nvkaftvlke encoko

Verbs

English	Mvskoke
to debate	nake setenkerretv
to elect someone	este ohmelletv
to vote	cokv ensatetv
to lead people	este enhomahtetv
to follow a leader	enhomahtv vcvkkayetv
to decide	fvccēcetv
to guess	mohmes kometv
to be elected	ohmelletv
to be honest	ēfvccēcetv
to be greedy	encakē
to be brave	fekhvnkē
or	fekhvmkē
to be strict	fetektvnēceko

Exercises

Exercise 1

Using the sentences in examples 7 through 11 above as the beginning of your story, complete the narrative concerning Rabbit and Bear. How do you think Rabbit responds to Bear's statement that he only cooks meat? Do you think Rabbit manages to get something edible from Bear, or does he eat meat, too, in this story? Does Rabbit play a trick on Bear while he is visiting him, or is he simply glad for Bear's generosity? Does Rabbit do something in return for Bear's generosity? These are some questions you may think about having your story answer—or you may focus on different topics in your version. Remember that Rabbit is usually, but not always, a tricky character, so it is permissible to have him do something mischievous in your story.

EXERCISE 2

Translate the following sentences from English to Mvskoke. After you have translated each sentence individually, rework this collection of sentences with the conjunctions and transitions presented in this chapter to make them flow in the way you would expect a speaker to produce them when talking with others. Be prepared to say your version of the narrative out loud in class, so that your classmates can hear how you think someone might produce it. Then, be prepared to discuss differences in phrasing and/or how your and your classmates' use of conjunctions and transitions differ. If your classmates created narratives that sound different from yours, do these make you react differently to the various characters and their actions?

1. Yesterday, I went to talk with the chief, who is honest and kind.
2. When I got to the council house, he was talking with a strict judge.
3. The chief stopped talking to the judge and greeted me.
4. I asked them about the new law that is going to be debated by the House of Warriors.
5. The judge said it is a good one.
6. The judge said the law will make our police stronger.
7. Thieves will be caught and jailed faster.
8. The chief said he had to think about it more before he decided.
9. I don't know if the law is good.
10. I will listen to the debate and will decide after I talk with my relatives and friends.

EXERCISE 3

Working with a classmate, create a conversation about some topic that interests you both. Be certain that each of you has extended periods of speech requiring the use of some of the conjunctions, transitions, or other narrative-connecting devices covered in this chapter. Rehearse your conversation so that you can perform it in front of your fellow students, should your teacher ask you to do so. If you need assistance with finding vocabulary words, it is recommended that you consult the glossary of this textbook and *Beginning Creek*, the Loughridge and Hodge dictionary (1890 [1964]), or the Martin and Mauldin dictionary (2000). For those of you who know other speakers of Mvskoke, you may also ask them for assistance with words or phrasing.

EXERCISE 4

The following are loose English translations of the lines in the conversation "Shopping for Groceries" (track 2 on the CD). The individual speakers' turns are recorded on tracks 9 through 32, should you want to listen to them individually. For each of the English lines (which do not indicate hesitations or all conjunctions), provide a Mvskoke translation. If you need assistance with vocabulary, recommended sources are: the glossaries in this text and *Beginning Creek*; Loughridge and Hodge's dictionary (1890 [1964]); and Martin and Mauldin's dictionary (2000). If you know of fluent speakers of Mvskoke, you may also ask them for help with vocabulary and/or phrasing. The track on which each speaker's turn appears is shown in parentheses at the opening of each line. Once you have written out your translations, practice them so that you will be prepared to say them in class.

> (track 9) I am going to the store.
> (track 10) What are you going to buy?
> (track 11) I am going to get milk, butter, eggs, and meat. I don't know what kind of meat I'll get.
> (track 12) Get whatever we need.
> (track 13) We also need flour.
> (track 14) Make a list of what we need to buy.
> (track 15) Ok, I am going now.

(track 16) Ok, go ahead and go.

After Bertha has returned from the store.

(track 17) Are you just getting back from the store?

(track 18) Yes, I just got back. I just looked around.

(track 19) What were you going to buy?

(track 20) I was going to buy meat. I looked around to see what they had.

(track 21) Did you buy anything?

(track 22) Yes.

(track 23) What did it cost?

(track 24) Twenty-five dollars was what they said, and that's what I paid.

(track 25) That's ok. We will be eating it.

(track 26) I looked at the watermelons and cantaloupes. They weren't very ripe and I didn't get any.

(track 27) We will wait awhile for those.

(track 28) You wanted beans, but they didn't have any.

(track 29) They will sell them. Just wait.

(track 30) The Farm-Market usually has some. I will go and see on Saturday.

(track 31) They usually have a variety. Buy what you think I will like.

(track 32) I will do that.

Listening Exercises

Use the Mvskoke translation you produced in exercise 4 as you work on this exercise. Listen closely to the conversation on the CD. Are there differences between what you have written and what the speaker says? If so, write these out. Do you understand why the speaker phrased things in the way that she did? Do you think your version would work just as well? If there are differences in the vocabulary used, check the words that are different. Do these words mean exactly the same things? Are there differences in what is being implied or said because of the use of slightly different vocabulary or grammatical constructions? Be ready to talk about these questions in class.

Listen to the conversation "Watching TV" (track 3) on the CD. The individual speakers' turns are located on tracks 33 through 46. Write down the conversation in Mvskoke. It may be helpful to review any notes you took on this conversation for the exercises in chapters 1 and 3. You may need to listen to the tracks several times to do this, but that is to be expected, particularly if you are not used to hearing extended discourse in Mvskoke. Once you have written down the Mvskoke version of the conversation, provide a loose translation in English. Do not worry about providing a morpheme-by-morpheme analysis—simply listen and try to understand the conversation as it is going. You may work with fellow students on this, as various people may be better able to interpret different portions of the conversation. In the end, come up with as complete a transcript of the Mvskoke as possible and a full translation in English.

Government

The Muscogee (Creek) and Seminole Nations of Oklahoma share traditional customs and language. The Seminoles were once part of the Lower Creeks but became dissatisfied with the Upper Creeks and began moving to Florida. Once there, they reestablished their tribal towns and began governing themselves separately from the Creeks. After they moved to Florida, they became known as the Seminoles (meaning 'wild' or 'runaway').

Tribal government is sometimes as complex as the United States federal government. Today the Seminoles and Muskogees have an elected chief, but the authority lies in the legislative body of the tribal government. Within Muscogee (Creek) Nation government, this body is called the Creek Council, and among the Seminoles it is known as the General Council.

Before removal of the Creeks and Seminoles from the Southeast, their governments were different. The Creeks had the House of Kings and the House of Warriors. The House of Kings was like the legislative body of the tribe, enacting laws and overseeing the policy of the tribe. The House of Warriors was the protector of the tribe, defending the tribe when necessary and playing a strong role in discussions when warfare or disagreements were topics.

The Seminoles appointed their chiefs before removal. Well-respected men from the different towns might be considered for the post, with one of these being selected by the people during talks in their towns. The same system was used to decide who would represent each town in large councils, so if a man was chosen at one time, it did not mean that he would represent the town all of the time or even at the next meeting.

Removal from their homelands to Indian Territory (Oklahoma) caused many changes for both tribes, including changes in their government. The federal government has been responsible for many of these changes. Among the latest were new constitutions written for both tribes in the 1970s, outlining how each tribe would organize its government from then on.

MUSCOGEE (CREEK) NATION

There were forty-four tribal towns within the Creek Tribe before Removal. The town was a village lying within a fenced area that was the living area for town members. This area contained several types of buildings, including some for storing grain, as well as houses and areas for planting and cooking. Also in this enclosure was the town's ceremonial ground and ball-playing field.

Each tribal town had its own system of government, made up of elders and respected male citizens. These town councils would make decisions about issues affecting individual towns and the families within them. A member of the town council would be selected to represent the town at the larger tribal meetings. At these meetings of the House of Kings and House of Warriors, issues relevant to all people and towns among the Creeks were debated.

Some of the tribal towns that came to Oklahoma from the Southeast during Removal are: Alabama; Arbeka; Arbekoce; Atusse; Ceyane; Hvccvcvpv; Kecopotake; Locvpokv; and Nuyakv. Today, the Creek Nation has sixteen ceremonial grounds, many of which have connections with these and other towns that were reestablished in Oklahoma after Removal. The Seminole Nation has one ground, which also has ties to older Seminole communities that were removed to Oklahoma.

After removal in 1867, a new constitution was written that made provisions for the offices of a Principal Chief, Assistant Chief, and National Council. At that time, the federal government had the responsibility of choosing who would fill each of these positions, so the Muskogee people did not have much say in their own government. In 1871 the constitution was revised to allow citizens to elect the Principal and Assistant Chiefs and the members of the National Council.

Today, the Creeks have a chief elected by registered tribal voters. The legislative body of the Creek government, the Creek Council, is also elected by the people. The Council has a speaker who oversees the meeting of the Council. Within the legislature, elected officials are assigned to committees that consider various matters affecting the tribe. If you have a problem, you have to go to a meeting of the appropriate committee to present your concerns. The committee discusses the issue and decides whether it should be presented to the larger Creek Council. If the matter is worthy of consideration by the Council, the representatives vote to make it an agenda item in a future Council meeting.

The Creek Nation is divided into districts. A representative is elected every four years from each district as the district's representative on the Creek Council. The Council meets in Okmulgee, which is the capitol of the Muscogee (Creek) Nation. The tribal headquarters, housing all of the executive offices, and the museum are located in Okmulgee.

The Muscogee (Creek) Nation has twelve active ceremonial grounds and three Euchee (Yuchi) grounds. The Creek grounds are: Alabama, Arbeka, Fish Pond, Greenleaf, Hickory Ground, Hillabee, Nuyaka, Okfuskee, Oyogofke, New Tulsa, and Pokkon Tallahassee. The Euchee grounds are Duck Creek, Iron Post, and Kellyville. All are located within the boundaries of the Muscogee (Creek) Nation.

SEMINOLE NATION OF OKLAHOMA

Prior to Removal to Indian Territory, the Seminoles were led by chiefs. The chiefs were selected by groups of elderly and/or respected men from each town. These men were chosen to represent their towns because of their good judgment and knowledge of the results coming from previous decisions and leaders.

The Seminoles were forced to move to Indian Territory after the Second Seminole War. Not all Seminole people moved, however; about three hundred to five hundred Seminoles stayed in Florida by evading the government soldiers responsible for rounding up all those who would move. Today, the descendents of these Seminoles make up the Seminole Tribe of Florida. The Seminoles of Florida have become a very prosperous tribe and now live on three reservations, headquartered in the Miami area.

The Seminoles who were moved to Indian Territory set up their government by dividing into Tribal Bands. They had fourteen of these bands, with two being made up of descendents of former slaves, called Freed-men Bands. Representatives from all of these bands made up the General Council. A chairman was selected from the representatives to lead and direct the Council.

In 1969, a new constitution was written to make provisions for the election of a Chief, Vice Chief, and members of the General Council. The people elected to these positions were to hold them for four years. The constitution also defined the actions of the Executive Department and the General Council. The General Council's objectives are to carry on business to improve the social, health, and economic welfare of tribal members and to promote economic development. The Executive Department carries out the decisions set forth by the General Council.

Representatives are responsible for meeting with band members to discuss business that will help the tribe to grow and meet members' needs. In turn, the representatives let the General Council know about the needs of people from their band. Members of the Council work together to meet the needs of the tribe. Once the Council agrees on what is important and sets priorities, Council members meet with members of the Executive Department to let them know what needs to be done. The Executive Department puts these plans into place and meets with other agencies that can assist them with meeting these goals, many of which are part of the Oklahoma state government or the federal government.

The Seminole Nation is located in Seminole County, Oklahoma. The executive offices are located in Wewoka, Oklahoma. While the Executive Department offices are in Wewoka, other tribal offices are located in Seminole, Oklahoma. The tribe still owns 320 acres of trust land (land that is under tribal control) south of Seminole. They have some of their programs located on this property. The Seminoles also have one active ceremonial ground, Cheyvhv (Gar Creek), located within the boundaries of the Seminole Nation.

Suggested Readings

Readers interested in knowing more about narrative-structuring devices in Mvskoke are directed to Bell (1983, 1984, 1985) and Hardy (2005). Each of these sources presents an analysis of at least one Mvskoke narrative. The analysis covers both the grammatical structures that help with cohesion and the stylistic features of the narrative(s) that make them distinctly Mvskoke texts. The content of the narratives is also interesting and, particularly in each of Bell's analyses, leads her to discuss cultural factors that affect the ways in which the speakers construct their discourse.

Those interested in Mvskoke narrative forms as represented in Mvskoke-language texts are directed again to Bell (1983, 1984, 1985) and also to Speck (1907), Swanton (1928b: 639–56), Innes (2004b), Martin, Mauldin, and McGirt (2004), and Martin, Mauldin, and McCarty (2005). Bell's writings (1983, 1984, 1985) present an analysis of narrative structures found in the formal speeches presented at the stompgrounds. These have a very distinctive form of speech, an example of which can be heard on disc B, included with *Beginning Creek*, track 25. The content and organization of topics in this type of oratory is closely tied to the ceremonial context in which it is produced.

Speck's (1907), Swanton's (1928b), and Innes's (2004b) texts provide examples of Mvskoke songs. Speck's (1907) work covers a range of song types, from those one would hear at a stompdance (like that found on track 8 of the CD included with this textbook) to the kind used by doctors in the healing process. The notations used to write out the songs in all three works are not in the Mvskoke orthography. Instead, Speck uses a technical linguistic writing system. Swanton (1928b) varies between a system similar to Speck's and the systems used by earlier writers, who often relied on English writing conventions to represent Mvskoke sounds. The one song in Innes's (2004b) chapter, which is taken from Swanton, presents the spelling of words in the system he used. Speck provides musical notations for some of the songs he discusses, and all three works provide good cultural background and description so as to situate the use of these songs for the reader.

At this time, the only large collection of stories in Mvskoke is Martin, Mauldin, and McGirt (2004). This book is a collection of stories written out by Earnest Gouge, one of John Swanton's informants. The book makes available Earnest's stories, the originals of which are housed in the Smithsonian Institution. Martin, Mauldin, and McCarty (2005) maintain a website on which copies of documents written in Mvskoke (including letters, pages from diaries, etc.) may be viewed. Sound recordings of readers reciting some of these items are also available on the website.

For those who are able to travel, a vast collection of Mvskoke stories is archived at the American Philosophical Library in Philadelphia. Mary R.

Haas's notes, which are kept there, contain over two hundred narratives she collected in Mvskoke during her fieldwork in Oklahoma in the 1930s to 1940s. These narratives are currently being prepared for publication by Jack Martin, and it is hoped that they will be widely available soon.

A final source containing a single story, the Mvskoke migration legend, is to be found in Gatschet (1884: 237–43). The text is written in an old linguistic phonetic notation, so may be difficult to decipher for those used to Mvskoke orthography. A translation, taken from a previously prepared German translation, is offered on pages 244–51. The commentary that Gatschet, an anthropologist, provides earlier in the book gives the reader interesting insights into Muskogee history and culture (as understood at the time) and helps to situate the text.

There are two highly regarded and varied collections of Mvskoke stories translated into English. Both of these works (Tuggle [1973] and Swanton [1929: 2–117]) present stories collected in the late 1800s and early 1900s. The stories range in scope from myths about the origin of corn to entertaining (and enlightening) stories about the escapades of Rabbit and other characters. Betty Mae Jumper (1994) presents stories of the Florida Seminoles in English, which readers may be interested in comparing with the stories in the collections by Swanton and Tuggle. The parallels and differences are interesting, demonstrating the importance of historic events and environment in the creation and retention of oral narratives in these communities.

Further information about the governmental structure of the Muscogee (Creek) and Seminole Nations of Oklahoma is available in Moore (1988, 1990), O'Brien (1989: 119–37), Opler (1937, 1952), Sattler (1987), and Spoehr (1941b, 1941c). These sources provide information about the governmental structures of the Muskogee Creeks and Seminoles just after Removal (in Sattler and, to a lesser extent, Moore [1988]), through the period of reorganization (in Opler 1937, 1952, and Spoehr, 1941b, 1941c), to the current period (in O'Brien and Moore [1990]). The various changes that the two nations have had to make in their governmental structures and styles since Removal to Oklahoma are described in excellent detail across these sources.

CHAPTER TEN

Discourse

To some extent, this chapter will move away from the type of material that the previous chapters have covered. In those chapters, you were acquainted with the most pertinent features of Mvskoke sentence structure and pronunciation. At this point, we will discuss how these phonological, morphological, and grammatical features are used as people put together constructions that are longer than single sentences. Constructions of this type are called **discourses**.

There are several kinds of discourses in which Mvskoke speakers take part. You have been introduced to several of these in this textbook and in *Beginning Creek*. Stories and conversations are among the various types of discourses created by Mvskoke speakers, and you have been presented with several examples of these two forms of discourse in these two textbooks. When you went through exercises in which you were to narrate stories, listened to the conversations on the CD, or created conversations of your own, you were performing these discourses. It is our hope that these types of exercises, along with the information provided in this chapter, will enable you to participate in several kinds of discourses with Mvskoke speakers.

The first discourse that we present in this chapter is the story about Turtle's shell, which you have been asked to listen to several times now on track 89 of the CD. You may notice that the version told on the CD is slightly different from the version printed here. Storytelling among Mvskoke speakers is just as creative a process as it is for English-speaking storytellers, so it should be no surprise that every time this story is told it will be a little different. Still, many of the words and, certainly, the order of actions described in the two versions are similar, so you should be able to follow the flow of the spoken version once you have become familiar with this printed version.

You will notice that Linda chants or sings at one point in the story. Turtle is given a powerful song to heal himself, presented in the short lines in the written version. If you are slightly confused by the words following *cvto* in each line, this is because they are not completely inflected verbs but are, instead, only the verbal roots. The first word, *sokoso*, is a partial reduplication (repetition) of the verb stem in *vsofotketv* 'to rub against.' In creating the form found in the song, the first vowel has been dropped, the consonant /k/ has been substituted for the /f/ in the stem, and the first two syllables are then pronounced with a repetition of the first syllable. This rhythmic and poetic manipulation of words is common in both English and Mvskoke song lyrics. The second line of the song finds the root from *liketv* 'to sit, be located (of one)' repeated twice. Again, this makes for a powerful poetic phrasing in the lyric.

Linda says that there are several morals to this story, each of which is important for understanding how one is to interact with other beings in life. First, Turtle asks for help from the Creator in his time of need, and the Creator comes through for him. This tells you that the Creator listens to all beings within the world, even the smallest of animals, and is responsive to calls for help. However, even though the Creator listens to Turtle's request for assistance, Turtle is left with a reminder of his arrogance and lack of attention to the women's directions. The pattern on the Turtle's back is evidence of his self-centeredness in the past, which he carries for all to see.

Locv Folahpv Nakonvkucen

Hofonof Locvt aretowat coko liken roret. Hoktvke hokkolet vce hocvkat welaken tempen vhoyet vpelhoyetomen, Locv keco likan roret, vhvrakvtēs. Vhvraketowan, hoktē hvnket yacekot Locv vharan "vcen arekos!" kicvtēs. Mowis Locv vharet monkan mv hoktētot ētimvt aret "ceyacekot!" kicet Locv vwikvtēs. Locv aret rvlaket keco hueran, elvwētot vce hockē vwenayet vhvretowan. Mv hoktē Locv hvtvm hecetowis, enhomecētomis, ohkueket kecvpen eset espvccetv mēcvtēs.

Locv cetakkose hahket, "Nakstowen heyv cvcetakkosēte? Vnnokkētos," vkerricet. "Ēmērkv vwikvs!" vkerricet. Ayat, etolvcce rakkē wakken ralikvtēs.

"Ennokkē ocit, stowen hericvhaniyv? Hiyowat cvlvhanetos." vkerricenowat. Etohwvlvpkekot, vyekot, likof enhonrkv hvlwen vtotvrēs. Mv likof Locv okat, "Cvwvnhēcicvhaneckv?" makvtēs.

Onvkv emvlakat okat, hvmmakecenowat yvn yvhiketv, hvlwe kicvtēs. "Hvmmakvs!" kicvtēs.

"Cvto sokoso,
cvto li li,
cvto sokoso,
cvto li li,
cvto sokoso,
cvto li li,
cvto sokoso,
cvto li li"
maket okenowat Locv likofv eccvrēs. Kicvtēs. Mowen Locv okat,
"cvto sokoso,
cvto li li,"
maket osticvtēs. Ehvrpetat hvlvlatkosen etelicvtēs. Mvn Locv hvrpe etekvpvkēt etelicvtat kerkēn owvtēs.

The next story is one that would have been told primarily for entertainment purposes. In this story, Rabbit is definitely in his role as Trickster. He offers to do something that seems nice, yet he finds a way to get what he wants out of the deal. In the end, one is left wondering how anyone would trust Rabbit!

Cufe Nak-vhockuce Hompes

Cufe nene wakkan arvtēs. Coko likat hoyanat nak-vhockuce ocen hēcet hoyanet, hvfvpeton hecvtēs. Mvn vkerricat fekhonniyet. "Hvfvpat enhvsvtecin ceyacv?" Cufet ocvn vpohit. Cufe vnoksēt mowis makenowat, "Enhvsvtecarēs." "Ehi," ocvt Cufen emvyoposkvtēs.

Vkerrickv ocet aretowat. Nake lokcē ocan hompetvn yacet vkerrickv ocēt tates. Emetektvniken, mv nettv hvsvtēcat, omvlkvn nakrvfkv enlokcē ocat, omvlkvn lokepet vyēpvtēs. "Mvn hvsvteckvtv?" nak-vhockuce ocvt kohmetos. Cufet yefolkekot, vyēpvtēs. Nakonvkucetontos.

The final story in this chapter begins with the sentences from examples 7–11 in chapter 9. This is another old-time story, describing yet another one of Rabbit's exploits. In this one, however, Rabbit does not come out ahead, because of his trickiness and ego. Instead, he pays the price for being too proud and self-confident for his own good.

The most obvious moral content of this story is that one should always treat unique powers and knowledge with great respect. As Rabbit's experience shows, to not do so can lead to painful and even fatal consequences. One should also not let pride lead one to do things that he or she has not been trained to do. Instead, one should acknowledge the special skills and knowledge of others, seek training from appropriate teachers if one wants to learn how to do something, and use that knowledge with wisdom and discipline. These are good rules to live by, and it is through stories such as this one that the Mvskoke elders transmitted these rules to younger generations.

Cufet Nokosen Hompetv Hayes

Hofonof Cufet arvtēt. "Cvlvwēt, cvhiyēt, cvhotosēs," kowet. "Stofvn cokon likat hehcit, fekhonnvhanis," Cufe kicvtēs. Monkv, stofvn Cufet Nokose encoko likat heciset, ohyvkvpvtēs. Nokoset Cufen coko ehomvn heciset, monkv yossvtēs. Nokose Cufe vsēken. Momet, "Likepvs ci!" kicen, momen Cufe okat, "Mvto, vnhesse," kicvtēs.

Nokose okat, "Hompetv cehayvhanit, mowis vpeswv vlkēn hompitos." Cufet okat, "Vpeswv henrētos. Cvlvwēt, omvlkvn hompvhanis," Cufe Nokosen akicvtēs. Nokose okat, "Vnhesse likepvs. Cokofvn ecēyvhanit, hompetv pohayvhanit. Rvtvrēs," kicvtēt, mowet cokofvn ecēyes.

Cufe coko ehomvn liket, hecvtēs. "Cvnockelēt, yvkvpvrit, vhoneciyvrēs," kowet. Mowet Cufe Nokose oponvyetvn pohet komvtēs. "Nake?" Cufe vpohen, momis Nokose vyoposkekotos. Cufe vhvoke ohvyet, cokofvn hecet, Nokosen iemapohvtēs.

Nokoset ohhompetv ehomvn huerat, yvhikvtēs. "Yvhiketv cvyacet, kerrvhanis," Cufe komvtēs. Hvte, Nokosen ēwarvtēt mowis catekot, hvkihkekot, vpeswv eset nak-svkmorēcv ofvn wakecvtēs. Cufe hēcofvn, Nokose vpeswvn svkmorecvtēs.

Stofvn Nokose vpeswvn esvtet cvfeknētos. Mowen Cufet Nokosen hvmkvn hecvtēn mowis lvfkatis lekwetis hecekvtēs. Nokose Cufen vpelet, okat, "Hompvs ci!" kicvtēs. Cufe hompet, Nokosen emponvyet. Vpeswv sulkēn hompvkvtēs. Cufet Nokosen enkvpakofvn, okat, "Pakse vncokopericeckvrēs. Vpeswv sulkē ocatis, vpeswv noricvhanis," kicvtēs. Nokose "Hēnrētos! Pakse cencokopericarēs," akicvtēs.

Cufe yvkvpofvn, Nokose yvhiketv enaken yvhikvtēs. Yvhiketv omvlkvn kerrekot, mowis ēnaoricekvtēs. Nokose vpeswv hompetvn kowofvt, Cufe vpelvtēs.

Rem paksen Nokose Cufen encokopericen, mowen Cufe okat, "Likepvs ci!" kicvtēn, etemponvyakvtēs. "Celvwēte?" Cufe Nokosen vpohis, mowen "Ehi, vpeswv cvyacetos," Nokose akicvtēs. "Likvs ci! Vpeswv sulkē svkmorecetv ocit. Hiyomat vpeswv sakmorecvhanis," Cufe kicet.

Cufe encoko ecēyet, ohhompetv ehomvn hueret, eslafkv fvskat atakkeset, mowet yvhiketvn yvhikvtēs. Yvhiketvn yvhiket osticofet hoyanat, Cufe esokson eslafkvn eslaffvtēs. "Oh!" Cufe selakket, mowis Cufe hvtvm ē-eslaffet, "Vnlekwē pvfnēn enwikvrēs," komvtēs. Ēwaret, ēwaret mēcvtēs. "Oh!" selakket, Cufe catat ocvtēs.

Nokose Cufe hvkihkan pohat, cokofv ecēyvtēs. Nokose Cufe okat, "Nake mēceckv? Cecatētos!" kicvtēs. Mowen Cufe okat, "Vpeswvn waris. Cehehcit, mowet mvn mēcit tayēt komis," kicvtēs. "Monks. Yvhiketvtis heleswvtis kerreckekotos. Ēwarenowat, ē-elēceckvrēs," kicvtēs. Nokose ekv norottet, Cufe encoko enkvpvkvtēs.

Nakonvkucetontos.

Vocabulary

STORY CHARACTERS AND OTHER ELEMENTS

English	*Mvskoke*
story, fairytale	nakonvkuce
story, tale, news	nakonvkv
tie-snake	estakwvnayv
turtle	locv
rabbit	cufe
buzzard	sule
buffalo	yvnvsv
bones	fone
mortar	kecvpe
pestle	keco
tree branch	etolvcce
blood	catv

Verbs

English	Mvskoke
to hit {I;II}	nvfketv
to crawl {I}	hvlketv
to annoy/bother {II}	naoricetv
to die (of one) {II}	eletv
to make fun of someone {I;II}	este nakhayetv
to return/come back (of one) {I;II}	rvlvketv
to be conceited, proud {II}	ēkvsvmetv
to be stupid {II}	nak-kerreko
to cry out, shout {I})	selakketv
to bleed {II}	catetv

Exercises

Exercise 1

Listen to the version of the story about Turtle's shell that Linda presents on track 89 on the CD included with this book. Compare the spoken version with the version presented in writing. What do you hear that is different? What parts are the same? In those things that are different between the two versions, do these changes radically alter the story or just point out features that Linda wanted to expand on in the spoken version? How will you change the story when you tell it?

Become familiar with the story and then try reciting it to another member of your class. Have your classmate do the same thing. Compare your two versions of the story with each other, then compare them with the version that Linda told on the CD. Again, what is the same and what is different? Which version do you like best? Why?

Exercise 2

Working from what you know of Rabbit's behavior, write a story about something he might have done. Your story can be as short as "Cufe Nak-vhockuce Hompes" or as long as "Cufe Nokosen Hompetv Hayes." In whatever you write about Rabbit, remember that he likes to play tricks but occasionally finds that his tricks actually benefit those he had hoped to outwit. As "Cufe Nak-vhockuce Hompes" demonstrates, though, he sometimes gets his own way. Be prepared to share your story with the rest of your classmates, both in written form and presented orally.

EXERCISE 3

Choose one of the Creek stories in Swanton's (1929) *Myths and Tales of the Southeastern Indians* or Tuggle's (1973) *Shem, Ham, and Japheth.* Try translating this story back into Mvskoke. What kinds of problems or difficulties do you have? What portions are easy? When you have it translated, present it to your class, both in written and spoken form. What do your classmates and teacher think of your translation? Does it sound like something Linda, Bertha, or another Mvskoke speaker would produce? If yes, why? If no, why not?

EXERCISE 4

What other kinds of life lessons or pieces of knowledge do you think Mvskoke elders want the younger generations to know? Choose one of the items that you think are important for younger people to know or understand and write a story in Mvskoke that communicates this knowledge. Be prepared to read it to your classmates and give them written copies. When you present them with the story, are they able to understand it? Do they think the message in your story is good to know? Did any of your classmates choose the same kind of issue for their story, too? Why?

   If your classmates are not certain that your message is important for younger Mvskoke people to know, why do you think that is? You might think about differences in cultural perspectives or differences that arise from socioeconomic, educational, or other differences between your own background and that of many Mvskoke people.

EXERCISE 5

Choose one of the conversations from tracks 2–6 on the CD and analyze it for use of transitions, switch-reference, and other discursive features that help a speaker create a meaningful discourse. Which devices do you find are used most in the conversation that you have chosen to investigate? Why do you think these particular devices are the ones used in this conversation? If you arranged the conversation differently (e.g., chopped it up more or had more or shorter turns for each speaker) do you think different devices would have been used? Why or why not?

Working with a fellow classmate, construct a conversation covering the same topic as one in any of the chapters of *Beginning Creek* or from tracks 2–6 on the CD. You may use some of the phrasings and/or turn-constructions that are already present in the conversation, or you may create it very differently. Be prepared to present your conversation in class and to discuss why you organized it in the way you did.

Exercise 6

Make up a story about some of the characters we have listed in the vocabulary for this chapter. (You may find ideas for stories about these characters in Martin, Mauldin and McGirt's (2004) *Totkv Mocuse*, Swanton's (1929) *Myths and Tales of the Southeastern Indians,* or Tuggle's (1973) *Shem, Ham, and Japheth*.) Do not simply copy any of the stories that you find in these sources, but create a new one yourself. The kinds of activities in which the characters Buffalo, Tie-snake, Buzzard, Turtle, and Rabbit participate in the stories contained in these other collections may give you ideas that you can use in your own story. You may create a teaching story, an entertaining story, or a story explaining how some aspect of these characters came into being. Be creative and have fun with this exercise.

Telling Stories

It was not an everyday occurrence for Muskogee men and women to sit around and tell stories, but sometimes people would do this when they visited with their neighbors. When guests came to visit and stayed most of the day or overnight, it was not uncommon for stories to be told for entertainment. Sometimes, too, stories were told by elders to younger people in order to make a point about life and behavior.

Snacks were usually offered when storytelling was going to take place. Sweet potatoes would be baked in an open fire or in the stove. Drinks like *sofke* and *vpvske* would be offered to everyone there. These drinks were made from dried corn. *Vpvske* was fixed by parching finely ground corn over coals and putting this in water with some kind of sweetener. *Sofke* was cooked and flavored with ash drippings. Before they were made into drinks, both the ground *vpvske* corn and *sofke* corn were kept in containers so they would stay dry and free of rot.

The kinds of stories that people told depended on what was happening at the time. People might gather for storytelling after a meeting or while visiting. The mood of the gathering set the tone for the types of stories that would be told. No matter what kind of mood people were in, there were always stories about animals that would fit.

The majority of stories are about animals: Rabbit for his crafty ways; Fox for being sly; Turtle for being slow. Stories about things that humans did were generally good for a laugh or for an educational or moral teaching. Even the animal stories had a moral. If you did not catch the moral the first time that you heard it, you might be told the story again another time. It was always good to think about what happened in the stories, because there was always a lesson.

The elders were very good about telling you a story that had a moral to it. They would tell you to think about it. They wanted you to be able to figure out what they wanted you to learn from the story. If you were unsure, you could ask an elder to tell the story again, or you could ask the elder what he or she thought about it. This was a very good way of teaching younger people to think for themselves, but also to ask the elders, who had much more knowledge and experience.

Life is about learning, whether it is from the experiences of animals or other people or experiences that you have. Reading or listening to someone tell about an incident or happening will help you learn. Always be a good listener, and you will learn something that will help you to grow as a person.

Suggested Readings

The majority of the literature that is relevant to the linguistic topic we discuss in this chapter was presented in the suggested readings section of chapter 9. Those more generally interested in the ways in which Native

Estahu[t]ke herake malekat vo. Seminole teaching a White Man's good things. *Lizzie D. Thomas Collection, Courtesy of the Oklahoma Historical Society. Negative #21104.56.*

American oral texts are structured—which has some relevance to the ways in which speakers indicate new, important, or background information— are referred to Hymes (1981, 1996, 2003), Tedlock (1983), and Wiget (1987). In each of these writings, the author demonstrates that speakers have linguistic means of highlighting new information and alerting a listener to when something different is being discussed. Some of the ways in which Mvskoke speakers weave together the portions of their texts, as demonstrated in the stories within this chapter, will be found to have correlates in the languages whose narratives are presented in the works by Hymes, Tedlock, and Wiget.

Narratives from other Southeastern groups may also be of interest to some readers. For those who would like to learn more about the narrative range among other groups, Kimball (1996) and Mould (2004) are good sources. Kimball presents some stories from the Koasati people, and Mould provides Choctaw tales. Both of these groups speak languages related to Mvskoke, and readers who have looked at the Creek tales in Swanton (1929) will find some of the motifs and topics are quite similar. However, the narratives in Kimball's and Mould's works are not mere facsimiles of any of the Creek stories, and they should be savored for their own beauty. Swanton (1929) also presents stories by groups besides the Creek, though none are given in the native language.

Issues of translation also come into play when one is interested in transcribing and presenting spoken language in a written form. As you have seen from your work on some of the exercises in this and earlier chapters, determining how and when to separate lines of text, as well as what punctuation (if any) to use to demarcate intonational or sentence-level divisions, are some of the features that come to the fore when one is writing down spoken discourse. Luthin (2002), Mattina (1987), and Mithun (2001) all grapple with these and other facets of producing printed versions of oral forms, as well as with how to translate oral narrative (e.g., closely or loosely, including showing hesitations or leaving them out, etc.).

This may also be a good opportunity to explore other types of discourse styles produced by Muskogee Creek and Seminole people. The work by the following authors covers a range of styles and topics, which some may find more and some less stimulating, depending on their personal interests. Joy Harjo (1990, 2000a, 2000b), Carolyn Dunn (2000; 2006; 2001, with Paula Gunn Allen), and Louis Oliver (1982, 1983, 1990) are well-respected, well-known Creek authors and poets. Their poetry and stories speak out on a wide range of issues, are at some times very challenging and at others easy to engage with, and are well worth exploring. Some of their writings make reference to Muskogee traditions, and they occasionally include Mvskoke phrases and words.

A number of academic writers of Muskogee Creek and/or Seminole heritage may also be of interest to readers. Troy Johnson (1997, with Joane Nagel and Duane Champagne; 1999, with Alvin Joseph, Jr., and Joane Nagel) has published extensively on American Indian activism. K. Tsianina Lomawaima (1994; 2002, with David E. Wilkins; 2006, with Teresa L. McCarty) explores the issues of Native American education and federal policy designed to "civilize" Native Americans in her books. Some of Craig Womack's works (1999; 2006, with Jace Weaver and Robert Warrior) are concerned with issues concerning the Native American literary canon and its recognition by academics generally. Womack's other book (2001) is a work of fiction rather than academic writing. Donald L. Fixico (1997; 1998; 2000; 2004, with B. Hosmer and C. O'Neill) writes about a number of issues concerning Native Americans generally, including economic development and the experience of Native Americans in urban areas. The range of topics covered by these academic writers is sweeping, and we expect that readers of this book will be interested in some of the books listed here.

A final author to mention is Cynthia L. Smith, another Muskogee Creek author whose works (2000; 2002; 2007; 2001, with Lori Earley) are produced for younger readers. She draws on her Muskogee heritage to inform the three earlier books. Like the works of the other authors mentioned above, her work is part of a varied and creative body emerging from the pens of Muskogee Creek and Seminole writers. The creativity, diversity, and artistry of the work by each of these authors surely deserve to be recognized. We encourage you to explore the diversity of the genres that Muskogee Creek and Seminole authors are producing.

APPENDIX 1

Nouns with Special Plural Forms

Smallcaps SECTION 1. Nouns Pluralized with –*vlk*-

English translation	Singular form	Plural form
Baptist/Baptists	Este-Aksomkv	Este-Aksomkvlke
Cherokee/the Cherokee	Cvlakke	Cvlakkvlke
Chickasaw/the Chickasaw	Cekvsv	Cekvsvlke
Choctaw/the Choctaw	Cahtv	Cahtvlke
French person/French people	Fvlvnce	Fvlvncvlke
Jewish person/Jewish people	Cos	Cosvlke
kin, blood relative/blood relatives	ennake	ennakvlke
mother/parents	ecke	eckvlke
Spaniard/Spaniards	Espane	Espanvlke
second chief/second chiefs	henehv	henehvlke
leader/leaders (of something)	homahtv	enhomahhotvlke
young person/young people	hvte-mahē	hvte-mahvlke
disciple/disciples	kerrēpv	kerrēpvlke
berry, brier/brier patch	kvco	kvco vlkat
Comanche person/the Comanches	Kvmince	Kvmincvlke
Muskogee person/the Muskogee	Mvskoke	Maskokvlke
Englishman/the English	Mēkelese	Mēkelesvlke
Mexican/Mexicans	Meksekvn	Meksekvlke
Christian/Christians	Emēkusapv	Emēkusapvlke
that person/those people	miste	mistvlke

SECTION 1. Nouns Pluralized with *–vlk-* (*continued*)

English translation	Singular form	Plural form
Natchez person/the Natchez	Nacce	Naccvlke
Presbyterian/Presbyterians	Ohfēskv	Ohfēskvlke
Methodist/Methodists	Ohkalv	Ohkalvlke
messenger/messengers	opunvkv-svhopakv	opunvkv-esfullvlke
ball player/ball team	pokkēccv	pokkēccvlke
Shawnee/the Shawnees	Sawvnoke	Sawvnokvlke
Seminole/the Seminoles	Semvnole	Semvnolvlke
Catholic/Catholics	(E)tohwelēpv	(E)tohwelēpvlke
warrior/warriors	tvstvnvke	tvstvnvkvlke

SECTION 2. Nouns Pluralized with *–vke* and *–vk-*

English translation	Singular form	Plural form
boy/boys	cēpvnē	cēpvnvke
immature girl/immature girls	hokloswv	hoklosvke
prostitute/prostitutes	hoktarv	hoktarvke
woman/women	hoktē	hoktvke
girl/girls	hoktuce	hoktvkuce
old woman/old women	hoktvlwv	hoktvlvke
scout, peacemaker/scouts, peacemakers	le-homahte	le-homahtvke
chief, king/chiefs, kings	mēkko	mēkkvke
old person, elder/old people, elders	vculē	vculvke

SECTION 3. Nouns taking *–take*

English translation	Singular form	Plural form
grandchild/grandchildren	em ososwv	em osostake
his sister/his sisters	ēwvnwv	ēwvntake
his son/his sons	eppuce, ēppuce	eppucetake
man/men	honvnwv	honvntake
wife/wives	ehiwv	ehitake

SECTION 3. Nouns taking –*take* (*continued*)

English translation	Singular form	Plural form
woman's child of either gender, woman's sister's child/woman's children, woman's sister's children	eccuswv, echuswv	eccustake
child/children	hopuewv	hopuetake

Nouns Based on Suppletive Verbs

English translation	Singular form	Plural form
giant/giants	este-capko	este-cvpcakv
member (of a church, council)/members	cuko-vpikv	cuko-vtēhkv
name/names	hocefkv	hocefhokv
thing, something/things	nake	nanvke
width/widths	entvphē	entvptvhē

SECTION 4. CLAN NAMES (Pluralized forms of nouns, in common usage, the noun itself does not take this plural form.)

Snake clan	Cettvlke
Goat clan	Cowatvlke
Fox clan	Culvlke
Alligator clan	Hvlpvtvlke
Raccoon clan	Wotkvlke
Beaver clan	Eccaswvlke, Echaswvlke, Echasvlke
Deer clan	Ecovlke
Bird clan	Foswvlke
Wind clan	Hotvlkvlke
Tiger clan	Kaccvlke
Cane clan (Florida)	Kohvsvlke
Skunk clan	Konepvlke
Bear clan	Nokosvlke
Turkey clan	Penwvlke
Sweet Potato clan	Vhvlvkvlke

APPENDIX 2

Suppletive Verb Forms

The following lists present the suppletive verbs in Mvskoke. Verbs having different forms for singular and plural (two or more) subjects are presented in section 1, followed by section 2, a list of those with different forms for singular, dual (two), or plural (three or more) subjects. Verbs that have two forms based upon the number of objects (singular or plural) are shown in section 3. Section 4 includes those verbs having different forms for singular, dual, and plural objects. The final list, section 5, presents two verbs that have singular and plural forms, one of which depends on how many times the action is performed and the other based upon the number of sounds resulting from the activity.

SECTION I. Suppletive Verbs Changing Form for Singular and Plural Subjects

English Translation	Singular Form	Plural Form
to ache (s)	tiyetv	tihoyetv
angry, mad (s)	cvpakkē	cvpakhokē
to back up, go backward (s)	vcekelletv	vcekelhoyetv
to be clean (s)	hvsvtkē	hvsvthvkē
to be dry (s)	kvrpē	kvrkvpē
to be in water, a low place, jail (s)	akpiketv	aktehketv
to be inside, get inside (s)	vpiketv	vtehketv
to become, turn into (s)	haketv	hahvketv
big (s)	rakkē	rakrvkē

233

SECTION I. Suppletive Verbs Changing Form for Singular and Plural Subjects (*continued*)

English Translation	Singular Form	Plural Form
black (s)	lvstē	lvslvtē
to burst into (s)	etefvlvpketv	etefvlahletv
chipped, broken off (s)	kvlkē	kvlkvkē
crooked (s)	fvyvtkē	fvyvtfvkē
dead (s)	elē	pvsvtkē
deep (of a body of water) (s)	lvokē	lvolvkē
deep (of a hole, a pot, but not of water) (s)	sofkē	sofsokē
to die (s)	eletv	pvsvtketv
to die in water (s)	akeletv	akpvsvtketv
different (s)	emvrahkv	emvrahrvkv
dirty (s)	vholwvkē	vholwahokē
dirty, filthy, nasty (s)	lekvcwē	lekvclewē
to do a somersault, turn over (s)	hvkvnceropotketv	hvkvnceropothoketv
to dry off, dry up, dry out (s)	vkvrpetv	vkvrkvpetv
dull (of a blade) (s)	tefnē	teftenē
empty (s)	tvnkē	tvntvkē
to fall over (as of a tree) (s)	tolketv	toltoketv
fast, quick (s)	pvfnē	pvfpvnē
flat, level (s)	tvpeksē	tvpestvkē
forked (as of a road) (s)	yakpē	yakyvpē
frozen stiff, numb (s)	cuehē	cuecuhē
full (s)	fvckē	fvcfvkē
to go between (s)	vsokketv	vsokhoketv
to go in, enter (s)	recēyetv	cukolvketv
gray (s)	sopakhvtkē	sopakhvthvkē
to hang, hang onto (s)	vtvrketv	vtvrtvketv
hard, brittle (s)	tvkvcwē	tvkvctvwē
hard, firm (s)	wvnhē	wvnwvhē
having a piece broken off (leaving a crescent shape) (s)	kvlaksē	kvlvskvkē
having (something) in it (s)	vcvnkē	vcvncvkē
heavy (in weight) (s)	honnē	honhoyē
high (in height or expensive) (s)	hvlwē	hvlhvwē

SECTION I. Suppletive Verbs Changing Form for Singular and Plural Subjects (*continued*)

English Translation	Singular Form	Plural Form
hot (as in temperature) (s)	hiyē	hihoyē
to hush up, be quiet, still (s)	cvyayvketv	cvyayvhoketv
to laugh, smile (s)	vpeletv	vpelhoyetv
limber, flexible, supple, weak, tender (s)	lowakē	lowalokē
long, tall (s)	cvpkē	cvpcvkē
to look up with the head tilted back (s)	vnvtaksetv	vnvtvsnvketv
lopsided (s)	fvleknē	fvlenfvkē
or	lvceksē	lvceslvkē
lying on the side, tilted, slanted (s)	vfvleknē	vfvlenfvkē
mashed (s)	cetakkē	cetakcekē
mushy (as of fruit) (s)	cvlaknē	cvlvncvkē
old (of something inanimate) (s)	leskē	leslekē
on tiptoe (s)	tekenkē	tekentekē
pale (s)	hvtwē	hvthvwē
paralyzed (s)	elē omē	pvsvtkē omē
pointed, coming to a point (s)	cufoknē	cufuncokē
precious, valuable, expensive (s)	vcakē	vcacvkē
pretty (s)	eshēnrusē	esherankusē
puffed up, inflated (s)	pakkē	pakpvkē
to put on clothing (s)	vccetv	vchoyetv
round (like a ball) (s)	polokē	polopokē
sewn (s)	vhorkē	vhorhokē
sharp (s)	fvskē	fvsfvkē
short (as in height) (s)	kocoknē	koconcokē
shut, closed (s)	akhotkē	akhothokē
sick (s)	enokkē	enokhokē
sideways, at an angle (s)	cvneksē	cvnescvkē
sliced, cut (s)	tvckē	warkē
sliced, split (of wood) (s)	selkē	selsekē
small (s)	cutkē	lopockē
soft (s)	lowvckē	lowvclokē
split (as of wood) (s)	fvlvpkē	fvlvpfvkē

Section I. Suppletive Verbs Changing Form for Singular and Plural Subjects (*continued*)

English Translation	Singular Form	Plural Form
spread out, flared (s)	tvleksē	tvlestvkē
to squat on the ground or floor (s)	taktekaksetv	taktekvstvketv
to stick to, be sticking to (s)	vlokpetv	vloklopetv
sticking in, projecting into (s)	vcakhē	vcakcvhē
sticking in, sticking up on the ground (s)	takcakhē	takcakcvhē
sticking in water or a low place (s)	akcakhē	akcakcvhē
sticking out behind (s)	akvcakhē	akvcakcvhē
sticking out on top of (s)	ohcakhē	ohcakcvhē
sticking out, projecting (s)	fvnkē	fvnfvkē
sticking up, sticking in, standing (of something inanimate) (s)	cakhē	cakcvhē
stinky, bad smelling (s)	fvmpē	fvmfvpē
to stoop over, bend over (s)	comokletv	comolcoketv
straight (of a road, line) (s)	lvpotkē	lvpotlvkē
sweet (s)	cvmpē	cvmcvpē
swollen, bloated, having an upset stomach, having diarrhea (s)	wvpaksē	wvpvswvkē
tall (s)	mahē	mahmvyē
thick (as of paper, cloth, etc.) (s)	cekfē	cekcefē
twisted (according to number of pairs of things being twisted) (s)	etepvllvkē	etepvllapvkē
ugly, bad, naughty, wicked (s)	holwvkē	holwahokē
uninhabited, barren (s)	hvyakpē	hvyakyvpē
well, healthy (s)	cvfeknē	cvfencvkē
to whisper (s)	wvswaketv	wvswahoketv
white (s)	hvtkē	hvthvkē
wide (s)	tvphē	tvptvhē

SECTION 2. Suppletive Verbs Changing Form for Singular, Dual, and Plural Subjects

English Translation	Singular Form	Dual Form	Plural Form
to arrive (s)	vlvketv	vlahoketv	yicetv
to arrive, get there, reach there (s)	roretv	rorhoyetv	roricetv
to arrive here (s)	vlvketv	vlahoketv	yicetv
asleep (s)	nucē	nucuepetv	nucuecvpetv
to bark (s)	wohketv	wohhoketv	wohecetv
to bark at (s)	vwohketv	vwohhoketv	vwohecetv
to be lost, get lost, disappear (s)	somketv	somhoketv	somecetv
to buck, spring up (s)	fvtosketv	fvtoshoketv	fvtosecetv
to climb (s)	vcemketv	vcemhoketv	vcemecetv
to climb on top of, climb into (s)	ohcemketv	ohcemhoketv	ohcemecetv
to come (s)	vtetv	vthoyetv	vwetv
to come in from (s)	acēyetv	acēhoyetv	acēyetv
to come in with, bring in (s)	ascēyetv	ascēhoyetv	ascēyetv
to come out of the water or a low place (s)	a-akossetv	a-akoshoyetv	a-sakossiketv
to come running (s)	aletketv	atokorketv	apefatketv
to come toward (s)	oh-vtetv	oh-vthoyetv	oh-vwetv
to crash into a ditch (s)	rasaklvtketv	rasakyurketv	rasakpvlvtketv
or	aklvtiketv	aklvthoketv	akpvlvtiketv
to crawl (s)	hvlketv	hvlhoketv	hvlecetv
to cross (a road/street) (s)	etewvlvpketv	etewvlvphoketv	etewvlvpecetv
to cross over, go over (s)	vwelvpketv	vwelvphoketv	vwelvpecetv
to cross water, traveling in the water or a low place (s)	aktiketv	aktihoketv	aktvyecetv
to cry (s)	hvkihketv	hvkihhoketv	hvkahecetv
to cry about (s)	vhvkihketv	vhvkihhoketv	vhvkahecetv
to dive into water (s)	a-aktasketv	a-aktashoketv	a-aktasecetv
to enter the water (s)	akcēyetv	akcokolvtketv	akcēyetv
to enter the water or a low place with (something) (s)	esakcēyetv	esakcokolvtketv	esakcēyetv

SECTION 2. Suppletive Verbs Changing Form for Singular, Dual, and Plural Subjects (*continued*)

English Translation	Singular Form	Dual Form	Plural Form
to enter with (something) (s)	ecak-ecēyetv	ecak-ecēhoyetv	ecak-escēyetv
to fall (s)	lvtketv	yurketv	pvlvtketv
to fall down in the water or a low place (s)	aklvtketv	akyurketv	akpvlvtketv
to fall down on the ground or floor (s)	taklvtketv	takyurketv	takpvlvtketv
to fall from, fall off (s)	alvtketv	ayurketv	apvlvtketv
to fall on top of (s)	ohlvtketv	ohyurketv	ohpvlvtketv
to float (s)	okotafketv	okotafhoketv	okotafecetv
to fly (s)	tvmketv	tvmhoketv	tvmecetv
to fly toward (s)	ohtvmketv	ohtvmhoketv	ohtvmecetv
to follow (s)	ecak-vyetv	ecak-vhoyetv	ecak-vpeyetv
to get out of jail (s)	ossetv	wvliketv	sossetv
to get out of the water, a low place (s)	akossetv	akoshoyetv	asvkossetv
or	akossetv	awvliketv	asvkossetv
to go (s)	vyetv	vhoyetv	vpeyetv
to go about, wander (s)	vretv	welvketv	fulletv
to go across water (s)	tiketv	tihoketv	tvyecetv
to go around (an obstacle) (s)	vfolotketv	vfolothoketv	vfolotecetv
to go around on top of, be around on top of (s)	oh-vretv	ohwelvketv	ohfulletv
to go around, be around on the ground or floor or within an enclosed space (s)	takvretv	takwelvketv	takfulletv
to go around (something), go to the other side of, pass (s)	vhvpalofketv	vhvpalofhoketv	vhvpalofecetv
to go back (s)	yefolketv	yefolhoketv	yefolecetv
to go back and forth (s)	etoh-vretv	etohwelvketv	etohfulletv
to go back toward (s)	yohfolketv	yohfolhoketv	yohfolecetv
to go down (s)	hvtvpketv	hvtvphoketv	hvtvpecetv
to go down (s)	akhvtvpketv	akhvtvphoketv	akhvtvpecetv
to go down on top of, step down on top of (s)	ohhvtvpketv	ohhvtvphoketv	ohhvtvpecetv

SECTION 2. Suppletive Verbs Changing Form for Singular, Dual, and Plural
Subjects (*continued*)

English Translation	Singular Form	Dual Form	Plural Form
to go in (s)	ecēyetv	ecēhoyetv	escēyetv
to go in the woods, the water, a low place (s)	akvyetv	akvhoyetv	akvpeyetv
to go out (s)	ossetv	wolketv	sossetv
to go out, get out (s)	ossetv	oshoyetv	sossetv
to go out of sight, disappear (s)	rvsomketv	rvsomhoketv	rvsomecetv
to go out with (someone) (s)	ecak-ossetv	ecak-oshoyetv	ecak-sossetv
to go outside (s)	wolketv	wolhoketv	wolecetv
or	ossetv	weliketv	sossetv
to go outside with (someone) (s)	ecak-wolketv	ecak-wolhoketv	ecak-wolecetv
or (with vb 'to go with')	ossetv	wolketv	sossetv
to go through, pass through (s)	ropottetv	ropothoyetv	ropotecetv
to go up to (something/ someone) (s)	oh-vyetv	oh-vhoyetv	oh-vpeyetv
to jump (s)	tasketv	tashoketv	tasecetv
to jump back over (s)	ratohtasketv	ratohtashoketv	ratohtasecetv
to jump in the water or a low place (s)	aktasketv	aktashoketv	aktasecetv
to jump over, jump across (s)	etohtasketv	etohtashoketv	etohtasecetv
to jump toward, jump onto (s)	ohtasketv	ohtashoketv	ohtasecetv
to lie down (s)	wakketv	wakhoketv	lomhetv
to lie, be situated, exist in the water or a low place (s)	akwakketv	akwakhoketv	aklomhetv
to lie on the ground or floor or within an enclosed space (s)	takwakketv	takwakhoketv	taklomhetv
to lie on top of (s)	ohwakketv	ohwakhoketv	ohlomhetv
to merge into, enter (a field, lawn, etc.) (s)	ohcēyetv	ohcēhoyetv	esohcēyetv
to move, move out of the way, get out of the way (s)	vkueketv	vkuehoketv	vkoyecetv

SECTION 2. Suppletive Verbs Changing Form for Singular, Dual, and Plural Subjects (*continued*)

English Translation	Singular Form	Dual Form	Plural Form
to move toward (s)	ohkueketv	ohkuehoketv	ohkoyecetv
to pass by (s)	hoyvnetv	hoyvnhoyetv	hoyvnēcetv
to pass someone (s)	etehoyvnetv	etehoyvnhoyetv	etehoyvnecetv
to pass through in the water or a low place (s)	akropottetv	akropothoyetv	akropotecetv
to return to (s)	ohfolketv	ohfolhoketv	ohfolecetv
to revolve, turn around (s)	hapalofketv	hapalofhoketv	hapalofecetv
to rise, go up (s)	kvwvpketv	kvwvphoketv	kvwvpecetv
to run (s)	letketv	tokorketv	pefatketv
to run from, escape from (s)	enletketv	entokorketv	enpefatketv
to run to (s)	vletketv	vtokorketv	vpefatketv
to run toward (s)	ohletketv	ohtokorketv	ohpefatketv
to sink, disappear, get lost in water *or* to be baptized (s)	aksomketv	aksomhoketv	aksomecetv
to sit (s)	liketv	kaketv	vpoketv
to sit at, sit on (s)	vliketv	vkaketv	vhvpoketv
to sit, be situated, exist in the water or a low place *or* to be stuck in the mud (s)	akliketv	akkaketv	akvpoketv
to sit, be situated on the ground or floor or inside an enclosed space (s)	takliketv	takkaketv	takvpoketv
to sit on top of (s)	ohliketv	ohkaketv	ohvpoketv
to sleep (s)	nocetv	nochoyetv	nocicetv
to slide, slip (s)	solotketv	solothoketv	solotecetv
to slide on top of, move over toward (s)	ohsolotketv	ohsolothoketv	ohsolotecetv
to stand (s)	hueretv	sehoketv	svpakletv
to stand against, stand at (s)	vhueretv	vsehoketv	vsvpakletv
to stand in the water or a low place *or* to step in (something) (s)	akhueretv	aksehoketv	aksvpakletv
to stand on, stand on top of, step on top of (s)	ohhueretv	ohsehoketv	ohsvpakletv

SECTION 2. Suppletive Verbs Changing Form for Singular, Dual, and Plural Subjects (*continued*)

English Translation	Singular Form	Dual Form	Plural Form
to stand up (s)	ahueretv	asehoketv	asvpakletv
to step down, get off (s)	hvtvpketv	hvtvphoketv	hvtvpecetv
to turn (s)	fiketv	fihoketv	fvyecetv
to turn around (s)	folotketv	folothoketv	folotecetv
to veer (s)	pvcēssetv	pvcēshoyetv	pvcēssecetv
to wade, walk in the water (s)	akyvkvpetv	akyvkvphoketv	akyvkvpvketv
to wade, wander in the water (s)	ak-vretv	ak-welvketv	ak-fulletv
to walk (s)	yvkvpetv	yvkvphoketv	yvkvpvketv
to wander around after, go after, be with (s)	ecak-vretv	ecak-welvketv	ecak-fulletv
to wander around, be near (s)	vhvretv	vwelvketv	vfulletv
to whoop, bray, neigh (s)	pihketv	pihhoketv	pahecetv
to whoop at (s)	ohpihketv	ohpihhoketv	ohpahecetv

SECTION 3. Suppletive Verbs Changing Form for Singular and Plural Objects

English Translation	Singular Form	Plural Form
to back up, make (someone/ something) back up (o)	vcekellicetv	vcekelhuecetv
to bend (something) into a curve or crook (o)	konhicetv	konkohicetv
to break up, take apart (o)	lekvfetv	lekvflēcetv
to clean (o)	hvsvtecetv	hvsvthicetv
to cut, slice (o)	tvcetv	waretv
to cut into pieces (o)	etewaretv	etewarwicetv
to cut, slice or tear off (o)	atvcetv	awaretv
to cut, trim (o)	tonetv	tontuecetv
to dip up (o)	ak-esetv	akcvwetv
to dip up (something) with (o)	esak-esetv	esakcvwetv
to dry (something) (o)	kvrpēcetv	kvrkvpēcetv
to embarrass, shame (o)	vlsēcetv	vlsvkuecetv
to empty, make void (o)	tvnecicetv	tvnticetv
to fatten, make fat (o)	vpessicetv	vpessvkuecetv

SECTION 3. Suppletive Verbs Changing Form for Singular and Plural Objects (*continued*)

English Translation	Singular Form	Plural Form
to fill (o)	fvcecetv	fvcficetv
to get dirty, make dirty (o)	vholwicetv	vholwahuecetv
or	seholwicetv	seholwahuecetv
to hang up (as clothing) (o)	vtvretv	vtvrticetv
to heal, make well, cure (o)	cvfeknicetv	cvfencicetv
to hit on, nail (o)	ohrvhetv	ohrahricetv
to hold (o)	hvlvtetv	hvlvthicetv
to hurt, injure, harm (o)	ennokkicetv	ennokhokicetv
to kill (o)	elēcetv	pvsvtetv
to kill in water, drown (o)	akelēcetv	akpvsvtetv
to knock over, fell (a tree) (o)	toletv	toltuecetv
to know (o)	kerretv	kerhoyetv
to lean (something) against (o)	vccayetv	vccacicetv
to make (someone) go down (o)	akhvtvpecicetv	akhvtvphēcetv
to make (something) go down, let (something) down (o)	sakhvtvpecicetv	sakhvtvphēcetv
to let (someone/something) go out, put out, cast out (o)	ossicetv	oshuecetv
to lose (something/someone) (o)	somecicetv	somhuecetv
to lower to the ground (o)	taklicetv	takvpohetv
to make (o)	hayetv	hahicetv
to make bigger, to raise (a plant) (o)	rakkuecetv	rakrvkuecetv
to make (someone/something) climb (o)	vcemecicetv	vcemhuecetv
to make (something) cross, lay across *or* to toss over, throw over (o)	vwelvpecicetv	vwelvphuecetv
to make (something) fly, flush (a bird) (o)	tvmecicetv	tvmhuecetv
to make (someone/something) go around (an obstacle) (o)	vfolotecicetv	vfolothuecetv
to make (someone) go back (o)	yefolecicetv	yefolhuecetv
to make (someone) go back toward (o)	yohfolecicetv	yohfolhuecetv

SECTION 3. Suppletive Verbs Changing Form for Singular and Plural Objects (*continued*)

English Translation	Singular Form	Plural Form
to make happy (o)	afvcecicetv	afvckvkuecetv
to make long (o)	cvpkuecetv	cvpcvkuecetv
to make sick (o)	enokkicetv	enokhokicetv
to make (someone/something) slide (o)	solotecicetv	solothuecetv
to make small (o)	cutecicetv	lopocecicetv
to make (someone) pass by (o)	hoyvnecicetv	hoyvnhuecetv
to make (someone/something) return, return (something) (o)	ohfolecicetv	ohfolhuecetv
to make (someone) sorry (o)	feknokkicetv	feknokhokicetv
to make (someone) step down (o)	hvtvpecicetv	hvtvphuecetv
to make (someone) take (something) (o)	esēpicetv	escvwepicetv
to make (someone) trip (o)	lentappuecetv	lentaphuecetv
to make (someone) turn (o)	fvyecicetv	fihuecetv
to make (someone) turn around (o)	folotecicetv	folothuecetv
to name (o)	hocefetv	hocefhuecetv
to paint (someone/something) with (o)	essiyetv	essisicetv
to pocket, put in one's pocket (o)	ēpiketv	vtēhetv
to pop (o)	tvpocecetv	tvpohlicetv
to pour into, fill (o)	vcvnetv	vcvncicetv
to pour (some liquid) into another large body of liquid (o)	akcvnetv	akcvncicetv
to pour (some liquid) into a small body of liquid (like a pot of soup) (o)	esakcvnetv	esakcvncicetv
to put in the water, a low place, jail (o)	akpiketv	aktehetv
to put inside (o)	vpiketv	vtehetv
to put (someone/something) in (o)	ohpiketv	ohtehetv
to put on (something) encircling a limb (o)	esvwvnvyetv	esvwvnawicetv
to save (someone or something) (o)	hesayēcetv	hesahuecetv
to sew, stitch (o)	vhoretv	vhorhuecetv

SECTION 3. Suppletive Verbs Changing Form for Singular and Plural Objects (*continued*)

English Translation	Singular Form	Plural Form
to sharpen (o)	fvsecetv	fvsficetv
to shove in, stick in, insert between (o)	vsoketv	vsoksuecetv
to show (o)	hecicetv	hecvkuecetv
to shut, close (o)	akhottetv	akhothuecetv
to slice, split (o)	seletv	selsēcetv
to snap, break (o)	kvcetv	kvcēyetv
or	kvcketv	kvcēketv
to snap (something) against, break (long items) against (o)	vkvcetv	vkvcēyetv
to spread (something) out (o)	pvticetv	pvtapicetv
to stick (something) in (o)	cakhēcetv	cakcvhēcetv
to stick (something) in an upright position on the head (o)	kohcakhēcetv	kohcakcvhēcetv
to stick (something) in the water or a low place (o)	akcakhēcetv	akcakcvhēcetv
to stick (something) into (o)	vcakhēcetv	vcakcvhēcetv
to stick (something) on, glue to (o)	vlokpicetv	vloklopicetv
to stick (something) out (o)	fvnecicetv	fvnficetv
to stretch (a rubber band, etc.) (o)	senēpecetv	senēpsēcetv
to take (o)	esetv	cvwetv
to take from the water or a low place (o)	akesetv	akcvwetv
to take off (items of clothing) (o)	roketv	rokruecetv
to take out, pick up (o)	a-esetv	a-cvwetv
to take out of the water or a low place (o)	akesetv	akcvwetv
to take (something) from (something/someone), to hold (a cloth item) for (someone) (o)	enesetv	encvwetv
to tame (o)	yvmvsēcetv	yvmvshuecetv
to tear, rip (something) (o)	sētetv	sētsēcetv
to tear up, grind, mash (o)	cetvketv	cetakcēcetv
to throw (liquids) at (o)	vkvletv	vkvlkicetv
to tie (o)	wvnvyetv	wvnawicetv

SECTION 3. Suppletive Verbs Changing Form for Singular and Plural Objects (*continued*)

English Translation	Singular Form	Plural Form
to tie (something/someone) on (o)	ohwvnvyetv	ohwvnawicetv
to torment (o)	estemerricetv	estemerrvkuecetv
to tow, pull behind (o)	safotecetv	hvlvtepicetv
to tow, pull behind in the water or a low place (o)	akhvlvtetv	akhvlvtepicetv
to translate (o)	etohtvlecicetv	etohtvlhuecetv
to turn (something) over (o)	rakpvletv	rakpvlricetv
to twist together (according to number of pairs of things being twisted) (o)	etepvllvyetv	etepvllapicetv
to unbutton, untie (o)	esetohrecvpetv	esetohrecvprēcetv
to untie, to release (o)	recvpetv	recvprēcetv
to wake (someone) up (o)	vhonecicetv	vhonechuecetv
to wash (o)	okkosetv	okkoskuecetv
to whip (o)	rokafetv	rokafruecetv
to whiten, make white (o)	hvtecetv	hvthicetv
to whittle, shave, plane, carve, peel (o)	kvlvfetv	kvlvfkicetv
to wreck, spoil, ruin, destroy, break (o)	vhopvnetv	vhopvnhuecetv

SECTION 4. Suppletive Verbs Changing Form for Singular, Dual, and Plural Objects

English Translation	Singular Form	Dual Form	Plural Form
to drop or throw down into the water or a low place (o)	akwitetv	akkayetv	akpulutetv
to lay down in the water or a low place (o)	akwvkecetv	akwvkhokicetv	aklomhicetv
to lay down, make lie down, put to bed (o)	wvkecetv	wakhokicetv	lomhicetv
to make (someone/something) come in (o)	acēyicetv	acēhecetv	acēyicetv
to make (something) come out, pull out from the mud (o)	akessetv	akcvhwetv	akcvwakketv

SECTION 4. Suppletive Verbs Changing Form for Singular, Dual, and Plural Objects (*continued*)

English Translation	Singular Form	Dual Form	Plural Form
to make (something) go around (o)	vrēcicetv	welvkuecetv	fullicetv
to make (something) go in, let (something) go in (o)	acēyicetv	acukolvkēcetv	ascēyecetv
to make mad, anger (o)	cvpakkuecetv	cvpakhuecetv	cvpakhokicetv
to make (someone) run to (o)	vletecicetv	vtokorhuecetv	vpefatecicetv
to make (someone/something) sit down (o)	likepicetv	kakepicetv	vpokepicetv
to make (someone/something) sit up (o)	alicetv	akayetv	apoyetv
to make (someone/something) stand up from a lying down position (o)	ahuericetv	asehoketv	asvpakletv
to pull out from a low place (o)	akossicetv	akoshuecetv	aksossicetv
to put down, spread (something) in the water, a low place (o)	aklicetv	akkayetv	akvpoyetv
to run off, make run (o)	letecicetv	tokorhuecetv	pefatecicetv
to seat, set (o)	licetv	kayetv	vpoyetv
to send (someone), make (someone) go (o)	vyēcicetv	vhoyecicetv	vpeyecicetv
to set down (o)	eslicetv	kayetv	vpoyetv
to set (something/someone) down on top of (o)	ohlicetv	ohkayetv	ohvpoyetv
to sink, be immersed, submerge in water (o)	aksomecicetv	aksomhuecetv	aksomecetv
to stand (someone/something) on top of, make stand up on top of (o)	ohhuericetv	ohsehoyetv	ohsvpaklēcetv
to stand (something) up (o)	huericetv	sehoyetv	svpaklēcetv
to throw or spill into the water or a deep space (o)	akwiketv	akkayetv	akpvlvtetv
to throw (something) out or away (as garbage), discard (o)	vwiketv	vkayetv	vpvlvtetv

SECTION 5. Suppletive Verbs Changing Form Based Upon Features Other Than Numbers of Subjects or Objects

English Translation	Singular Form	Plural Form
to creak (a number of creaks)	wekēcketv	wekēcwēketv
to smear on (depends on number of places smeared)	vlofetv	vlofluecetv

Glossary

Mvskoke to English

A

acvwetv (a:·ca·wí·ta {I;3}): to take two or more items down

acvwēcetv (a:·ca·wi:·ci·tá {I;3}): to take something out of a container; *also* iem esetv

aesetv (a:·i·sí·ta {I;3}): to take one item down

afvcfvkē (a:·fac·fa·kí: {II}): happy, glad (of two or more)

afvckē (a:·fác·ki: {II}): happy, glad (of one)

ahkopvnetv (a:h·ko·pa·ni·tá {I}): to play

ahueretv (a:·hoy·li·tá {I}): to stand up (of one)

ahvlvtetv (a:·ha·la·ti·tá {I;II}): to pull in the direction of the speaker

ahvtvpecetv (a:·ha·ta·pi·cí·ta {I}): to come down (of three or more); *also* akhvtvpecetv

ahvtvphoketv (a:·ha·tap·ho·kí·ta {I}): to come down (of two); *also* akhvtvphoketv

ahvtvpketv (a:·ha·tap·ki·tá {I}): to come down (of one); *also* akhvtvpketv

akaketv (a:·ka:·ki·tá {I}): to rise up, sit up (as from lying down) (of two), to set aside (two items)

akesetv (ak·i·si·tá {I;II}): to take (one) from the water or a low place

akhecetv (ak·hi·ci·tá {I}): to look into the water or a low place

akhvtvpecetv (a:k·ha·ta·pi·cí·ta {I}): to come down (of three or more); *also* ahvtvpecetv

249

akhvtvphoketv (a:k·ha·tap·ho·kí·ta {I}): to come down (of two); *also* ahvtvphoketv

akhvtvpketv (a:k·ha·tap·ki·tá {I}): to come down (of one); *also* ahvtvpketv

akicetv (a:·ke:·ci·tá {I;II}): to answer back, reply; *also* vyoposketv

akketv (a:k·ki·tá {I;II}): to bite

akletketv (ak·lit·ki·tá {I}): to run in the water or a low place (of one)

akossetv (ak·os·si·tá {I}): to get out of the water or a low place (of one)

aktashoketv (ak·ta:s·ho·kí·ta {I}): to jump, hop, leap into the water or a low place (of two)

aletketv (a:·lit·ki·tá {I}): to come running (of one)

aliketv (a:·le:·ki·tá {I}): to rise up, sit up (as from lying down) (of one)

a-ohyvkvpetv (a·oh·ya·ka·pi·tá {I}): to walk a short distance toward (of one)

apvlvtetv (a:·pa·la·ti·tá {I;3}): to drop three or more items

asehoketv (a:·si·ho:·ki·tá {I}): to stand up (of two)

asvpakletv (a:·sa·pa:k·li·tá {I}): to stand up (of three or more)

aswiyetv (a:s·we:·yi·tá {I;3;D}): to pass (something) to someone

atakkayetv (a:·tak·ka:·yi·tá {I;3}): to put down, drop two items or something made of fabric

atakkesetv (a:·tak·ki·sí·ta {I;II}): to pick up one item

ataklicetv (a:·tak·le:·ci·tá {I;3}): to put down one item

atakvpoyetv (a:·tak·a·po·yi·tá {I;3}): to put down three or more items

atasketv (a:·ta:s·ki·tá {I}): to jump up from lying down (of one)

atomo (a:·to·mó): car, automobile

a-vpoketv (a:·a·po·ki·tá {I}): to rise up, sit up (as from lying down) (of three or more)

avtēhkuce (a:·a·ti:h·ko·cí): cereal bowl, small bowl

avtēhkv (a:·a·tí:h·ka): serving bowl; *also* hompetv-vcvnetv

a-vwenayetv (a:·a·wi·na:·yi·tá {I;II/II;3}): to smell, sniff from a short distance; *also* awenayetv

a-vyetv (a:·a·yí·ta {I}): to go a short distance (of one)

awenayetv (a:·wi·na:·yi·tá {I;II/II;3}): to smell, sniff from a short distance; *also* a-vwenayetv

awiketv (a:·we:·ki·tá {I;3}): to drop one item

awiyetv (a:·we:·yi·tá {I;3}): to hold out (a hand, paper, etc.)

ayēccicetv (a:·yi:c·ce:·ci·tá {I;D}): to let go, set someone free; *also* enrecvpetv

ayo (á:·yo): hawk

C

catē (cá:·ti: {II}): red

catetv (ca:·ti·tá {II}): to bleed

catv (cá:·ta): blood

cē (cî:): a particle added to the ends of declarative or imperative sentences to show the speaker's feelings are strong and/or sincere; *also* ci

cekfē (cík·fi: {II}): to be thick (of paper, cloth, or of liquids such as gravy, soup, etc.)

Cekvsvlke (ci·ka·sâl·ki): Chickasaws, Chickasaw Tribe

celayetv (ci·la:·yi·tá {I;II}): to touch, feel

cēme (cí:·mi): you

cēmeu (ci:·mió): you and (something/someone else)

Cemme (cím·mi): Jimmy

cenvpaken (ci·na·pâ:·kin): eight

cēpvne (ci:·pa·ní): boy

cēpvnvke (ci:·pa·ná·ki): boys

cesse (cís·si): mouse

cetakkosē (ci·tă:k·ko·si: {II}): mashed (as of potatoes), torn up

cetto (cít·to): snake

cetto hvce svkvsicv (cít·to há·ci sa·ka·sé:·ca): rattlesnake; *also* cetto-mēkko

cetto-mēkko (cit·to·mí:k·ko): rattlesnake; *also* cetto hvce svkvsicv

cetvketv (ci·ta·ki·tá {I;3}): to mash (potatoes) or grind meat

'cēyetv (ci:·yi·tá {I;3}): to go in, enter (of one); *also* ecēyetv

ci (cê:): a particle added to the ends of declarative or imperative sentences to show the speaker's feelings are strong and/or sincere; *also* cē

cofe (co·fí): rabbit, Rabbit of legends; *also* cufe

cofonwv (co·fón·wa): fork (eating utensil); *also spelled* cufunwv

coko (co·kó): house; *also spelled* cuko

coko enmēkko (co·kó in·mí:k·ko): House of Kings

coko entvstenvke (co·kó in·tas·te·ná·ki): House of Warriors

coko-ohrvnkv (co·ko·oh·łán·ka): roof; *also* coko-onvpv

coko-onvpv (co·ko·o·ná·pa): roof; *also* coko-ohrvnkv

cokofv-ohrvnkv (co·ko·fa·oh·łán·ka): ceiling; *also* vtopv

cokopericetv (co·ko·pi·łe:·ci·tá {I;D}): to visit someone; *also* cukopericetv

cokuce (co·kó·ci): bathroom

cokv (có:·ka): book, paper

cokv ensatetv (có:·ka in·sa:·ti·tá {I}): to vote

cokv-hayv (co:·ka·há:·ya): secretary

cokv-hēcv (co:·ka·hí:·ca): student

cokv-tohahwv (co:·ka·to·há:h·wa): paper bag

cokv-tvlvme (co:·ka·ta·la·mí): newspaper

cufe (co·fí): rabbit, Rabbit of legends; *also* cofe

cufokonhe (co·fo·kón·hi): fishhook; *also* rvro rakcvwetv

cufunwv (co·fón·wa): fork (eating utensil); *also spelled* cofonwv

cuko (co·kó): house; *also spelled* coko

cukopericetv (co·ko·pi·łe:·ci·tá {I;D}): to visit someone; *also*
     cokopericetv

cuntv (cón·ta): worm

custake (cos·tá:·ki {D}): egg

cutkē (cót·ki {II}): small (of one)

cutkosē (cot·ko·sí: {II}): little (of one)

cvfeknē (ca·fík·ni: {II}): well, healthy (of one)

cvfeknicetv (ca·fik·ne:·ci·tá {I;II}): to cure, heal (one person/thing)

cvfencicetv (ca·fin·ce:·ci·tá {I;II}): to cure, heal (two or more
     persons/things); *also* cvfencvkuecetv

cvfencvkē (ca·fin·ca·kí: {II}): well, healthy, smart (of two or more)

cvfencvkuecetv (ca·fin·ca·koy·ci·tá {I;II}): to cure, heal (two or more
     persons/things); *also* cvfencicetv

cvhkēpen (cah·kî:·pin): five

cvkotvkse (ca·ko·ták·si): archery bow

cvkotvkse enrē (ca·ko·ták·si in·łí:): arrow

Cvlakkvlke (ca·la:k·kâl·ki): Cherokees, Cherokee Tribe

cvlaknē (ca·lá:k·ni: {II}): mushy (as of one piece of fruit)

cvmpuce (cam·po·cí): candy

cvpakhokē (ca·pa:k·ho·kí: {II}): angry (of two or more)

cvpakkē (ca·pá:k·ki: {II}): angry (of one)

cvpcvkē (cap·ca·kí: {II}): long, tall (of two or more)

cvpkē (cáp·ki: {II}): long, tall (of one)

cvpofv (ca·pó:·fa): field

cvsketv (cas·ki·tá {I;3}): to chop (wood)

cvstvlē (cas·ta·łí:): watermelon

cvto (ca·tó): stone, rock, stove; *also* totkv-hute, for 'stove' cvtvhakv (ca·ta·há:·ka): blue bread

cvwetv (ca·wí·ta {I;II}): to take, catch, carry, hold two or more things

cvyayvkē (ca·ya:·ya·kí: {II}): quiet (of one)

cvyayvhokē (ca·ya:·ya·hó·ki: {II}): quiet (of two or more)

E

eccetv (ic·cí·ta {I;II}): to fire, shoot

eccus hoktē (ic·cós hók·ti: {II}): a woman's daughter

eccustake (ic·cos·tá:·ki {II}): a woman's children

ecerwv (i·cíɫ·wa {II}): a woman's brother

ecerwv mvnetosat (i·cíɫ·wa ma·ni·to·sá:t {II}): a man's younger brother

ecēyetv (i·ci:·yi·tá {I;3}): to go in, enter (of one); also ʻcēyetv

eccv (íc·ca): gun

ecke (íc·ki {II}): his/her mother

eckuce (ic·kó·ci {II}): his/her maternal aunt

eco (i·có): deer

efolo (i·fó·lo): owl, screech owl

efone (i·fó·ni {II}): his/her bone/bones; also fone

efv (i·fá) :dog

ehen (i·hín): interjection, similar to "um" or "uh"

ehi (i·hé:): yes

ehiwv (i·hé:·wa {II}): his wife

ehomv (i·hó·ma {II}): in front of; also homv

ehvce (i·há·ci {II}): his/her tail; also hvce

ehvcko (i·hác·ko {II}): his/her ear

ehvpo (i·ha·pó: {II}): his/her camp; also hvpo

ehvrpe (i·háɫ·pi {II}): his/her/its skin, hide, casing, shell; also hvrpe

ekv (i·ká {II}): his/her head

elē (i·lí: {II}): dead (of one)

elecv (i·lí·ca {II}): under, beneath, below; also lecv

eletv (i·lí·ta {II}): to die (of one)

elvwē (i·lá·wi: {II}): hungry

em ahkopvnetv (im ah·ko·pa·ni·tá {I;D}): to play with someone,
     something

em akhottetv (im a:k·hot·ti·tá {I;3;D}): to close something for someone

em akwiyetv (im a:k·we:·yi·tá {I}): to fish, catch fish

em ēhetv (im i:·hi·tá {I;D}): to hide something from someone

em enhonretv (im in·hon·łi·tá {I;D/II;D}): to believe in, trust, depend on (something or someone)

em enhotetv (im in·ho·tí·ta {II;D}): to be uneasy about

emērkv (i·mí:ł·ka): self-pity

em etektvnkē (im i·tik·tán·ki: {II}): to have permission, have a chance at

emetv (i·mí·ta {I;3;D}): to give something to someone

em mapohicetv (im ma:·po·he:·ci·tá {I;D}): to listen to; *also* mapohicetv

em mēkusvpetv (im mi:·ko·sa·pi·tá {I;D}): to pray for

em merretv (im mił·łi·tá {II;D}): to have compassion for, have mercy for, feel sorry for

em mvyattēcetv (im·ma·ya:t·ti:·ci·tá {I;D}): to wave at

em onvyetv (im·o·na·yí·ta {I;3;D}): to tell (something) to (someone), say to

em oponvyetv (im o·po·na·yí·ta {I;D}): to talk to someone; *also* em ponvyetv

em penkvlē (im pin·ka·lí: {I;D/II;D}): to be afraid of

em ponvyetv (im po·na·yí·ta {I;D}): to talk to someone; *also* em oponvyetv

em vcvnēyetv (im a·ca·ni:·yi·tá {I;D}): to peek at

em vliketv (im·a·le:·ki·tá {D}): clan

em vlostetv (im a·los·ti·tá {II;3/3;D}): to like, be fond of

em vlvketv (im·a·la·kí·ta {I;D}): for (one) to arrive, come to (another one)

em vnicetv (im a·ne:·ci·tá {I;D}): to help someone

em vrokafetv (im·a·ło·ka:·fi·tá {I;II}): to slap (someone on a body part)

em vsehetv (im a·si·hí·ta {I;D}): to give a warning to, caution

em vyoposketv (im a·yo·pos·ki·tá {I;D}): to answer (a person), give an answer to

enahvmkvlke (i·na:·ham·kâl·ki {II}): relatives; *also* enahvnkvlke

enahvnkvlke (i·na:·han·kâl·ki {II}): relatives; *also* enahvmkvlke

enake (i·nâ:·ki): his/her/its (follows the possessed noun)

encakē (in·cá:·ki: {II}): to be greedy; *also* vnoksē

encvpakkē (in·ca·pá:k·ki: {II;D}): to be angry at someone (of one)

encvpakhokē (in·ca·pa:k·ho·kí: {II;D}): to be angry at someone (of two or more)

enfolotetv (in·fo·lo·tí·ta {I;3}): to grind (coffee, corn, etc.)

enhesse (in·hís·si {D}): his/her friend

enhomahtv (in·ho·má:h·ta {D}): his/her leader

enhomahtv vcvkkayetv (in·ho·má:h·ta a·cak·ka:·yi·tá {I;II}): to follow a leader

enhomecē (**in·ho·mí·ci**: {**II;D**}): to be mad/furious with someone

enhonrkv (**in·hónł·ka**): hope, trust

enhorrē (**in·hół·li**: {**II**}): lazy

enhvwēcetv (**in·ha·wi:·ci·tá** {**I;3;D**}): to open something for someone

enke (**in·kí** {**II**}): his/her hand

en kecētketv (**in ki·ci:t·ki·tá** {**I;II**}): to take a single bite of something/someone

enkvpvketv (**in·ka·pa·ki·tá** {**I;D**}): to leave (someone, someplace)

enletketv (**in·lit·ki·tá** {**I;D**}): to run away from someone, something (of one)

enokhokē (**i·nok·ho·kí**: {**II**}): to be sick (of two or more)

ennokkē (**in·nók·ki**: {**3;D**}): hurting, soreness, pain

enokkvlke-vfastv (**i·nok·kâl·ki a·fá:s·ta**): nurse; *also* nokke-vfastv

enpefatketv (**in·pi·fa:t·ki·tá** {**I;D**}): to run away from someone, something (of three or more)

enrecvpetv (**in·łi·ca·pí·ta** {**I;D**}): to let go, set someone free; *also* ayēccicetv

entokorketv (**in·to·koł·ki·tá** {**I;D**}): to run away from someone, something (of two)

enwiketv (**in·we:·ki·tá** {**I**}): to heal (of a wound)

epose (**i·pó·si** {**II**}): his/her grandmother, paternal aunt; *also* pose

epoyetv (**i·po:·yi·tá** {**I**}): to win; *also* vkosletv

eppuce (**ip·po·cí** {**II**}): a man's son

erke (**íł·ki** {**II**}): his/her father

erkenvkv (**ił·ki·ná·ka**): preacher

ero (**i·łó**): squirrel

ervhv (**i·łá·ha** {**II**}): his/her older sibling of the same sex

(e)sem vfikv (**(i)s·im·a·fé:·ka**) screw/screws

(e)sem vfikv em esetv (**(i)s·im·a·fé:·ka im i·sí·ta** {**I;3**}): to unscrew something

(e)sem vfiyetv (**(i)s·im a·fe:·yi·tá** {**I**}): to screw something in

(e)sem vtehke (**(i)s·ím a·tíh·ki**): pie; *also* (e)sem vtehkv

(e)sem vtehkv (**(i)s·ím a·tíh·ka**): pie; *also* (e)sem vtehke

(e)sesketv (**(i)s·is·ki·tá**): cup, glass

eseteyametv (**is·i·ti·ya:·mi·tá** {**I;3**}): to stir things using an implement

esetv (**i·sí·ta** {**I;II**}): to catch, carry, take, hold one thing

esfekcakhetv (**is·fik·ca:k·hi·tá** {**I;II**}): to be jealous about or toward

esfokv (**is·fó:·ka**): saw (cutting implement)

eshecetv (is·hi·ci·tá {I;3}): to find (something)

eshoccickv (is·ho:c·cé:c·ka): pen, pencil, writing implement

es hopoyetv (is ho·po·yi·tá {I;II}): to hunt around for, look for (with something)

eshvkahecetv (is·ha·ka:·hi·cí·ta {I;3}): to cry about something (of three or more)

eskayetv (is·ka:·yi·tá {I;3}): to set (two things, an item made of cloth) down; *also* kayetv

esketv (is·ki·tá {I;3}): to drink

eslafkv (is·lá:f·ka): knife

esletketv (is·lit·ki·tá {I}): to run off with something (of one)

eslicetv (is·le:·ci·tá {I;3}): to set (one item) down

esliketv (is·le:·ki·tá {I}): to sit, be situated, exist (of a clump of things)

esohlicetv (is·oh·le:·ci·tá {I;3}): to set (one item) down on (something)

esohtēhkv ((i)s·oh·tí:h·ka): boots; *also* morvfkv; (e)stelepik-morvfkv; sohtēhkv

esokso (i·sók·so {II}): his/her hip

estakwvnayv (ist·ak·wa·ná:·ya): tie-snake

Espane (is·pá:·ni): Spaniard

Espanvlke (is·pa:n·âl·ki): Spaniards, Spanish people

espvccetv (is·pac·ci·tá {I;3}): to pound, crush, beat, shatter, crack

Este-Aksomkvlke (is·ti·a:k·som·kâl·ki): Baptists

este-capko (is·ti·cá:p·ko): a giant

este enhomahtetv (is·ti·in·ho·ma:h·ti·tá {I;D}): to lead people

(e)stelepik-morvfkv ((i)st·i·li·pe:k·mo·łáf·ka): boot/boots; *also* esohtēhkv; morvfkv; sohtēhkv

(e)stelepikv ((i)st·i·li·pé:·ka): shoe/shoes

estele-svhocackv ((is·ti·li) sa·ho·cá:c·ka): sock/socks; *also* svhocickv, svhocackv

este nakhayetv (is·ti·nâ:k·ha:·yi·tá {I;II}): to make fun of someone

(e)stenke-hute ((i)st·in·ki·hó·ti): glove

(e)stenkesakpikv ((i)st·in·ki·sa:k·pé:·ka): ring (as one wears on a finger)

este ohmelletv (is·ti·oh·mil·li·tá {I;II}): to elect someone

estewvnayv (is·ti·wa·ná:·ya): policeman

estewvnayvlke (is·ti·wa·na:·yâl·ki): the police

estimvt (is·te:·mát): who; *also* stimvt

estomē (is·to·mí:): how; *also* estomēcet, stomēcet

estomēcet (is·to·mí:·cit): how; *also* estomē, stomēcet

estonko (is·tón·ko): how do you feel?; a phrase offered to ask how one is doing, as when greeting someone

estvmen (is·ta·mín): where; *also* stvmen

(e)sem vlvketv ((i)s·im·a·la·ki·tá {I;3;D}): to bring (something) to (someone)

etecetv (i·ti·ci·tá {I;3}): to light a fire/stove; *also* tak-etecetv

etehecetv (i·ti·hi·cí·ta {I}): to look at one another

etehoyvnēcv (i·ti·ho·ya·ní:·ca): hallway

(e)tehoyvnetv ((i)·ti·ho·ya·ni·tá {I;II}): to pass by someone (of one)

etekvpvkē (i·ti·ka·pá·ki: {II}): separated, apart

etelicetv (i·ti·le:·ci·tá {I}): to put together, come together

etemontvlē (i·ti·mon·ta·lí: {II}): to be uneven (as of boards or the ground)

etem vyoposketv (it·im a·yo·pos·ki·tá {I;D}): to argue with each other; *also* isemayecetv

(e)tennvrkvpv ((i)·tin·naɫ·ka·pá): between; *also* (e)tenrvwv

(e)tenrvwv ((i)·tin·ɫa·wá): between; *also* (e)tennvrkvpv

eteyametv (i·ti·ya:·mi·tá {I;3}): to stir things

etkolē (it·ko·lí: {II}): to feel cold (of an animate being)

eto (i·tó): tree, wood

etohkayetv (i·toh·ka:·yi·tá {I;3}): to stack two things on top of another

etohlicetv (i·toh·le:·ci·tá {I;3}): to stack one thing on top of another

etohwelēpkv (it·oh·wi·lí:p·ka): cross, crucifix; *also* tohwelēpkv

etohwvlvpketv (i·toh·wa·lap·ki·tá {I}): to cross over (of one)

etohvpoyetv (i·toh·a·po·yi·tá {I;3}): to stack three or more things on top of another

etolvcce (e·to·lác·ci): tree branch; *also* 'tolvcce

eto-vlke (i·to·âl·ki): forest; *also* pelofv

ewvnhkē (i·wánh·ki: {II}): thirsty

eyvcetv (i·ya·ci·tá {II;3}): to want, need, like

Ē

ē-elēcetv (i:·i·li:·ci·tá {I}): to kill oneself

ēfvccēcetv (i:·fac·ci:·ci·tá {II}): to be honest

ēhecetv (i:·hi·cí·ta {I}): to see oneself, look at oneself

ēhetv (i:·hi·tá {I;II}): to hide something or someone

ēkayetv (i:·ka:·yi·tá {I}): to remove one's own clothes

(ē)kvnhvlwe ((i:)·kan·hál·wi): hill

ēkvnhvlwe-rakko (i:·kan·hal·wi·rá:k·ko): mountain; *also* kvnhvlwe-rakko

(ē)kvnhvlwuce ((i:)·kan·hal·wo·cí): small hill

ēkvn-korke (i:·kan·kół·ki): hole dug in the ground

ēkvntvckv (i:·kan·tác·ka): district; *also* 'kvntvckv

ēkvnv (i:·ka·ná): land, ground, earth

ēkvnv otē nvrkvpv (i:·ka·ná o·tí: nał·ka·pá): island; *also* ēkvnv owv
    ohliketv

ēkvnv owv ohliketv (i:·ka·ná o·wá oh·le:·ki·tá): island; *also* ēkvnv otē
    nvrkvpv

ēkvn(v)-rolahvlēcv (i:·ka·na·ło·la:·ha·lí:·ca): gopher; *also* vcetekv,
    hvcetekv

ēkvsvmetv (i:·ka·sa·mi·tá {II}): to be proud, conceited

ēnaoricetv (i:·na:·o·łe:·ci·tá {I}): to worry

ēpaken (i:·pâ:·kin): six

ērolopetv (i:·ło·lo·pi·tá {II}): to be stubborn

ēsso (í:s·so): ash drippings; *also* kvpe

ētimv (i:·té:·ma): another, different

ēwaretv (i:·wa:·łi·tá {I}): to slice oneself repeatedly

ēwvntake (i:·wan·tá:·ki {II}): a man's sisters

ēwvnwv (i:·wán·wa {II}): a man's sister

F

fayetv (fa:·yi·tá {I}): to hunt

fayv (fá:·ya): hunter

fayvlke (fa:·yâl·ki): hunters

fekce (fík·ci): pig intestines, cleaned well and fried

fekefeketv (fi·ki·fi·kí·ta {I}): to wiggle, wriggle (like a worm); *also*
    wenowēyetv

fekhonnetv (fik·hon·ni·tá {I}): to stop

fekhvmkē (fik·hám·ki: {II}): brave; *also* fekhvnkē

fekhvnkē (fik·hán·ki: {II}): brave; *also* fekhvmkē

fetektvnēceko (fi·tik·ta·ni:·cí·ko {II}): to be strict

fo-encvmpē (fo:·in·cam·pí:): honey

foco (fo·có): duck; *also* fuco

folahpv (fo·lá:h·pa): shell

fone (fó·ni {II}): his/her bone/bones; *also* efone

foswv (fós·wa): bird; *also* fuswv
fotketv (fo:t·ki·tá {I}): to whistle
foyetv (fo:·yi·tá {I;3}): to saw
fuco (fo·có): duck; *also* foco
fulletv (fol·li·tá {I}): to go about, wander, be located (of three or more)
fuswv (fós·wa): bird; *also* foswv
fvccēcetv (fac·ci:·ci·tá {I;3}): to decide
fvccēcv (fac·cí:·ca): judge
fvccv (fác·ca {II}): toward
fvccvlik hoyanen (fac·ca·lé:k ho·yâ:·nin): afternoon
fvleknē (fa·lík·ni: {II}): lopsided
Fvlvncvlke (fa·lan·câl·ki): French people
fvmfvpē (fam·fa·pí: {II}): smelly, stinky (of two or more)
fvmpē (fám·pi: {II}): smelly, stinky (of one)
fvsfvkē (fas·fa·kí: {II}): sharp (of two or more)
fvskē (fás·ki: {II}): sharp (of one)

H

hahicetv (ha:·he:·ci·tá {I}): to build or make two or more things
haketv (ha:·ki·tá {I}): to become
hakkuce (ha:k·ko·cí): teaspoon
hakkv (há:k·ka): spoon
haktēsketv (ha:k·ti:s·ki·tá {II/I}): to sneeze; *also* hvtēsketv
halo-pvlaknv (ha:·lo·pa·lá:k·na): pan; *also* nak-vtehetv
hayetv (ha:·yi·tá {I;3;D}): to build or make one thing, to build/make
    something for someone
hecetv (hi·cí·ta {I;II}): to see, look at
heleswv (hi·lís·wa): medicine
henehv (hi·ní·ha): second chief (of a tribal town)
henehvlke (hi·ni·hâl·ki): second chiefs (of a tribal town)
henrē (hin·ɫí: {II}): good
hensci (híns·ce:) hello
hericetv (hi·ɫe:·ci·tá {I;3}): to put away, store
heromē (hi·ɫó·mi: {II}): kind, generous
heromosē (hi·ɫô:·mo·si: {II;D}): kind, generous to
Hesaketvmesē (hi·sa:·ki·ta·mi·sí:): the Creator, God
hetotē (hi·to·tí:): snow, ice

hetoticetv (hi·to·te:·ci·tá {I;3}): to freeze something

heyv (hi·yá): this, this one, here; *also* yv

hiyē (hé:·yi: {II}): heat, warmth (of one)

hiyomat (he:·yô:·ma:t): now; *also* hiyowat

hiyowat (he:·yô:·wa:t): now; *also* hiyomat

hoccicetv (hoc·ce:·ci·tá {I;3}): to write

hocefhoketv (ho·cif·ho·kí·ta): names

hocefketv (ho·cif·ki·tá): name

hocetv (ho·cí·ta {I;3}): to pound or beat something in a container, as
    when pounding corn in a kecvpe; *see also* pvccetv

hockē (hóc·ki: {II}): beaten, pounded

hockvte (hoc·ka·tí): flour

hofonof(en) (ho·fô:·nof or ho·fô:·no·fin): a long time ago

hokkolen (hok·kô:·lin): two

hoktē (hok·tí:): woman

hoktē ehessē (hok·tí: i·hís·si:): married woman

hoktuce (hok·to·cí): girl

hoktvke (hok·ta·kí): women

hoktvkuce (hok·ta·kó·ci): girls

hoktvlē (hok·ta·lí:): old woman

holattē (ho·lá:t·ti: {II}): blue

holwvkē (hol·wa·kí: {II}): bad, naughty

holwvyēcē (hol·wa·yí:·ci: {II}): bad, naughty, cruel

hompetv (hom·pi·tá {I;3}): to eat; food

hompetv-coko (hom·pi·ta·co·kó): kitchen; *also* hompetv-hakcoko

hompetv-hakcoko (hom·pi·ta·ha:k·co·kó): kitchen; *also* hompetv-coko

hompetv hayv (hom·pi·ta há:·ya): cook (food preparer)

hompetv-vcvnetv (hom·pi·ta-a·ca·ni·tá): serving bowl; *also* avtēhkv

hompicetv (hom·pe:·ci·tá {I;3;II}): to feed something to someone

homuce (ho:·mo·cí): black pepper

homv (hó·ma {II}): in front of; *also* ehomv

honhoyē (hon·ho·yí: {II}): heavy (of two or more)

honnē (hón·ni: {II}): heavy (of one)

honnv (hón·na {D}): dress

honnv kocoknosat (hon·na ko·cok·no·sá:t {D}): skirt (article of
    clothing); *also* honnv-lecv

honnv-lecv (hon·na·lí·ca {D}): skirt (article of clothing); *also* honnv
    kocoknosat

honvntake (ho·nan·tá:·ki): men

honvnwv (ho·nán·wa): man

hopoyetv (ho·po·yi·tá {I;II}): to hunt for, look around for

hopuetake (ho·poy·tá:·ki): children

horkopv (hoł·kó:·pa): thief

hotopetv (ho·to·pi·tá {I;3}): to bake, broil, roast

hotosē (ho·tó·si: {II}): skinny, tired (of one)

hotosvkē (ho·to·sa·kí: {II}): skinny, tired (of two or more)

hotvlē (ho·ta·lí:): wind

hoyanat (ho·ya:·nâ:t): after, when it is past

hoyv (ho·yá): net

hoyvnetv (ho·ya·ni·tá {I;II}): to pass by (of one)

hueretv (hoy·łi·tá {I}): to stand (of one)

hvcce (hác·ci): river

hvccenvpv (hac·ci·ná·pa): riverbank; *also* hvcconvpv, hvcce onvpv

hvcce onvpv (hác·ci o·ná·pa): riverbank; *also* hvccenvpv, hvcconvpv

hvcconvpv (hac·co·ná·pa): riverbank; *also* hvccenvpv, hvcce onvpv

hvccuce (hac·co·cí): ditch, stream

hvce (há·ci {II}): his/her tail; *also* ehvce

hvcetekv (ha·ci·ti·ká): gopher; *also* ēkvn(v)-rolahvlēcv, vcetekv

hvfvpē (ha·fá·pi:): weedy, overgrown place

hvkihketv (ha·ke:h·ki·tá {I}): to cry (of one)

hvlhvwē (hal·ha·wí: {II}): high (of two or more)

hvlketv (hal·ki·tá {I}): to crawl

hvloneske (ha·lo·nís·ki): devil's shoestring (plant used to stun fish); *also*
    hvnoleske

hvlpvtv (hal·pa·tá): alligator

Hvlpvtvlke (hal·pa·tâl·ki): Alligator Clan

hvlvlatkē (ha·la·lá:t·ki: {II}): slow

hvlwe (hál·wi): heaven

hvmken (hám·kin): one; *also* hvnken

hvmkvn (hám·kan): all over

hvmmaketv (ham·ma:·ki·tá {I;II}): to make another say

hvnken (hán·kin): one; *also* hvmken

hvnoleske (ha·no·lís·ki): devil's shoestring (plant used to stun fish); *also*
    hvloneske

hvpo (ha·pó: {II}): camp; *also* ehvpo

hvpohayvke (ha·po·ha:·ya·kí): camps

hvrēssē (ha·łi:s·sí:): moon

hvrpe (háł·pi {II}): his/her/its skin, hide, casing, shell; *also* ehvrpe

hvse (ha·sí): sun

hvse-(e)skērkuce (ha·si·(i)s·ki:ł·ko·cí): watch, timepiece

hvsossv (ha·só:s·sa): the East, sunrise

hvsvtecetv (ha·sa·ti·cí·ta {I;3}): to clean (one)

hvsvthicetv (ha·sat·he:·ci·tá {I;II}): to clean (two or more items)

hvsvthvkē (ha·sat·ha·kí: {II}): to be clean (of two or more)

hvsvtkē (ha·sát·ki: {II}): to be clean (of one)

hvte (ha·tí): just now, recently

hvtekpikv (ha·tik·pé:·ka): pants

hvtēsketv (ha·ti:s·ki·tá {II/I}): to sneeze; *also* haktēsketv

hvthvkē (hat·ha·kí: {II}): white (of two or more); *also* hvtkvlke

hvthvwē (hat·ha·wí: {II}): pale (of two or more)

hvtkē (hát·ki: {II}): white (of one)

hvtkvlke (hat·kâl·ki {II}): white (of two or more); *also* hvthvkē

hvtvm (ha·tâm): again, next time, more

hvwecetv (ha·wi·ci·tá {I;3}): to open (a door, window, etc.)

hvyayvkē (ha·ya:·ya·kí: {II}): to be light (as the out-of-doors, the sun, etc.)

I

iem apohetv (e:·im a:·po·hí·ta {I;D}): to eavesdrop on

iem esetv (e:·im i·si·tá {I;3}): to take something out of a container; *also* acvwēcetv

isemayecetv (e:·si·ma:·yi·cí·ta {I;D}): to argue with someone; *also* etem vyoposketv

K

kaccv (ká:c·ca): tiger, mountain lion

kafe (ká:·fi): coffee

kaketv (ka:·ki·tá {I}): to sit, be seated, exist (of two)

kakompv-saktehke (ka:·kom·pa·sa:k·tíh·ki): pickle—Mvskoke pronunciation; *also* takompv—Seminole pronunciation

kapv (ká:·pa): coat (article of clothing)

kayetv (ka:·yi·tá {I;II}): to set (two, an item made of cloth) down; *also* eskayetv

keco (ki·có): mortar

kecvpe (ki·cá·pi): pestle, pounding stick

kerkē (kíł·ki: {II}): known

kerretv (kił·li·tá {I;II}): to know, learn

kicetv (ke:·ci·tá {I;II}): to tell, say (something) to someone in particular

kocecvmpv (ko·ci·cám·pa): star

kolēppa (ko·li:p·pá:): firefly

kolvpaken (ko·la·pâ:·kin): seven

kometv (ko:·mi·tá {I;3}): to think, believe, try, hope, want; *also* kowetv

konawv (ko·ná:·wa): necklace, beads

kono (ko·nó): skunk

kowetv (ko:·wi·tá {I;3}): to think, believe, try, hope, want; *also* kometv

kvmoksē (ka·mók·si: {II}): to be sour (not of milk)

kvnhvlwe-rakko (kan·hal·wi·rá:k·ko): mountain; *also* ēkvnhvlwe-rakko

'kvntvckv (kan·tác·ka): district; *also* ēkvntvckv

kvpe (ka·pí): ash drippings; *also* ēsso

kvperv fvccvn (ka·pí·ła fác·can): to the right

kvpotokv (ka·po·tó·ka {D}): hat; *also* kvtopokv

kvrkvpēcetv (kał·ka·pi:·ci·tá {I;3}): to dry two or more items

kvrpē (kał·pí: {II}): to be dry

kvrpēcetv (kał·pi:·ci·tá {I;3}): to dry one item

kvskvnv fvccvn (kas·ka·ná fác·can): to the left

kvsvmrē (ka·sám·łi: {II}): to be thin (of gravy, soup, etc.); *also* wētvlkē

kvsvppē (ka·sáp·pi: {II}): cold (of weather, water, something touched)

kvtopokv (ka·to·pó·ka {D}): hat; *also* kvpotokv

kvtopoyetv (ka·to·po·yí·ta {I;3}): to wear something on one's head (as a hat, turban, etc.)

L

lanē (lá:·ni: {II}): yellow, green

lecv (lí·ca {II}): under, beneath, below; *also* elecv

lekothofv (li·kot·hó:·fa): the south

lekothofv fvccvn (li·kot·hó:·fa fác·can): toward the south

lekvclewē (li·kac·li·wí: {II}): nasty, dirty, filthy (of two or more)

lekwē (lík·wi: {II}): a sore, wound

leslekē (lis·li·kí: {II}): old (of two or more inanimate things)

letketv (lit·ki·tá {I}): to run (of one)

letvfetv (li·ta·fi·tá {**I**}): to tear down
liketv (le:·ki·tá {**I**}): to sit, be seated, exist (of one)
locv (lo·cá): turtle, turtle-shell rattles (for dancing), Turtle (in stories)
lokcē (lók·ci: {**II**}): to be fertile, ripe (as of fruit)
lokcicetv (lok·ce:·ci·tá {**I;3**}): to farm/grow things
loketv (lo·kí·ta {**I;3**}): to devour, eat all of, finish off
lomhetv (lom·hi·tá {**I**}): to lie down (of three or more)
lopicē (lo·pé:·ci: {**I/II**}): to be kind
lopockē (lo·póc·ki: {**II**}): small (of two or more)
lowvckē (lo·wác·ki: {**II**}): to be tender (like meat), mushy or soft (of one)
lowvclokē (lo·wac·lo·kí: {**II**}): soft (of two or more)
lvffetv (laf·fi·tá {**I;II**}): to cut with a knife
lvfkē (láf·ki: {**II**}): cut, gashed
lvmhe (lám·hi): eagle
lvokē (láw·ki: {**II**}): deep (of one body of water)
lvolvkē (law·la·kí: {**II**}): deep (of two or more bodies of water)
lvpkē (láp·ki: {**II**}): quick
lvslvtē (las·la·tí: {**II**}): black (of two or more)
lvstē (lás·ti: {**II**}): black (of one)
lvtketv (lat·ki·tá {**II/I**}): to fall (of one)

M

mahē (má:·hi: {**II**}): tall (of one)
mahmvyē (ma:h·ma·yí: {**II**}): tall (of two or more)
maketv (ma:·ki·tá {**I;II**}): to say
mapohicetv (ma:·po·he:·ci·tá {**I; D**}): to listen to; *also* em mapohicetv
mēcetv (mi:·ci·tá {**I;II**}): to do, perform an activity
mēkko (mí:k·ko): chief
mēkkvke (mi:k·ka·kí): chiefs
mēkusvpkv-cuko (mi:·ko·sáp·ka có·ko): church
melletv (mil·li·tá {**I**}): to point
meteliketv (mi·ti·le:·ki·tá {**D**}): band (Seminole political division)
mi (mé:): place, location; *also* miyewv
miste (mé:s·ti): that person (usually used to refer to a male)
miste vculē (mé:s·ti a·có·li:): old man
mistvlke (me:s·tâl·ki): those people, those men
miyewv (me:·yi·wá): place, location; *also* mi

mohmes kometv (**moh·mís ko·mí·ta** {**I;3**}): to guess

momen (**mo:·mín**): and, then (with different subject in following clause); *also* mont, mowen

momet (**mo:·mít**): and, then (with same subject in following clause); *also* mowet

momis (**mô:·me:s**): but, however; *also* mowis

monkan (**món·ka:n**): or; *also* monkat

monkat (**món·ka:t**): or; *also* monkan

monks (**mónks**): no

monkv (**món·ka**): so, therefore

mont (**mó:nt**): and, then (with different subject in following clause); *also* momen, mowen

morecetv (**mo:·łi·cí·ta** {**I;3**}): to boil, make bubble

morvfkv (**mo·łáf·ka**): boots; *also* esohtēhkv; (e)stelepik-morvfkv; sohtēhkv

mowen (**mo:·wín**): and, then (with different subject in following clause); *also* momen, mont

mowet (**mo:·wít**): and, then (with same subject in following clause); *also* momet

mowis (**mô:·we:s**): but, however; *also* momis

mowof (**mo:·w·ô:f**): when it happens—contraction of mowen owof

mucv-nettv (**mo·ca·nít·ta**): today

mv (**má**): that, that one, he/she/it

mvhakv-cuko (**ma·ha:·ka·có·ko**): school house, school

mvhayv (**ma·há:·ya** {**D**}): teacher

mvhayetv (**ma·ha:·yi·tá** {**I;D**}): to teach

mvnettē (**ma·nít·ti:** {**II**}): young

mvnhēretv (**man·hi:·łi·tá** {**II;D**}): to enjoy

Mvnte (**mán·ti**): Monday

Mvnte enhvyvtke (**mán·ti in·ha·yát·ki**): Tuesday

Mvskokvlke (**mas·ko:·kâl·ki**): the Mvskoke people

N

nake (**nâ:·ki**): thing, something

nake 'setenkerretv (**nâ:·ki (i)s·it·in·kił·łi·tá** {**I;II**}): to debate

nak en hecicetv (**nâ:k in hi·ce:·ci·tá** {**I;II**}): one person to show something to someone

nak en hecicēyetv (**nâ:k in hi·ce:·ci:·yi·tá** {**I;II**}): two or more persons to show something to someone

nak (e)sem vfiyetv (**nâ:k (i)s·im·a·fe:·yi·tá**): screwdriver

nak-eshoccickv cokv (**nâ:k·is·ho:c·cé:c·ka co·ká**): notebook

nak-kerreko (**nâ:k·kił·łí·ko {II}**): to be stupid

naklokcicv (**nâ:k·lok·cé:·ca**): farmer

naklokcicvlke (**nâ:k·lok·ce:·câl·ki**): farmers

nakonvkuce (**nâ:k·o·na·ko·cí**): short story, fairytale

nakonvkv (**nâ:k·oná·ka**): story, tale, news

nakrvfkv (**nâ:k·łaf·ka**): transplanted plants

nakstomen (**na:k·sto:·mín**): why; *also* nakstowen, stomen, stowen

nakstowen (**na:k·sto:·wín**): why; *also* nakstomen, stomen, stowen

nak-svkmorēcv (**nâ:k·sak·mo·łí:·ca**): frying pan

nak-vfastv (**nâ:k·a·fá:s·ta**): general council

nak-vfastv-emetohkvlketv (**nâ:k·a·fá:s·ta·i·mi·toh·kâl·ki·ta**): general council meeting

nak-vhockuce (**nâ:k·a·hoc·ko·cí**): small garden

nak-vtehetv (**nâ:k·a·ti·hi·tá**): pan; *also* halo-pvlaknv

nakwiyv (**nâ:k·wé:·ya**): shopkeeper, salesperson

nanvke (**nâ:·na·kí**): things

naoricetv (**na:·o·łe:·ci·tá {I;II}**): to bother, annoy

nehē (**ni·hí: {II}**): fat

nekattetv (**ni·ka:t·ti·tá {II}**): to nod once

nekēyetv (**ni·ki:·yi·tá {I}**): to move, shake

nekēyicetv (**ni·ki:·ye:·ci·tá {I;II}**): to move, shake around

nekricetv (**nik·łe:·ci·tá {I;II}**): to burn; *also* nokricetv

nene (**ni·ní**): road, path

nerē-isē (**ni·łí:·ê:·si:**): last night

nesetv (**ni·sí·ta {I;3}**): to buy

nettv (**nít·ta**): day

nocetv (**no·cí·ta {II/I}**): to sleep, go to sleep, be asleep (of one); *also* nucetv

nochoyetv (**noc·ho·yí·ta {II/I}**): to sleep, go to sleep, be asleep (of two); *also* nuchoyetv

nocicetv (**no·ce:·ci·tá {II/I}**): to sleep, go to sleep, be asleep (of three or more); *also* nucicetv

nockelē (**noc·ki·lí: {II}**): sleepy; *also* nuckelē

nockv-coko (**no:c·ka·có·ko**): bedroom; *also* wakketv-cokofv

nokke-vfastv (**nók·ki a·fá:s·ta**): nurse; *also* enokkvlke-vfastv

nokose (**no·kó·si**): bear

nokricetv (**nok·ɬe:·ci·tá {I;II}**): to burn; *also* nekricetv
noricetv (**no·ɬe:·ci·tá {I;3}**): to cook or bake
norickv-hute (**no·ɬe:c·ka·hó·ti**): oven; *also* tvklik-noricv
norottetv (**no·ɬo:t·ti·tá {I}**): to shake the head
nowat (**nó:·wa:t**): conditional suffix
nucē (**no·cí: {II}**): asleep (of one)
nucetv (**no·cí·ta {II/I}**): to sleep, go to sleep, be asleep (of one); *also* nocetv
nuchoyetv (**noc·ho·yí·ta {II/I}**): to sleep, go to sleep, be asleep (of two); *also* nochoyetv
nucicetv (**no·ce:·ci·tá {II/I}**): to sleep, go to sleep, be asleep (of three or more); *also* nocicetv
nuckelē (**noc·ki·lí: {II}**): sleepy; *also* nockelē
nute (**nó·ti {II}**): his/her tooth
nvcomusē (**na·cǒ:^{n}·mo·si:**): very few, very little (in size), a little bit
nvfketv (**naf·ki·tá {I;II}**): to hit
nvkaftvlke encoko (**na·ka:f·tâl·ki in·có·ko**): council house

O

ocē-cvpkuce mvpe (**o·ci:·cap·ko·cí má·pi**): pecan tree
ocetv (**o·ci·tá {I;3}**): to have
ocv (**ó:·ca**): owner
ofiketv (**o·fe:·ki·tá**): underwear; *also* ofv-vccetv
ofv (**ó:·fa**): inside of, during
ofv-vccetv (**o:·fa·ac·ci·tá**): underwear; *also* ofiketv
oh (**ôh**): ouch
ohenockv (**oh·i·nó:c·ka**): tie, scarf, anything worn around the neck
ohfolhuecetv (**oh·fol·hoy·ci·tá {I;II}**): to make (two or more) return something
ohhaktēsketv (**oh·ha:k·ti:s·ki·tá {I;II}**): to sneeze on someone or something
ohhecetv (**oh·hi·ci·tá {I;II}**): to look down (from something), to look over (something)
ohhompetv (**oh·hom·pi·tá**): table
ohhonvyetv (**oh·ho·na·yi·tá {I;II}**): to read
Ohkalvlke (**oh·ka:·lâl·ki**): Methodists; *also* Uewv Ohkalvlke
ohkayetv (**oh·ka:·yi·tá {I;3}**): to set (two items, something made of cloth) on top of (something else)

ohkueketv (oh·koy·ki·tá {I;II}): to move toward (of one)

ohliketv (oh·le:·ki·tá): chair

ohliketv (oh·le:·ki·tá {I;II}): to sit on, ride (of one)

ohliketv-ohlikv (oh·le:·ki·ta-oh·lé:·ka): chairman, chairperson

ohliketv-ohlikv-vpoktv (oh·le:·ki·ta-oh·le:·ka-a·pók·ta): vice-chairman, vice-chairperson

ohmelletv (oh·mil·li·tá {I}): to be elected

ohoketv (o·ho:·ki·tá {II/I}): to cough

ohranetv (oh·ła:·ni·tá {I;II}): to cover

ohrolopēyof (oh·ło·lo·pí:·yof): next year

ohrvnkv cvwetv (oh·łán·ka ca·wí·ta {I;II}): to uncover two or more things

ohrvnkv esetv (oh·łán·ka i·sí·ta {I;II}): to uncover one thing

ohtvmhoketv (oh·tam·ho·kí·ta {I;II}): to fly toward, fly over (of two)

ohtvmketv (oh·tam·ki·tá {I;II}): to fly toward, fly over (of one)

ohvpoketv (oh·a·po:·ki·tá {I;II}): to sit on top of, ride (of three or more)

oh-vthoyetv (oh·at·ho·yí·ta {I;II}): to come toward (of two)

ohvyetv (oh·a·yí·ta {I;II}): to go up to (something or someone) (of one)

ohyvkvpetv (oh·ya·ka·pí·ta {I;II}): to walk toward (of one)

ohyvkvpvketv (oh·ya·ka·pa·ki·tá {I;II}): to walk toward (of three or more)

okat (o:·kâ:t): says, is saying

oketv (o·kí·ta {I}): to mean, say

okholattē (ok·ho·lá:t·ti: {II}): purple; *also* pvrkomē

okkoset mēcetv (ok·ko·sít mi:·ci·tá {I;II}): to wash over and over, as the fekce

okkosetv (ok·ko·si·tá {I;II}): to wash (of one), wash one item

okkoskuecetv (ok·kos·koy·ci·tá {I;II}): wash (of two or more), to wash two or more items

oklanē (ok·lá:·ni {II}): brown

Okmvlke (ok·mál·ki): Okmulgee, Oklahoma

okneha (ok·ni·há:): gravy

okofkē (o·kóf·ki: {II}): muddy, dirty (of water)

oktahv (ok·tá:·ha): sand

oktahv-topv (ok·ta:·ha·tó·pa): sandbar

ometv (o·mí·ta {I}): to be; *also* owetv

omvlke (o·mâl·ki): all; may be used as a plural pronoun by inserting type I suffixes

omvlkv (o·mál·ka): all, everything, every

onvkv (o·ná·ka): word, saying

onvpv (o·ná·pa {II}): above, over

opanv (o·pá:·na): dancer

oponayv (o·po·ná:·ya): speaker

oponvkv hērv honayetv (o·po·na·ká hí:·ła ho·na:·yi·tá): sermon

(o)ponvyetv ((o)·po·na·yí·ta {I}): to talk, speak, give a speech

opvnetv (o·pa·ni·tá {I}): to dance

oretv (o·łí·ta {I;3}): to reach, achieve (a goal, position, etc.) (of one)

ossetv (os·sí·ta {I}): to get out of jail or some confined space (of one)

osten (ô:s·tin): four

osticetv (os·te:·ci·tá {I;3}): to do four times

ostvpaken (os·ta·pâ:·kin): nine

owetv (o·wí·ta {I}): to be; also ometv

owv (ó:·wa): water; also uewv

owvlvste eshoccickv (o:·wa·lás·ti is·ho:c·cé:c·ka): writing pen

P

pakpvkoce (pa:k·pa·kó·ci): flower

pakse (pá:k·si): tomorrow; also vpakse

pakse vsimv (pá:k·si a·sé:·ma): day after tomorrow; also vpakse vsimv

paksvnkē (pa:k·san·kí:): yesterday

pasetv (pa:·si·tá {I;3}): to sweep

pefatketv (pi·fa:t·ki·tá {I}): to run (of three or more)

pelofv (pi·łó:·fa): forest; also eto-vlke

penanv (pi·ná:·na): banana

penkvlē (pin·ka·lí: {II}): afraid, scared

penwv (pín·wa): turkey

perofv (pi·łó·fa): forest; also eto-vlke

pipuce (pe:·po·cí): baby

poca (po·cá: {II}): his/her grandfather; also puca

pocoswv (po·cós·wa): axe; also woceswv

Poca Rakko (po·cá: łá:k·ko): Wolf (in stories)

pohetv (po·hí·ta {I;II}): to hear

pohkē (póh·ki: {II}): loud

pokkēccvlke (pok·ki:c·câl·ki): ball team

pokko (pók·ko): ball

polokē (po·łó:·ki: {II}): round (like a ball or sphere) (of one)

pome (pó:·mi): we, us

pose (pó·si {II}): his/her grandmother or paternal aunt; *also* epose
pose (pó:·si): cat
posuce (po:·so·cí): kitten
puca (po·cá: {II}): his/her grandfather; *also* poca
pvccetv (pac·ci·tá {I;3}): to pound, smash, break up, shatter, as when hitting something with a hammer or mallet; *see also* hocetv
pvfnē (páf·ni: {II}): quick, fast (of one)
pvfpvnē (paf·pa·ní: {II}): quick, fast (of two or more)
pvkohlicetv (pak·oh·le:·ci·tá {I;3}): to fold
pvlaknv (pa·lá:k·na): plate, dish
pvlaknv-rakko (pa·la:k·na·łá:k·ko): serving platter
pvlvtetv (pa·la·ti·tá {I;3}): to pour a liquid out, as when emptying a bucket, jar, etc.
pvlvtketv (pa·lat·ki·tá {I}): to fall, drop (of three or more)
pvrko-afke (pał·ko·á:f·ki): grape dumpling; *also* pvrko-sakporoke, pvrko-svpkonepke
pvrkomē (pał·ko·mí: {II}): purple; *also* okholattē
pvrko-sakporoke (pał·ko·sa:k·po·łó·ki): grape dumpling; *also* pvrko-svpkonepke, pvrko-afke
pvrko-svpkonepke (pał·ko·sap·ko·níp·ki): grape dumpling; *also* pvrko-afke, pvrko-sakporoke
pvrvnkē (pa·łán·ki:): on the other side of
pvsvtkē (pa·sát·ki: {II}): dead (of two or more)
pvwv (pá·wa {II}): his/her maternal uncle

R

rahecetv (ła:·hi·cí·ta {I;II}): to see a long distance
rakkē (łá:k·ki: {II}): big (of one)
rakko (łá:k·ko): horse
rakrvkē (ła:k·ła·kí: {II}): big (of two or more)
raliketv (ła:·le:·ki·tá {I}): to sit down after going a distance
rē (łí:): bullet, arrow
refolhoketv (łi·fol·ho·kí·ta {I;II}): to return to a location, come back to a location (of two)
rem paksen (łim pá:k·sin): the next day
rohyvkvpetv (łoh·ya·ka·pi·tá {I;II}): to walk a long distance toward (of one)
roketv (ło·kí·ta {I;3}): to take off one piece of clothing

rokruecetv (łok·łoy·ci·tá {I;3}): to take off more than one piece of clothing

ropotecetv (ło·po:·ti·cí·ta {I}): to go through, pass through (of three or more)

ropothoyetv (ło·po:t·ho·yí·ta {I}): to go through, pass through (of two)

ropottetv (ło·po:t·ti·tá {I}): to go through, pass through (of one)

roretv (ło·łi·tá {I}): to arrive, get there, reach there (of one)

rvlvketv (ła·la·ki·tá {I;II}): to return to, come back to a location (of one)

rvro (ła·łó): fish

rvro akhopoyv (ła·łó a:k·ho·pó:·ya): fisherman; *also* rvro em akwiyv

rvro aswiketv (ła·łó a:s·we:·ki·tá {I;3}): to catch a fish; *also* rvro esetv

rvro em akwiyetv (ła·łó im a:k·we:·yi·tá {I}): to fish; *also* em akwiyetv

rvro em akwiyv (ła·łó im a:k·wé:·ya): fisherman; *also* rvro akhopoyv

rvro esetv (ła·łó i·sí·ta {I;3}): to catch a fish; *also* rvro aswiketv

rvro rakcvwetv (ła·łó ła:k·ca·wí·ta): fishhook; *also* cufokonhe

rvtetv (ła·ti·tá {I}): to come back, return (of one)

S

sahkopvnetv (sa:h·ko·pa·ni·tá {I;II}): to play a prank on someone

sakpv-seko (sa:k·pa·sí·ko): vest

sasvkwv (sâ:·sak·wa): goose

sehoketv (si·ho:·ki·tá {I}): to stand (of two)

seholwahuecetv (si·hol·wa:·hoy·ci·tá {I;II}): to make (two or more) dirty; *also* vholwahuecetv

selakketv (si·la:k·ki·tá {I}): to shout, cry out

setēfketv (si·ti:f·ki·tá {I}): to melt

sētetv (si:·ti·tá {I;3}): to tear, rip

sofke (sóf·ki): a drink made from corn and lye (ash drippings)

sofkē (sóf·ki: {II}): to be deep, not of water (of one)

sofsokē (sof·so·kí: {II}): to be deep, not of water (of two or more)

sohtēhkv (soh·tí:h·ka): boot/boots; *also* (e)stelepik-morvfkv, esohtēhkv, morvfkv

sokcv (sók·ca): bag; *also spelled* sukcv

sokhv (sók·ha): pig, hog

sokhv-hatkv (sok·ha·há:t·ka): opossum

somecicetv (so·mi·ce:·ci·tá {I;3}): to lose (one thing or one game)

somhoketv (som·ho·kí·ta {II}): to be lost (of two or of a cloth item)

somhuecetv (som·hoy·ci·tá {I;3}): to lose (more than one thing, more than once)

somketv (som·ki·tá {II}): to be lost (of one); *also* sonketv

sonketv (son·ki·tá {II}): to be lost (of one); *also* somketv

sopakhvtkē (so·pa:k·hát·ki: {II}): grey (of one)

sopakhvthvkē (so·pa:k·hat·ha·kí: {II}): grey (of two or more)

sopaktv (so·pá:k·ta): toad, frog

sote (só:·ti): baking soda

stimvt (ste:·mát): who; *also* estimvt

stofvn (sto:·fán): when

stomēcet (sto·mí:·cit): how; *also* estomē, estomēcet

stomen (sto:·mín): why; *also* nakstomen, nakstowen, stowen

stowen (sto:·wín): why; *also* nakstomen, nakstowen, stomen

stvmen (sta·mín): where; *also* estvmen

sukcv (sók·ca): bag; *also spelled* sokcv

sule (so·lí): buzzard, Buzzard (of stories)

sulkē (sól·ki: {II}): many, much, numerous

svcakhetv (sa·ca:k·hi·tá {I}): to crash (of a car)

svhocackv (sa·ho·cá:c·ka): sock/socks; *also* estele-svhocackv, svhocickv

svhocickv (sa·ho·cé:c·ka): sock/socks; *also* estele- svhocackv, svhocackv

svholwvkē (sa·hol·wa·kí: {II}): to be dirty, unclean (of one)

svkmorecetv (sak·mo·li·ci·tá {I;3}): to fry

svlvfkēcetv (sa·laf·ki:·ci·tá {I;II}): to arrest, imprison; *also* svlvfkuecetv

svlvfkuecetv (sa·laf·koy·ci·tá {I;II}): to arrest, imprison; *also* svlvfkēcetv

svpakletv (sa·pa:k·li·tá {I}): to stand (of three or more)

svtokuce (sa·to:·ko·cí): hammer

svtv (sa·tá): apple/apples

T

tafvmpe (ta:·fám·pi): onion/onions

tafvmpuce (ta:·fam·po·cí): wild onions

tak-etecetv (ta:k·i·ti·ci·tá {I;3}): to light a fire/stove; *also* etecetv

takfulletv (tak·fol·li·tá {I}): to be around at ground level or on the floor (of three or more); to be around in an enclosed space/building (of three or more)

takketv (ta:k·ki·tá {I;II}): to kick

taklomhetv (tak·lom·hi·tá {I}): to lie down on the floor or ground (of three or more)

takompv (**ta:·kóm·pa**): pickle—Seminole pronunciation; *also* kakompv-saktehke—Mvskoke pronunciation

taktopvtake (**ta:k·to·pa·tá:·ki**): floor

takyurketv (**tak·yoɬ·ki·tá** {**I**}): to fall on the ground or floor (of two)

tasecetv (**ta:·si·cí·ta** {**I**}): to hop, jump (of three or more)

tashoketv (**ta:s·ho·kí·ta** {**I**}): to hop, jump (of two)

tasketv (**ta:s·ki·tá** {**I**}): to hop, jump (of one)

taskuecetv (**ta:s·koy·ci·tá** {**I;II**}): to make (one) jump

tat (**ta:t**): adds mild focus to a preceding phrase, often to resume a topic; *also* tate

tate (**tá:·ti**): adds mild focus to a preceding phrase, often to resume a topic; *also* tat

tayē (**tá:·yi:**): enough

tefnē (**tíf·ni:** {**II**}): to be dull (as of a knife)

tēkvnv (**ti:·ka·ná**): deacon

telomhv (**ti·lóm·ha**): quilt

tempē (**tím·pi:**): close to, near

tenaspē (**ti·ná:s·pi:** {**II**}): slippery, slick

tenēpicetv (**ti·ni:·pe:·ci·tá** {**I;3**}): to iron

tepvkē (**ti·pa·kí:**): together

tofketv (**tof·ki·tá** {**I;II**}): to spit

tofvpetv (**to·fa·pi·tá** {**I;3;D**}): to crumble (something)

tohahwv (**to·há:h·wa**): box

tohlikē (**toh·le:·kí:** {**II**}): to be piled up (as of laundry, brush, etc.); *also* tohvpokē

tohvpokē (**toh·a·po·kí:** {**II**}): to be piled up (as of laundry, brush, etc.); *also* tohlikē

tohwelēpkv (**toh·wi·lí:p·ka**): cross, crucifix; *also* etohwelēpkv

tokonhe (**to·kón·hi**): stickball stick, ball stick

tokorketv (**to·koɬ·ki·tá** {**I**}): to run (of two)

toksē (**tók·si** {**II**}): to be sour (of milk)

tolose (**to·lô:·si**): chicken

'tolvcce (**to·lác·ci**): tree branch; *also* etolvcce

topv (**to·pá**): bed

topvrv (**to·pá·ɬa**): in back of a building

torkowv (**to:ɬ·ko·wá** {**II**}): knee

torofv (**to·ló:·fa** {**II**}): his/her face

torsakhēckv (**toɬ·sa:k·hí:c·ka** {**II**}): glasses, eyeglasses

tosēnv (to·sí:·na): salt pork
totkv (tó:t·ka): fire
totkv-hute (to:t·ka·hó·ti): fireplace, stove; *also* cvto for 'stove'
totkv-vslēcv (to:t·ka·as·lí:·ca): fireman
tutcēnen (tot·cî:·nin): three
tvcetv (ta·cí·ta {I;3}): to cut once
tvklik (tak·lé:k): bread; *also* tvklike
tvklik-cvmpuce (tak·le:k·cam·po·cí): cookie
tvklik-cvmpv (tak·le:k·cám·pa): cake
tvklike (tak·lé:·ki): bread; *also* tvklik
tvklik-noricv (tak·le:k·no·łé:·ca): oven; *also* norickv-hute
tvklik-svkmorke (tak·le:k-sak·mó:ł·ki): fried bread
tvko (ta·kó): mole or vole
tvkocetv (ta·ko·ci·tá {I;3}): to break, crack (one egg, glass, etc.)
tvkohlicetv (tak·oh·le:·ci·tá {I;3}): to break, crack (two or more eggs,
    glasses, etc.)
tvlofv (ta·ló:·fa): town
tvlvswē (ta·lás·wi: {II}): to be tough, like meat or clay
Tvlsv (tál·sa): Tulsa, Oklahoma
tvmecetv (ta·mi·ci·tá {I}): to fly (of three or more)
tvmhoketv (tam·ho·kí·ta {I}): to fly (of two)
tvmketv (tam·ki·tá {I}): to fly (of one)
tvpeksē (ta·pík·si: {II}): level, flat
tvphē (táp·hi: {II}): to be wide (of one)
tvptvhē (tap·ta·hí: {II}): to be wide (of two or more)
tvskocē (tas·ko·cí: {II}): to be thin (of cloth, paper, etc.)
tvstvnvke (tas·ta·ná·ki): warrior
tvstvnvkvlke (tas·ta·na·kâl·ki): warriors

U

uewv (óy·wa): water; *also* owv
Uewv Ohkalvlke (óy·wa oh·ka:·lâl·ki): Methodists; *also* Ohkalvlke

V

vcayēcetv (a·ca:·yi:·ci·tá {I;3}): to store something, to protect, save
    something

vccakv (ac·cá:·ka): ladder

vccetv (ac·cí·ta {I;3}): to put on clothing that slips over the head or is wrapped around the body (of one)

vce (a·cí): corn

vcemecetv (a·ci·mi·cí·ta {I}): to climb up (of three or more)—Mvskoke pronunciation; *also* vcvmecetv

vcemhoketv (a·cim·ho·kí·ta {I}): to climb up (of two)—Mvskoke pronunciation; *also* vcvmhoketv

vcemketv (a·cim·ki·tá {I}): to climb up (of one)—Mvskoke pronunciation; *also* vcumketv, vcunketv

vcetekv (a·ci·ti·ká): gopher; *also* hvcetekv, ēkvn(v)-rolahvlēcv

vchoyetv (ac·ho·yi·tá {I;3}): to put on clothing that slips over the head or is wrapped around the body (of two or more)

vcokv (a·có:·ka): nail/nails; *also* vcopv

vcopv (a·có:·pa): nail/nails; *also* vcokv

vculē (a·có·li: {II}): old, aged, elderly (of one animate being)

vcumecetv (a·co·mi·cí·ta {I}): to climb up (of three or more)—Seminole pronunciation; *also* vcemecetv

vcumhoketv (a·com·ho·kí·ta {I}): to climb up (of two)—Seminole pronunciation; *also* vcemhoketv

vcumketv (a·com·ki·tá {I}): to climb up (of one)—Seminole pronunciation; *also* vcemketv, vcunketv

vcunketv (a·con·ki·tá {I}): to climb up (of one)—Mvskoke pronunciation; *also* vcemketv, vcumketv

vcvkē (a·ca·kí: {II}): short (of an animate being)

vcvmecetv (a·ca·mi·cí·ta {I}): to climb up (of three or more)—Mvskoke pronunciation; *also* vcemecetv, vcumecetv

vcvmhoketv (a·cam·ho·kí·ta {I}): to climb up (of two)—Mvskoke pronunciation; *also* vcemhoketv, vcumhoketv

vfopkē (a·fó:p·ki:): by, next to

vhakv (a·há:·ka): law

vhakv-empvtakv (a·há:·ka·im·pa·tá:·ka): constitution

vhakv-hayv (a·ha:·ka·há:·ya): lawyer

vhayetv (a·ha:·yi·tá {I;II}): to paint (a picture, a house, etc.)

vhēhketv (a·hi:h·ki·tá {I;II}): to growl at

vhoccickv (a·ho:c·cé:c·ka): blackboard

vholwahokē (a·hol·wa:·ho·kí: {II}): dirty (of two or more)

vholwahuecetv (a·hol·wa:·hoy·ci·tá {I;II}): to make (two or more) dirty; *also* seholwahuecetv

vholwvkē (a·hol·wa·kí: {II}): dirty (of one)

vhonecetv (a·ho·ni·cí·ta {I}): to wake up, awaken

vhopvketv (a·ho·pa·kí·ta {I;II}): to push, shove

vhoretv (a·ho·li·tá {I;3}): to sew (one item)

vhorhuecetv (a·hoł·hoy·ci·tá {I;3}): to sew (two or more items)

vhoyetv (a·ho·yi·tá {I}): to go (of two)

vhv (a·há): potato

vhvce-rēhe (a·ha·ci·łí:·hi): Irish potato/potatoes

vhvoke (a·háw·ki): door

vhvokuce (a·haw·ko·cí): window

vhvretv (a·ha·li·tá {I;II}): to wander around, be near (of one)

vkerricetv (a·kił·łe:·ci·tá {I;II}): to think about, wonder about

vkerrickv (a·kił·łé:c·ka): a thought (about something)

vkhottetv (ak·hot·ti·tá {I;3}): to close (a door, window, etc.)

vkosletv (a·kos·li·tá {I}): to win; *also* epoyetv

vlēkcv (a·lí:k·ca): doctor

vlkē (ál·ki:): only, nothing but

vloso (a·ló:·so): rice

vlvtketv (a·lat·ki·tá {I;II}): to fall against (of one)

vmelletv (a·mil·li·tá {I;II}): to point at

vne (a·ní): I

vnokecetv (a·no·ki·cí·ta {I;II}): to love someone

vnoksē (a·nók·si: {II}): greedy; *also* encakē

vnrvpetv (an·ła·pí·ta {I;II}): to meet another

vpakse (a·pá:k·si): tomorrow; *also* pakse

vpakse vsimv (a·pá:k·si a·sé:·ma): day after tomorrow; *also* pakse vsimv

vpefatecicetv (a·pi·fa:·ti·ce:·ci·tá {I;II}): to make three or more run

vpeletv (a·pi·li·tá {I}): to laugh, smile (of one)

vpelhoyetv (a·pil·ho·yí·ta {I}): to laugh, smile (of two or more)

vpelicetv (a·pi·le:·ci·tá {I;II}): to laugh at

vpeshockē (a·pis·hóc·ki:): boiled meat (meat that has been dried, boiled, and then cooked with onions)

vpeswv (a·pís·wa): meat

vpeyetv (a·pi·yi·tá {I}): to go (of three or more)

vpiketv (a·pe:·ki·tá {I;3}): to put on one shoe or one item pulled up on a body part, to put one item on another

vpohetv (a·po·hi·tá {I;II}): to ask for, ask about, buy

vpoketv (a·po·ki·tá {I}): to sit, be seated, exist (of three or more)

vpvlvtetv (a·pa·la·tí·ta {I;3}): to throw out (three or more items)

vretv (a·łí·ta {I}): to go around, wander (of one)

vrvhkv (a·łáh·ka): because of

vsēketv (a·si:·ki·tá {I;II}): to shake hands with, greet

vslēcetv (as·li:·ci·tá {I;3}): to put out a fire, turn off a lamp, erase, rub out

vsofotketv (a·so·fo:t·ki·tá {I}): to rub against (as when washing clothes on a washboard)

vsse (ás·si): tea

vtehketv (a·tih·ki·tá {I;3}): to put on pants or two things pulled up on a body part, to put two or more items on another, to get or be inside something (of two or more)

vtokorketv (a·to·koł·ki·tá {I;II}): to run to (of two)

vtopv (a·tó·pa): ceiling; *also* cokofv-ohrvnkv

vtotetv (a·to·ti·tá {I;3}): to send something

vtotketv (a·tot·ki·tá {I}): to work

vtotkv (a·tó:t·ka): worker

vtvretv (a·ta·łi·tá {I;3}): to hang up one item

vtvrticetv (a·tał·te:·ci·tá {I;3}): to hang up two or more items

vwenayetv (a·wi·na:·yi·tá {I;II/II;3}): to smell something

vwiketv (a·we:·ki·tá {I;3}): to throw (one) out or away

vwohketv (a·wo:h·ki·tá {I;II}): to bark at (of one)

vwenayetv (a·wi·na:·yi·tá {I;II/II;3}): to smell, sniff

vwvnhēcicetv (a·wan·hi:·ce:·ci·tá {I;II/I;3}): to make firm, harden

vwvnvyetv (a·wa·na·yí·ta {I;3}): to tie something to someone

vyepetv (a·yi·pi·tá {I}): to leave, go away from (of one)

vyetv (a·yí·ta {I}): to go (of one)

vyocetv (a·yo:·ci·tá {I}): to gather, pick fruits or vegetables

vyoposketv (a·yo·pos·ki·tá {I;II}): to answer back, reply; *also* akicetv

W

wakketv (wa:k·ki·tá {I}): to lie down (of one)

wakketv-cokofv (wa:k·ki·ta·co·kó·fa): bedroom; *also* nockv-coko

wakv (wá:·ka): cow

wakvneha (wa:·ka·ni·há:): butter; *also* wakvpesē-neha

wakvpesē (wa:·ka·pi·sí:): milk

wakvpesē-neha (wa:·ka·pi·sí: ni·há:): butter; *also* wakvneha

waretv (wa:·łi·tá {I;3}): to slice, cut more than once (as bread, meat, etc.)

welvketv (wi·la·ki·tá {I}): to go about, be located, wander (of two)

wenowēyetv (wi·no·wi:·yi·tá {I}): to wiggle, wriggle (like a worm); *also* fekefeketv

wētvlkē (wi:·tâl·ki: {II}): to be thin (of gravy, soup, etc.); *also* kvsvmrē

wiyetv (we:·yi·tá {I;3}): to sell, offer

woceswv (wo·cís·wa): axe; *also* pocoswv

wotko (wó:t·ko): raccoon

Wotkvlke (wo:t·kâl·ki): Raccoon clan

wvkecetv (wa·ki·ci·tá {I;II}): to lay (a person, long object) down

wvnvkē (wa·ná·ki: {II}): tied up

Y

yefolhoketv (yi·fol·ho·kí·ta {I}): to go back (of two)

yefolketv (yi·fol·ki·tá {I}): to go back (of one)

yekcē (yík·ci: {II}): strong

yokkofketv (yok·ko:f·ki·tá): shirt

yomockē (yo·móc·ki: {II}): to be dark, as the out-of-doors; *also* yvpockē

yopv (yó·pa {II}): behind, in back of

yossetv (yos·si·tá {I;II}): to go out (toward something) (of one)

yurketv (yoł·ki·tá {I}): to fall (of two)

yvhiketv (ya·he:·ki·tá): song

yvhiketv (ya·he:·ki·tá {I}): to sing

yvkvpetv (ya·ka·pi·tá {I}): to walk (of one)

yvlahv (ya·lá:·ha): orange (fruit)

yvlonkv-lanet (ya·lon·ka·lá:·nit): carrot

yv (yá): this, this one, here; *also* heyv

yvnvsv (ya·ná·sa): buffalo, Buffalo (of stories)

yvpockē (ya·póc·ki: {II}): to be dark, as the out-of-doors; *also* yomockē

Glossary

English to Mvskoke

A

above, over: onvpv (o·ná·pa {II})

achieve, reach (a goal, a position, etc.) (of one), to: oretv (o·łí·ta {I;3})

afraid, scared: penkvlē (pin·ka·lí: {II})

afraid of, to be: em penkvlē (im pin·ka·lí: {I;D/II;D})

after, when it is past: hoyanat (ho·ya:·nâ:t)

afternoon: fvccvlik hoyanen (fac·ca·lé:k ho·yâ:·nin)

again, next time, more: hvtvm (ha·tâm)

aged, old, elderly (of one animate being): vculē (a·có·li: {II})

all, may be used as a plural pronoun by inserting type I suffixes: omvlke (o·mâl·ki)

all, everything, every: omvlkv (o·mál·ka)

all over: hvmkvn (hám·kan)

alligator: hvlpvtv (hal·pa·tá)

Alligator clan: Hvlpvtvlke (hal·pa·tâl·ki)

and, then (with different subject in following clause): momen (mo:·mín); *also* mont (mó:nt); mowen (mo:·wín)

and, then (with same subject in following clause): momet (mo:·mít); *also* mowet (mo:·wít)

angry (of one): cvpakkē (ca·pá:k·ki: {II})

angry (of two or more): cvpakhokē (ca·pa:k·ho·kí: {II})

angry at someone (of one), to be: encvpakkē (in·ca·pá:k·ki: {II;D})

279

angry at someone (of two or more), to be: encvpakhokē
  (in·ca·pa:k·ho·kí: {II;D})

annoy, bother, to: naoricetv (na:·o·łe:·ci·tá {I;II})

another, different: ētimv (i:·té:·ma)

answer (a person), give an answer to, to: em vyoposketv (im
  a·yo·pos·ki·tá {I;D})

answer back, reply, to: akicetv (a:·ke:·ci·tá {I;II}); *also* vyoposketv
  (a·yo·pos·ki·tá {I;II})

apart, separated: etekvpvkē (i·ti·ka·pá·ki: {II})

apple, apples: svtv (sa·tá)

archery bow: cvkotvkse (ca·ko·ták·si)

argue with each other, to: etem vyoposketv (it·im a·yo·pos·ki·tá {I;D});
  also isemayecetv (e:·si·ma:·yi·cí·ta {I;D})

**around at ground level or on the floor (of three or more); to be around
  in an enclosed space/building (of three or more):** takfulletv
  (tak·fol·li·tá {I})

arrest, imprison, to: svlvfkēcetv (sa·laf·ki:·ci·tá {I;II}); *also* svlvfkuecetv
  (sa·laf·koy·ci·tá {I;II})

arrive (for one to), come to (another one): em vlvketv (im·a·la·kí·ta
  {I;D})

arrive there, get there, reach there (of one), to: roretv (ło·li·tá {I})

arrow: cvkotvkse enrē (ca·ko·ták·si in·łí:)

arrow, bullet: rē (łí:)

ash drippings (used to flavor sofke): ēsso (í:s·so); *also* kvpe (ka·pí)

ask for, ask about, buy, to: vpohetv (a·po·hi·tá {I;II})

asleep (of one): nucē (no·cí: {II})

aunt (his/her maternal): eckuce (ic·kó·ci {II})

aunt (his/her paternal), grandmother: epose (i·pó·si {II}); *also* pose
  (pó·si {II})

automobile, car: atomo (a:·to·mó)

awaken, wake up, to: vhonecetv (a·ho·ni·cí·ta {I})

axe: pocoswv (po·cós·wa); *also* woceswv (wo·cís·wa)

B

baby: pipuce (pe:·po·cí)

bad, naughty: holwvkē (hol·wa·kí: {II})

bad, naughty, cruel: holwvyēcē (hol·wa·yí:·ci: {II})

bag: sokcv (sók·ca); *also* sukcv (sók·ca)

bake, cook, to: noricetv (no·ɫe:·ci·tá {I;3})

bake, roast, broil, to: hotopetv (ho·to·pi·tá {I;3})

baking soda: sote (só:·ti)

ball: pokko (pók·ko)

ball team: pokkēccvlke (pok·ki:c·câl·ki)

banana: penanv (pi·ná:·na)

band (Seminole political division): meteliketv (mi·ti·le:·ki·tá {D})

Baptists: Este-Aksomkvlke (is·ti·a:k·som·kâl·ki)

bark at (of one), to: vwohketv (a·wo:h·ki·tá {I;II})

bathroom: cokuce (co·kó·ci)

be, to: ometv (o·mí·ta {I}); *also* owetv (o·wí·ta {I})

beads, necklace: konawv (ko·ná:·wa)

bear (animal): nokose (no·kó·si)

beat, shatter, pound, crush, crack, to: espvccetv (is·pac·ci·tá {I;3})

beat, pound something in a container, as when pounding corn in a
  kecvpe, **to:** hocetv (ho·cí·ta {I;3}); *see also* pvccetv (pac·ci·tá {I;3})

beaten, pounded: hockē (hóc·ki: {II})

because of: vrvhkv (a·ɫáh·ka)

become, to: haketv (ha:·ki·tá {I})

bed: topv (to·pá)

bedroom: nockv-coko (no:c·ka·có·ko); *also* wakketv-cokofv
  (wa:k·ki·ta·co·kó·fa)

behind, in back of: yopv (yó·pa {II})

believe, want, think, try, hope, to: kometv (ko:·mi·tá {I;3}); *also* kowetv
  (ko:·wi·tá {I;3})

believe in, trust, depend on (something or someone), to: em enhonretv
  (im in·hon·ɫi·tá {I;D/II;D})

below, beneath, under: elecv (i·lí·ca {II}); *also* lecv (lí·ca {II})

beneath, under, below: elecv (i·lí·ca {II}); *also* lecv (lí·ca {II})

between: (e)tennvrkvpv ((i)·tin·naɫ·ka·pá); *also* (e)tenrvwv ((i)·tin·ɫa·wá)

big (of one): rakkē (ɫá:k·ki: {II})

big (of two or more): rakrvkē (ɫa:k·ɫa·kí: {II})

bird: foswv (fós·wa); *also* fuswv (fós·wa)

bite, to: akketv (a:k·ki·tá {I;II})

bite (take a single bite of something/someone), to: en kecētketv (in
  ki·ci:t·ki·tá {I;II})

black (of one): lvstē (lás·ti: {II})

black (of two or more): lvslvtē (las·la·tí: {II})

blackboard: vhoccickv (a·ho:c·cé:c·ka)

bleed, to: catetv (ca:·ti·tá {II})

blood: catv (cá:·ta)

blue: holattē (ho·lá:t·ti: {II})

bluebread: cvtvhakv (ca·ta·há:·ka)

boil, make bubble, to: morecetv (mo:·łi·cí·ta {I;3})

boiled meat (meat that has been dried, boiled, and then cooked with onions): vpeshockē (a·pis·hóc·ki:)

bone/bones (his/her/its): efone (i·fó·ni {II}); *also* fone (fó·ni {II})

book, paper: cokv (có:·ka)

boots: esohtēhkv ((i)s·oh·tí:h·ka); *also* morvfkv (mo·łáf·ka); (e)stelepik-morvfkv ((i)st·i·li·pe:k·mo·łáf·ka); sohtēhkv (soh·tí:h·ka)

bother, annoy, to: naoricetv (na:·o·łe:·ci·tá {I;II})

bowl, large or serving: avtēhkv (a:·a·tí:h·ka); *also* hompetv-vcvnetv (hom·pi·ta·a·ca·ni·tá)

bowl, small or cereal: avtēhkuce (a:·a·ti:h·ko·cí)

box, a: tohahwv (to·há:h·wa)

boy: cēpvne (ci:·pa·ní)

boys: cēpvnvke (ci:·pa·ná·ki)

brave, to be: fekhvmkē (fik·hám·ki: {II}); *also* fekhvnkē (fik·hán·ki: {II})

bread: tvklik (tak·lé:k); *also* tvklike (tak·lé:·ki)

break, crack (one egg, glass, etc.), to: tvkocetv (ta·ko·ci·tá {I;3})

break, crack (two or more eggs, glasses, etc.), to: tvkohlicetv (tak·oh·le:·ci·tá {I;3})

break up, pound, smash, shatter, as when hitting something with a hammer or mallet, to: pvccetv (pac·ci·tá {I;3}); *see also* hocetv (ho·cí·ta {I;3})

bring (something) to (someone), to: (e)sem vlvketv ((i)s·im·a·la·ki·tá {I;3;D})

broil, roast, bake, to: hotopetv (ho·to·pi·tá {I;3})

brother (a man's younger): ecerwv mvnetosat (i·cíł·wa ma·ni·to·sá:t {II})

brother (a woman's): ecerwv (i·cíł·wa {II})

brown: oklanē (ok·lá:·ni: {II})

bubble (make), boil, to: morecetv (mo:·łi·cí·ta {I;3})

Buffalo (of stories), buffalo: yvnvsv (ya·ná·sa)

build, make one thing; build or make something for someone, to: hayetv (ha:·yi·tá {I;3;D})

build, make two or more things, to: hahicetv (ha··he:·ci·tá {I})
bullet, arrow: rē (łí:)
burn, to: nekricetv (nik·łe:·ci·tá {I;II}); *also* nokricetv (nok·łe:·ci·tá {I;II})
but, however: momis (mô··me:s); *also* mowis (mô··we:s)
butter: wakvneha (wa:·ka·ni·há:); *also* wakvpesē-neha (wa:·ka·pi·sí: ni·há:)
buy, to: nesetv (ni·sí·ta {I;3})
buy, ask for, ask about, to: vpohetv (a·po·hi·tá {I;II})
Buzzard (of stories), buzzard: sule (so·lí)
by, next to: vfopkē (a·fó:p·ki:)

C

cake: tvklik-cvmpv (tak·le:k·cám·pa)
camp (his/her): ehvpo (i·ha·pó: {II}); *also* hvpo (ha·pó: {II})
camps: hvpohayvke (ha·po·ha:·ya·kí)
candy: cvmpuce (cam·po·cí)
car, automobile: atomo (a:·to·mó)
carrot: yvlonkv-lanet (ya·lon·ka·lá:·nit)
carry, catch, take, hold (one thing), to: esetv (i·sí·ta {I;II})
carry, take, catch, hold (two or more things), to: cvwetv (ca·wí·ta {I;II})
casing, shell, skin, hide (his/her/its): ehvrpe (i·háł·pi {II}); *also* hvrpe (háł·pi {II})
cat: pose (pó:·si)
catch, carry, take, hold (one thing), to: esetv (i·sí·ta {I;II})
catch, take, carry, hold (two or more things), to: cvwetv (ca·wí·ta {I;II})
catch a fish, to: rvro aswiketv (ła·łó a:s·we:·ki·tá {I;3}); *also* rvro esetv (ła·łó i·sí·ta {I;3})
catch fish, fish, to: em akwiyetv (im a:k·we:·yi·tá {I}); *also* rvro em akwiyetv (ła·łó im a:k·we:·yi·tá {I})
caution, give a warning to, to: em vsehetv (im a·si·hí·ta {I;D})
ceiling: cokofv-ohrvnkv (co·ko·fa·oh·łán·ka); *also* vtopv (a·tó·pa)
cereal bowl, small bowl: avtēhkuce (a:·a·ti:h·ko·cí)
chair: ohliketv (oh·le:·ki·tá)
chairman, chairperson: ohliketv-ohlikv (oh·le:·ki·ta-oh·lé:·ka)
Cherokees, Cherokee tribe: Cvlakkvlke (ca·la:k·kâl·ki)
Chickasaws, Chickasaw tribe: Cekvsvlke (ci·ka·sâl·ki)
chicken: tolose (to·lô:·si)
chief: mēkko (mí:k·ko)

chiefs: mēkkvke (mi·k·ka·kí)

children: hopuetake (ho·poy·tá:·ki)

children (a woman's): eccustake (ic·cos·tá:·ki {II})

chop (wood), to: cvsketv (cas·ki·tá {I;3})

church: mēkusvpkv-cuko (mi:·ko·sáp·ka có·ko)

clan: em vliketv (im·a·le:·ki·tá {D})

clean (one), to: hvsvtecetv (ha·sa·ti·cí·ta {I;3})

clean (two or more items), to: hvsvthicetv (ha·sat·he:·ci·tá {I;II})

clean (of one), to be: hvsvtkē (ha·sát·ki: {II})

clean (of two or more), to be: hvsvthvkē (ha·sat·ha·kí: {II})

climb up (of one), to: vcemketv (a·cim·ki·tá {I}); *also* vcumketv
     (a·com·ki·tá {I}); vcunketv (a·con·ki·tá {I})

climb up (of three or more), to: vcemecetv (a·ci·mi·cí·ta {I}); *also*
     vcvmecetv (a·ca·mi·cí·ta); vcumecetv (a·co·mi·cí·ta {I})

climb up (of two), to: vcemhoketv (a·cim·ho·kí·ta {I}); *also* vcvmhoketv
     (a·cam·ho·kí·ta {I}); vcumhoketv (a·com·ho·kí·ta {I})

close (a door, window, etc.), to: vkhottetv (ak·hot·ti·tá {I;3})

close (something) for (someone), to: em akhottetv (im a:k·hot·ti·tá {I;3;D})

close to, near: tempē (tím·pi:)

coat (article of clothing): kapv (ká:·pa)

coffee: kafe (ká:·fi)

cold (of an animate being), to feel: etkolē (it·ko·lí: {II})

cold (of weather, water, something touched): kvsvppē (ka·sáp·pi: {II})

come back, return (of one), to: rvtetv (ła·ti·tá {I})

come back to a location, return back to a location (of one), to: rvlvketv
     (ła·la·ki·tá {I;II})

come back to a location, return back to a location (of two), to: refol-
     hoketv (łi·fol·ho·kí·ta {I;II})

come down (of one), to: ahvtvpketv (a:·ha·tap·ki·tá {I}); *also* akhvtvpketv
     (a:k·ha·tap·ki·tá {I})

come down (of three or more), to: ahvtvpecetv (a:·ha·ta·pi·cí·ta {I}); *also*
     akhvtvpecetv (a:k·ha·ta·pi·cí·ta {I})

come down (of two), to: ahvtvphoketv (a:·ha·tap·ho·kí·ta {I}); *also*
     akhvtvphoketv (a:k·ha·tap·ho·kí·ta {I})

come running (of one), to: aletketv (a:·lit·ki·tá {I})

come to (another one), for one to arrive: em vlvketv (im·a·la·kí·ta {I;D})

come together, put together, to: etelicetv (i·ti·le:·ci·tá {I})

come toward (of two), to: oh·vthoyetv (oh·at·ho·yí·ta {I;II})

conceited, proud, to be: ēkvsvmetv (i:·ka·sa·mi·tá {II})

conditional suffix: nowat (nó:·wa:t)

constitution: vhakv-empvtakv (a·há:·ka·im·pa·tá:·ka)

cook (food preparer): hompetv hayv (hom·pi·ta há:·ya)

cook, bake, to: noricetv (no·łe:·ci·tá {I;3})

cookie: tvklik-cvmpuce (tak·le:k·cam·po·cí)

corn: vce (a·cí)

cough, to: ohoketv (o·ho:·ki·tá {II/I})

Council House: nvkaftvlke encoko (na·ka:f·tâl·ki in·có·ko)

cover, to: ohranetv (oh·ła:·ni·tá {I;II})

cow: wakv (wá:·ka)

crack, break (one egg, glass, etc.), to: tvkocetv (ta·ko·ci·tá {I;3})

crack, break (two or more eggs, glasses, etc.), to: tvkohlicetv
    (tak·oh·le:·ci·tá {I;3})

crack, shatter, pound, crush, beat, to: espvccetv (is·pac·ci·tá {I;3})

crash (of a car), to: svcakhetv (sa·ca:k·hi·tá {I})

crawl, to: hvlketv (hal·ki·tá {I})

Creator, God: Hesaketvmesē (hi·sa:·ki·ta·mi·sí:)

cross, crucifix: etohwelēpkv (it·oh·wi·lí:p·ka); *also* tohwelēpkv
    (toh·wi·lí:p·ka)

cross over (of one), to: etohwvlvpketv (i·toh·wa·lap·ki·tá {I})

crucifix, cross: etohwelēpkv (it·oh·wi·lí:p·ka); *also* tohwelēpkv
    (toh·wi·lí:p·ka)

cruel, naughty, bad: holwvyēcē (hol·wa·yí:·ci: {II})

crumble (something), to: tofvpetv (to·fa·pi·tá {I;3;D})

crush, crack, shatter, pound, beat, to: espvccetv (is·pac·ci·tá {I;3})

cry (of one), to: hvkihketv (ha·ke:h·ki·tá {I})

cry about something (of three or more), to: eshvkahecetv
    (is·ha·ka:·hi·cí·ta {I;3})

cry out, shout, to: selakketv (si·la:k·ki·tá {I})

cup, glass: (e)sesketv ((i)s·is·ki·tá)

cure, heal (one person/thing), to: cvfeknicetv (ca·fik·ne:·ci·tá {I;II})

cure, heal (two or more persons/things), to: cvfencicetv (ca·fin·ce:·ci·tá
    {I;II}); *also* cvfencvkuecetv (ca·fin·ca·koy·ci·tá {I;II})

cut, gashed: lvfkē (láf·ki: {II})

cut, slice more than once (as bread, meat, etc.), to: waretv (wa:·łi·tá {I;3})

cut once, to: tvcetv (ta·cí·ta {I;3})

cut with a knife, to: lvffetv (laf·fi·tá {I;II})

D

dance, to: opvnetv (o·pa·ni·tá {I})

dancer: opanv (o·pá·na)

dark (as the out-of-doors), to be: yomockē (yo·móc·ki: {II}); *also* yvpockē (ya·póc·ki: {II})

daughter (a woman's): eccus hoktē (ic·cós hók·ti: {II})

day: nettv (nít·ta)

day after tomorrow: pakse vsimv (pá:k·si a·sé:·ma); *also* vpakse vsimv (a·pá:k·si a·sé:·ma)

deacon: tēkvnv (ti:·ka·ná)

dead (of one): elē (i·lí: {II})

dead (of two or more): pvsvtkē (pa·sát·ki: {II})

debate, to: nake 'setenkerretv (nâ:·ki (i)s·it·in·kił·łi·tá {I;II})

decide, to: fvccēcetv (fac·ci:·ci·tá {I;3})

deep, not of water (of one), to be: sofkē (sóf·ki: {II})

deep, not of water (of two or more), to be: sofsokē (sof·so·kí: {II})

deep (of one body of water): lvokē (láw·ki: {II})

deep (of two or more bodies of water): lvolvkē (law·la·kí: {II})

deer: eco (i·có)

depend on, trust, believe in (something or someone), to: em enhonretv (im in·hon·łi·tá {I;D/II;D})

devil's shoestring (plant used to stun fish): hvloneske (ha·lo·nís·ki); *also* hvnoleske (ha·no·lís·ki)

devour, finish off, eat all of, to: loketv (lo·kí·ta {I;3})

die (of one), to: eletv (i·lí·ta {II})

different, another: ētimv (i:·té:·ma)

dirty (of one): vholwvkē (a·hol·wa·kí: {II})

dirty (of two or more): vholwahokē (a·hol·wa:·ho·kí: {II})

dirty, unclean (of one): svholwvkē (sa·hol·wa·kí: {II})

dirty, nasty, filthy (of two or more): lekvclewē (li·kac·li·wí: {II})

dirty (of water), muddy: okofkē (o·kóf·ki: {II})

dirty, to make two or more: seholwahuecetv (si·hol·wa:·hoy·ci·tá {I;II}); *also* vholwahuecetv (a·hol·wa:·hoy·ci·tá {I;II})

dish, plate: pvlaknv (pa·lá:k·na)

district: ēkvntvckv (i:·kan·tác·ka); *also* 'kvntvckv (kan·tác·ka)

ditch, stream: hvccuce (hac·co·cí)

do, perform an activity: mēcetv (mi:·ci·tá {I;II})

doctor: vlēkcv (a·lí:k·ca)

dog: efv (i·fá)

door: vhvoke (a·háw·ki)

dress: honnv (hón·na {D})

drink, to: esketv (is·ki·tá {I;3})

drink made from corn and lye (ash drippings): sofke (sóf·ki)

drop (one item), to: awiketv (a:·we:·ki·tá {I;3})

drop, fall (of three or more), to: pvlvtketv (pa·lat·ki·tá {I})

drop (three or more) items, to: apvlvtetv (a:·pa·la·ti·tá {I;3})

drop, put down (two items or something made of fabric), to: atakkayetv (a:·tak·ka:·yi·tá {I;3})

dry, to be: kvrpē (kał·pí: {II})

dry one item, to: kvrpēcetv (kał·pi:·ci·tá {I;3})

dry two or more items, to: kvrkvpēcetv (kał·ka·pi:·ci·tá {I;3})

duck (waterfowl): foco (fo·có); *also* fuco (fo·có)

dull (as of a knife), to be: tefnē (tíf·ni: {II})

during, inside of: ofv (ó:·fa)

dying, to die (of one): eletv (i·lí·ta {II})

E

eagle: lvmhe (lám·hi)

ear (his/her/its): ehvcko (i·hác·ko {II})

earth, land, ground: ēkvnv (i:·ka·ná)

east (the), sunrise: hvsossv (ha·só:s·sa)

eat, to: hompetv (hom·pi·tá {I;3})

eat all of, finish off, devour, to: loketv (lo·kí·ta {I;3})

eavesdrop on, to: iem apohetv (e:·im a:·po·hí·ta {I;D})

egg: custake (cos·tá:·ki {D})

eight: cenvpaken (ci·na·pâ:·kin)

elderly, old, aged (of one animate being): vculē (a·có·li: {II})

elect someone, to: este ohmelletv (is·ti·oh·mil·li·tá {I;II})

elected, to be: ohmelletv (oh·mil·li·tá {I})

enjoy, to: mvnhēretv (man·hi:·łi·tá {II;D})

enough: tayē (tá:·yi:)

enter, go in (of one), to: ꞌcēyetv (ci:·yi·tá {I;3}); *also* ecēyetv (i·ci:·yi·tá {I;3})

erase, turn off a lamp, put out a fire, rub out, to: vslēcetv (as·li:·ci·tá {I;3})

every, all, everything: omvlkv (o·mál·ka)

everything, all, every: omvlkv (o·mál·ka)

exist, be seated, sit (of one), to: liketv (le:·ki·tá {I})

exist, be seated, sit (of three or more), to: vpoketv (a·po·ki·tá {I})

exist, be seated, sit (of two), to: kaketv (ka:·ki·tá {I})

exist, sit, be situated (of a clump of things), to: esliketv (is·le:·ki·tá {I})

eyeglasses, glasses: torsakhēckv (toł·sa:k·hí:c·ka {II})

F

face (his/her/its): torofv (to·łó:·fa {II})

fairytale, short story: nakonvkuce (nâ:k·o·na·ko·cí)

fall (of one), to: lvtketv (lat·ki·tá {II/I})

fall (of two), to: yurketv (yoł·ki·tá {I})

fall, drop (of three or more), to: pvlvtketv (pa·lat·ki·tá {I})

fall against (of one), to: vlvtketv (a·lat·ki·tá {I;II})

fall on the ground or floor (of two), to: takyurketv (tak·yoł·ki·tá {I})

farm, grow things, to: lokcicetv (lok·ce:·ci·tá {I;3})

farmer: naklokcicv (nâ:k·lok·cé:·ca)

farmers: naklokcicvlke (nâ:k·lok·ce:·câl·ki)

fast, quick (of one): pvfnē (páf·ni: {II})

fast, quick (of two or more): pvfpvnē (paf·pa·ní: {II})

fat: nehē (ni·hí: {II})

father (his/her): erke (íł·ki {II})

feed something to someone, to: hompicetv (hom·pe:·ci·tá {I;3;II})

feel, touch, to: celayetv (ci·la:·yi·tá {I;II})

feel sorry for, have compassion for, have mercy on, to: em merretv (im mił·łi·tá {II;D})

fertile, ripe (as a fruit), to be: lokcē (lók·ci: {II})

few (very), very little (in size), a little bit: nvcomusē (na·cŏ:ⁿ·mo·si:)

field: cvpofv (ca·pó:·fa)

filthy, nasty, dirty (of two or more): lekvclewē (li·kac·li·wí: {II})

find (something), to: eshecetv (is·hi·ci·tá {I;3})

finish off, devour, eat all of, to: loketv (lo·kí·ta {I;3})

fire, a: totkv (tó:t·ka)

fire, shoot, to: eccetv (ic·cí·ta {I;II})

firefly: kolēppa (ko·li:p·pá:)

fireman: totkv-vslēcv (to:t·ka·as·lí:·ca)

fireplace, stove: totkv-hute (to:t·ka·hó·ti); *also* cvto (ca·tó) for stove

firm (to make), harden, to: vwvnhēcicetv (a·wan·hi:·ce:·ci·tá {I;II/I;3})

fish, a: rvro (ła·łó)

fish, catch fish, to: em akwiyetv (im a:k·we:·yi·tá {I}); *also* rvro em akwiyetv (ła·łó im a:k·we:·yi·tá {I}); *see also* catch a fish

fisherman: rvro akhopoyv (ła·łó a:k·ho·pó:·ya); *also* rvro em akwiyv (ła·łó im a:k·wé:·ya)

fishhook: cufokonhe (co·fo·kón·hi); *also* rvro rakcvwetv (ła·łó ła:k·ca·wí·ta)

five: cvhkēpen (cah·kî:·pin)

flat, level: tvpeksē (ta·pík·si {II})

floor: taktopvtake (ta:k·to·pa·tá:·ki)

flour: hockvte (hoc·ka·tí)

flower: pakpvkoce (pa:k·pa·kó·ci)

fly (of one), to: tvmketv (tam·ki·tá {I})

fly (of three or more), to: tvmecetv (ta·mi·ci·tá {I})

fly (of two), to: tvmhoketv (tam·ho·kí·ta {I})

fly over, fly toward (of one), to: ohtvmketv (oh·tam·ki·tá {I;II})

fly over, fly toward (of two), to: ohtvmhoketv (oh·tam·ho·kí·ta {I;II})

fold, to: pvkohlicetv (pak·oh·le:·ci·tá {I;3})

follow a leader, to: enhomahtv vcvkkayetv (in·ho·má:h·ta a·cak·ka:·yi·tá {I;II})

fond of (to be), to like: em vlostetv (im a·los·ti·tá {II;3/3;D})

food: hompetv (hom·pi·tá)

forest: eto-vlke (i·to·âl·ki); *also* pelofv (pi·ló:·fa)

fork (eating utensil): cofonwv (co·fón·wa); *also* cufunwv (co·fón·wa)

four: osten (ô:s·tin)

four times, to do: osticetv (os·te:·ci·tá {I;3})

freeze something, to: hetoticetv (hi·to·te:·ci·tá {I;3})

French people, the: Fvlvncvlke (fa·lan·câl·ki)

fried bread: tvklik-svkmorke (tak·le:k-sak·mó:ł·ki)

friend (his/her): enhesse (in·hís·si {D})

frog, toad: sopaktv (so·pá:k·ta)

fry, to: svkmorecetv (sak·mo·łi·ci·tá {I;3})

frying pan: nak-svkmorēcv (nâ:k·sak·mo·łí:·ca)

furious with, mad at someone, to be: enhomecē (in·ho·mí·ci: {II;D})

G

garden (small): nak-vhockuce (nâ:k·a·hoc·ko·cí)

gashed, cut: lvfkē (láf·ki: {II})

gather, pick fruits or vegetables, to: vyocetv (a·yo:·ci·tá {I})

General Council: nak-vfastv (nâ:k·a·fá:s·ta)

General Council meeting: nak-vfastv-emetohkvlketv
   (nâ:k·a·fá:s·ta·i·mi·toh·kâl·ki·ta)

generous, kind: heromē (hi·łó·mi: {II})

generous, kind to: heromosē (hi·łô:·mo·si: {II;D})

get out of jail or some confined space (of one), to: ossetv (os·sí·ta {I})

get out of the water or a low place (of one), to: akossetv (ak·os·si·tá {I})

get there, arrive there, reach there (of one), to: roretv (ło·łi·tá {I})

giant, a: este-capko (is·ti·cá:p·ko)

girl: hoktuce (hok·to·cí)

girls: hoktvkuce (hok·ta·kó·ci)

give a speech, speak, talk, to: (o)ponvyetv ((o)·po·na·yí·ta {I})

give a warning to, caution, to: em vsehetv (im a·si·hí·ta {I;D})

give (something) to (someone), to: emetv (i·mí·ta {I;3;D})

glad, happy (of one): afvckē (a:·fác·ki: {II})

glad, happy (of two or more): afvcfvkē (a:·fac·fa·kí: {II})

glass, cup: (e)sesketv ((i)s·is·ki·tá)

glasses, eyeglasses: torsakhēckv (toł·sa:k·hí:c·ka {II})

glove: (e)stenke-hute ((i)st·in·ki·hó·ti)

go (of one), to: vyetv (a·yí·ta {I})

go (of three or more), to: vpeyetv (a·pi·yi·tá {I})

go (of two), to: vhoyetv (a·ho·yi·tá {I})

go a short distance (of one), to: a-vyetv (a:·a·yí·ta {I})

go about, wander, be located (of three or more), to: fulletv (fol·li·tá {I})

go about, wander, be located (of two), to: welvketv (wi·la·ki·tá {I})

go around, wander (of one), to: vretv (a·łí·ta {I})

go away from, leave (of one), to: vyepetv (a·yi·pi·tá {I})

go back (of one), to: yefolketv (yi·fol·ki·tá {I})

go back (of two), to: yefolhoketv (yi·fol·ho·kí·ta {I})

go in, enter (of one), to: ʾcēyetv (ci:·yi·tá {I;3}); *also* ecēyetv (i·ci:·yi·tá
   {I;3})

goose: sasvkwv (sâ:·sak·wa)

go out (toward something) (of one), to: yossetv (yos·si·tá {I;II})

go through, pass through (of one), to: ropottetv (ło·po:t·ti·tá {I})

go through, pass through (of three or more), to: ropotecetv
   (ło·po:·ti·cí·ta {I})

go through, pass through (of two), to: ropothoyetv (ło·po:t·ho·yí·ta {I})

go up to (something or someone) (of one), to: ohvyetv (oh·a·yí·ta {I;II})
God, Creator: Hesaketvmesē (hi·sa:·ki·ta·mi·sí:)
good: henrē (hin·łí: {II})
gopher: ēkvn(v)-rolahvlēcv (i:·ka·na·ło·la:·ha·lí:·ca); *also* vcetekv
  (a·ci·ti·ká); hvcetekv (ha·ci·ti·ká)
grandfather (his/her): poca (po·cá: {II}); *also* puca (po·cá: {II})
grandmother, paternal aunt (his/her): epose (i·pó·si {II}); *also* pose
  (pó·si {II})
grape dumpling: pvrko-afke (pał·ko·á:f·ki); *also* pvrko-sakporoke
  (pał·ko·sa:k·po·łó·ki); pvrko-svpkonepke (pał·ko·sap·ko·níp·ki)
gravy: okneha (ok·ni·há:)
greedy, to be: encakē (in·cá:·ki: {II}); *also* vnoksē (a·nók·si: {II})
green, yellow: lanē (lá:·ni: {II})
greet, shake hands with, to: vsēketv (a·si:·ki·tá {I;II})
grey (of one): sopakhvtkē (so·pa:k·hát·ki: {II})
grey (of two or more): sopakhvthvkē (so·pa:k·hat·ha·kí: {II})
grind (coffee, corn, etc.), to: enfolotetv (in·fo·lo·tí·ta {I;3})
grind meat, mash (potatoes), to: cetvketv (ci·ta·ki·tá {I;3})
ground, earth, land: ēkvnv (i:·ka·ná)
grow things, farm, to: lokcicetv (lok·ce:·ci·tá {I;3})
growl at, to: vhēhketv (a·hi:h·ki·tá {I;II})
guess, to: mohmes kometv (moh·mís ko·mí·ta {I;3})
gun: eccv (íc·ca)

H

hallway: etehoyvnēcv (i·ti·ho·ya·ní:·ca)
hammer: svtokuce (sa·to:·ko·cí)
hand (his/her): enke (in·kí {II})
hang up (one item), to: vtvretv (a·ta·łi·tá {I;3})
hang up (two or more items), to: vtvrticetv (a·tał·te:·ci·tá {I;3})
happy, glad (of one): afvckē (a:·fác·ki: {II})
happy, glad (of two or more): afvcfvkē (a:·fac·fa·kí: {II})
harden, make firm, to: vwvnhēcicetv (a·wan·hi:·ce:·ci·tá {I;II/I;3})
hat: kvpotokv (ka·po·tó·ka {D}); *also* kvtopokv (ka·to·pó·ka {D})
have, to: ocetv (o·ci·tá {I;3})
have a chance at, have permission, to: em etektvnkē (im i·tik·tán·ki: {II})
have compassion for, have mercy on, feel sorry for, to: em merretv (im
  mił·łi·tá {II;D})

have mercy on, have compassion for, feel sorry for, to: em merretv (im mił·li·tá {II;D})

have permission, have a chance at, to: em etektvnkē (im i·tik·tán·ki: {II})

hawk: ayo (á:·yo)

head (his/her): ekv (i·ká {II})

heal (of a wound), to: enwiketv (in·we:·ki·tá {I})

heal, cure (one person/thing), to: cvfeknicetv (ca·fik·ne:·ci·tá {I;II})

heal, cure (two or more persons/things), to: cvfencicetv (ca·fin·ce:·ci·tá {I;II}); *also* cvfencvkuecetv (ca·fin·ca·koy·ci·tá {I;II})

healthy, well, smart (of one): cvfeknē (ca·fík·ni: {II})

healthy, well, smart (of two or more): cvfencvkē (ca·fin·ca·kí: {II})

hear, to: pohetv (po·hí·ta {I;II})

heat, warmth (of one): hiyē (hé:·yi: {II})

heaven: hvlwe (hál·wi)

heavy (of one): honnē (hón·ni: {II})

heavy (of two or more): honhoyē (hon·ho·yí: {II})

hello: hensci (híns·ce:)

help someone, to: em vnicetv (im a·ne:·ci·tá {I;D})

here, this, this one: heyv (hi·yá); *also* yv (yá)

hide, casing, shell, skin (his/her/its): ehvrpe (i·háł·pi {II}); *also* hvrpe (háł·pi {II})

hide (something or someone), to: ēhetv (i:·hi·tá {I;II})

hide (something) from (someone), to: em ēhetv (im i:·hi·tá {I;D})

high (of two or more): hvlhvwē (hal·ha·wí: {II})

hill: (ē)kvnhvlwe ((i:)·kan·hál·wi)

hill (small): (ē)kvnhvlwuce ((i:)·kan·hal·wo·cí)

hip (his/her): esokso (i·sók·so {II})

his/her/its (follows the possessed noun): enake (i·nâ:·ki)

hit, to: nvfketv (naf·ki·tá {I;II})

hog, pig: sokhv (sók·ha)

hold, catch, carry, take (one thing), to: esetv (i·sí·ta {I;II})

hold, take, carry, catch (two or more things), to: cvwetv (ca·wí·ta {I;II})

hold out (a hand, a paper, etc.), to: awiyetv (a:·we:·yi·tá {I;3})

hole dug in the ground: ēkvn-korke (i:·kan·kół·ki)

honest, to be: ēfvccēcetv (i:·fac·ci:·ci·tá {II})

honey: fo-encvmpē (fo:·in·cam·pí:)

hop, jump (of one), to: tasketv (ta:s·ki·tá {I})

hop, jump (of three or more), to: tasecetv (ta:·si·cí·ta {I}) hop, jump (of two), to: tashoketv (ta:s·ho·kí·ta {I})

hop, leap, jump into the water or a low place (of two), to: aktashoketv
(ak·ta:s·ho·kí·ta {I})

hope, trust: enhonrkv (in·hónɬ·ka)

hope, want, think, believe, try, to: kometv (ko:·mi·tá {I;3}); *also* kowetv
(ko:·wi·tá {I;3})

horse: rakko (ɬá:k·ko)

house: coko (co·kó); *also* cuko (co·kó)

House of Kings: coko enmēkko (co·kó in·mí:k·ko)

House of Warriors: coko entvstvnvke (co·kó in·tas·ta·ná·ki)

how: estomē (is·to·mí:); *also* estomēcet (is·to·mí:·cit); stomēcet
(sto·mí:·cit)

**How do you feel?, a phrase offered to ask how one is doing, as when
greeting someone:** estonko (is·tón·ko)

however, but: momis (mô:·me:s); *also* mowis (mô:·we:s)

hungry: elvwē (i·lá·wi: {II})

hunt, to: fayetv (fa:·yi·tá {I})

hunt around for, look for, to: hopoyetv (ho·po·yi·tá {I;II})

hunt around for, look for (with something), to: es hopoyetv (is
ho·po·yi·tá {I;II})

hunter: fayv (fá:·ya)

hunters: fayvlke (fa:·yâl·ki)

hurting, soreness, pain: ennokkē (in·nók·ki: {3;D})

I

I (pronoun): vne (a·ní)

ice, snow: hetotē (hi·to·tí:)

imprison, arrest, to: svlvfkēcetv (sa·laf·ki:·ci·tá {I;II}); *also* svlvfkuecetv
(sa·laf·koy·ci·tá {I;II})

in back of, behind: yopv (yó·pa {II})

in back of a building: topvrv (to·pá·ɬa)

in front of: ehomv (i·hó·ma {II}); *also* homv (hó·ma {II})

inside of, during: ofv (ó:·fa)

inside something (of two or more) (to get or be), put on pants or two
things pulled up on a body part, to put two or more items on
another: vtehketv (a·tih·ki·tá {I;3})

interjection similar to "um" or "uh": ehen (i·hín)

intestines (pig), cleaned well and fried: fekce (fík·ci)
iron, to: tenēpicetv (ti·ni:·pe:·ci·tá {I;3})
island: ēkvnv otē nvrkvpv (i:·ka·ná o·tí: naɫ·ka·pá); *also* ēkvnv owv ohliketv (i:·ka·ná o·wá oh·le:·ki·tá)

J

jealous about or toward, to be: esfekcakhetv (is·fik·ca:k·hi·tá {I;II})
Jimmy (proper name): Cemme (cím·mi)
judge: fvccēcv (fac·cí:·ca)
jump, hop (of one), to: tasketv (ta:s·ki·tá {I})
jump, hop (of three or more), to: tasecetv (ta:·si·cí·ta {I})
jump, hop (of two), to: tashoketv (ta:s·ho·kí·ta {I})
jump, hop, leap into the water or a low place (of two), to: aktashoketv (ak·ta:s·ho·kí·ta {I})
jump, to make one: taskuecetv (ta:s·koy·ci·tá {I;II})
jump up from lying down (of one), to: atasketv (a:·ta:s·ki·tá {I})
just now, recently: hvte (ha·tí)

K

kick, to: takketv (ta:k·ki·tá {I;II})
kill oneself, to: ē-elēcetv (i:·i·li:·ci·tá {I})
kind, to be: lopicē (lo·pé:·ci: {I/II})
kind, generous: heromē (hi·ɫó·mi: {II})
kind, generous to: heromosē (hi·ɫô:·mo·si: {II;D})
kitchen: hompetv-coko (hom·pi·ta·co·kó); *also* hompetv-hakcoko (hom·pi·ta·ha:k·co·kó)
kitten: posuce (po:·so·cí)
knee (his/her/its): torkowv (to:ɫ·ko·wá {II})
knife: eslafkv (is·lá:f·ka)
know, learn, to: kerretv (kiɫ·ɫi·tá {I;II})
known: kerkē (kíɫ·ki: {II})

L

ladder: vccakv (ac·cá:·ka)
land, earth, ground: ēkvnv (i:·ka·ná)

last night: nerē-isē (ni·łí:·ê:·si:)
laugh, smile (of one), to: vpeletv (a·pi·li·tá {I})
laugh, smile (of two or more), to: vpelhoyetv (a·pil·ho·yí·ta {I})
laugh at, to: vpelicetv (a·pi·le:·ci·tá {I;II})
law: vhakv (a·há:·ka)
lawyer: vhakv-hayv (a·ha:·ka·há:·ya)
lay down (a person, long object), to: wvkecetv (wa·ki·ci·tá {I;II})
lazy: enhorrē (in·hół·łi: {II})
lead people, to: este enhomahtetv (is·ti·in·ho·ma:h·ti·tá {I;D})
leader (his/her): enhomahtv (in·ho·má:h·ta {D})
leap, hop, jump into the water or a low place (of two), to: aktashoketv
  (ak·ta:s·ho·kí·ta {I})
learn, know, to: kerretv (kił·łi·tá {I;II})
leave (someone, someplace), to: enkvpvketv (in·ka·pa·ki·tá {I;D})
leave, go away from (of one), to: vyepetv (a·yi·pi·tá {I})
left, to the: kvskvnv fvccvn (kas·ka·ná fác·can)
let go, set someone free, to: ayēccicetv (a:·yi:c·ce:·ci·tá {I;D}); *also*
  enrecvpetv (in·łi·ca·pí·ta {I;D})
level, flat: tvpeksē (ta·pík·si: {II})
lie down (of one), to: wakketv (wa:k·ki·tá {I})
lie down (of three or more), to: lomhetv (lom·hi·tá {I})
lie down on the floor or ground (of three or more), to: taklomhetv
  (tak·lom·hi·tá {I})
light (as the out-of-doors, the sun, etc.), to be: hvyayvkē (ha·ya:·ya·kí: {II})
light a fire/stove, to: etecetv (i·ti·ci·tá {I;3}); *also* tak-etecetv (ta:k·i·ti·ci·tá
  {I;3})
like, be fond of: em vlostetv (im a·los·ti·tá {II;3/3;D})
like, want, need, to: eyvcetv (i·ya·ci·tá {II;3})
listen to, to: em mapohicetv (im ma:·po·he:·ci·tá {I;D}); *also* mapohicetv
  (ma:·po·he:·ci·tá {I;D})
little (of one): cutkosē (cot·ko·sí: {II}); *see also* small
little (very, in size), few (very), a little bit: nvcomusē (na·čǒ:^{n}·mo·si:)
located (be), wander, go about (of three or more), to: fulletv (fol·li·tá {I})
located (be), wander, go about (of two), to: welvketv (wi·la·ki·tá {I})
location, place: mi (mé:); *also* miyewv (me:·yi·wá)
long, tall (of one): cvpkē (cáp·ki: {II})
long, tall (of two or more): cvpcvkē (cap·ca·kí: {II})
long time ago, a: hofonof(en) (ho·fô:·nof) or (ho·fô:·no·fin)

lopsided: fvleknē (fa·lík·ni: {II})

look at, see, to: hecetv (hi·cí·ta {I;II})

look at one another, to: etehecetv (i·ti·hi·cí·ta {I})

look at oneself, see oneself, to: ēhecetv (i:·hi·cí·ta {I})

look down (from something), look over (something), to: ohhecetv
    (oh·hi·ci·tá {I;II})

look for, hunt around for, to: hopoyetv (ho·po·yi·tá {I;II})

look for, hunt around for (with something), to: es hopoyetv (is
    ho·po·yi·tá {I;II})

look into the water or a low place, to: akhecetv (ak·hi·ci·tá {I})

lose (one thing or one game), to: somecicetv (so·mi·ce:·ci·tá {I;3})

lose (more than one thing, more than once), to: somhuecetv
    (som·hoy·ci·tá {I;3})

lost (of one), to be: somketv (som·ki·tá {II}); *also* sonketv (son·ki·tá {II})

lost (of two or of a cloth item), to be: somhoketv (som·ho·kí·ta {II})

loud: pohkē (póh·ki: {II})

love someone, to: vnokecetv (a·no·ki·cí·ta {I;II})

M

mad at, furious with someone, to be: enhomecē (in·ho·mí·ci: {II;D})

make, build one thing; build, make something for someone, to: hayetv
    (ha:·yi·tá {I;3;D})

make, build two or more things, to: hahicetv (ha:·he:·ci·tá {I})

make another say, to: hvmmaketv (ham·ma:·ki·tá {I;II})

make fun of someone, to: este nakhayetv (is·ti·nâ:k·ha:·yi·tá {I;II})

man: honvnwv (ho·nán·wa)

man, old: miste vculē (mé:s·ti a·có·li:)

many, numerous, much: sulkē (sól·ki: {II})

mash (potatoes), grind meat: cetvketv (ci·ta·ki·tá {I;3})

mashed (as of potatoes), torn up: cetakkosē (ci·tă:k·ko·si: {II})

mean, say, to: oketv (o·kí·ta {I})

meat: vpeswv (a·pís·wa)

medicine: heleswv (hi·lís·wa)

meet another, to: vnrvpetv (an·ła·pí·ta {I;II})

melt, to: setēfketv (si·ti:f·ki·tá {I})

men: honvntake (ho·nan·tá:·ki)

men (those), those people: mistvlke (me:s·tâl·ki)

Methodists: Ohkalvlke (oh·ka:·lâl·ki); *also* Uewv Ohkalvlke (óy·wa
   oh·ka:·lâl·ki)

milk: wakvpesē (wa:·ka·pi·sí:)

mole, vole: tvko (ta·kó)

Monday: Mvnte (mán·ti)

moon: hvrēssē (ha·łi:s·sí:)

more, next time, again: hvtvm (ha·tâm)

mortar: keco (ki·có)

mother (his/her): ecke (íc·ki {II})

mountain: kvnhvlwe-rakko (kan·hal·wi·rá:k·ko); *also* ēkvnhvlwe-rakko
   (i:·kan·hal·wi·rá:k·ko)

mountain lion, tiger: kaccv (ká:c·ca)

mouse: cesse (cís·si)

move, shake, to: nekēyetv (ni·ki:·yi·tá {I})

move around, shake around, to: nekēyicetv (ni·ki:·ye:·ci·tá {I;II})

move toward (of one), to: ohkueketv (oh·koy·ki·tá {I;II})

much, numerous, many: sulkē (sól·ki: {II})

muddy, dirty (of water): okofkē (o·kóf·ki: {II})

mushy (as of one piece of fruit): cvlaknē (ca·lá:k·ni: {II})

mushy, tender (like meat), soft (of one), to be: lowvckē (lo·wác·ki: {II})

Mvskoke people: Mvskokvlke (mas·ko:·kâl·ki)

N

nail, nails: vcokv (a·có:·ka); *also* vcopv (a·có:·pa)

name: hocefketv (ho·cif·ki·tá)

names: hocefhoketv (ho·cif·ho·kí·ta)

nasty, dirty, filthy (of two or more): lekvclewē (li·kac·li·wí: {II})

naughty, bad: holwvkē (hol·wa·kí: {II})

naughty, bad, cruel: holwvyēcē (hol·wa·yí:·ci: {II})

near, close to: tempē (tím·pi:)

near (to be), wander around (of one), to: vhvretv (a·ha·łi·tá {I;II})

necklace, beads: konawv (ko·ná:·wa)

need, want, like, to: eyvcetv (i·ya·ci·tá {II;3})

net: hoyv (ho·yá)

news, story, tale: nakonvkv (nâ:k·oná·ka)

newspaper: cokv-tvlvme (co:·ka·ta·la·mí)

next day, the: rem paksen (łim pá:k·sin)

next time, again, more: hvtvm (ha·tâm)
next to, by: vfopkē (a·fó:p·ki:)
next year: ohrolopēyof (oh·ło·lo·pí:·yof)
nine: ostvpaken (os·ta·pâ:·kin)
no: monks (mónks)
nod once, to: nekattetv (ni·ka:t·ti·tá {II})
notebook: nak-eshoccickv cokv (nâ:k·is·ho:c·cé:c·ka co·ká)
nothing but, only: vlkē (ál·ki:)
now: hiyomat (he:·yô:·ma:t); *also* hiyowat (he:·yô:·wa:t)
numerous, many, much: sulkē (sól·ki: {II})
nurse: enokkvlke-vfastv (i·nok·kâl·ki a·fá:s·ta); *also* nokke-vfastv (nók·ki
    a·fá:s·ta)

O

offer, sell, to: wiyetv (we:·yi·tá {I;3})
Okmulgee, Oklahoma: Okmvlke (ok·mál·ki)
old, aged, elderly (of one animate being): vculē (a·có·li: {II})
old (of two or more inanimate things): leslekē (lis·li·kí: {II})
one: hvmken (hám·kin); *also* hvnken (hán·kin)
onion, onions: tafvmpe (ta:·fám·pi)
only, nothing but: vlkē (ál·ki:)
open (a door, window, etc.), to: hvwecetv (ha·wi·ci·tá {I;3})
open something for someone, to: enhvwēcetv (in·ha·wi:·ci·tá {I;3;D})
opossum: sokhv-hatkv (sok·ha·há:t·ka)
or: monkan (món·ka:n); *also* monkat (món·ka:t)
orange (fruit): yvlahv (ya·lá:·ha)
other side of, on the: pvrvnkē (pa·łán·ki:)
ouch: oh (ôh)
oven: norickv-hute (no·łe:·c·ka·hó·ti); *also* tvklik-noricv (tak·le:k·no·łé:·ca)
over, above: onvpv (o·ná·pa {II})
overgrown, weedy place: hvfvpē (ha·fá·pi:)
owl, screech owl: efolo (i·fó·lo)
owner: ocv (ó:·ca)

P

pain, soreness, hurting: ennokkē (in·nók·ki: {3;D})
paint (a picture, a house, etc.), to: vhayetv (a·ha:·yi·tá {I;II})

pale (of two or more): hvthvwē (hat·ha·wí: {II})

pan: halo-pvlaknv (ha:·lo·pa·lá:k·na); *also* nak-vtehetv (nâ:k·a·ti·hi·tá)

pants: hvtekpikv (ha·tik·pé:·ka)

paper, book: cokv (có:·ka)

paper bag: cokv-tohahwv (co:·ka·to·há:h·wa)

particle added to the end of a declarative or imperative sentence to show the speaker's feelings are strong and/or sincere: cē (cî:); *also* ci (cê:)

pass by (of one), to: hoyvnetv (ho·ya·ni·tá {I;II})

pass by someone (of one), to: (e)tehoyvnetv ((i)·ti·ho·ya·ni·tá {I;II})

pass through, go through (of one), to: ropottetv (ło·po:t·ti·tá {I})

pass through, go through (of three or more), to: ropotecetv (ło·po:·ti·cí·ta {I})

pass through, go through (of two), to: ropothoyetv (ło·po:t·ho·yí·ta {I})

pass (something) to someone, to: aswiyetv (a:s·we:·yi·tá {I;3;D})

path, road: nene (ni·ní)

pecan tree: ocē-cvpkuce mvpe (o·ci:·cap·ko·cí má·pi)

peek at, to: em vcvnēyetv (im a·ca·ni:·yi·tá {I;D})

pen, pencil, writing implement: eshoccickv (is·ho:c·cé:c·ka)

pencil, pen, writing implement: eshoccickv (is·ho:c·cé:c·ka)

people, those people, those men: mistvlke (me:s·tâl·ki)

pepper (black): homuce (ho:·mo·cí)

perform an activity, do, to: mēcetv (mi:·ci·tá {I;II})

person, that person (usually used to refer to a male): miste (mé:s·ti)

pestle, pounding stick: kecvpe (ki·cá·pi)

pick, gather fruits or vegetables, to: vyocetv (a·yo:·ci·tá {I})

pick up (one item), to: atakkesetv (a:·tak·ki·sí·ta {I;II})

pickle: kakompv-saktehke (ka:·kom·pa·sa:k·tíh·ki)—Mvskoke pronunciation; *also* takompv (ta:·kóm·pa)—Seminole pronunciation

pie: (e)sem vtehke ((i)s·ím a·tíh·ki); *also* (e)sem vtehkv ((i)s·ím a·tíh·ka)

pig, hog: sokhv (sók·ha)

piled up, as of brush, laundry, etc., to be: tohlikē (toh·le:·kí: {II}); *also* tohvpokē (toh·a·po·kí: {II})

place, location: mi (mé:); *also* miyewv (me:·yi·wá)

plants (transplanted): nakrvfkv (nâ:k·łaf·ka)

plate, dish: pvlaknv (pa·lá:k·na)

platter (serving): pvlaknv-rakko (pa·la:k·na·łá:k·ko)

play, to: ahkopvnetv (a:h·ko·pa·ni·tá {I})

play with (someone/something), to: em ahkopvnetv (im·ah·ko·pa·ni·tá {I;D})

point, to: melletv (mil·li·tá {I})

point at, to: vmelletv (a·mil·li·tá {I;II})

police: estewvnayvlke (is·ti·wa·na:·yâl·ki)

policeman: estewvnayv (is·ti·wa·ná:·ya)

potato: vhv (a·há)

potato (Irish): vhvce-rēhe (a·ha·ci·łí:·hi)

pound, shatter, crush, beat, crack, to: espvccetv (is·pac·ci·tá {I;3})

pound, break up, smash, shatter, as when hitting something with a hammer or mallet, to: pvccetv (pac·ci·tá {I;3}); *see also* hocetv (ho·cí·ta {I;3})

pound, pound something in a container, as when pounding corn in a *kecvpe*, **to:** hocetv (ho·cí·ta {I;3}); *see also* pvccetv (pac·ci·tá {I;3})

pounded, beaten: hockē (hóc·ki: {II})

pounding stick, pestle: kecvpe (ki·cá·pi)

pour a liquid out, as when emptying a bucket, jar, etc., to: pvlvtetv (pa·la·ti·tá {I;3})

prank, to play one on someone: sahkopvnetv (sa:h·ko·pa·ni·tá {I;II})

pray for, to: em mēkusvpetv (im mi:·ko·sa·pi·tá {I;D})

preacher: erkenvkv (ił·ki·ná·ka)

protect, store, save (something), to: vcayēcetv (a·ca:·yi:·ci·tá {I;3})

proud, conceited, to be: ēkvsvmetv (i:·ka·sa·mi·tá {II})

pull (in the direction of the speaker), to: ahvlvtetv (a:·ha·la·ti·tá {I;II})

purple: okholattē (ok·ho·lá:t·ti: {II}); *also* pvrkomē (pał·ko·mí: {II})

push, shove, to: vhopvketv (a·ho·pa·kí·ta {I;II})

put away, store, to: hericetv (hi·łe:·ci·tá {I;3})

put down (one item), to: ataklicetv (a:·tak·le:·ci·tá {I;3})

put down (three or more items), to: atakvpoyetv (a:·tak·a·po·yi·tá {I;3})

put down, drop (two items or something made of fabric), to: atakkayetv (a:·tak·ka:·yi·tá {I;3})

put on clothing that slips over the head or is wrapped around the body (of one), to: vccetv (ac·cí·ta {I;3})

put on clothing that slips over the head or is wrapped around the body (of two or more), to: vchoyetv (ac·ho·yi·tá {I;3})

put on one shoe or one item pulled up on a body part, put one item on another, to: vpiketv (a·pe:·ki·tá {I;3})

put on pants or two things pulled up on a body part, put two or more items on another, to get or be inside something (of two or more), to: vtehketv (a·tih·ki·tá {I;3})

put out a fire, turn off a lamp, erase, rub out, to: vslēcetv (as·li:·ci·tá {I;3})

put together, come together, to: etelicetv (i·ti·le:·ci·tá {I})

Q

quick: lvpkē (láp·ki: {II})

quick, fast (of one): pvfnē (páf·ni: {II})

quick, fast (of two or more): pvfpvnē (paf·pa·ní: {II})

quiet (of one): cvyayvkē (ca·ya:·ya·kí: {II})

quiet (of two or more): cvyayvhokē (ca·ya:·ya·hó·ki: {II})

quilt: telomhv (ti·lóm·ha)

R

Rabbit (of legends), rabbit: cofe (co·fí); *also* cufe (co·fí)

raccoon: wotko (wó:t·ko)

Raccoon clan: Wotkvlke (wo:t·kâl·ki)

rattlesnake: cetto hvce svkvsicv (cít·to há·ci sa·ka·sé:·ca); *also* cetto-mēkko (cit·to·mí:k·ko)

reach, achieve (a goal, a position, etc.) (of one), to: oretv (o·łí·ta {I;3})

reach there, arrive there, get there (of one), to: roretv (ło·łi·tá {I})

read, to: ohhonvyetv (oh·ho·na·yí·ta {I})

recently, just now: hvte (ha·tí)

red: catē (cá:·ti: {II})

relatives: enahvmkvlke (i·na:·ham·kâl·ki {II}); *also* enahvnkvlke (i·na:·han·kâl·ki {II})

remove one's own clothes, to: ēkayetv (i:·ka:·yi·tá {I})

reply, answer back, to: akicetv (a:·ke:·ci·tá {I;II}); *also* vyoposketv (a·yo·pos·ki·tá {I;II})

return, come back (of one), to: rvtetv (ła·ti·tá {I})

return back to a location, come back to a location (of one), to: rvlvketv (ła·la·ki·tá {I;II})

return back to a location, come back to a location (of two), to: refolhoketv (łi·fol·ho·kí·ta {I;II})

return something (to make two or more), to: ohfolhuecetv (oh·fol·hoy·ci·tá {I;II})

rice: vloso (a·ló:·so)

ride, sit on (of one), to: ohliketv (oh·le:·ki·tá {I;II})

ride, sit on (of three or more), to: ohvpoketv (oh·a·po:·ki·tá {I;II})

right, to the: kvperv fvccvn (ka·pí·ła fác·can)

ring (as one wears on a finger): (e)stenkesakpikv ((i)st·in·ki·sa:k·pé:·ka)

rip, tear, to: sētetv (si:·ti·tá {I;3})

ripe (as a fruit), fertile, to be: lokcē (lók·ci: {II})

rise up, sit up (as from lying down) (of one), to: aliketv (a:·le:·ki·tá {I})

rise up, sit up (as from lying down) (of three or more), to: a-vpoketv (a:·a·po·ki·tá {I})

rise up, sit up (as from lying down) (of two), set aside (two items), to: akaketv (a:·ka:·ki·tá {I})

river: hvcce (hác·ci)

riverbank: hvccenvpv (hac·ci·ná·pa); *also* hvcce onvpv (hác·ci o·ná·pa); hvcconvpv (hac·co·ná·pa)

road, path: nene (ni·ní)

roast, bake, broil, to: hotopetv (ho·to·pi·tá {I;3})

rock, stone: cvto (ca·tó)

roof: coko-ohrvnkv (co·ko·oh·łán·ka); *also* coko-onvpv (co·ko·o·ná·pa)

round (like a ball or sphere) (of one): polokē (po·ló:·ki: {II})

rub against (as when washing clothes on a washboard), to: vsofotketv (a·so·fo:t·ki·tá {I})

rub out, turn off a lamp, put out a fire, erase, to: vslēcetv (as·li:·ci·tá {I;3})

run (of one), to: letketv (lit·ki·tá {I})

run (of three or more), to: pefatketv (pi·fa:t·ki·tá {I})

run (of two), to: tokorketv (to·koł·ki·tá {I})

run away from someone/something (of one), to: enletketv (in·lit·ki·tá {I;D})

run away from someone/something (of three or more), to: enpefatketv (in·pi·fa:t·ki·tá {I;D})

run away from someone/something (of two), to: entokorketv (in·to·koł·ki·tá {I;D})

run in water or a low place (of one), to: akletketv (ak·lit·ki·tá {I})

run (to make three or more), to: vpefatecicetv (a·pi·fa:·ti·ce:·ci·tá {I;II})

run off (with something) (of one), to: esletketv (is·lit·ki·tá {I})

run to (of two), to: vtokorketv (a·to·koł·ki·tá {I;II})

S

salesman, shopkeeper: nakwiyv (nâ:k·wé:·ya)
salt pork: tosēnv (to·sí:·na)
sand: oktahv (ok·tá:·ha)
sandbar: oktahv-topv (ok·ta:·ha·tó·pa)
save, store, protect (something), to: vcayēcetv (a·ca:·yi:·ci·tá {I;3})
saw (cutting implement): esfokv (is·fó:·ka)
saw, to: foyetv (fo:·yi·tá {I;3})
say, to: maketv (ma:·ki·tá {I;II})
say, mean, to: oketv (o·kí·ta {I})
say to, tell (something) to (someone), to: em onvyetv (im·o·na·yí·ta {I;3;D})
say (something) to someone in particular, tell, to: kicetv (ke:·ci·tá {I;II})
saying, word: onvkv (o·ná·ka)
says, is saying: okat (o:·kâ:t)
scared, afraid: penkvlē (pin·ka·lí: {II})
scarf, tie, anything worn around the neck: ohenockv (oh·i·nó:c·ka)
school, schoolhouse: mvhakv-cuko (ma·ha:·ka·có·ko)
schoolhouse, school: mvhakv-cuko (ma·ha:·ka·có·ko)
screech owl, owl: efolo (i·fó·lo)
screw/screws: (e)sem vfikv ((i)s·im·a·fé:·ka)
screw something in, to: (e)sem vfiyetv ((i)s·im a·fe:·yi·tá {I})
screwdriver: nak (e)sem vfiyetv (nâ:k (i)s·im·a·fe:·yi·tá)
second chief (of a tribal town): henehv (hi·ní·ha)
second chiefs (of a tribal town): henehvlke (hi·ni·hâl·ki)
secretary: cokv-hayv (co:·ka·há:·ya)
seated (be), sit, exist (of one), to: liketv (le:·ki·tá {I})
seated (be), sit, exist (of three or more), to: vpoketv (a·po·ki·tá {I})
seated (be), sit, exist (of two), to: kaketv (ka:·ki·tá {I})
see, look at, to: hecetv (hi·cí·ta {I;II})
see a long distance, to: rahecetv (ła:·hi·cí·ta {I;II})
see oneself, look at oneself, to: ēhecetv (i:·hi·cí·ta {I})
self-pity: emērkv (i·mí:ł·ka)
sell, offer, to: wiyetv (we:·yi·tá {I;3})
send something, to: vtotetv (a·to·ti·tá {I;3})
separated, apart: etekvpvkē (i·ti·ka·pá·ki: {II})
sermon: oponvkv hērv honayetv (o·po·na·ká hí:·ła ho·na:·yi·tá)

serving bowl, large bowl: avtēhkv (a:·a·tí:h·ka); *also* hompetv-vcvnetv (hom·pi·ta-a·ca·ni·tá)

set aside (two items), rise up, sit up (as from lying down) (of two), to: akaketv (a:·ka:·ki·tá {I})

set down (one item), to: eslicetv (is·le:·ci·tá {I;3})

set down (one item) on (something), to: esohlicetv (is·oh·le:·ci·tá {I;3})

set down (two things, an item made of cloth), to: eskayetv (is·ka:·yi·tá {I;3}); *also* kayetv (ka:·yi·tá {I;II})

set (two things, something made of cloth) on top of (something else), to: ohkayetv (oh·ka:·yi·tá {I;3})

set someone free, let go, to: ayēccicetv (a:·yi:c·ce:·ci·tá {I;D}); *also* enrecvpetv (in·ɬi·ca·pí·ta {I;D})

seven: kolvpaken (ko·la·pâ:·kin)

sew (one item), to: vhoretv (a·ho·ɬi·tá {I;3})

sew (two or more items), to: vhorhuecetv (a·hoɬ·hoy·ci·tá {I;3})

shake, move, to: nekēyetv (ni·ki:·yi·tá {I})

shake around, move around, to: nekēyicetv (ni·ki:·ye:·ci·tá {I;II})

shake hands with, greet, to: vsēketv (a·si:·ki·tá {I;II})

shake the head, to: norottetv (no·ɬo:t·ti·tá {I})

sharp (of one): fvskē (fás·ki: {II})

sharp (of two or more): fvsfvkē (fas·fa·kí: {II})

shatter, break up, pound, smash, as when hitting something with a hammer or mallet, to: pvccetv (pac·ci·tá {I;3}); *see also* hocetv (ho·cí·ta {I;3})

shatter, pound, crush, beat, crack, to: espvccetv (is·pac·ci·tá {I;3})

shell: folahpv (fo·lá:h·pa)

shell, skin, hide, casing (his/her/its): ehvrpe (i·háɬ·pi {II}); *also* hvrpe (háɬ·pi {II})

shirt: yokkofketv (yok·ko:f·ki·tá)

shoe/shoes: (e)stelepikv ((i)st·i·li·pé:·ka)

shoot, fire, to: eccetv (ic·cí·ta {I;II})

shopkeeper, salesperson: nakwiyv (nâ:k·wé:·ya)

short (of an animate being): vcvkē (a·ca·kí: {II})

shout, cry out, to: selakketv (si·la:k·ki·tá {I})

shove, push, to: vhopvketv (a·ho·pa·kí·ta {I;II})

show something to someone (of one), to: nak en hecicetv (nâ:k in hi·ce:·ci·tá {I;II})

show something to someone (of two or more persons), to: nak en
    hecicēyetv (nâ:k in hi·ce:·ci:·yi·tá {I;II})
sibling (older and of the same sex as speaker): ervhv (i·łá·ha {II})
sick (of two or more), to be: enokhokē (i·nok·ho·kí: {II})
sing, to: yvhiketv (ya·he:·ki·tá {I})
sister (a man's): ēwvnwv (i:·wán·wa {II})
sisters (a man's): ēwvntake (i:·wan·tá:·ki {II})
sit, be seated, exist (of one), to: liketv (le:·ki·tá {I})
sit, be seated, exist (of three or more), to: vpoketv (a·po·ki·tá {I})
sit, be seated, exist (of two), to: kaketv (ka:·ki·tá {I})
sit, be situated, exist (of a clump of things), to: esliketv (is·le:·ki·tá {I})
sit down after going a distance, to: raliketv (ła:·le:·ki·tá {I})
sit on, ride (of one), to: ohliketv (oh·le:·ki·tá {I;II})
sit on, ride (of three or more), to: ohvpoketv (oh·a·po:·ki·tá {I;II})
sit up (as from lying down), rise up (of one), to: aliketv (a:·le:·ki·tá {I})
sit up, rise up (as from lying down) (of three or more), to: a-vpoketv
    (a:·a·po·ki·tá {I})
sit up (as from lying down), rise up (of two), set aside (two items), to:
    akaketv (a:·ka:·ki·tá {I})
situated (to be), sit, exist (of a clump of things): esliketv (is·le:·ki·tá {I})
six: ēpaken (i:·pâ:·kin)
skin, casing, shell, hide (his/her/its): ehvrpe (i·háł·pi {II}); *also* hvrpe
    (háł·pi {II})
skinny, tired (of one): hotosē (ho·tó·si: {II})
skinny, tired (of two or more): hotosvkē (ho·to·sa·kí: {II})
skirt (article of clothing): honnv kocoknosat (hon·na ko·cok·no·sá:t); *also*
    honnv-lecv (hon·na·lí·ca {D})
skunk: kono (ko·nó)
slap (someone on a body part), to: em vrokafetv (im·a·ło·ka:·fi·tá {I;II})
sleep, be asleep, go to sleep (of one), to: nocetv (no·cí·ta {II/I}); *also*
    nucetv (no·cí·ta {II/I})
sleep, be asleep, go to sleep (of three or more), to: nocicetv (no·ce:·ci·tá
    {II/I}); *also* nucicetv (no·ce:·ci·tá {II/I})
sleep, be asleep, go to sleep (of two), to: nochoyetv (noc·ho·yí·ta {II/I});
    also nuchoyetv (noc·ho·yí·ta {II/I})
sleepy: nockelē (noc·ki·lí: {II}); *also* nuckelē (noc·ki·lí: {II})
slice, cut more than once (as bread, meat, etc.), to: waretv (wa:·łi·tá {I;3})

slice one's self repeatedly, to: ēwaretv (i:·wa:·łi·tá {I})

slick, slippery: tenaspē (ti·ná:s·pi: {II})

slippery, slick: tenaspē (ti·ná:s·pi: {II})

slow: hvlvlatkē (ha·la·lá:t·ki: {II})

small (of one): cutkē (cót·ki: {II}); *see also* little

small (of two or more): lopockē (lo·póc·ki: {II})

smart, healthy, well (of two or more): cvfencvkē (ca·fin·ca·kí: {II})

smash, break up, pound, shatter as when hitting something with a hammer or mallet, to: pvccetv (pac·ci·tá {I;3}); *see also* hocetv (ho·cí·ta {I;3})

smell, sniff, to: vwenayetv (a·wi·na:·yi·tá {I;II/II;3})

smell, sniff from a short distance, to: a-vwenayetv (a:·a·wi·na:·yi·tá {I;II/II;3}); *also* awenayetv (a:·wi·na:·yi·tá {I;II/II;3})

smell something, to: vwenayetv (a·wi·na:·yi·tá {I;II/II;3})

smelly, stinky (of one): fvmpē (fám·pi: {II})

smelly, stinky (of two or more): fvmfvpē (fam·fa·pí: {II})

smile, laugh (of one), to: vpeletv (a·pi·li·tá {I})

smile, laugh (of two or more), to: vpelhoyetv (a·pil·ho·yí·ta {I}

snake: cetto (cít·to)

sneeze, to: haktēsketv (ha:k·ti:s·ki·tá {II/I}); *also* hvtēsketv (ha·ti:s·ki·tá {II/I})

sneeze on someone/something, to: ohhaktēsketv (oh·ha:k·ti:s·ki·tá {I;II})

sniff, smell from a short distance, to: a-vwenayetv (a:·a·wi·na:·yi·tá {I;II/II;3}); *also* awenayetv (a:·wi·na:·yi·tá {I;II/II;3})

snow, ice: hetotē (hi·to·tí:)

so, therefore: monkv (món·ka)

socks/sock: estele-svhocackv ((is·ti·li) sa·ho·cá:c·ka); *also* svhocickv (sa·ho·cé:c·ka); svhocackv (sa·ho·cá:c·ka)

soft, tender (like meat), mushy (of one), to be: lowvckē (lo·wác·ki: {II})

soft (of two or more): lowvclokē (lo·wac·lo·kí: {II})

something, thing: nake (nâ:·ki)

son (a man's): eppuce (ip·po·cí {II})

song: yvhiketv (ya·he:·ki·tá)

sore, wound: lekwē (lík·wi: {II})

soreness, hurting, pain: ennokkē (in·nók·ki: {3;D})

sour (of milk), to be: toksē (tók·si: {II})

sour (not of milk), to be: kvmoksē (ka·mók·si: {II})

south: lekothofv (li·kot·hó:·fa)

southward, toward the south: lekothofv fvccvn (li·kot·hó:·fa fác·can)

Spaniard: Espane (is·pá:·ni)

Spaniards, Spanish people: Espanvlke (is·pa:n·âl·ki)

speak, talk, give a speech, to: (o)ponvyetv ((o)·po·na·yí·ta {I})

speaker: oponayv (o·po·ná:·ya)

spit, to: tofketv (tof·ki·tá {I;II})

spoon: hakkv (há:k·ka)

squirrel: ero (i·łó)

stack (one thing) on top of another, to: etohlicetv (i·toh·le:·ci·tá {I;3})

stack (three or more things) on top of another, to: etohvpoyetv (i·toh·a·po·yi·tá {I;3})

stack (two things) on top of another, to: etohkayetv (i·toh·ka:·yi·tá {I;3})

stand (of one), to: hueretv (hoy·łi·tá {I})

stand (of three or more), to: svpakletv (sa·pa:k·li·tá {I})

stand (of two), to: sehoketv (si·ho:·ki·tá {I})

stand up (of one), to: ahueretv (a:·hoy·łi·tá {I})

stand up (of two), to: asehoketv (a:·si·ho:·ki·tá {I})

stand up (of three or more), to: asvpakletv (a:·sa·pa:k·li·tá {I})

star: kocecvmpv (ko·ci·cám·pa)

stickball stick, ball stick: tokonhe (to·kón·hi)

stinky, smelly (of one): fvmpē (fám·pi: {II})

stinky, smelly (of two or more): fvmfvpē (fam·fa·pí: {II})

stir things, to: eteyametv (i·ti·ya:·mi·tá {I;3})

stir things using an implement, to: eseteyametv (is·i·ti·ya:·mi·tá {I;3})

stone, rock: cvto (ca·tó)

stop, to: fekhonnetv (fik·hon·ni·tá {I})

store, protect, save (something), to: vcayēcetv (a·ca:·yi:·ci·tá {I;3})

store, put away, to: hericetv (hi·łe:·ci·tá {I;3})

story, news, tale: nakonvkv (nâ:k·oná·ka)

story (short), fairytale: nakonvkuce (nâ:k·o·na·ko·cí)

stove, fireplace: cvto (ca·tó); *also* totkv-hute (to:t·ka·hó·ti)

stream, ditch: hvccuce (hac·co·cí)

strict, to be: fetektvnēceko (fi·tik·ta·ni:·cí·ko {II})

strong: yekcē (yík·ci: {II})

stubborn, to be: ērolopetv (i:·ło·lo·pi·tá {II})

student: cokv-hēcv (co:·ka·hí:·ca)

stupid, to be: nak-kerreko (nâ:k·kił·łí·ko {II})

sun: hvse (ha·sí)

sunrise, the east: hvsossv (ha·só:s·sa)
sweep, to: pasetv (pa:·si·tá {I;3})

T

table: ohhompetv (oh·hom·pi·tá)
tail (his/her/its): ehvce (i·há·ci {II}); *also* hvce (há·ci {II})
take, catch, carry, hold (one thing): esetv (i·sí·ta {I;II})
take, carry, catch, hold (two or more things): cvwetv (ca·wí·ta {I;II})
take (one item) down: aesetv (a:·i·sí·ta {I;3})
take (two or more items) down: acvwetv (a:·ca·wí·ta {I;3})
take (one) from water or a low place: akesetv (ak·i·si·tá {I;II})
take off more than one piece of clothing, to: rokruecetv (łok·łoy·ci·tá {I;3})
take off one piece of clothing, to: roketv (ło·kí·ta {I;3})
take (something) out of a container: acvwēcetv (a:·ca·wi:·ci·tá {I;3}), *also* iem esetv (e:·im i·si·tá {I;3})
tale, news, story: nakonvkv (nâ:k·oná·ka)
talk, speak, give a speech, to: (o)ponvyetv ((o)·po·na·yí·ta {I})
talk to (someone), to: em oponvyetv (im o·po·na·yí·ta {I;D}); *also* em ponvyetv (im po·na·yí·ta {I;D})
tall (of one): mahē (má:·hi: {II})
tall (of two or more): mahmvyē (ma:h·ma·yí: {II})
tall, long (of one): cvpkē (cáp·ki: {II})
tall, long (of two or more): cvpcvkē (cap·ca·kí: {II})
tea: vsse (ás·si)
teach, to: mvhayetv (ma·ha:·yi·tá {I;D})
teacher: mvhayv (ma·há:·ya {D})
tear, rip, to: sētetv (si:·ti·tá {I;3})
tear down, to: letvfetv (li·ta·fi·tá {I})
teaspoon: hakkuce (ha:k·ko·cí)
tell (something) to (someone), say to, to: em onvyetv (im·o·na·yí·ta {I;3;D})
tell, say (something) to someone in particular, to: kicetv (ke:·ci·tá {I;II})
tender (like meat), mushy or soft (of one), to be: lowvckē (lo·wác·ki: {II})
that, that one, he/she/it: mv (má)
then, and (with different subject in following clause): momen (mo:·mín); *also* mont (mó:nt); mowen (mo:·wín)

then, and (with same subject in following clause): momet (mo:·mít);
   also mowet (mo:·wít)

thick (as of paper, cloth, or of liquids such as gravy, soup, etc.): cekfē
   (cík·fi: {II})

thief: horkopv (hoɫ·kó:·pa)

thin (of cloth, paper, etc.), to be: tvskocē (tas·ko·cí: {II})

thin (of gravy, soup, etc.), to be: kvsvnrē (ka·sán·ɫi: {II}); *also* wētvlkē
   (wi:·tâl·ki: {II})

thing, something: nake (nâ:·ki)

things: nanvke (nâ:·na·kí)

think, want, believe, try, hope, to: kometv (ko:·mi·tá {I;3}); *also* kowetv
   (ko:·wi·tá {I;3})

think about, wonder about, to: vkerricetv (a·kiɫ·ɫe:·ci·tá {I;II})

thirsty: ewvnhkē (i·wánh·ki: {II})

this, here, this one: heyv (hi·yá); *also* yv (yá)

this one, here, this: heyv (hi·yá); *also* yv (yá)

thought about something, a: vkerrickv (a·kiɫ·ɫé:c·ka)

three: tutcēnen (tot·cî:·nin)

throw (one item) out or away, to: vwiketv (a·we:·ki·tá {I;3})

throw out (three or more), to: vpvlvtetv (a·pa·la·tí·ta {I;3})

tie, scarf, anything worn around the neck: ohenockv (oh·i·nó:c·ka)

tie something to someone, to: vwvnvyetv (a·wa·na·yí·ta {I;3})

tied up: wvnvkē (wa·ná·ki: {II})

tie-snake: estakwvnayv (ist·ak·wa·ná:·ya)

tiger, mountain lion: kaccv (ká:c·ca)

timepiece, watch: hvse-(e)skērkuce (ha·si·(i)s·ki:ɫ·ko·cí)

tired, skinny (of one): hotosē (ho·tó·si: {II})

tired, skinny (of two or more): hotosvkē (ho·to·sa·kí: {II})

toad, frog: sopaktv (so·pá:k·ta)

today: mucv-nettv (mo·ca·nít·ta)

together: tepvkē (ti·pa·kí:)

tomorrow: pakse (pá:k·si); *also* vpakse (a·pá:k·si)

tooth (his/her/its): nute (nó·ti {II})

torn up, mashed (as of potatoes): cetakkosē (ci·tă:k·ko·si: {II})

touch, feel, to: celayetv (ci·la:·yi·tá {I;II})

tough (like meat or clay), to be: tvlvswē (ta·lás·wi: {II})

toward: fvccv (fác·ca {II})

town: tvlofv (ta·ló:·fa)

tree, wood: eto (i·tó)

tree branch: etolvcce (i·to·lác·ci); *also* 'tolvcce (to·lác·ci)

trust, believe in, depend on (something or someone): em enhonretv (im in·hon·łi·tá {I;D/II;D})

trust, hope: enhonrkv (in·hónł·ka)

try, want, think, believe, hope, to: kometv (ko:·mi·tá {I;3}); *also* kowetv (ko:·wi·tá {I;3})

Tuesday: Mvnte enhvyvtke (mán·ti in·ha·yát·ki)

Tulsa, Oklahoma: Tvlsv (tál·sa)

turkey: penwv (pín·wa)

turn off a lamp, put out a fire, erase, rub out, to: vslēcetv (as·li:·ci·tá {I;3})

Turtle (in stories), turtle, turtle-shell rattles (for dancing): locv (lo·cá)

two: hokkolen (hok·kô:·lin)

U

uncle (his/her maternal): pvwv (pá·wa {II})

unclean, dirty: svholwvkē (sa·hol·wa·kí: {II})

uncover (one thing), to: ohrvnkv esetv (oh·łán·ka i·sí·ta {I;II})

uncover (two or more things), to: ohrvnkv cvwetv (oh·łán·ka ca·wí·ta {I;II})

under, below, beneath: elecv (i·lí·ca {II}); *also* lecv (lí·ca {II})

underwear: ofiketv (o·fe:·ki·tá); *also* ofv-vccetv (o:·fa·ac·ci·tá)

uneasy about, to be: em enhotetv (im in·ho·tí·ta {II;D})

uneven (as boards or the ground), to be: etemontvlē (i·ti·mon·ta·lí: {II})

unscrew something, to: (e)sem vfikv em esetv ((i)s·im·a·fé:·ka im i·sí·ta {I;3})

us, we: pome (pó:·mi)

V

vest: sakpv-seko (sa:k·pa·sí·ko)

vice-chairman, vice-chairperson: ohliketv-ohlikv-vpoktv (oh·le:·ki·ta-oh·le:·ka-a·pók·ta)

visit someone, to: cokopericetv (co·ko·pi·łe:·ci·tá {I;D}); *also* cukopericetv (co·ko·pi·łe:·ci·tá {I;D})

vole, mole: tvko (ta·kó)

vote, to: cokv ensatetv (có:·ka in·sa:·ti·tá {I})

W

wake up, awaken, to: vhonecetv (a·ho·ni·cí·ta {I})

walk (of one), to: yvkvpetv (ya·ka·pi·tá {I})

walk a long distance toward (of one), to: rohyvkvpetv (łoh·ya·ka·pi·tá {I;II})

walk a short distance toward (of one), to: a-ohyvkvpetv (a·oh·ya·ka·pi·tá {I})

walk toward (of one), to: ohyvkvpetv (oh·ya·ka·pí·ta {I;II})

walk toward (of three or more), to: ohyvkvpvketv (oh·ya·ka·pa·ki·tá {I;II})

wander, go around (of one), to: vretv (a·łí·ta {I})

wander, go about, be located (of three or more), to: fulletv (fol·li·tá {I})

wander, go about, be located (of two), to: welvketv (wi·la·ki·tá {I})

wander around, be near (of one), to: vhvretv (a·ha·łi·tá {I;II})

want, need, like, to: eyvcetv (i·ya·ci·tá {II;3})

want, think, believe, try, hope, to: kometv (ko:·mi·tá {I;3}); *also* kowetv (ko:·wi·tá {I;3})

warmth, heat (of one): hiyē (hé:·yi: {II})

warrior: tvstvnvke (tas·ta·ná·ki)

warriors: tvstvnvkvlke (tas·ta·na·kâl·ki)

wash (of one), to wash one item: okkosetv (ok·ko·si·tá {I;II})

wash (of two or more), to wash two or more items: okkoskuecetv (ok·kos·koy·ci·tá {I;II})

wash over and over (like the fekce), to: okkoset mēcetv (ok·ko·sít mi:·ci·tá {I;II})

watch, timepiece: hvse-(e)skērkuce (ha·si·(i)s·ki:ł·ko·cí)

water: owv (ó:·wa); *also* uewv (óy·wa)

watermelon: cvstvlē (cas·ta·lí:)

wave at, to: em mvyattēcetv (im·ma·ya:t·ti:·ci·tá {I;D})

we, us: pome (pó:·mi)

wear something on one's head (as a hat, turban, etc.), to: kvtopoyetv (ka·to·po·yi·tá {I;3})

weedy, overgrown place: hvfvpē (ha·fá·pi:)

well, healthy (of one): cvfeknē (ca·fík·ni: {II})

well, smart, healthy (of two or more): cvfencvkē (ca·fin·ca·kí: {II})

when: stofvn (sto:·fán)

when it happens—contraction of mowen owof: mowof (mo:w·ô:f)

when it is past, after: hoyanat (ho·ya:·nâ:t)

where: estvmen (is·ta·mín); *also* stvmen (sta·mín)

whistle, to: fotketv (fo:t·ki·tá {I})

white (of one): hvtkē (hát·ki: {II})

white (of two or more): hvthvkē (hat·ha·kí: {II}); *also* hvtkvlke (hat·kâl·ki {II})

who: estimvt (is·te:·mát); *also* stimvt (ste:·mát)

why: nakstomen (na:k·sto:·mín); *also* nakstowen (na:k·sto:·wín); stomen (sto:·mín); stowen (sto:·wín)

wide (of one), to be: tvphē (táp·hi: {II})

wide (of two or more), to be: tvptvhē (tap·ta·hí: {II})

wife (his): ehiwv (i·hé:·wa {II})

wiggle, wriggle (like a worm), to: fekefeketv (fi·ki·fi·kí·ta {I}); *also* wenowēyetv (wi·no·wi:·yi·tá {I})

wild onions: tafvmpuce (ta:·fam·po·cí)

win, to: epoyetv (i·po:·yi·tá {I}); *also* vkosletv (a·kos·li·tá {I})

wind: hotvlē (ho·ta·lí:)

window: vhvokuce (a·haw·ko·cí)

Wolf (in stories): Poca Rakko (po·cá: łá:k·ko

woman: hoktē (hok·tí:)

woman, married: hoktē ehessē (hok·tí: i·hís·si:)

woman, old: hoktvlē (hok·ta·lí:)

women: hoktvke (hok·ta·kí)

wonder about, think about, to: vkerricetv (a·kił·łe:·ci·tá {I;II})

word, saying: onvkv (o·ná·ka)

worm: cuntv (cón·ta)

wood, tree: eto (i·tó)

work, to: vtotketv (a·tot·ki·tá {I})

worker: vtotkv (a·tó:t·ka)

worry, to: ēnaoricetv (i:·na:·o·łe:·ci·tá {I})

wound, sore: lekwē (lík·wi: {II})

wriggle, wiggle (like a worm), to: fekefeketv (fi·ki·fi·kí·ta {I}); *also* wenowēyetv (wi·no·wi:·yi·tá {I})

write, to: hoccicetv (hoc·ce:·ci·tá {I;3})

writing implement, pen, pencil: eshoccickv (is·ho:c·cé:c·ka)

writing pen: owvlvste eshoccickv (o:·wa·lás·ti is·ho:c·cé:c·ka)

Y

yellow, green: lanē (lá:·ni: {II})

yes: ehi (i·hé:)

yesterday: paksvnkē (pa:k·san·kí:)
you: cēme (cí:·mi)
you and (something/someone else): cēmeu (ci:·mío)
young: mvnettē (ma·nít·ti: {II})

Bibliography

Baker, T. Lindsay, and Julie P. Baker, eds.
1996   *The WPA Oklahoma Slave Narratives*. Norman: University of Oklahoma Press.

Bartram, William
1928   *Travels Through North and South Carolina, Georgia, East and*
[1791] *West Florida, the Cherokee Country, the Extensive Territories of the Muscogulges, or Creek Confederacy, and the Country of the Choctaws*, edited by M. Van Doren. New York: Dover Publications.

Bell, Amelia Rector
1983   Performative Effectiveness of Textual Cohesive Structures in Creek Long Talks. In *1982 Mid-America Linguistics Conference Papers*, edited by F. Ingemann, pp. 335–48. Lawrence: University of Kansas Press.
1984   Creek Ritual: The Path to Peace. Ph.D. dissertation, University of Chicago.
1985   Discourse Parallelisms and Poetics in Contemporary Creek Formal Language. In *In Honor of Roman Jakobson: Papers from the 1984 Mid-America Linguistics Converence*, edited by G. Youmans and D. M. Lance, pp. 323–30. Columbia: University of Missouri Press.
1990   Separate People: Speaking of Creek Men and Women. *American Anthropologist* 92(2):332–45.

Blackard, David M., and Patsy West
2004   Seminole Clothing: Colorful Patchwork. Seminole Tribe of Florida. http://www.seminoletribe.com/culture/clothing.shtml.

Blitz, John H.
1993   *Ancient Chiefdoms of the Tombigbee.* Tuscaloosa: University of Alabama Press.

Booker, Karen M.
1980   Comparative Muskogean: Aspects of Proto-Muskogean Verb Morphology. Ph.D. dissertation, University of Kansas.
1984   Directional Prefixes in Creek. In *Proceedings of the 1983 Mid-America Linguistics Conference,* edited by D. S. Rood, pp. 59–67. Boulder: University of Colorado Press.

Bosch, Anna
1984   *A Handbook of Creek (Muskogee) Grammar.* Muskogee, Okla.: Indian University Press, Bacone College.

Bourne, Edward Gaylor, ed.
1922   *Narratives of the Career of Hernando de Soto in the Conquest of Florida, as Told by a Knight of Elvas and in a Relation by Luys Hernandez de Biedma, Factor of the Expedition.* 2 vols. New York: Allerton Book Co.

Cohn, Abigail
1987   Causative Formation in the Oklahoma Seminole Dialect of Creek. In *Muskogean Linguistics,* edited by P. Munro, pp. 51–65. Occasional Papers in Linguistics no. 6. Los Angeles: Department of Linguistics, University of California.

Cox, Beverly, and Martin Jacobs
1991   *Spirit of the Harvest: North American Indian Cooking.* New York: Stewart, Tabori and Chang.

Dunn, Carolyn
2000   *Outfoxing Coyote.* San Pedro, Calif.: That Painted Horse Press.
2006   *Echo Location.* San Pedro, Calif.: That Painted Horse Press.

Dunn, Carolyn, and Paula Gunn Allen
2001   *Hozho, Walking in Beauty: Short Stories by American Indian Writers.* Los Angeles: Lowell House.

Finger, John R., and Theda Perdue
2004   History of the Old South since Removal. In *Handbook of North American Indians,* vol. 14, *Southeast,* edited by R. Fogelson, pp. 152–61. Washington, D.C.: Smithsonian Institution Press.

Fixico, Donald L.
1997   *Rethinking American Indian History*. Albuquerque: University of
        New Mexico Press.
1998   *The Invasion of Indian Country in the Twentieth Century: American
        Capitalism and Tribal Natural Resources*. Boulder: University Press
        of Colorado.
2000   *The Urban Indian Experience in America*. Albuquerque: University
        of New Mexico Press.
2004   History of the Western Southeast since Removal. In *Handbook of
        North American Indians*, vol. 14, *Southeast*, edited by R. Fogelson,
        pp. 162–73. Washington, D.C.: Smithsonian Institution Press.
Fixico, Donald L., Brian C. Hosmer, and Colleen O'Neill
2004   *Native Pathways: American Indian Culture and Economic
        Development in the Twentieth Century*. Boulder: University Press
        of Colorado.
Fogelson, Raymond, ed.
2004   *Handbook of North American Indians*, vol. 14, *Southeast*.
        Washington, D.C.: Smithsonian Institution Press.
Gatschet, Albert S.
1884   *A Migration Legend of the Creek Indians, with a Linguistic, Historic
        and Ethnographic Introduction*. Philadelphia: D. G. Brinton.
Haas, Mary R.
1948   Classificatory Verbs in Muskogee. *International Journal of
        American Linguistics* 14(4):244–46.
Hally, David J., and Robert C. Mainfort, Jr.
2004   Prehistory of the Eastern Interior after 500 B.C. In *Handbook of
        North American Indians*, vol. 14, *Southeast*, edited by R. Fogelson,
        pp. 265–85. Washington, D.C.: Smithsonian Institution Press.
Hardy, Donald E.
1988   The Semantics of Creek Morphosyntax. Ph.D. dissertation, Rice
        University.
1994   Middle Voice in Creek. *International Journal of American
        Linguistics* 60(1):39–68.
2005   Creek. In *Native Languages of the Southeastern United States*,
        edited by H. K. Hardy and J. Scancarelli, pp. 200–45. Lincoln:
        University of Nebraska Press.
Harjo, Joy
1990   *In Mad Love and War*. Middletown, Conn.: Wesleyan University
        Press.

Harjo, Joy (*continued*)
2000a *The Good Luck Cat.* San Diego, Calif.: Harcourt Brace.
2000b *A Map to the Next World: Poetry and Tales.* New York: W. W. Norton
Harwell, Henry O., and Delores T. Harwell
1981 *The Creek Verb.* Muskogee, Okla.: Indian University Press, Bacone College.
Hawkins, Benjamin
1848 A Sketch of the Creek Country, in 1798 and 99. Georgia Historical Society Collections, vol. 3. Savannah: Georgia Historical Society.
1980 *Letters, Journals, and Writings of Benjamin Hawkins,* vol. 1, edited by C. L. Grant, Savannah, Ga.: Beehive Press.
Henri, Florette
1986 *The Southern Indians and Benjamin Hawkins 1796–1816.* Norman: University of Oklahoma Press.
Hitchcock, Ethan Allen
1996 *A Traveler in Indian Territory: The Journal of Ethan Allen Hitchcock,* edited by G. Foreman. Norman: University of Oklahoma Press.
Howard, James H., and Willie Lena
1984 *Oklahoma Seminoles: Medicines, Magic, and Religion.* Norman: University of Oklahoma Press.
Hymes, Dell
1981 *"In Vain I Tried to Tell You": Essays in Native American Ethnopoetics.* Philadelphia: University of Pennsylvania Press.
1996 Narrative Form as a Grammar of Experience: Native Americans and a Glimpse of English. In *Ethnography, Linguistics, Narrative Inequality: Toward an Understanding of Voice,* pp. 121–41. London: Taylor and Francis.
2003 *Now I Know Only So Far: Essays in Ethnopoetics.* Lincoln: University of Nebraska Press.
Innes, Pamela
2004a Creek in the West. *Handbook of North American Indians,* vol. 14, *Southeast,* edited by R. Fogelson, pp. 393–403. Washington, D.C.: Smithsonian Institution Press.
2004b How Changing Attitudes Toward Fluency Among the Muskogee/Creek Affect Retention of Medicine-Making Language. In *Linguistic Diversity in the South: Changing Codes, Practices,*

and Ideology, edited by M. Bender, pp. 90–103. Athens: University of Georgia Press.

2006   The Interplay of Linguistic Genres, Gender, and Language Ideology Among the Muskogee. *Language in Society* 35(2):231–59.

Innes, Pamela, Linda Alexander, and Bertha Tilkens

2004   *Beginning Muskogee: Mvskoke Emponvkv*. Norman: University of Oklahoma Press.

Johnson, Troy, Alvin Joseph, Jr., and Joane Nagel, eds.

1999   *Red Power: The American Indian's Fight for Freedom*. Lincoln: University of Nebraska Press.

Johnson, Troy, Joane Nagel, and Duane Champagne, eds.

1997   *American Indian Activism: Alcatraz to the Longest Walk*. Urbana: University of Illinois Press.

Jumper, Betty Mae

1994   *Legends of the Seminoles*. Sarasota, Fla.: Pineapple Press.

Kimball, Geoffrey

1996   Two Koasati Traditional Narratives. In *Coming to Light: Contemporary Translations of the Native Literatures of North America*, edited by B. Swann, pp. 704–14. New York: Vintage.

Lewis, David, Jr., and Ann T. Jordan

2002   *Creek Indian Medicine Ways: The Enduring Power of Mvskoke Religion*. Albuquerque: University of New Mexico Press.

Littlefield, Daniel F., Jr.

1992   *Alex Posey: Creek Poet, Journalist, and Humorist*. Lincoln: University of Nebraska Press.

Lomawaima, K. Tsianina

1994   *They Called It Prairie Light: The Story of Chilocco Indian School*. Lincoln: University of Nebraska Press.

Lomawaima, K. Tsianina, and Teresa L. McCarty

2006   *To Remain an Indian: Lessons in Democracy from a Century of Native American Education*. New York: Teachers College Press.

Lomawaima, K. Tsianina, and David E. Wilkins

2002   *Uneven Ground: American Indian Sovereignty and Federal Law*. Norman: University of Oklahoma Press.

Loughridge, R. M., and David M. Hodge

1890   *Dictionary of Muskokee and English*. Okmulgee, Okla.: Baptist
[1964] Home Mission Board.

Luthin, Herbert W.
2002   Making Texts, Reading Translations. In *Surviving Through the Days: Translations of Native California Stories and Songs*, pp. 21–56. Berkeley: University of California Press.
Martin, Jack B.
1989   Some Strange Plurals in Muskogean. Ms. in author's possession.
1991   Lexical and Syntactic Aspects of Creek Causatives. *International Journal of American Linguistics* 57(2):194–229.
Martin, Jack B., and Margaret McKane Mauldin
2000   *A Dictionary of Creek/Muskogee*. Lincoln: University of Nebraska Press.
Martin, Jack B., Margaret McKane Mauldin, and Gloria McCarty
2005   Creek Language Archive: Resources for the Study of the Creek (Muskogee) Language. http://www.wm.edu/linguistics/creek.
Martin, Jack B., Margaret McKane Mauldin, and Juanita McGirt
2004   *Totkv Mocvse/New Fire: Creek Folktales by Earnest Gouge*. Norman, Okla.: University of Oklahoma Press.
Mattina, Anthony
1987   North American Indian Mythography: Editing Texts for the Printed Page. In *Recovering the Word: Essays on Native American Literature*, edited by B. Swann and A. Krupat, pp. 129–48. Berkeley: University of California Press.
Mithun, Marianne
2001   Who Shapes the Record: The Speaker and the Linguist. In *Linguistic Fieldwork*, edited by P. Newman and M. Ratliff, pp. 34–54. Cambridge: Cambridge University Press.
Moore, John H.
1988   The Mvskoke Question in Oklahoma. *Science and Society* 52(2):163–90.
1990   *A Short History of the Mvskoke Creek Tribal Towns*. Okemah, Okla.: Tribal Towns Center.
Mould, Tom
2004   *Choctaw Tales*. Jackson: University Press of Mississippi.
Muscogee Nation News
2007   The Art of Longbow Making Carried on by Schulter Resident. January, section B, p. 2.
Nairne, Thomas
1988   *Nairne's Muskhogean Journals: The 1708 Expedition to the Mississippi River*, edited by A. Moore. Jackson: University Press of Mississippi.

Nathan, Michele
1977   Grammatical Description of the Florida Seminole Dialect of Creek. Ph.D. dissertation, Tulane University.

O'Brien, Sharon
1989   *American Indian Tribal Governments*. Norman: University of Oklahoma Press.

Oliver, Louis
1982   *The Horned Snake*. Merrick, N.Y.: Cross-Cultural Communications.
1983   *Caught in a Willow Net: Poems and Stories*. Greenfield Center, N.Y.: Greenfield Review Press.
1990   *Chasers of the Sun: Creek Indian Thoughts*. Greenfield Center, N.Y.: Greenfield Review Press.

Opler, Morris E.
1937   *Report on the History and Contemporary State of Aspects of Creek Social Organization and Government*. Washington, D.C.: Bureau of Indian Affairs.
1952   The Creek "Town" and the Problem of Creek Indian Political Reorganization. In *Human Problems in Technological Change: A Casebook*, edited by E. H. Spicer, pp. 165–80. New York: Russell Sage Foundation.

Paredes, Anthony J.
2004   Creek in the East since Removal. *Handbook of North American Indians*, vol. 14, *Southeast*, edited by R. Fogelson, pp. 404–406. Washington, D.C.: Smithsonian Institution Press.

Preston, Vera, and Mary Hannigan
1998   The Mathematics of Seminole Patchwork. Austin Community College. http://www2.austin.cc.tx.us/hannigan/Presentations/NSF Mar1398/MathofSP.html.

Rush, Beverly, and Lassie Wittman
1994   *The Complete Book of Seminole Patchwork*. Mineola, N.Y.: Dover Publications.

Sattler, Richard A.
1987   *Siminoli Italwa: Socio-Political Change Among the Oklahoma Seminoles Between Removal and Allotment, 1836–1905*. Ph.D. dissertation, University of Oklahoma.
2004   Seminole in the West. *Handbook of North American Indians*, vol. 14, *Southeast*, edited by R. Fogelson, pp.450–64. Washington, D.C.: Smithsonian Institution Press.

Schuetze-Coburn, Stephan
1987   Exceptional -*t*-/-*n*- Marking in Oklahoma Seminole Creek. In *Muskogean Linguistics*, edited by P. Munro, pp. 146–60. Occasional Papers in Linguistics no. 6. Los Angeles: Department of Linguistics, University of California.
Smith, Cynthia Leitich
2000   *Jingle Dancer*. New York: Morrow Junior Books.
2002   *Indian Shoes*. New York: Harper Collins.
2007   *Tantalize*. Cambridge, Mass.: Candlewick Press.
Smith, Cynthia Leitich, and Lori Earley
2001   *Rain Is Not My Indian Name*. New York: Harper Collins.
Snow, Alice Micco, and Susan Enns Stans
2001   *Healing Plants: Medicine of the Florida Seminole Indians*. Gainesville: University Press of Florida.
Speck, Frank G.
1907   The Creek Indians of Taskigi Town. *Memoirs of the American Anthropological Association.* 2(part 2):99–164.
Spoehr, Alexander
1941a   Camp, Clan, and Kin Among the Cow Creek Seminole of Florida. *Field Museum of Natural History Anthropological Series, Publication 498* 33(1):1–27. Chicago: Field Museum of Natural History.
1941b   Oklahoma Seminole Towns. *Chronicles of Oklahoma* 19(4):377–80.
1941c   Creek Inter-town Relations. *American Anthropologist* 43(1):132–33.
1942   Kinship System of the Seminole. *Field Museum of Natural History Anthropological Series, Publication 513* 33(2). Chicago: Field Museum of Natural History.
1947   Changing Kinship Systems: A Study in the Acculturation of the Creek, Cherokee, and Choctaw. *Field Museum of Natural History Anthropological Series, Publication 583* 33(4):151–235. Chicago: Field Museum of Natural History.
Sturtevant, William C., and Jessica R. Cattelino
2004   Florida Seminole and Miccosukee. *Handbook of North American Indians*, vol. 14, *Southeast*, edited by R. Fogelson, pp. 429–49. Washington, D.C.: Smithsonian Institution Press.
Swanton, John R.
1928a   Social Organization and Social Usages of the Indians of the Creek Confederacy. *Forty-Second Annual Report of the Bureau of American Ethnology*, pp. 23–472. Washington, D.C.: Government Printing Office.

1928b Religious Beliefs and Medical Practices of the Creek Indians. *Forty-Second Annual Report of the Bureau of American Ethnology,* pp. 473–672. Washington, D.C.: Government Printing Office.

1929 *Myths and Tales of the Southeastern Indians.* Washington, D.C.: Government Printing Office.

Tedlock, Dennis

1983 *The Spoken Word and the Work of Interpretation.* Philadelphia: University of Pennsylvania Press.

Tuggle, William Orrie

1973 *Shem, Ham, and Japheth: The Papers of W. O. Tuggle, Comprising His Indian Diary, Sketches and Observations, Myths, and Washington Journal in the Territory and at the Capital, 1879–1882,* edited by E. Current-Garcia and D. B. Hatfield. Athens: University of Georgia Press.

Walker, Willard B.

2004 Creek Confederacy Before Removal. In *Handbook of North American Indians,* vol. 14, *Southeast,* edited by R. Fogelson, pp. 373–92. Washington, D.C.: Smithsonian Institution Press.

Welch, Paul D.

1991 *Moundville's Economy.* Tuscaloosa: University of Alabama Press.

Wiget, Andrew

1987 Telling the Tale: A Performance Analysis of a Hopi Coyote Story. In *Recovering the Word: Essays on Native American Literature,* edited by B. Swann and A. Krupat, pp. 297–336. Berkeley: University of California Press.

Womack, Craig

1999 *Red on Red: Native American Literary Separatism.* Minneapolis: University of Minnesota Press.

2001 *Drowning in Fire.* Tucson: University of Arizona Press.

Womack, Craig, Jace Weaver, and Robert Warrior

2006 *American Indian Literary Nationalism.* Albuquerque: University of New Mexico Press.

Index

Contents of Accompanying CD